Stalkers and their victims

Over recent years, stalking has emerged as a major social and legal issue, and also as a clinical problem for mental health professionals. This absorbing and informative book draws on the authors' extensive experience of working with stalkers and their victims in the clinical setting, and makes a major contribution toward understanding the nature, causes, impact and management of stalking.

Topics covered include:
- The growing recognition of stalking as an issue of public, legal and scientific concern
- The definition, classification and epidemiology of stalking
- The impact on victims, and how this may be reduced
- Same gender stalking, stalking by proxy, workplace stalking, and the stalking of professionals, such as doctors and teachers
- The association of stalking with physical and sexual assault
- Anti-stalking laws internationally
- Support and practical advice for victims of stalking
- Assessing and managing the stalker

With many case histories, and an approach that is at once scholarly and highly practical, this will be the definitive guide and reference for anyone with a professional or academic interest in this complex behaviour.

Paul Mullen is Professor of Forensic Psychiatry at Monash University in Australia, and he is also Medical Director of the Victorian Institute of Forensic Mental Health.

Michele Pathé is Honorary Senior Lecturer at Monash University, and Consultant Forensic Psychiatrist at the Victorian Institute of Forensic Mental Health in Brunswick, Australia.

Rosemary Purcell is based in the Department of Psychological Medicine at Monash University.

Stalkers and their Victims is a brilliant fusion of cutting-edge scientific research and riveting clinical account. Written with genuine eloquence, argued with unfailing insight, and suffused with compassion, the book ups the ante on all future work on stalking. An extraordinary scholarly accomplishment of both international and enduring significance.

John Monahan
Doherty Professor of Law
University of Virginia

This lucid, encyclopaedic and dispassionate review of stalking views it not merely in terms of the participants – protagonist and victim – but as a social pathology reflecting distortions in personal and communal relations. The history of stalking, the classification of its various forms, its phenomenology as well as practical ways of responding to it are amongst the issues examined in a fashion which is both impressive in its detachment and admirable in its depth. The skilful use of case histories illustrating the forensic and clinical aspects of stalking makes it a particularly readable and useful text for professionals and provides a rare insight into the motives and behaviours of those who prey and prowl and pester. Given the intense media interest, it is vital that there be a resource of hard, factual and tested information available to offset the more lurid and mistaken views on the subject. Paul Mullen and his colleagues have provided exactly that. There is little doubt that this book will remain for many years the definitive account of one of the pathological phenomena of our fractured times, of gripping fascination to lay and professional readers alike.

Anthony W. Clare
Department of Psychiatry
St James's Hospital, Dublin

STALKERS
and their victims

Paul E. Mullen

Michele Pathé

and

Rosemary Purcell

CAMBRIDGE
UNIVERSITY PRESS

PUBLISHED BY THE PRESS SYNDICATE OF THE UNIVERSITY OF CAMBRIDGE
The Pitt Building, Trumpington Street, Cambridge, United Kingdom

CAMBRIDGE UNIVERSITY PRESS
The Edinburgh Building, Cambridge CB2 2RU, UK   http://www.cup.cam.ac.uk
40 West 24th Street, New York, NY 10011–4211, USA   http://www.cup.org
10 Stamford Road, Oakleigh, Melbourne 3166, Australia
Ruiz de Alarcón 13, 28014 Madrid, Spain

First published 2000

Printed in the United Kingdom at the University Press, Cambridge

Typeface Minion 10.5/14pt   *System* QuarkXPress™   [SE]

A catalogue record for this book is available from the British Library

Library of Congress Cataloguing in Publication data

Mullen, Paul E.
Stalkers and their victims/Paul E. Mullen, Michele Pathé, and Rosemary Purcell.
  p.   cm.
ISBN 0 521 66950 2 (pbk.)
1. Stalking.   2. Stalkers.   3. Women – Crimes against – Prevention.   I. Pathé, Michele,
1959–   II. Purcell, Rosemary, 1969–   III. Title.
HV6594.M85   2000
362.88 – dc21   99-044607

ISBN 0 521 66950 2 paperback

Contents

| 14 | **Defining and prosecuting the offence of stalking** | 249 |

Acknowledgements

Our thanks to Julie King for her constant help and good-humoured forbearance in preparing the manuscript. We received advice and feedback from a number of friends and colleagues. We would particularly like to acknowledge Dr John Hamill, Laura Cronin, Professor Louis Waller, Dr Tim Lindsay and John Carruthers. Our thanks also to Richard Barling for encouragement and patience. Finally we would like to thank the many victims of stalking, and the occasional stalker, who willingly provided information through interviews and filling in questionnaires at the cost of their time and their emotional energies, knowing it was in pursuit of our scientific enquiries not their own management.

Introduction

Until a little more than a decade ago the word 'stalking' was attached, almost exclusively, to the activities of hunters who called the pursuit of deer and other animals sport. To stalk and to be stalked have today acquired radically different and even more sinister resonances. Stalkers are now the frightening pursuers who haunt not merely the famous but potentially all of us. To stalk is a crime. To be a stalker is to transgress the all important boundaries that protect individuals from incursions by those they perceive as threatening. To be stalked is to be a victim.

The new language of stalking was born in the sensationalism of the media who first appropriated the term stalker to name the persistent pursuers of celebrities. The term was taken up with alacrity and rapidly generalized to cover unwanted following, approaching and harassing in all its many and varied forms. Now stalking forms part of legal and scientific discourses as well as having acquired a privileged status among the descriptors of our society's categories of fear.

Stalking established itself as a social problem and as a specific type of criminal offence before clear definitions of its nature, its causes, its possible impacts and its natural history were established. In a short history, stalking has metamorphosed from the pursuit of the famous by the deranged, to the harassment of women by insensitive ex-partners, to a broad categorization of repeated intrusions that induce apprehension in a wide range of targets. Gradually, systematic studies have begun to elucidate the nature of stalking behaviours, the prevalence of such activities, their potential impact on victims, and finally some of their causes and cures. This book reviews the present state of knowledge on stalkers and their victims. We draw on the general, legal and social, and psychological literatures. This is, however, still an emerging academic discourse. Even the use of the word 'stalker' is challenged by some who would prefer a less sensational term such as obsessional follower. The substituting of obsessional follower for stalker, although appearing technical and precise, is perhaps flawed, as stalkers are rarely obsessional and not exclusively followers. Stalking as a crime, and as an area of study, was born out of a media cry of scandal, and we happily acknowledge those origins by retaining the terminology of stalker and stalking. We also favour these terms because it was exactly this dramatic language that was able to provoke the public concern which finally evoked an appropriate response to the harassment and fear produced by these behaviours and without which this book would not exist.

The approach we have taken is first and foremost descriptive and phenomenological. The book begins with a clarification of the nature and range of stalking behaviours and how these differ from behaviours that are currently accepted, if not necessarily welcomed. The definition of stalking requires a cultural and historical perspective. The emergence of stalking is at least, in part, a product of changing attitudes toward personal relationships and acceptable social behaviours. To understand stalking it is necessary to explore the motivations of the stalker. This begins with the detailed description of the desires, hopes and aspirations of those who pursue. Similarly, the study of the impact of stalkers on their victims has to be grounded in a clear descriptive analysis of the effects of the special forms of stress imposed by being stalked.

The frequent use of case examples through this book serves the need for an emphasis on descriptive and phenomenological approaches. The case examples are drawn in part from published accounts of scholarly and popular works but, equally importantly, from our own clinical experience. The accounts from people, provided to us in our professional work as clinicians and researchers, have been carefully rewritten to preserve anonymity. This has been accomplished by altering all identifying and many nonessential details in every case. We have also on occasion combined aspects of two separate narratives in a manner that does not change essential relationships but does further protect confidentiality. The internal world of the stalker is predominantly a secret world of someone who is often also a social isolate. The experience of being stalked is all too often an equally isolating private hell. What is potentially identifiable by others are the actions and dramas in which stalker and victim have played their part. It is these observable and public elements of the stalking experience that have been altered in our accounts. This book may be read by some of the over 200 stalkers and victims that we have encountered in our work. Even among those of whose stories we have made use it would be our hope that few, if any, would be able to identify themselves with confidence and nobody else would have any knowledge of their identities. A number of our patients, mostly from among victims, but including a few stalkers, have actively volunteered to have their stories told in the hope that it will help others. Even here, however, we have taken the same precautions against the possibility of inadvertently identifying the subject. In some ways the most complex situation is provided by instances where the stalking and the associated drama received wide media coverage and where either the victim or the stalker was seen in our service. To avoid any inadvertent breach of confidentiality we have not mixed information from the public and clinical domains. We have also avoided describing cases in which linkages could be made, for example, with media reports and our clinical description of a participant. We have occasionally alluded to media accounts of cases of which we have knowledge from other sources but in such instances no information is to be found in this book drawn from, or influenced by, information not in the public domain.

We have in the past been confronted by patients who believed they recognized themselves in accounts of cases in our published papers. Such accusations were perfectly reasonable, given that the cases described bore a remarkable similarity to the individuals' circumstances. Fortunately, these fears were allayed once we were able to demonstrate that the papers had been written prior to the patients having been seen at the clinic and to our having acquired any knowledge of their circumstances. It is in the nature of stalking, and particularly of descriptions chosen to exemplify aspects of the phenomena, that there will be commonalities between the experiences of stalkers and between the experiences of their victims. We hope those who read this book who have been stalked, or have been a stalker, will recognize aspects of their own experience in the accounts. We hope also that none of those from whose experiences we have learned will feel their trust has been broken or in any way exploited.

Stalking is a situation in which one individual imposes on another unwanted and fear-inducing intrusions in the form of communications or approaches. It is, we believe, appropriate that our first concern is with the victims of such activities and how to relieve them from this burden. We favour the term victim, and occasionally the descriptor target, over the even more emotive 'survivor' or the overly distanced 'object of'.

We work with stalkers as well as victims. We have come to realize that many stalkers inflict considerable pain and damage on themselves in the pursuit of their victim. The price often paid by stalkers may be considerable in terms of time, emotional distress, money and their own self-esteem. This is not to argue for an equivalence of suffering between perpetrator and victim but to note the obvious; for most stalkers there is much to be gained from freeing themselves from the behaviour. There is a place on occasion for sympathy for the stalker and there is certainly a place for working with the stalker to end the behaviour for their own as well as for the victim's sake.

The purpose of this book is to interest and inform. You cannot, in our view, do the latter without the former. The hope is that the information will ultimately contribute to an understanding of how to respond to and manage stalking in ways that relieve the victim and stop the behaviour, as rapidly as possible.

Part of society's response to the recognition of stalking as a problem has been through the criminal justice system. This book contains a consideration of the anti-stalking laws and the associated responses by courts and law enforcement agencies. We are of the view that legal sanctions have a central part to play in stopping some stalkers. Equally they are totally ineffective in others. Our view is that of clinicians interested in relieving suffering, not that of lawyers, let alone those who would advance agendas of retribution and revenge. It is in that spirit that we have approached the legal and law enforcement responses to the stalker.

This book was written jointly by the three of us. It is not a book with three parts written by the three authors. Although initial drafts of each chapter were written by one author the final product is very much a joint effort. We hope this will have produced a reasonably consistent style, a consistency of approach and, perhaps most importantly, reduce repetition to the unavoidable minimum.

1

Stalking – a new categorization of human behaviour

Le grand malheur, de ne pouvoir être seul.

La Bruyère[1]

Introduction

Stalkers and stalking are words that have acquired new connotations by being increasingly applied to individuals who persistently pursue, or otherwise intrude on, others. Stalking has emerged as a social problem that not only commands considerable public attention but is now, in many jurisdictions, a specific form of criminal offence. Stalking is increasingly attracting clinical and research interest among behavioural scientists and mental health professionals.

The word 'stalk' has the meaning of both the act of following one's prey and walking stealthily. To label someone a stalker has been, at least from the sixteenth century, to imply that he or she is a prowler or a poacher (*Oxford English Dictionary*, 1971). When the media appropriated the word to describe those who pestered and harassed others they provided a new focus for this ancient indictment.

'Stalking' is now part of our culture's language. It has become a category with which we describe and understand our experiences. If someone is repeatedly followed by a stranger, or is distressed at receiving numerous unwanted letters from an estranged partner then, in today's world, they are likely to describe themselves as being stalked. Looking back over their life they may now recall having been stalked in the past. At the time they might have described the experience as having been persistently pestered but now, retrospectively, it is recognized as their having been stalked.

This is not just the substitution of one word for another. Stalking and being stalked are constructs with particular implications and resonance. Stalking is now a warning of future violence. Stalking is a cause of psychological damage. Stalking is a form of victimization. Stalkers are dangerous. Stalkers are criminals. Stalkers are disturbed and unpredictable. Stalking implies the inflicting of distress and damage

---

[1] Quoted at the beginning of Edgar Allen Poe's (1967/1840). *The Man of the Crowd.* [This greatest of misfortunes, not being able to be alone.]

(whether or not the perpetrator consciously intends such damage). Being stalked evokes the self-perception of being violated and hurt. In attributing to ourselves the experience of being stalked (and occasionally of being, or having been, a stalker) we potentially change our evaluation of ourselves. We change our moral judgement of what is occurring. There is an alteration in our expectations of what will happen and what we have a right to expect from society. The question of whether this reframing is 'a good thing' is not at issue here; the concern is recognizing the potential changes inherent in the emergence of stalking as a social category. The experience of certain types of interaction and certain forms of relatedness have been changed forever.

The capacity of new social constructs such as stalking to reframe the past so as to endow it with new meanings and new resonance is not confined to personal experience. The rediscovery and publishing of the long ignored first novel of Louisa May Alcott (1832–1888) provides a curious illustration of this phenomenon. *A Long Fatal Love Chase* (1997) was written in 1866, two years prior to *Little Women*. The plot involves the protracted pursuit of the heroine, Rosamond, by her estranged husband. When Rosamond flees her marriage as a result of discovering both his polygamy and murderous past, he refuses to accept that the relationship is at an end. His reaction is initially portrayed as a desire for reconciliation and a wish to continue their relationship. As she continues to try to escape him he becomes increasingly resentful and angry: 'with his own unabated passion was now mingled a resentful desire to make her expiate her contempt by fresh humiliation or suffering' (ibid., p. 329). The novel climaxes with the murder of Rosamond and the suicide of her killer who dies uttering 'mine first – mine last – mine even in the grave!' (ibid., p 346).

According to its editor, this overheated example of the gothic languished in a university library until resuscitated and published in 1993. It re-emerged as a tale of stalking. On the cover of the paperback version appears the following, 'He stalked her every step – for she had become his obsession'. Inside the book are numerous endorsements and quotes from reviews including that from *USA Today*, 'A tale of obsessive love, stalking and murder that seems ripped off today's tabloids'. Although it might be more correct to say today's tabloids have endowed this nineteenth century novel not only with new relevance but with new meaning and a new relationship to our culture's current preoccupations.

Defining stalking

Meloy & Gothard (1995, p. 259), defined stalking, or as they prefer to call it obsessional following, as 'an abnormal or long term pattern of threat or harassment directed toward a specific individual'. The pattern of threat or harassment was further clarified as being 'more than one overt act of unwanted pursuit of the victim that was perceived by the victim as being harassing', although more than one may seem a generous rendering of a long-term pattern. Meloy (1998b) further states that in distinction to legal definitions, which are set forth to define and prosecute criminal behaviour, this definition was designed to further scientific investigation and clinical understanding. The advantage of this definition is that it directs attention to actions that are repeated and are perceived as unwanted by the object of these attentions. A further potential strength of this definition is that, disavowals notwithstanding, it closely parallels many of the statutory definitions of the offence of stalking.

Pathé & Mullen (1997, p. 12) defined stalking as 'a constellation of behaviours in which one individual inflicts on another repeated unwanted intrusions and communications'. The intrusions are further characterized as 'following, loitering nearby, maintaining surveillance and making approaches' and the communications via 'letter, the telephone, electronic mail, graffiti or notes attached, for example, to the victim's car'. The authors added that, although not part of the core and defining behaviours, there were the associated activities of ordering goods on the victim's behalf, interfering with their property, making false accusations, issuing threats and in some cases assaulting the victim. Pathé & Mullen (1997) attempted a definition that can be operationalized and depends on observable activities, with the qualification that the activities be unwanted by the victim. It defines a course of conduct but, as it stands, offers no temporal or numerical limits to that conduct. In a subsequent publication, the authors suggested that, to constitute stalking, the behaviour should consist of at least ten separate intrusions and/or communications, the conduct spanning a period of at least four weeks (Mullen et al., 1999). This was an intentionally conservative set of limitations which ensured that the study group were unequivocally stalkers.

Westrup & Fremouw (1998) noted a conspicuous lack of agreement among definitions of stalking in the literature. They are of the view that the term stalking is employed indiscriminately to cover both a class of behaviours and the specific act of following someone. Westrup (1998) called for a clear definition of stalking, with precise inclusion criteria comparable with those provided in the fourth edition of the American Psychiatric Association, (1994) *Diagnostic and Statistical Manual of Mental Disorders* (DSM). Westrup (1998, p. 276) proposed the following definition: 'stalking behaviour is one or more of a constellation of behaviours that (a) are directed repeatedly towards a specific individual (the target); (b) are experienced by the target as unwelcome and intrusive, and (c) are reported to trigger fear or concern in the target'. In their paper Westrup & Fremouw castigated virtually all existing literature, noting: 'Our comprehension of stalking behaviour has not been appreciably increased from these efforts' (ibid., p, 269). They offered as a solution a functional analytical approach which in the future could potentially clarify the antecedent conditions for a stalking event, the overt behaviour engaged in by, and the reinforcing consequences for, the stalker which tend to encourage repetition. In individual cases this approach offers a prospect of intervening to modify the controlling variables that sustain stalking behaviours.

Given that most definitions emphasize that the course of conduct constituting stalking be a pattern or repeated actions, the behaviour must occur on more than one occasion, but how many more times than one? Meloy & Gothard (1995) opted for two or more instances and in this they are in accord with most statutory definitions of the crime of stalking (for a full discussion of the legal discourse on stalking, see Chapter 14). Thus the ex-partner who makes a second unwanted phone call enters the ranks of stalkers. Equally, so does the hopeful suitor who puts himself for a second time in the way of the woman he desires, if as a result she feels harassed. The problem with such a low threshold is that it leaves little if any gap between stalking and those behaviours that may well be irritating but are certainly extremely common. By placing the lower end of the spectrum of stalking so close to many mundane activities, one captures a very wide range of commonplace behaviours. On the other hand why shouldn't a woman followed home by a strange man on two sequential nights be eligible to claim that she is a victim of stalking?

The impetus to cast the net as widely as possible in defining stalking reflects at least three influences. The first is the tendency noted by Westrup (1998) to conflate stalking as a description of surreptitious following, with stalking as the overarching term for a variety of unwanted attempts to maintain contact. Being followed on one occasion is, for most of us, an unsettling experience and when it is repeated most reasonable people would become concerned about their safety. This is all the more so if the follower is a man, unknown, or worse still, known to hold a grudge. Secondly, stalking is constructed, particularly by law enforcement agencies, as a warning sign of imminent violence. If stalking is viewed primarily as the harbinger of assault then the quicker it is recognized and responded to the better. The third influence is that more than once seems less arbitrary than more than five, more than ten, more than seventeen times. Nobody would want to advise a terrified victim who has had a man stand outside the house looking up at the window on nine consecutive nights that, according to Mullen et al. (1999), there was another night to go before he or she could lay claim to being stalked. Central to the concern not to place an inevitably arbitrary barrier to the recognition and potential response to stalking is the proper concern to respond to fear and distress in a potential victim.

The resolution of the dilemma of the threshold for the number of intrusions that constitute stalking should, we believe, be a function of the purpose for which the behaviours are being labelled as stalking. The law may plausibly claim a need, in pursuit of public safety, to respond promptly to the first signs of risk. Given the all too often tardy and partial responses of police and the courts to even gross and extended stalking activities, anxieties about overreaction may seem misplaced. It should be noted, however, that the low threshold for committing a stalking offence tempts police to use this as a so called 'loading' charge to add to other offences. We have seen at our clinic a number of men charged with stalking in association with child molestation offences, where the so-called stalking was integral to the sexual offence. One man was charged with stalking on the basis of following a child around a playground and subsequently approaching the child in the street, where he exposed himself. The two approaches were enough to trigger the stalking charge, which in our jurisdiction (Victoria, Australia) carries a potential sentence many times greater than that for the indecent act of exhibitionism. Although the child molester's plight may evoke little sympathy, the use of anti-stalking laws in this context risks diluting their effectiveness in situations where no other legal protections exist. If penalties for indecent exposure to children are inadequate the solution is to change the penalty. Inappropriately employing anti-stalking laws that are still in the process of having their role and scope determined by the criminal justice system puts in jeopardy reforms whose purpose was to extend protection to a previously ignored group of victims.

If we place only brief time constraints on behaviour constituting stalking, then walking past someone and looking at them on three or four occasions in the space of an hour or so at, for example, an open air market could conceivably be construed as stalking. Equally, to return to our example of the nocturnal observer outside the front gate, is it reasonable to deny the protection of the law until four weeks have elapsed?

It would be comforting to believe that common sense would arbitrate between irritating but broadly sanctioned behaviours and those that are sufficiently intrusive and so potentially fear-inducing to justify their being labelled, and potentially prosecuted, as stalking. But such common sense depends on shared common values. It is at least arguable that the emergence of stalking as an issue reflects a process of change, if not fragmentation, in our culture's previously shared notions of privacy, personal safety and the proper limits on the forms of contact and approach sanctioned by courtship and even marriage. Central to the construction of stalking are the perceptions of the person who is the object of the unwanted attentions that these behaviours are harassing and frightening. It is not the intentions of the putative stalker that are the defining element but the reactions of the recipients of the unwanted attentions who, in the act of experiencing themselves as victimized, create a stalking event.

In the final analysis, stalking lies in the eye of the beholder. Stalking is those repeated acts, experienced as unpleasantly intrusive, which create apprehension and can be understood by a reasonable fellow citizen (the ordinary man or woman) to be grounds for becoming fearful. A case example will illustrate the extent to which perpetrator and victim may construct the behaviours differently.

Case example

When first seen, Mr C was in prison on remand for charges relating to the stalking of his ex-wife. His imprisonment had followed the repeated phoning and approaching of his ex-wife, despite both his bail conditions and a previous court order, which specifically forbade such contact. He was a practising Catholic, had been married for five years and there was one child. He regarded marriage as a permanent union. From his perspective he had fulfilled all his obligations to his wife and child; he had worked long hours to provide a substantial income; he had never, whilst they were together, been threatening let alone violent. He believed he had always been loving and considerate, and he had never even looked at another woman. He had complied, albeit reluctantly, when his wife asked him to move out of the marital home for what he claimed she said would be a brief period because she 'needed space' and had 'some personal issues'. When, however, a few weeks later she had indicated that she wished the separation to become permanent, he described himself as devastated. He saw his behaviour over the subsequent year as reasonable and constituting legitimate attempts to attain a reconciliation with his ex-wife.

He claimed his repeated phone calls and multiple attempts to approach his wife simply indicated how important she was to him and how enthusiastic he was for a reconciliation. Following her and watching the house at night were in his view the natural result of her seeing another man with sufficient frequency to stimulate in him fears about her fidelity. He acknowledged that on occasions he had become enraged by his wife's repeated rejections of his advances and that he had several times threatened her and on one occasion torn up the garden fence when refused entry to the house. Although he was prepared to accept that he should not have lost control, he was firmly of the view that any reasonable man in his position would have been likely to have responded similarly. Mr C is an enormous man standing over two metres tall and weighing more than 120 kg but, in his view, he could not be held responsible for his size and it was of no relevance to whether he might have been seen as intimidating. Mr C was an intelligent man who was perfectly capable of calculating his own advantage. Despite this he had given the magistrate, who told him he must not continue trying to contact his ex-wife, an extended and forceful lecture on the magistrate's moral failings in trying to put asunder those whom God had joined. At a later stage he gave the Parole Board a similar piece of his mind. Such outbursts, he was aware, virtually guaranteed his detention but he felt he could not in all decency refrain.

Mr C's ex-wife's perspective was clear from her various statements to police and from two thorough victim-impact reports prepared as part of the court's consideration of sentencing options. She had been initially attracted to Mr C because he seemed so strong and stable and at that time in her life, following the breakdown of a previous relationship, these had been important qualities. She stated that she had wanted them to live together but she had acquiesced in his wishes for marriage. From her perspective the relationship had soon foundered as she was exposed to the extent of Mr C's demanding dependence. She stated that she felt as if she had a family of two small children, not one. She described repeated attempts to negotiate a separation which Mr C had ignored, threatening suicide should she leave. Her statements did not attempt to hide that she had established a new relationship with an old boyfriend prior to finally persuading Mr C to move out. Nor did she deny that she had managed finally to evict Mr C by misleading him into believing that this was a temporary separation. Equally clear was the devastating impact of Mr C's repeated intrusions on his ex-wife. She was terrified. She described barricading herself in her house, never going out without an escort, being too frightened to answer the phone, being constantly vigilant, expecting yet another intrusion. She reported fearing not only for her own life but for that of her child. She had broken off her relationship with the other man for fear of further provoking Mr C. She now lived the life of a recluse. She was for the first time in her life using sleeping tablets and had been prescribed antidepressants.

Over the subsequent two years, Mr C spent several periods in prison and made two serious suicide attempts. His ex-wife finally fled to another state, changing her name, breaking off all contact with friends and family and attempting to 'disappear'. Two lives were devastated and that ignores the possible impact on their child. Mr C's sense of entitlement to his wife and child are unchanged. He still believes he acted in the only ways open to him.

This was a clear case of stalking in the context of a relationship breakdown. Mr C's behaviour was not only illegal but would be likely to have been regarded by most of his fellow citizens as unconscionable. Not so long ago, however, in most Western societies it would have been the ex-wife's behaviour that would have been likely to have attracted most criticism, if not frank outrage. There are still many societies in which the premises that Mr C appealed to in justification of his behaviour would find considerable resonance among established practice and even legal entitlements. Stalking is new, partly because of changes in our society's understanding of the nature of the relationship between people.

Stalking as popular, legal and scientific discourses

Initially the term stalking was used by the media to describe the behaviour of the unwanted followers of the famous. It was later extended to include those who harassed ex-partners, co-workers, casual acquaintances and a whole range of fellow citizens. The intense media attention that stalking and stalkers has attracted in the last decade has generated a public consciousness and concern which has found political expression in a series of anti-stalking laws. The first such law was enacted in California, the other states in the union, the sole exception being Maine, clamouring to follow suit. Currently, most Western nations have either passed anti-stalking laws or are in the process of doing so. The legal definitions of stalking are often framed in response to local preoccupations, be it with protecting the famous, preventing the harassment of ex-partners or strengthening the laws against persistent nuisance. The emergence of what has amounted to a new category of criminal behaviour in its turn has generated interest amongst mental health professionals and behavioural scientists, particularly those working within the criminal justice area and forensic mental health services.

In the last decade stalking has generated three areas of discussion, almost simultaneously: a legal discourse, particularly around how to define the offence of stalking; a popular discourse carried forward with no signs of flagging interest, not only in the media but through novels, films and television drama; and finally there is emerging a scientific discourse. The scientific discourse initially focussed on the nature and motivations of stalkers and latterly on the reactions of the victims and the impact of being stalked on their health and safety. This emergence of a new way of describing and talking about the world provides an opportunity to examine how these popular, legal and scientific discourses have developed and interacted, and in turn how they have created new categories of fear, crime and scientific study. The rapid acceptance of the word's new connotations and purpose was in large part because the categories of stalking and stalker filled a need that, if not perceived previously, became obvious once coined and accepted. It defined an area of human behaviour that caused distress to others. The behaviour itself is not new but once labelled could in rapid succession be discussed, defined, prohibited and studied. In short, the coining of the word 'stalking' and its establishment as a significant social problem allowed us to recognize and act upon a previously unregarded area of human activity.

Stalking, like any form of complex human activity, can be the end point of a range of intentions and influences. Similarly, like many other forms of behaviour that cause distress to others, it forms the extreme end of a spectrum of activities ranging from the usually welcomed and mundane to the terrifying and fortunately rare. One of the consequences of the identification and naming of stalking as a form of deviance has been to focus attention on which types of related behaviour are, in current society, acceptable, questionable or to be outlawed. The carving off of certain forms of activity usually aimed at establishing or maintaining interpersonal contact as not only unacceptable but criminal and deviant has occurred with scant discussion of boundary problems except in law journals. Little attempt has been made to reconcile the emerging ideas of what constitutes stalking with what in marginal cases amounts to a disjunction between the intentions and attitudes of those involved in establishing a relationship or negotiating an end to a relationship. The legal literature has focussed extensively on legitimate versus criminal following and intrusion, as well as subjective versus objective definitions of offending. This has, however, been strictly within discussions of legal process and the framing of effective legislation. In part the uncritical acceptance of stalking as a social evil has been because initially the actions so described were obviously dangerous to the victim. Prominent among the first well-publicised cases of stalking were examples in which victims were eventually murdered by their stalkers. That many stalkers are at best a distressing nuisance and at worst dangerous is beyond dispute, but this still leaves unresolved the boundary issues. In, for example, an ex-partner, where is the line that divides the acceptable pursuit of reconciliation and the stalking of that erstwhile love? In the would-be suitor, how many phone calls denote enthusiasm and how many stalking? In the dismissed worker, how many angry letters and enquiries constitute the legitimate pursuit of clarification and assertion of rights and how many stalking? This book not only attempts to describe unequivocally damaging stalking behaviours but examines the boundaries and continuities between stalking and related forms of human behaviour.

Stalking is a problem because it evokes, in the object of the unwanted attention, distress and on occasion fear. There are real grounds in some cases for the victims to fear for their physical safety, and even their lives. Equally, there are good reasons to suppose that the disruptions produced by persistent stalking will have deleterious effects on a victim's mental health. It should not be forgotten that the lives of the stalkers are also severely disrupted by their actions. At the root of much stalking lie such states as loneliness, the pain of loss, nostalgia and the longing for intimacy. This is not to excuse or to argue for some equivalence of suffering, merely to state the obvious: in many cases of stalking, both victim and perpetrator have everything to gain from resolution and an end to the behaviour. The successful management of stalking, it is argued in this book, requires that the stalker be exposed to an appropriate balance of therapeutic help and legal sanction. For some, such as the individual with erotomanic delusions, treatment is paramount. In the calculating and vengeful ex-partner, confrontation with the personal costs of continuing to stalk, in terms of legal consequences, can have a gratifyingly salutary influence. For most stalkers a mixture of treatment and external control is optimal. Victims, even if the burden of the stalking has been relieved, are often left sufficiently traumatized to be in need of considerable help. In those still being stalked, practical help and appropriate support may go some way to relieving the burden and speeding its removal.

The question of how certain activities come to be identified as stalking has only occasionally been directly considered. As already emphasized, it is the victim who ultimately defines stalking, but what are the cues for recognizing oneself as being stalked?

Emerson et al. (1998) attempted to address this question by considering stalking as a social process. They based their analysis on a variety of accounts of individuals who had been followed and harassed. They argued 'stalking is keyed to a variety of hitches and disjunctures surrounding relational coming together and splitting apart' (ibid., p. 295). What they describe as the 'core dynamic' is a one-sided attempt to create or sustain a close relationship. Central is the notion of one party being indifferent or opposed to the establishing, or re-establishing, of a relationship with the other eager for such an outcome.

Many intimate relationships begin with the meeting of strangers. The encounter with another person who is either previously unknown or largely unregarded is a common but none the less frequently charged event. This is particularly true when the context is one that promises the beginning of an important relationship. As we move from encountering someone to relating to that person we travel across a complex social and interpersonal minefield. Traversing the pitfalls that lie between encountering and relating is rarely straightforward. The opportunities are many, not just for failure but for producing unsolicited responses of anger or fear. Perceiving the other as intrusive and harassing, and oneself as stalked, is a measure of the experienced disjunction between the intentions and perceptions of the protagonist of the relationship and that of the unwilling object of those aspirations. When intimate relationships founder and fail, one partner usually perceives (or even pursues) the imminent termination before the other. Again this is fruitful ground for those disjunctions that make possible the self-definitions of being a stalking victim. In the quest for a new intimacy the initiator risks being defined as a stalker. In the dissolution of intimacy it is the initiator of the break-up who risks provoking a response in which they experience themselves as a stalking victim.

Each and every struggle toward, or away from, intimacy does not inevitably occur under the threat of the evocation of the label 'stalking'. Any unlucky individual could find themselves accused of being a stalker by an oversensitive, overanxious or even self-serving target of their affections. In practice, however, most reasonable individuals give a fair degree of latitude to those whose advances they intend to resist or reject. Sometimes that generosity stems from guilt, sometimes from sympathy, occasionally from simple politeness, but it is usually offered. In most cases the pursuers need to be possessed of a good dose of insensitivity and an overwhelming sense of entitlement to place themselves at risk of their behaviour being construed as stalking.

The archaeology of stalking

The emergence of stalking as a term for a particularly egregious form of harassment has clarified and specified the possible perspectives from which repeated unwanted intrusions can properly be viewed. It has also constrained the extent to which similar behaviours can be presented in a positive light. One construction of courtly love was the unrequited love of the persistent suitor who merely admired from afar the unattainable perfections of the loved one (see Singer, 1984).

The great Italian poets Petrarch (1304–1374) and Dante Alighieri (1265–1321) both celebrated in their works life-long devotions to women with whom they had had little or no actual contact. Dante writes of his love of Beatrice in *La Vita Nuova* (circa 1292). Although some have held Beatrice to be a symbol she is usually identified with Beatrice Portinari. For Dante she is 'an abstract, almost allegorical, embodiment of beauty, goodness and the other perfections' (Singer 1984, p. 156). T. S. Eliot (1930) regarded Dante as having a pathological obsession with Beatrice, with whom he had no real contact but nevertheless used her as the focus and inspiration of his idealized love. Petrarch had a similar infatuation and idealized love for Laura (thought to be Laura de Noves, married 1325 died 1348, the mother of eleven children). It is not the reality of Beatrice or Laura but entirely their imagined properties that moves these poets. De Rougemont (1950, p. 178) wrote: 'but here again the woman, whether absent or present, is never but the *occasion* for a torment he cherishes above all else'. Petrarch wrote of Laura: 'I know to follow while I flee my fire: I freeze when present: absent my desire is hot' (quoted in de Rougemont, 1950). We do not know in what manner Dante pursued his Beatrice (though the Pre-Raphaelites portray him as furtively spying). It is not known whether Laura felt harassed by Petrarch's 365 daily poems, assuming he sent them to their inspiration (number 366 was dedicated to the Virgin Mary). What is clear is that for their contemporaries, and for many generations to come, Dante and Petrarch pursuing loves that took no account of the realities or feelings of the beloved were a subject not of scandal but of admiration. Western society at that period accepted as an ideal an autistic love constructed by a man out of projections and fantasies that took no account of the realities of the actual woman.

Søren Kierkegaard (1813–1855), the Danish philosopher, theologian and founder member of the existential elite, wrote a curious collection of pieces published as *Either/Or* (1987/1843). The first volume, *Either*, is ostensibly written by 'A,' a young self-styled aesthete and includes the narrative *The Seducer's Diary*. This is said to be the fictionalized account of Kierkegaard's pursuit of a young woman, Regine Olsen, renamed Cordelia Wahl in the book. The pursuit consists of surreptitious following, spying upon her, gathering information about her and engineering repeated encounters in public places. Kierkegaard in the fictionalized account describes his (or A's) first contact with the supposed beloved as follows.

A figure appears, enveloped to the eyes in a cape. It is not possible to see where he is coming from . . . He passes by you just as you are entering the front door. At precisely the crucial moment a sidelong glance falls on its object. You blush; your bosom is too full to unburden itself in a single breath. There is indignation in your glance, a proud contempt. There is a plea, a tear in your eye, both are equally beautiful. I accept them both with equal right . . . I certainly shall meet her again sometime; I certainly shall recognize her, and she may recognize me – my sidelong glance is not forgotten so easily . . . I promise she will recall the situation. No impatience no greediness – everything will be relished in slow draughts; she is selected, she will be overtaken. (Kierkegaard, 1987/1843, pp. 314–315)

In the author's mind a relationship is created in the moment of eye contact. It is for him an exchange. An exchange of vows, a moment of recognition and reciprocity. The 'she may recognize me' at some time in the future is rapidly superseded by 'she will recall the situation'. The relationship is established, albeit autistically. His claim 'she is selected, she will be overtaken' takes no account of her; it is a statement of entitlement.

The relationship established is for A one of worship and service: 'my beautiful stranger . . . I am at your service in every way' (Kierkegaard, 1987/1843, p. 320). There is a recognition that at least in the first few weeks there is no real reciprocity, only the hope and expectation of a favourable response: 'in a certain sense my profits are meagre but then I do have the prospect of the grand prize' (ibid., p. 326). The course of the following manufactured contracts and information gathering are documented in the account, which is in the form of a diary. He follows her 'with the intention of passing by her and dropping behind her many times until I discovered where she lived' (ibid., p. 333). He spies: 'I will know who you are – why else do you think the police keep census records?' (ibid., p. 327). He watches her house: 'Today I learned something about the house into which she disappeared' (ibid., p. 337) and plans, for 'if it is necessary for me to gain entrance to the house . . . I am prepared' (ibid., p. 338).

The behaviours appear to us to be those of stalking, although this is not how either Kierkegaard or his contemporaries would have constructed this story, even assuming the vocabulary existed for such a labelling. Even more interesting is the description of A's internal world as he creates for himself an intimate relationship. First there is the fantasy of the loved one's inevitable succumbing. Then he bestows on her characteristics, desires and intentions in a vacuum, for at this stage he knows only her appearance and the appearance of her house. She 'lives in a world of fantasy' (ibid., p. 341). He is convinced that 'she is an isolated person' (ibid., p. 339), that she is 'proud' (ibid., p. 342), she has 'imagination, spirit, passion' and even 'maybe at particular moments she wishes that she were not a girl but a man' (ibid., p. 343). It is difficult to avoid the suspicion that the beloved is being constructed, or reconstructed, in the image of the lover. A rich world is created out of glimpsed moments and stolen observations. *The Seducer's Diary* seems a window into the world of one particular type of person we would now call a stalker.

But is Kierkegaard's account really that of stalking, and to what extent is it, as is often assumed, a true account of his initial pursuit of Regine Olsen? Regine Olsen did eventually have an actual relationship with Kierkegaard, although it did not last. She survived him, living until 1904 and becoming a celebrity on the basis of *The Seducer's Diary*. Her later memories of Kierkegaard are not those of the stalker but of the man she eventually met and to whom for a time she was engaged. Kierkegaard remained preoccupied (obsessed even) with Regine for the rest of his life and even in his last will and testament claimed 'my estate is her [Regine's] due exactly as if I had been married to her' (Kierkegaard, 1996 p. 657). The extent to which *The Seducer's Diary* accurately portrays the actions and mental life of Kierkegaard in his early pursuit of Regine Olsen must remain questionable. It could be more fictional than factual, it could conflate (or even transpose) other episodes of such stalking-like behaviour. Kierkegaard (1996, p. 417) claimed: '*The Seducer's Diary* was written for her sake, to help repulse her'. What it does unquestionably is provide an insight into the thinking and behaviour of someone whom we would now label a stalker. At the time, however, A could have legitimately, in the eyes of his culture and his contemporaries, styled himself a lover.

We do not know the impact on the victim, who must, to some extent, have been aware of the undeclared observer. If this is an account of the stalking of Ms Olsen it is difficult retrospectively to view her as unduly disturbed, let alone traumatized, given that she later accepted his attentions and offer of marriage and given that she accepted, in later life, the role of the great philosopher's great love. We would speculate that the experience of being followed and spied upon would have been experienced very differently for Regine Olsen in the Copenhagen of the mid-nineteenth century than it would be by a teenager (she was 16 or 17 years old) in London or New York at the end of the twentieth century. The man, though unknown, would not have been a stranger in the same sense, given that his identity, if not already suspected, could easily have been established in the relatively small community. His appearance would have defined him in terms of probable social class and role to a far greater extent than in today's world. His behaviour would have had acceptable explanations in terms of the shy suitor, the gauche admirer or even the romantic stranger. The threatening and sinister were not imminent to anything like the same degree in the attentions of a stranger.

John Updike (1997) described Kierkegaard's behaviour as revealed in *The Seducer's Diary* as convoluted gallantry, although he does also describe it as stalking. Updike gave stalking a curious resonance, however, when he wrote: 'The hero's long and loving stalking of a girl too young to approach provides, in fiction as in reality, the peak of erotic excitement' (ibid., p. xiii). Kierkegaard's alter ego A does not appear in *The Seducer's Diary* to be desisting from direct contact because Cordelia is a schoolgirl, so the reader is left in some doubt as to whose reality it is that finds stalking young girls the peak of erotic excitement. That such people exist will become clear as this book progresses; that Kierkegaard was an example is, one can hope, a misinterpretation.

The social construction of stalking

In an outstanding article Lowney & Best (1995) examined the emergence of the construction of stalking as a social problem. They examined media coverage between 1980 and 1994 in the form of newspapers, tapes of television and radio broadcasts and magazine articles, together with scholarly journals and court and congressional proceedings. The focus was on how and in what form claims about stalking were brought to public attention and how this led to the construction of a new crime problem. They identify three phases, or periods, in the emergence of stalking as a widely recognized social problem.

The first period described by Lowney & Best (1995) was from 1980 to 1988, when there were articles and discussions under such headings as 'psychological rape' and 'obsessive following'. The word 'stalking' hardly ever appeared. The psychological rape and obsessive following that were made manifest in various forms of sexual harassment and intrusiveness were typified by the nonviolent, but persistent, pursuit of a victim (usually, but not exclusively, female). The victims, though distressed and exposed by the limitations of the criminal justice system's ability to protect them, were nevertheless often portrayed as at least partly complicit in their plight. Although the behaviours were accepted as problematic they were not 'packaged and presented so as to command public attention' (Lowney & Best, 1995, p. 39).

The second phase from 1989 to 1991 was, Lowney & Best (1995) argued, marked by the increasing use of the term stalker, usually in the form of 'star stalkers'. These were men and women who persistently followed and harassed the famous. The murder of the American sitcom actress Rebecca Schaeffer by a disordered fan, Robert Bardo, gave a dramatic focus to this new construction. Victims were now celebrities and the perpetrators typically mentally disturbed and/or inappropriately obsessed with their victims. Stalking became a form of random violence for which the victim bore no responsibility. The behaviour of the stalker was now seen as the harbinger of violence and often as the product of mental disorder. The new construction captured public attention, captured the attention and harnessed the energies of the media and entertainment industries, and finally captured both the attention and (self) interest of the law makers.

The final construction articulated by Lowney & Best (1995) was the redefinition, in the period 1992–1994, of stalking as a product of failed relationships and male violence. Stalking was reframed as a 'women's issue, a widespread precursor to serious violence . . . a common problem . . . a form of domestic violence against women . . .' (ibid., p. 42–3). These authors illustrate how juxtaposing domestic violence and stalking could create new evidence. Thus a statement that 90% of women killed by their partners had previously called the police was equated with 90%

having previously been stalked. This in turn generated the outrageous claim that nine women a day (in the USA) are killed by stalkers. Stalking had been reconstructed into a violent crime, usually committed against women by former or current husbands or lovers and also labelled by some as an 'epidemic' (e.g. Gilligan, 1992). The new construction virtually excluded psychological explanations, let alone psychiatric accounts, of the perpetrator's motivations. Typifying examples of stalking, when not an extension of the battering of women, feature children and adolescents as victims. Such examples made clear the stalking paedophile's responsibilities and made manifest the essentially evil nature of the perpetrator's intentions and actions.

Stalking's emergence as a social issue and a new category of crime shares features with other similar categories that have come to prominence, including child sexual abuse, mugging and road rage (Scott, 1995; Fergusson & Mullen, 1999). Each in their different ways have acquired the status of social facts whose existence is no longer challenged. The process of constructing a social problem, for example child abuse, has been conceptualized as occurring in the four overlapping stages of discovering, diffusion, consolidation and reification (Parton, 1979; Scott, 1995).

The key question about the 'discovery' of stalking is why these particular forms of harassing behaviours were defined as a special problem at that particular historical moment, and why stalking suddenly gained such prominence. As has been emphasized, there was nothing new about behaving in the manner we now call stalking, nor in considering such behaviour to be a problem. What was new was increasingly regarding such behaviour as a problem separable from other forms of inappropriate intrusiveness and as having peculiarly sinister implications. The discovery of stalking does not reflect a single influence but the concatenation of a number of trends and concerns, many of which had remained inchoate before the concept and the very word 'stalking' gave them a medium for expression.

The elements from which stalking's initial articulation as the persistent following and intrusion on the famous (star stalking) emerged include the following:

1 The 1970s and 1980s were marked by an increasing public concern about privacy and the capacity of others to monitor and pry into the lives of fellow citizens. These concerns were particularly acute for those in the public eye who were more and more the object of the intrusions of gossip columnists, photographers (the paparazzi), investigative journalists and the multiplicity of TV and radio shows that claimed to expose or reveal the doings of the famous. For the famous, be they entertainers, politicians, sports people or royalty, nothing was now sacred. Every action, or rumour of action, was potentially grist for the exposure mill. In response, privacy gained a reciprocally increased valuation, with the protection of such privacy becoming a social good.

2 There has occurred over the last century or so a continuing change in how people

experience themselves in relation to other members of their society. The emergence of large urban conurbations inevitably led to people living among those about whom they had no knowledge. As early as 1798 a Parisian police agent was complaining: 'It is almost impossible to maintain good behaviour in a thickly populated area where an individual is, so to speak, unknown to all others and thus does not have to blush in front of anyone, (quoted in Benjamin, 1968, p. 40). The stranger, in contrast to the foreigner, was of the same society but was an unknown element within your own community. In literature the stranger as potential threat and as the carrier of evil became an increasingly common theme, illustrated in the work of, for example, Edgar Allen Poe, whose quote from *The Man of the Crowd* prefaced this chapter.

At the very moment in the 1980s when the word 'community' was rising to ideological prominence, the reality for most of those in Western society was a dissolution and virtual disappearance of community. The bonds of common interest, which linked individuals to those other individuals with whom they lived in some proximity, were disappearing. In urban life neighbours were increasingly becoming strangers. The individuals' interests were rarely experienced as linked to those among whom they lived. The latter became sources not of mutual support but of irritation, intrusiveness and even risk. Fear became even more likely to be a central mediator between the individual and the stranger. In this climate the transformation of the stranger into predator was readily accomplished. Again the famous shared in the emerging fear of fellow citizens. The sense of vulnerability experienced by public figures was enhanced by such events as the assassinations of President John F. Kennedy and of singer John Lennon. There was apparently an escalation in the frequency with which the famous received threatening letters and communications. Part of achieving prominence became the acquisition of a need for protection. Whatever the real level of threat to the famous, the perception of risk spawned a specialist security industry with new technologies and new forms of expertise to assess risk, manage risk and protect. It would be difficult not to become increasingly sensitive to threat if surrounded by security experts who advise, and induce, the spending of large sums of money on protection from as yet undeclared dangers.

3 The 1980s were marked by a perception that our society contained increasing numbers of strange people who might intrude and threaten. Public awareness, and wariness of, groups such as the mentally ill, the addicted and the intellectually disabled were fed partly by the reality of increased numbers of such people in the community, but equally by constructions of such disorders and disabilities as predisposing to impulsive and aggressive conduct. The Secret Service in the USA maintain extensive dossiers on mentally disordered individuals who are considered to present a risk, however remote, to the President or other politi-

cians. The threat to the famous is constructed as a threat from the irrational and the disordered; after all, who but the mad could bear such animosity toward politicians, let alone entertainers?

These and other preoccupations found expression in the notion of stalking. The murder of Rebecca Schaeffer provided the case around which concerns with privacy, safety and the threat presented by the disordered crystallized in the form of the new issue of stalking. Those claiming that stalking should be recognized as a specific and serious crime were able to organize their advocacy around this dramatic example.

The phase of diffusion of the awareness of stalking through the wider society was remarkably rapid. Given that stalking was initially viewed primarily as a threat to which media personalities were peculiarly vulnerable, it is not surprising that coverage was as extensive as it was effective. Equally, the combination of the famous, sinister pursuit, violence and in many cases disordered affection proved irresistible to the watching and reading public. Doubtless, experts expounding on exotic and potentially titillating subjects such as erotomania and obsessional following added to the fascination.

The ready acceptance of stalking as a social problem was accompanied by a dramatic widening of the concept. What began as a description of behaviour directed at the famous was rapidly generalized to include similar behaviours directed at ordinary individuals. A social problem that was relatively uncommon, because it was circumscribed by the contingency of being a star, was transformed into an experience open to all. Nobody was safe, or at least in the early stages of the genesis of stalking as a social problem, no woman or child was safe.

These developments in part mirror the acceptance of child sexual abuse as a major social problem. Child sexual abuse emerged in the late 1970s in the form of claims for society's attention and concern made by adult women usually recalling their victimization as children by incestuous abuse. This soon generalized to incorporate claims about a wide range of child molestation affecting a significant proportion of the population (Fergusson & Mullen, 1999).

The first and most important phase in the generalizing of stalking occurred when well-established concerns about the harassment of women by their male partners were annexed to the emergent phenomenon of stalking. The bracketing of stalking with domestic violence was dramatically successful for those who had been advocating more recognition and greater protection for battered women. The media fascination with stalking, together with the public and political acceptance of it as a serious form of criminal activity, was readily transferred to stalking as a form of domestic violence. For a period the construction of stalking was almost completely colonized by legitimate, but previously discounted, attempts to extend legal protections to women harassed and pursued by current or previous partners. The first anti-stalking legislation in California reflected concerns with the stalking of the famous, although subsequent legislation increasingly gave primacy to the protection of women, some anti-stalking statutes even confining stalking to the harassment of those who had previously either cohabited or had had intimate relationships with their stalker (e.g. original legislation in West Virginia in the USA and New South Wales in Australia). Stalking made one of its earliest entries into the scholarly behavioural science literature firmly coupled with domestic violence (Kurt, 1995). The first community study to be published of the prevalence of stalking surveyed only women (Australian Bureau of Statistics, 1996). The USA Department of Justice, which has played an important role in documenting stalking and supporting legislative responses in the USA, produced its reports under the title 'Domestic Violence and Stalking' and reported to Congress under the Violence Against Women Act. Despite this, to its credit, the research commissioned by the US Department of Justice surveyed males as well as females. This research has been important in widening notions of who stalks and who is stalked. (National Institute of Justice, 1997; Tjaden & Thoennes, 1998).

To understand how it was possible for stalking to be so successfully translated into an aspect of domestic violence it is necessary to examine developments over the prior decade. The intimidation and battering of women by their male partners attained substantial prominence as a social problem in the 1970s and 1980s. The success of advocates for abused women in evoking appropriate social and legislative responses was, however, limited with regard to harassment that did not involve overt physical violence (Follingstad et al., 1990; Walker, 1989). The media gave considerable attention in the early 1980s to the following and harassing of women after the revelation that actress Jodie Foster had been persistently pursued in the USA by John Hinckley Jr, who later attempted to assassinate President Ronald Reagan. Although the media at this time tended to focus on the famous it did generalize into the broader issue of the harassing of women by their male partners (Wilcox, 1982). Female harassment was the term usually employed for this phenomenon, though 'psychological rape' briefly had currency in the media (Jason et al., 1984; Lowney & Best, 1995). An interesting study by Jason and colleagues, which appeared in 1984, examined female harassment. They defined female harassment as 'a male persistently using psychological or physical abuse in an attempt to begin or continue a dating relationship with a female who had indicated a desire to terminate the dating relationship' (Jason et al., 1984, p. 261). Their study amounts to arguably the first study of this form of stalking in a community sample. Female harassment did not continue to receive sufficient media coverage to establish its position on either the public or political agendas. Further systematic studies also had to wait for the stimulus provided by the emergence of the stalking phenomena in 1989 and 1990. Although female harassment failed in the wider public arena to hold attention, it remained firmly on the agenda of activists and advocates. The women's movement was only too aware of its frequency and its destructive potential. When stalking exploded onto the media as a hot issue, female harassment was a ready-made claimant for a share of the attention, a claim pushed home with considerable success by the domestic violence lobby.

As part of this phase of diffusion the emphasis on the stalker being mentally disordered or at the very least an obsessional follower was replaced by a characterization of a male who brutalized and potentially battered his female partner. Mental disorder was replaced by brutality and criminality, and the stalker became more strongly gendered.

Stalking conceptually and legislatively has not remained so closely tied to domestic violence. It is not clear exactly which influences led to a further generalization of stalking and a partial return to a concern with pursuit by disordered admirers. Certainly, when studies of stalkers began to appear they suggested a wider range of victims and perpetrators than could be accommodated within either the domestic violence paradigm or the notion of stalkers to the stars. Initial studies of victims also indicated a wide range of relationships between stalker and victim (see Chapter 3). The media continued to give prominence to accounts of the stalking of men as well as women and one of the outstanding journalistic accounts during this period was of the stalking of a male surgeon by a female journalist (Brenner, 1991). Perhaps what was most important in driving the increasingly broad conceptualization of the relationship between stalkers and their victims was the practical experience of both courts and researchers. Beginning with the behaviour of persistent intrusions and unwanted communications rather than with causal theories (be that around domestic violence or obsessional following), then a far richer reality is revealed in the phenomena of stalking. Courts have perforce to consider first and foremost behaviour, not theories of causation. Behavioural scientists should start with the behavioural phenomena, not their pet theory about those phenomena. As this book will illustrate, we hope, if you begin with the behaviours that constitute stalking you reveal a varied and rich tapestry of intentions, motivations and forms of relatedness that frustrates attempts to restrict stalking and stalkers to any single context or overarching theory of causation.

The phase of consolidation of a new social problem occurs when a social agency or agencies come to be held responsible for responding to the perceived needs created by this new social and political agenda. Stalking once given life by the media was rapidly transformed into a specific type of criminal offence. It was to the police and the courts that the responsibility of dealing with stalkers fell. Stalkers were initially regarded as drawn from the disturbed and the mentally disordered of the community. Despite the powerful impact of the subsequent absorption of forms of domestic violence into stalking the notion that stalkers were at least in part a mental health problem persisted. The first organizational structure to emerge specifically to manage stalkers was the Los Angeles Police Department's Threat Management Unit (Zona et al., 1993, 1998). This combined the skills of police, legal and mental health professionals in a system aimed to manage, and where possible prevent, stalking. They employed a range of interventions including those of mental health professionals. In our own mental health clinic in Melbourne the first initiative was directed at providing support to victims of stalking but this soon led to a parallel concern with the assessment and management of perpetrators of stalking. This book is predicated on the assumption that the approaches and skills of mental health professionals and behavioural scientists are central to understanding and managing stalking.

The final stage of the reification of a social problem involves the ossifying of the issue into something taken for granted as a natural area of concern by the general community (Scott, 1995). The questions become not 'What is stalking?', 'What brings it about?' or even 'How much of it is out there?', but merely 'Who should deal with it?' and 'Why haven't they dealt with it?'. The issue becomes one for professional competencies and institutional technologies. The problem itself becomes an accepted part of the social landscape, which may raise concerns but not curiosity. If stalking has reached that stage by the time this book has been published then only a select few of our professional colleagues are likely to be reading this sentence.

There are problems over the use of theories of social construction. In attempting to describe the way in which a phenomenon becomes an object of knowledge and a topic of concern within a particular culture, it is all too easy to appear to be overly sceptical or even mocking. Persistently inflicting on someone else repeated unwanted intrusions and communications is a totally unacceptable way of behaving, which, in our view, has rightly been made criminal in most Western jurisdictions. Such behaviour induces fear and can produce in the victim considerable psychological damage and extensively disrupt their functioning. It is a real social evil. It was a social evil before the word and the concept of stalking emerged in 1989 and 1990. Stalking is nevertheless a construction. Neither the reality of the pain and distress that so often accompanies both being stalked and being a stalker, nor the fact that stalking is a construction, should be in question (for an exemplary discussion of these issues with regard to multiple personality disorder, see Hacking, 1995).

Conclusions

The social construction of stalking began around instances that typically involved extensive and prolonged intrusions and culminated not infrequently in assaults that could be lethal. The incorporation of female harassment into the rubric of stalking widened the net but maintained a clear association with assault, battery and even murder. Stalking has now been greatly extended to encompass behaviours that, although distressing, are typically far less likely to involve either such extensive intrusions or such obvious risks of serious assault as did the earlier typifying cases. This extension has not to date been accompanied by an equivalent modification in the meanings and expectations attached to being stalked. As a result, a radical restructuring of our understanding of the social world may be occurring.

A similar trajectory was followed when child sexual abuse, initially constructed around severely physically intrusive and often prolonged incestuous abuse, was broadened to incorporate a wide range of forms of the sexual molestation of children. The benefits of this process were the recognition of the true extent of the sexual exploitation of children and the emergence of a social consensus that such behaviour should be stopped and victims accorded appropriate protection (and in some societies treatment and monetary recompense). The downside was a widespread confusion about the nature, extent and effects of child sexual abuse in all its forms, which impaired effective responses (Fergusson & Mullen, 1999). It also brought about a change in how victims understood themselves and their pasts, which was certainly not without its problems. The attempt more accurately to inform professionals and the public about the realities of stalkers and stalking is central to this book. We are at a relatively early stage in the development of stalking as a social issue and an area of scientific study but already the need to confront growing myths and unexamined assumptions about stalkers and stalking is clear.

2

The epidemiology of stalking

Introduction

The various metamorphoses experienced by the meaning attached to stalking were described in Chapter 1. Understandably, the potential prevalence and nature of stalking shifted dramatically as the definitional constraints on the behaviour changed. The prevalence of stalking differs according to whether we confine its use to the pursuit of the famous, the harassing of women, the obsessive following of others or, finally, to the specific patterns of repeatedly intrusive behaviour that occasion fear. The changing constructions throw up different typifying instances with different propositions about what constitutes stalking and what are its likely implications. The stalking of Rebecca Schaeffer was the paradigm case of 'star stalking'. The construction of stalking within a domestic violence paradigm offered equally frightening defining instances in, for example, the killing of American Kristin Lardner by her ex-boyfriend (Lardner, 1995) and the understandably extensively reported pursuit of Joy Silverman by her ex-lover, Chief Judge Sol Wachtler in the USA (see Gross, 1994; Kurt, 1995).

As the net represented by stalking widens to catch an ever larger range of behaviours and perpetrators, there has not always been an appropriate shift in the image conjured up by the label stalking. When the lifetime prevalence of stalking was reported to be between 8% and 12% for women in the USA (Tjaden & Thoennes, 1998), the image conjured up for many was of vast numbers of women living in fear for their lives and at the mercy of potential killers. These researchers were careful in their definitions and in the presentation of their data and can in no way be held responsible for the ways in which such figures were utilized in the public arena. The problem is the familiar one of once a dramatic and memorable image of a particular activity has been established in the public mind, this becomes the defining instance. Whenever stalkers, or for that matter child molesters or muggers, are referred to, it conjures up an image drawn from the extreme and most damaging end of the spectrum encompassed by such descriptions. At the present stage of research into the epidemiology of stalking, questions are couched in the form of the broadly defined category of stalking. Widely different activities are grouped under the single rubric. The small number of community studies that have been undertaken are inevitably bracketed with the far larger number of case reports and series drawn from clinic or court samples. This reinforces the tendency to view the data as a function of the more extreme aspects of the stalking phenomenon. Case studies and clinical series are usually drawn from samples of people whose stalking activities have been sufficiently outrageous to lead to their arrest, admission to hospital or at least referral to a mental health clinic. These are likely to be a different population from those who harassed the randomly selected community respondents endorsing such enquiries as 'Have you ever been followed or spied upon?' or 'Have you ever been sent unsolicited letters?'. These were among the entirely appropriate screening questions from the study of Tjaden & Thoennes (1998), which were intended to capture a wide sample of the harassed. No equivalence should be automatically assumed between such community respondents considered to have been stalked and the victims described in clinic-based populations (see, e.g. Pathé & Mullen, 1997).

As research develops, prevalence figures are likely to be increasingly expressed in terms of more tightly defined types of stalking behaviours. Tjaden & Thoennes (1998) took an important step in this direction by quoting figures for stalking victims defined more or less stringently in terms of the level of fear induced by the stalking behaviour (equivalent in some senses to child sexual abuse being separated into contact and noncontact abuse). We can expect increasingly sophisticated analyses of stalking in terms of its constituent behavioural elements, its frequency, impact and associations, most particularly to other forms of violence.

The epidemiology of stalking in practice is the epidemiology of the reporting of having been stalked. Epidemiology attempts to establish the prevalence of the phenomenon, what correlates with its occurrence and what are its consequences. Prevalence refers to the portion of the population who have the condition (or in this case, the experience) at a given time. With stalking, what has been reported is not a true prevalence, but a cumulative incidence, as when the percentage of those reporting having been stalked is given over the previous year or over the subject's lifetime. We will acquiesce, here, in common practice by referring to a cumulative incidence as a prevalence qualified by the specified period.

The estimates of stalking will be affected by how stalking is defined. It will also be influenced by the way in which questions eliciting information about being stalked are framed. The selection of the sample to be surveyed can also have considerable influence, as can variability within and between such samples. If stalking is taken as two or more episodes of some form of harassing behaviour, the prevalence will be considerably higher than if the threshold is set at, say, ten such incidents. If a criterion for a stalking event includes that it did in fact occasion fear, this will reduce prevalence estimates from those obtained by including reports of having been subjected to the behaviours irrespective of their impact. Similarly, as will be seen below, the degree of fear required to qualify the stalking event affects prevalence. In the study by Tjaden & Thoennes (1998), figures were provided for both thresholds of 'significantly frightened or fearful' and 'somewhat or a little frightened'. At this early stage in the epidemiological enquiries into stalking it is desirable that results be presented in a manner that allows the potential variables in the definition to be applied to the data. Thus, on the issue of how many events constitute stalking, data can be provided for populations reporting varying frequencies of harassment. Equally, the temporal constraints can be shifted if the results are presented with an analysis of the varying lengths of time involved in the stalking events.

The manner of framing enquiries will also influence ascertainment rates (for discussions of this issue in the child sexual abuse literature, see Peters et al., 1986; Dill et al., 1991; Martin et al., 1993; Fergusson & Mullen, 1999). Overarching questions such as 'Have you ever been stalked?', even if a definition of stalking is provided as a guide, is likely to produce lower ascertainment rates than a series of specific questions about particular experiences. Thus: 'Have you ever been subjected to unwanted telephone calls?' 'How often did these calls occur?' (with directions such as once, twice, three to five times, etc), 'For how long did the calls continue?', and finally, 'How much fear did they cause?'. A far richer and more flexible data base is generated by using properly structured questions that constrain the respondent to detailing what happened, how often, over what period of time, and with what level of distress being generated.

Sample selection can also have significant effects on estimates of prevalence. Using convenience population samples such as students, or those from a particular occupation, will provide prevalence estimates that are difficult to generalize beyond the group from which the sample was drawn. Even more restricted in terms of generalizability will be samples drawn from clinics or attendees of health professionals, given that the variables associated with being stalked and certainly the effects of being stalked may increase or decrease the chances of attending such services. Restricting sampling to women, or the young, or those from neighbourhoods with a particular class structure, can all profoundly influence prevalence estimates. A representative random community sample is the preferred sampling method likely to produce the most widely applicable prevalence estimates. This design is not, however, without its problems. The prevalence of stalking behaviours and the extent to which such behaviours are experienced by their target as fear inducing will almost certainly vary between cultures, between communities and even within communities. The willingness to participate in surveys of stalking will differ, affecting response rates. Systematic errors in prevalence estimates will reflect the extent to which the willingness to participate in a survey of stalking experiences is directly influenced by whether or not the subject has been stalked. Those who have been stalked may be more eager to participate, or, conversely, may experience any letter containing intrusive enquiries as a re-victimization they can well do without. In either case, response rates would directly reflect the experience of stalking and bias the resulting prevalence estimate.

The bulk of information regarding the nature of stalking and the characteristics of both stalkers and their victims has been derived from clinical studies conducted in forensic mental health settings. To date, few epidemiological studies of stalking have been conducted or published. This chapter reviews and analyses the findings from the few community-based studies of stalking, focussing on the rates of stalking in the community, the behaviours involved, and the characteristics of victims and their stalkers.

The prevalence of stalking

Initial guesses at the prevalence of stalking suggested that each year in the USA, 200000 stalkers were pursuing victims. It was further speculated that one in twenty women would at some time in their lives experience the unwanted attentions and intrusions of a stalker, although predictions regarding the scale of male victimization were not proffered. These early estimates were tentatively advanced by a prominent US forensic psychiatrist, Dr Park Dietz, who properly qualified the figure as an educated guess. Subsequently, these figures took on a life of their own, being re-iterated through popular and scholarly publications and being endorsed by the US government (Senate Judiciary Committee, 1992). Dietz had in part extrapolated from a series of studies that examined threatening and inappropriate letters sent to Hollywood celebrities and members of the US Congress (Dietz et al., 1991a, b). The authors of these disturbing letters all reportedly sent numerous missives to their targets, typically at least ten but in some cases up to several hundred, their communications persisting for on average twelve months or more. Dietz and colleagues noted that it was not uncommon for the writers to enclose relatively mundane items with their messages, such as photographs or media clippings, but other enclosures ranged through the abhorrent (e.g. syringes of blood or semen) and the bizarre (one Hollywood celebrity received a bed pan) to the grotesque (a coyote's head was reportedly sent to one member of Congress). It is certainly likely that many of these letter writers shared motivations (e.g. infatuation or resentment) and diagnoses (e.g. erotomania, paranoia) similar to those encountered in stalking populations. However, it should be noted that firm diagnostic ascriptions could not be made solely on the basis of the subjects' correspondence. None the less, this group could by no means be regarded as representative of stalkers per se, given the highly selective population to whom they directed their communications and their unitary method of pursuit. Inferring the prevalence of stalking on the basis of these individuals alone undoubtedly underestimated the true extent of this phenomenon in the community.

Australia

Despite its media cachet, remarkably few studies have attempted to examine the prevalence or nature of stalking in the community. The first epidemiological study of stalking was conducted in Australia in 1996. The Australian Bureau of Statistics (ABS) conducted a national survey of women's experiences of physical and sexual violence, part of which included questions related to stalking and harassment. A random and representative community sample of 6300 adult women were asked during confidential interviews whether they had ever been 'stalked' by a man. Stalking was defined as being followed or watched, having a man loiter outside the home, workplace or places of leisure, being telephoned or sent mail (including electronic mail), receiving offensive material, or experiencing property interference or damage. This definition was based on a composite of Australian state anti-stalking laws (see Chapter 14), which broadly define the criminal offence of stalking as two or more acts that the victim believes are undertaken with the intention to frighten or harm. Those respondents who acknowledged experiencing two or more stalking behaviours, or who had experienced the same unwanted behaviour on more than one occasion, were for the purposes of this study defined as victims of stalking.

Based on this definition, the ABS survey found that 15% of women reported being stalked by a man at some time in their lives, which would imply that an estimated one million Australian women will have experienced this type and level of stalking. A further 2.4% reported having been stalked in the twelve months preceding the survey. Almost a quarter of the respondents who acknowledged having been stalked in the preceding twelve months were experiencing ongoing victimization. Those who reported stalking were drawn from the entire age spectrum, although young women aged 18–24 were the most likely group to have been pursued in the previous twelve months. Contrary to the findings of case reports and nonrandom studies of stalking (see Chapter 3), most women reported being stalked by a stranger, as opposed to a prior intimate partner or acquaintance.

The duration of the stalking experiences were reported as less than a month in over 30% of subjects. Almost a quarter, however, were pursued for six months to two years. Some 15% of subjects indicated they had been stalked for a period of two or more years. Those who were pursued by strangers experienced the shortest duration of stalking (the majority stalked for less than a month). This was in marked contrast to ex-intimate partners who typically pursued their victims for at least six months and not infrequently for over two years. Thus, while women were more often stalked by a stranger than someone they knew, the duration of stalking was greatest when there had been a previous relationship with the perpetrator.

The methods of pursuit and harassment reported to have been employed against the subjects in this survey were remarkably consistent. Most said they received unwanted telephone calls and letters or cards, notes frequently being attached to their property. Being kept under surveillance, particularly within the home, and being followed, were also common experiences. In contrast, the incidence of property damage, receiving offensive material and loitering outside the victim's workplace or places of leisure was reportedly low. Unfortunately the survey did not examine the frequency of explicit threats directed at the victim and/or third parties, nor the incidence of violence, either physical or sexual, directly associated with the stalking.

Many of the women who had been stalked in the twelve months prior to the survey said they were living in fear for their personal safety, irrespective of whether the stalking was continuing or had ceased. Over a third of victims had changed their social activities in response to the stalking, while others modified their shopping routines (16%), or arranged alternative child care or voluntary work arrangements (10%). One in ten victims in paid employment claimed that they had had to take time off work as a consequence of the stalking. Surprisingly though, for the majority of women who were stalked (60%), the experience was not acknowledged to have produced safety fears. Furthermore, only 38% of victims notified the police of the unwanted contacts or communications. Unfortunately, the survey did not examine whether the impact of stalking on its victims was mediated to any extent by the duration of their pursuit, the methods used to stalk and intimidate, or the prior relationship to the perpetrator. Similarly, victims were not questioned as to whether their reluctance to notify the police related to fear of inciting their stalker, concerns that they would not be believed, or a lack of appreciation of the criminal ramifications of such conduct (particularly as most state anti-stalking laws in Australia had been in operation for less than a year at the time of the survey). It is possible that many victims, especially those who had been prior intimates or acquaintances of the stalker, may have minimized or underestimated the threat to their safety posed by the stalkers' actions, and thus suffered fewer effects. It is also possible that for a large proportion of victims in this study, the events experienced, while sufficient to meet the legal criteria of stalking, were not perceived as serious enough to warrant police intervention.

The ABS survey demonstrated that, far from being a rare occurrence, broadly defined, stalking is a relatively frequent experience within the community. Stalking affected nearly 15% of Australian women at some time in their lives. This rate is likely to be an underestimate given that male victimization and same gender stalking were not considered. It should be noted, however, that in this study respondents qualified as victims of stalking if they had experienced as few as *two* unwanted contacts or intrusions at some time in their lives. Importantly, being stalked in this study was not contingent upon the experience of fear. It is conceivable that on the basis of such criteria, essentially inadvertent behaviours (e.g. following someone in traffic, or standing outside their home), rather than being considered as isolated though unsettling events, were redefined, or reinterpreted by some respondents and/or interviewers as stalking. This is implied to some extent by the observation that many of the victims were stalked for less than a month (indeed possibly for only a day, although this cannot be established from the data) and frequently by a stranger. Thus, while up to 15% of women may at some time experience unwanted contacts or communications that meet the broad definition of stalking employed in this study, it remains uncertain how many were subjected to stalking behaviours that caused significant apprehension and distress. None the less, for many women, the unwanted intrusions persisted over a number of months, and in several cases extended over years, causing significant fear and apprehension and often resulted in disruptive changes to their lifestyle (for further discussion, see Chapter 3).

USA

Important though the ABS survey is as the first published epidemiological study of the prevalence of stalking in a community sample, there are major limitations. As already noted, the study excluded male victims and female perpetrators. The definition of stalking was very broadly based and not qualified by the requirement that the behaviour induce fear or distress in the victim. Furthermore, the study does not allow any analysis of the association between stalking and future violence. The US National Institute of Justice commissioned a study to specifically examine the extent of stalking in the US population (National Institute of Justice, 1997; Tjaden & Thoennes, 1998). This study is, at the time of writing, the most informative and influential treatise on the experiences of stalking among the wider community. Like the Australian survey, its primary purpose was to examine the incidence and patterns of violence against women, particularly within the domestic context. Additionally, however, the study collected information related to stalking, including the frequency of this behaviour, the nature of the relationship between stalkers and their victims, and its impact on victims. Importantly, the design incorporated male as well as female respondents. A representative random sample of 8000 adult women and 8000 men from across the USA participated in telephone-based interviews. Unlike the Australian survey, the US study did not explicitly ask respondents whether they had ever been 'stalked', as this approach necessarily – and perhaps erroneously – assumes that respondents know to what 'stalking' refers. The question 'Have you ever been stalked?' also requires the respondents to be able to perceive themselves as victims of this conduct. Instead, the study employed a behavioural definition (derived from US state anti-stalking laws) that intentionally omitted the word 'stalking'. Respondents were asked to indicate whether any person, male *or* female (but not including debt collectors, telephone solicitors or other sales people), had ever: followed or spied on them; sent them unsolicited letters or written correspondence; made unsolicited telephone calls; stood outside their home, school or workplace; showed up at the same places even though they had no business being there; left them unwanted items; tried to communicate with them against their will; vandalized their property, or destroyed something they loved. As in the Australian survey, a legal definition of stalking was utilized for the study, and therefore considered as possible victims all those respondents who had experienced such behaviours on two or more occasions. However, only those respondents who additionally acknowledged that the assailant's behaviour rendered them 'significantly frightened' or 'fearful of bodily harm' were defined as stalking victims in the US study.

The study found that 8% of women and 2% of men had experienced stalking at some time in their lives. The twelve-month prevalence of stalking was 1% for women and 0.4% for men, a rate only half that reported in the Australian sample. The study also examined the prevalence of stalking on the basis of less stringent criteria, whereby respondents were required to feel 'only a little' or 'somewhat frightened'. Using this definition, the prevalence increased substantially, from 8% to 12% for women, and from 2% to 4% for men, while the twelve-month prevalence jumped from 1% to 6% for women, and from 0.4% to 1.5% for men. These figures more closely resemble the earlier Australian findings, indicating that the requirement of a low standard of fear boosts the reported rates of stalking significantly.

The US study confirmed that women were most likely to be victims of stalking, although men were by no means immune from this conduct, accounting for 22% of all those having been stalked at some time in their lives. There were no differences in the prevalence of stalking among white and minority respondents of both sexes (African–American, Hispanic, Asian/Pacific Islanders, American Indians/Native Alaskans), although Native American Indian and Alaskan women were found to be at greater risk of stalking than women from other minority ethnic backgrounds. (The rates of fatal and nonfatal violence within these populations are also increased, however, suggesting that stalking may be one aspect of a broader pattern of violence in these indigenous communities; Tjaden & Thoennes, 1998.)

The majority of victims in the US sample were aged between 18 and 29 years when the stalking first commenced. Indeed, stalkers in the USA showed a preference for young victims, apparently few pursuing victims aged over 40 years. Female victims reported being stalked almost always by a male perpetrator (94%). In contrast, males indicated that they were as likely to be harassed by men as by women. One third of male victims reported pursuit by a current or ex-intimate partner (most cases involving heterosexual relationships), 34% by an acquaintance and

36% by a stranger. Interestingly, for the majority of men who reported being stalked by a nonintimate, the perpetrator was in almost all instances also a male. The researchers were at a loss to explain this unexpectedly high proportion of same gender stalking, but speculated that this may be motivated by homosexual attraction, homophobia or even gang-related activities (for further discussion, see Chapter 9).

Women claimed to be stalked principally by someone with whom they had a current or prior intimate relationship, be it a spouse, de facto husband or casual date. The survey did not differentiate between stalkers who were current or former intimate partners, nor did it separate spouses from other types of romantic partner. This practice of treating what are disparate groups as a unified whole unfortunately obstructs the understanding of what may be significant differences in the prevalence, nature, impact and risks of violence associated with stalking in these distinct groups. Furthermore, the failure in this study to distinguish current from former intimate relationships confuses the phenomenon of stalking with the control and manipulation of spouses that occurs in the broader context of domestic violence. The study certainly demonstrated a strong association between domestic violence and stalking, with up to 80% of women who were stalked by a current or former partner reporting having previously been assaulted by the perpetrator. Similarly, in 60% of cases involving intimate partner stalking, the pursuit commenced *before* the relationship had ended. None the less, as the results of this study also demonstrate, the experience of stalking occurs in a variety of contexts, as well as in the context of diverse intentions, thus warranting its status as a separable phenomenon, rather than an annex of domestic violence.

The US survey examined the duration of stalking according to years, rather than the more illuminating index of months. Some 50% of victims stated that they were pursued for less than a year, while a quarter had been harassed for between two and five years. Approximately 10% said they had been stalked for five years or more. In keeping with the Australian findings, the average duration of stalking was longer when the perpetrator was an intimate partner (2.2 years) than a nonintimate (1.1 years). The methods of pursuit employed by stalkers were similar to those observed in other Western countries, most victims in the US reporting following, receiving unwanted telephone calls and letters, as well as being kept under various forms of surveillance. Almost 50% of victims reported being explicitly threatened by their stalker and a third experienced property damage. Women were significantly more likely to be spied upon, followed and to receive unwanted telephone calls compared with male victims, although threats, property damage, unsolicited materials and letters were directed equally to both groups. One in ten stalkers reportedly killed or threatened to kill their victim's pets, although curiously the incidence of physical violence against the victims themselves or third parties was not examined.

Half the victims in the US study indicated that they notified the police of their stalking. Those who chose not to report the offences frequently claimed that 'it was not a police matter', that 'the police couldn't do anything' and that they feared reprisal from the stalker. Equal proportions of males and females informed the police, although police intervention appeared to be heavily dependent on the gender of the complainant. Perhaps not surprisingly, the police were more likely to arrest or detain a male suspect accused of stalking a woman, and were also more likely to refer women than men to appropriate victim services. Less than a fifth of victims who reported their stalking to the police actually had their case prosecuted and only 50% of these cases resulted in a conviction. The study found that women were more likely to obtain a restraining or protective order against their stalker than male victims (28% versus 10%), which reflects to some extent the greater incidence of intimate partner stalking against women, many of whom had previously been assaulted by their stalker. The use of restraining orders, however, proved largely ineffective, as 70% of female and 80% of male victims who had obtained such an order reported its violation. Of those victims who notified the police of their harassment, only half approved of the police response and intervention. The remainder claimed to be dissatisfied in that the police had not detained or arrested their stalker, their complaint had not been taken seriously, or that the police had failed to offer them sufficient protection.

Victims of stalking in the US study were also asked their perceptions of why the stalker had pursued them. The most common attribution was that the stalker was trying to control them. Other postulated motivations were the desire to forcefully maintain a relationship, or to instil fear. Few perceived the stalking to be explained by mental illness. When asked their thoughts on why their stalker had ceased his or her pursuit (in the 92% of cases where the behaviour had discontinued), most victims considered the stalker's relocation or preoccupation with a new love interest to be salient factors. They were far less likely to attribute the cessation of the stalking to police and criminal justice interventions.

Consistent with the Australian findings, the impact of stalking on victims in the US survey varied. A third of victims stated that they were fearful that they would be stalked again by another perpetrator and 20% took 'additional precautions' as a consequence of their experience. Other victims enlisted the help of family and friends (18%), relocated (11%) or even went to the extreme of obtaining a gun as a protective measure (17%). A third of women and 20% of men sought psychological counselling to deal with the trauma, and 25% of victims reported losing time from work, usually up to ten days (for attendance at court or counselling, or for consultations with police or solicitors), although some 7% claimed they were unable to return to work at all. For many victims, the experience of being stalked produced a range of deleterious effects; yet in keeping with the Australian results a significant proportion (50%) indicated that they were not concerned for their personal safety, nor did the majority of victims (80%) acknowledge taking any extra precautions in response to the stalker's conduct. However, the mediating effects of the methods and duration of pursuit, or the nature of the prior relationship with the perpetrator were again not considered when examining the victim's emotional and practical responses to stalking.

Summary

These first community surveys suggest that, at least within Western industrialized countries, the experience of stalking is remarkably consistent in terms of the patterns and methods of pursuit, and, depending on the nature of the prior relationship with the perpetrator, the likely duration of such conduct. Most victims of stalking reported following and surveillance, and communications via the telephone and postal services were commonly encountered. Less frequent, although arguably more threatening when they occurred, were associated behaviours such as property vandalism, the killing of pets, explicit threats to harm and the receipt of offensive materials. In both studies, victims of all ages, from teenagers to the elderly, were at some time prey to such conduct. Men were the primary perpetrators of stalking behaviours, and in the US study they constituted a fifth of the victims. Stalking for the majority of victims persisted for several months, although an unfortunate few experienced a more protracted course of harassment over several years. Where these community surveys diverge is in the nature of the prior relationship between stalkers and their victims. In Australia, victims were more likely to report being pursued by a stranger than by a known perpetrator, whereas in the USA intimate partner stalking predominated. This high level of prior intimates stalking in the US study was due to some extent to the combining of current with former partners whose relationships varied markedly in their degree of intimacy. The political conceptualization of stalking in the USA, which firmly places the behaviour within the context of domestic abuse and violence against women, rather than acknowledging the range of contexts (e.g. social, occupational or professional) in which stalking can, and all too frequently does, emerge, has also gained momentum in Australia (McMahon & Davids, 1993) and Canada (Way, 1994). The unquestioned acceptance of this conceptualization of stalking, which derives more from specific political and financial motivations than clinical and epidemiological evidence, runs the very real risk of swamping the study and understanding of stalking, as well as deflecting attention and already scant service provisions away from other equally deserving victims of this conduct (such as male victims, victims of workplace stalking, or victims of stranger and same gender stalking, to name but a few).

Within the community, stalking is a not uncommon experience, with some 8% of women and 2% of men likely to experience at some time in their lives unwanted contacts and intrusions sufficient to cause significant fear and apprehension. Community surveys conducted to date capture well the spectrum of stalking, from the limited yet unsettling acts that constitute the legal criteria of criminal stalking, to the persistent and corrosive conduct that may extend over months and years, prompting not only distress in the victim and those around them, but disruptive and often expensive lifestyle changes. These studies also advance a rudimentary understanding of the impact of stalking on victims within the community. None the less, further population-based studies examining the effects of this conduct on the victim's social, psychological and occupational functioning are warranted, as are valuable, although undoubtedly even more difficult to undertake, community studies that advance our understanding of stalkers themselves.

3

The victims of stalkers

Stalking is like no other violent crime in that it is repeated, prolonged and engulfs not only the mental well-being of the victim and their family, but their entire lives.

Renee Goodale, stalking victim and founder of Survivors of Stalking (SOS)

Introduction

The past decade has seen an intensification of curiosity and concern relating to stalkers and their activities, but interest in the victims of stalking is a relatively recent development. Much common knowledge of victims was gleaned initially from media reports of celebrities and other public figures who had fallen prey to crazed fans or resentful constituents (see Dietz et al., 1991a,b; de Becker, 1997) and it was generally thought that such activities rarely involved ordinary citizens. In recent times researchers and legislators, recognizing major shortcomings in our understanding of stalking behaviours and their management, have focussed their attention upon stalking victims as a source of data that is not necessarily reflected in official records or in studies of perpetrators (Hall, 1998).

As a consequence of systematic enquiry into victims' experiences many earlier notions about stalkers and those they target are being revised. Victims of stalking certainly exist in the wider community and are not a rarity (some authorities believing that this crime has already reached epidemic proportions), nor can any citizen claim immunity from a stalker's unwanted attentions by virtue of gender, age, socioeconomic status, occupation or cultural background, although there is little doubt that some, such as celebrities, are at greater risk than others.

While we have been largely ignorant of the magnitude of this societal menace there has been, at least until the surge of stalking awareness that culminated in widespread anti-stalking legislation, a disregard for the plight of stalking victims. There was little appreciation of the impact of trauma of this nature upon those unlucky enough to become the object of a stalker's fixation. Public sympathies and any therapeutic efforts were more likely to be directed at those who sustained tangible physical injuries, because it was assumed that these were the cases who suffered the most disruption and emotional damage. Because little was understood of stalking itself, medical health workers were poorly equipped to offer its victims constructive interventions, any more than we were able to prevent our patients, loved ones and indeed ourselves from ever falling victim to such activities.

This chapter profiles the victims of stalkers and the links that exist between the two. It describes the various contexts in which stalkers choose their victims, and proposes a typology of victims based on the status of the prior relationship between victim and stalker, and the context in which the stalking arises. The chapter concludes by examining the impact of stalking upon its victims.

Victim studies

In what is probably the earliest empirical study of stalking victims, Jason et al. (1984) surveyed females who had been harassed by males after ending a relationship or refusing to enter into one. The researchers interviewed fifty women from Chicago, all of whom had been subject to harassment that persisted for at least one month and included repeated telephone calls (92%), unwanted approaches at work or at home (48%), following and surveillance (26%), unwanted letters and other unsolicited material (24%), and threats and physical attacks (30%). Sixty-nine per cent of the sample had dated their harassers on fewer than ten occasions and 14% had never dated them. While 42% claimed nothing unusual occurred during the period they dated, 24% indicated that their boyfriends were becoming too serious, discussing marriage and the like, 20% noted strange behaviours and 14% were reportedly subjected to physical or verbal abuse. Upon ending the relationship or refusing to date a would-be lover, harassment was experienced for on average 13 months (range 1–120 months), with 26% of the sample experiencing ongoing harassment.

A noteworthy study from the University of Toronto (Jones, 1996) examined the nature of stalking by drawing on victims' reports to police of 'criminal harassment' (the offence used to prosecute stalking in Canada) during the period 1994–5. The study analysed data from the Uniform Crime Reporting Survey, an annual review that encompasses 130 police departments throughout Canada, accounting for some 43% of the volume of reported crime nationally.

During the study period 7472 victims reported incidents of stalking and harassment to the police. The majority of these victims (80%) were women. The victims' demographic characteristics were not examined, the research instead focussing on the nature of the prior relationship with the stalker and the outcome of reporting stalking to the police. Most victims were pursued by an ex-spouse (33%) or, in 14% of cases, someone with whom they had had an intimate relationship. In 28% of cases the stalker had been a casual acquaintance. Five per cent of victims said they had been stalked by a family member (other than a spouse), 5% by a workmate or business associate, and 8% were pursued by a stranger. A current spouse was the perpetrator in 2% of cases, while 4% were unable to identify who was harassing them. Women were more likely to be pursued by an ex-intimate partner (56%), in contrast to men, who were typically stalked by a casual acquaintance (46%) or someone known through a work or business relationship (11%). The proportion of victims stalked by a stranger or a family member was similar for both men and women.

In the Canadian study one in four stalking incidents known to the police involved associated behaviours not contained within the Criminal Harassment Code, including the utterance of threats, assault, breach of probation or bail, and breaking and entering. Few victims reported being physically assaulted by their stalker, though many claimed to have suffered severe emotional trauma as a result of their pursuit and harassment, particularly when the stalking occurred at the victim's home (where indeed the majority of stalking incidents took place.) One should be cautious in interpreting this apparently low level of associated physical violence, given that, at the time, assault was an offence carrying a substantially heavier penalty and the lesser offence of harassment may in some instances have been absorbed into the more serious charge. In 20% of the cases reported to the police, no charges were laid owing to reluctance on the victims' part to pursue such a course. This reluctance was most commonly encountered in cases where the victim knew the perpetrator through a business relationship, or when a man was being pursued by an ex-wife. In contrast, women stalked by an ex-intimate were more likely to proceed with criminal justice intervention.

These findings indicate that stalking is not infrequently brought to the attention of law enforcers, with over 7000 people reporting crimes of this nature in two years. Males were found to be the primary perpetrators of stalking, although they were also at risk of victimization, accounting for 20% of self-referred victims. The majority of victims were stalked by an ex-intimate partner or a casual acquaintance, although the study characterized well the variation that exists in the prior relationship between stalkers and their targets. While most cases proceeded to prosecution of the perpetrator (the exceptions being those cases in which the victim was reluctant to pursue such a course), the outcome in most instances was probation rather than incarceration.

Fremouw and colleagues (1997) conducted the first epidemiological study on a nonforensic population of approximately 600 college students. Anonymous questionnaires administered to psychology undergraduates sought to establish the prevalence of both stalkers and stalking victims in this sample, the prior relationship between stalker and victim and the coping strategies employed by the latter. The survey revealed that 30% of females and 17% of males experienced being victims of stalking behaviours at some time. Conversely, a mere 1% (all three of whom were male) admitting to having acted as a stalker. Among those reporting stalking victimization, the stalker was known to his or her victim in 80% of cases, with 43% of females and 24% of males reporting a previous romantic involvement with their stalker. In fewer than 20% of cases the stalker was not previously known to the victim. The study also noted some discrepancies between reported coping strategies among female and male victims. While both either confronted or avoided the stalker, women also carried repellent spray weapons such as mace. An additional strategy reported by men, but not women, was to *reconcile* with their stalker, at least in instances where there had been a prior intimate relationship. Reporting the harassment to police and legal remedies such as protective injunctions were less popular options amongst this cohort.

The study of Tjaden & Thoennes (1998), detailed in Chapter 2, found a lifetime prevalence of stalking victimization among female and male respondents of 8% and 2%, respectively. The victim population was 78% female, while stalkers were male in 87% of cases. The majority of victims were between 18 and 29 years of age. In most cases the stalker was known to his or her victim, 23% of female and 36% of male victims indicating that they were stalked by a stranger. In 59% of female and 30% of male victims the stalker was an intimate partner. Half the victim sample had reported the crime to police. Of those who obtained a restraining order, 81% of male and 69% of female victims claimed that their stalker violated the order.

Hall (1998) recruited 145 stalking victims through press releases and media interviews that promoted the research in six major urban centres in the USA. In addition, flyers were distributed in several target regions to major victim centres, such as those for domestic violence and sexual abuse clinics. The author acknowledged that this selection process resulted in a nonrandom and skewed sample of self-defined victims, all of whom were willing to initiate contact with the researcher and provide their contact details. This is a significant undertaking for victims of stalking who are typically (and understandably) wary of divulging any personal information to strangers. That a significant proportion of victims were also drawn from domestic and sexual violence centres also limits the representativeness of the study, as these agencies traditionally do not attract male victims of violence or stalking. The study did not employ any objective criteria to define the parameters of stalking, thus possibly including in the sample victims with the infrequent experience of unwanted contact that would not qualify as stalking for more stringent clinical and research purposes.

The participants were a diverse group demographically and incorporated those who had made contact with police or victim organizations as well as those who had not previously divulged their victimization. Females constituted 83% of the sample, in keeping with the findings of the other clinical and epidemiological studies reviewed. Most victims were single or in intimate relationships and were typically aged in their mid thirties. A third of victims were employed in professional positions, 20% in an executive capacity and 16% had clerical jobs. In the majority of cases (57%), victims and their stalkers were prior intimates (89% of these stalkers being male), although 35% of respondents were pursued by prior acquaintances and 6% by strangers. The duration of stalking ranged from less than a month to over thirty-one years, the modal duration being between one and three years (although it should be recognized that the reported duration of stalking is likely to be an underestimate in many instances, given the inability of victims, especially those stalked by strangers or acquaintances, to be confident about the time at which they first became aware of the problem). For half the victims the stalking had ceased, but 25% of those surveyed continued to be harassed and a further 21% were unsure whether their stalking was ongoing. Most respondents believed that their pursuit was motivated by the inability of the stalker to accept the termination of a relationship, an 'obsession' with the victim (frequently involving suspected mental illness in the perpetrator), retaliation for a real or imagined slight, jealousy, or an attempt to initiate a relationship.

The majority of these victims experienced multiple forms of harassment, most often involving telephone calls (87%), surveillance (84%) and following (80%), while unwanted approaches, malicious gossip and unsolicited gifts or packages were reported by nearly half the sample. A number of victims recounted less common incidents designed to intimidate and control, such as entering the victim's home and interfering with household objects. It was often difficult for the victim to enlist police support when reporting subtle intrusions of this nature and these were virtually impossible to prosecute in the absence of other criminal activities such as breaking and entering or theft. Sixty-three victims said their property was damaged by the stalker, fifty-five reported physical assaults and thirty-two victims indicated that they had been sexually assaulted by their pursuer; there was no elaboration on the nature of these attacks. Over 40% of stalkers had threatened to harm a third party, although the incidence of overt threats against the primary victims was not reported, prohibiting any assessment of the relationship between threats and subsequent violence in this sample.

Pathé & Mullen (1997) examined the experiences of 100 victims of stalking, focussing predominantly on the impact on the victims' psychological, social and occupational functioning. The victims who participated in the study were derived from two sources, the first being persons referred to the authors' forensic mental health clinic, and the second comprising individuals who contacted the authors directly following a series of articles on stalking that appeared in the print media. The participants represented a broad cross-section of the community but, given the nonrandom nature of the sample, could not be assumed to be representative of the general population of stalking victims. For the purposes of this study, only those individuals who reported repeated intrusions or being persistently contacted for a period of at least four weeks were defined as stalking victims. Individuals who recounted isolated instances of following or unwanted communications, or who experienced occasional instances of unwanted contact or intrusions over the course of several years, especially where the identity of the perpetrator was uncertain and may have differed on different occasions, were not included in the study, however distressing the encounters.

The 100 individuals who fulfilled the criteria for stalking victims completed a detailed fifty-item questionnaire that examined their demographic characteristics (and those of the perpetrator where known); the nature and the duration of the harassment; the prior relationship between the stalker and the victim; the impact of the stalking on the victim's mental and physical health and their social and occupational functioning; and the availability and perceived adequacy of traditional and professional sources of assistance. Many victims provided additional comments and those seen individually at the clinic gave extensive personal accounts, often remarking that the opportunity to discuss their ordeal in a sympathetic and constructive setting was, in itself, therapeutic.

Eighty-three per cent of the stalking victims in this study were female. The victims ranged in age from 9 to 66 years, most being in their mid to late thirties. In the majority of cases, the victim reported some form of previous contact with their stalker, most commonly a prior intimate relationship (29%), although 25% in this study knew their perpetrator through a professional alliance (particularly doctor/patient), through other work-related contexts (9%) and in 21% the victim and stalker were prior acquaintances, usually meeting through social and familial networks. In 16% of cases, the victim and perpetrator were strangers. A significant proportion of the victims in this sample (36%) were, at the onset of stalking, employed in professional occupations such as medicine, teaching and law. The median duration of stalking was twenty-four months (ranging between one month and twenty years), 52% of the cohort claiming they were still being pursued.

All victims described multiple forms of harassment. Seventy-eight per cent received unsolicited telephone calls, often at inconvenient venues and frequently at times when they felt most vulnerable and violated, such as during the early hours. Those victims employed in professional occupations were more likely than other occupational groups to receive harassing telephone calls, usually at their workplace. Sixty-two per cent of the sample received unwanted letters from their stalkers, some receiving several missives per day. Two victims employed in professional occupations were harassed via email. Nearly 80% of victims reported unwanted approaches by their stalker, most often at their home, workplace or school, their assailants commonly seeking to express their love in person, plead for a reconciliation or verbally threaten. A further 71% were kept under surveillance, most being acutely aware of their stalker's ubiquitous presence, typically outside their home or places the victim frequented. Several stalkers menaced their victims by making the extent of their surveillance frighteningly apparent, often calling their victims at various locations throughout the day and night (several victims received calls from their stalker when visiting friends' homes), or calling the victim the moment they arrived home. Some described the outfit the victim was currently wearing or the people he or she was with.

Half the cohort received unsolicited material from their stalker, typically in the form of 'gifts' (flowers, perfume and chocolates prevailing), although others reported audiotapes, self-help books, magazines (often pornographic) or photographs (most often of the stalker). In several instances victims were sent mutilated animals, one finding a pig's head on her doorstep and another a parcel containing her missing, now dismembered, cat. Property damage was reported by 36% of victims, with cars bearing the brunt of vandalism, typically in the form of graffiti, scratched paintwork and slashed or deflated tyres, although homes were also frequently targeted, sustaining broken windows, damaged fences, upended letter boxes and ruined gardens.

More than half of this sample (58%) said they received overt threats from their stalker, usually directed at themselves as well as at third parties such as relatives, current intimate partners, friends or work colleagues. Threats included promises to destroy the victim unless he or she succumbed to the stalker's demands. Death threats were received by several victims, being both explicit and implicit in the form of cards bearing gravestones, or in one case a fake notice in the 'deaths' column in a newspaper. Other victims were threatened with rape, and several were tormented with threats to harm their children. Assaults by the stalker were reported by thirty-four subjects: thirty-one physically and seven sexually. Violence was most often directed toward the victim rather than third parties who, although frequently threatened with harm, appeared at less risk of an escalation to assault. The majority of victims who reported physical assaults sustained bruises, abrasions and lacerations, usually as a result of being hit, kicked, slapped or pushed. However, one victim was fortunate to survive strychnine poisoning and a further two victims survived strangling quite literally at the hands of their stalker. One woman recounted in chilling detail her abduction by her ex-spouse stalker who, over the course of several days, consumed a large quantity of alcohol, watched pornographic videos and raped her. In 76% of victims assaulted by their stalker previous threats of personal violence were received. In this study, violence was most likely to be perpetrated when there was a pre-existing relationship of an intimate nature between victim and stalker.

All victims had sought assistance to deal with their stalking, most commonly from family or friends (78%) and the police (69%), but many also attended medical practitioners (44%) and lawyers (38%). Police and lawyers were consulted predominantly by those victims suffering property damage, or when there was a prior intimate relationship in which violence was more likely to be a feature. Most victims noted that the stated desire of people and agencies to help was infrequently matched by their effectiveness, common examples being police who could not act to detain a stalker in the absence of physical harm or property damage (most of these cases presenting prior to the enactment of anti-stalking legislation in Australia). The victims' poignant, and at times astonishing, accounts of the impact of stalking upon their lives will be presented in detail later.

Typology of stalking victims

Several classifications of stalking victims have been proposed, all based on the premorbid relationship between victim and stalker. Zona et al. (1993) simply divided victims into two categories, either 'prior relationship' or 'no prior relationship', the former subdivided into 'acquaintance', 'customer', 'neighbour', 'professional relationship', 'dating' and 'sexual intimates'. Meloy & Gothard (1995) advocated categorization of victims as either 'stranger' or 'former (sexual) intimate', while Harmon et al. (1995) were rather more inclusive, classifying the victim's prior relationship as 'personal', 'professional', 'employment', 'media', 'acquaintance', 'none' or 'unknown'. Subsequently, Meloy (1996) argued for a simplification of this relational typology into three broad, mutually exclusive groupings: 'prior sexual intimates', 'prior acquaintances' and 'strangers'. Fremouw et al. (1997) divided the prior relationship between victim and stalker into 'friend', 'casual date', 'serious date' and 'stranger', while Emerson et al. (1998) introduced the terms 'unacquainted stalking', 'pseudoacquainted stalking' (where the victim is a publicly identified figure) and 'semi-acquainted stalking', where there has been some contact between victim and stalker in the past, as in co-workers.

We advance the following typology of stalking victims in which they are categorized according to their former relationship with the stalker and the context in which they are targeted. These are not entirely mutually exclusive groupings and the allocation of a victim will in some instances be a matter of judgement. The groupings are as follows: prior intimates, casual acquaintances and friends, professional contacts, workplace contacts, strangers and the famous.

Ex-intimates

This is the largest category, the commonest victim profile being a woman who has previously shared an intimate relationship with her (usually male) stalker. Although 'prior intimates' has been defined as 'current or former spouses, current or former co-habitants (of the same or opposite sex), or current or former boy-friends or girlfriends' (Tjaden & Thoennes, 1998), we include as stalking only those cases in which the relationship has been terminated, the victim having made his or her wishes known unequivocally to the other party. It has been noted that approx-imately half of these cases will have been stalked by their partner while still in the relationship, being even at this stage subjected to behaviours such as following, sur-veillance and damage to personal property. These relationships are often character-ized by the offending partner's emotional abuse, controlling behaviour and violence. Indeed, it has been found in one survey that over 80% of women stalked by current or former partners have, while still in the relationship, been physically assaulted by them, with a further 30% reporting sexual assaults prior to their sep-aration (Tjaden & Thoennes, 1998). The stalking behaviours often indulged in whilst the relationship is still in progress serve to intimidate and control the victim. Stalking a partner isolates them from outside supports such that the victim can less easily leave the relationship.

Stalked ex-intimates are exposed to the widest range of harassment methods. Repeated phone calls and persistent following, threats and violence are more likely to be experienced by this group, the latter particularly if the perpetrator has prior criminal convictions (Mullen et al., 1999). Walker & Meloy (1998, p. 142) con-tended that, within the realm of domestic violence, 'stalking is a risk factor for further physical abuse or a lethal incident just by virtue of the tenacious proximity seeking toward the victim, and especially if it occurs in combination with several other high risk behaviours'.

The victims of ex-intimate partners can expect the pursuit to be more persistent, although legal sanctions may persuade their ex-partner to refrain from further harassment. This is often more complicated if victim and stalker share children; the stalker may have legitimate visitation rights (although these are often exceeded) or may embark on a custody battle fuelled by a strong sense of entitlement, vengeance and determination to maintain contact with the rejecting party. In one instance, a stalker made false allegations that his ex-wife was abusing their two young children, a malicious tactic that very nearly resulted in the victim losing her children and facing criminal charges. Morbidly jealous ex-intimates are also more refractory to legal interventions, their victim typically reporting that they were subject to stalk-ing behaviours, particularly surveillance, during the relationship. One woman left her ex-partner when he became increasingly suspicious of her innocent interac-tions with male work peers. He had been monitoring her day-to-day activities by appearing unexpectedly at her workplace or at other venues including cafés and shops, wiretapping the home phone, scrutinizing her mobile phone bills for un-familiar numbers, and reading her letters. This behaviour escalated when the relationship ended, the woman being subjected to almost constant surveillance and repeated threats.

'Date' stalkers with whom the victim may have had only a brief romantic liaison are less likely to exhibit violence than ex-partners whose emotional investment in the victim is considerably greater. The victim of a date stalker often gives a history of discomfort early in the relationship. They are, however, often reluctant to hurt their (most commonly) boyfriend's feelings and they may accept further dates beyond the point at which they perceive any future in the relationship. These cases lend some truth to the maxim 'men who cannot let go choose women who cannot say no' (de Becker, 1997, p. 203). When victims do make an assertive attempt to extricate themselves, their partners typically react badly, often in a childlike or pathetic manner that exploits the victims' guilt and sympathy.

The guilt frequently experienced by victims in this category can be reinforced by the propensity of others to judge their predicament. Family and friends may express their disapproval of the victim's relationship choices and helping agencies may convey their suspicions that the victim in some way *encouraged* the stalking. Ex-intimate victims are more likely than those in other categories to seek police help and legal advice, where they may encounter similar attitudes. The response of the criminal justice system does not always live up to the victim's expectations, leading to calls for comprehensive training for workers in the criminal justice system in the special needs of victims of intimate partner stalking (Tjaden & Thoennes, 1998).

Casual acquaintances and friends

Victims in this category include neighbours and friends. It is probably the commonest category for male stalking victims (Hall, 1998). Intimacy seekers and incompetent stalkers may commence their activities after a casual social encounter, while the pursuit of the rejected stalker may be subsequent to the breakdown of a friendship or estrangement from a family member (one man following his stepsister to the opposite side of the world, driven by anger and jealousy at her decision to leave *him* so that she could study overseas).

Neighbour stalking is generally perpetrated by the resentful stalker. The victim may be involved in a dispute with a neighbour about a fence, garden or noise. The perpetrator develops a grudge against the victim and becomes increasingly focussed on revenge. His or her activities escalate, with personal threats directed at the victim, malicious complaints to police and government departments, property damage, the theft or killing of pets, letters and notes affixed to the victim's car or property, house break-ins, the leaving of unsolicited material such as dead rodents on the victim's doorstep, monitoring of the victim's movements from a vantage point such as a front or side window in the stalker's home (sometimes aided by binoculars and cameras), repeated accusatory approaches when the victim ventures out and even full-blown assaults. The stalker in these situations generally involves the primary victim's family or other co-habitants, children especially becoming pawns in the conflict. Protective injunctions are problematic and difficult to enforce in these circumstances, the victim or victims frequently resorting to a change of residence to escape their highly stressful home environment. Though drastic and disruptive to the victim's entire family this strategy is frequently curative in these situations.

Professional contacts

Health care providers, lawyers and teachers are especially vulnerable to stalking. These professions are at increased risk of stalkers from all motivational categories, although intimacy seekers, incompetent and resentful stalkers predominate. The termination of a therapeutic relationship may occasionally give rise to 'rejected' stalking patterns, and this group of victims can also be prone to the sexually predatory behaviours of their patients, clients or students.

Psychiatrists and primary care physicians share an enhanced risk of being stalked by intimacy seekers and incompetents by virtue of their regular contact with the lonely and mentally unstable. Any profession which 'comes into contact with the isolated and disordered and in whom sympathy and attention is easily reconstructed as romantic interest' may be vulnerable (Mullen et al., 1999). Psychotherapists are assailable as a consequence of transference phenomena that can be a stimulus for the development of erotomanic attachments (Leong, 1994). Plastic and orthopaedic surgeons as well as lawyers are more typically the focus of resentful individuals who feel wronged, mistreated or misshaped.

Lion & Herschler (1998) presented nine cases of clinicians stalked by patients. Five of the victims were male psychiatrists (one a resident-in-training), two were female psychiatrists, one a female psychologist and the other a plastic surgeon. One of the psychiatrists in this series ultimately strangled his stalker. In a survey conducted by Romans et al. (1996) 10 out of 178 university counsellors (5.6%) reported that they had been stalked by a current or former client, with up to 63% claiming to have experienced 'stalking-related events', which presumably did not meet the stringent criteria for stalking as defined in this study. As many as 60% of respondents indicated that they lacked formal training to deal with these situations.

Increasingly, recognition is being given to the problem of sexual harassment of health professionals by patients (Phillips & Schneider, 1993). Female general practitioners in particular report experiences involving, for example, male patients who repeatedly present with a genital rash that mysteriously vanishes on physical examination (Quayle, 1994). For some doctors, these inappropriate sexual advances may continue despite explanations, confrontations, referral to another practice and even threats of legal action.

These cases are universally frustrating and frequently distressing to the professional, because the harassment is undeserved ('I try to be a good doctor/teacher/social worker and this is how I'm rewarded'). The support of colleagues is not always forthcoming (they may even be regarded with suspicion) and many victims in these circumstances feel ill-prepared to deal with the situation. Although it is thought that harassing phone calls, gifts and letters are encountered more frequently by these victims than is following, surveillance or violence, the scant literature on this subject may not accurately reflect the true extent and nature of the problem. Medical educators, and those in other 'high-risk' professions, are now beginning to address the unpreparedness of this category of victims by including appropriate training in their curricula.

Workplace contacts

For some individuals, stalking victimization arises in a work-related context. In these settings the victim–stalker relationship is characteristically employer/supervisor–employee, fellow employees or service provider–customer. In the workplace, stalking is frequently motivated by resentment and the victim may be an individual or an entire organization. These victims find themselves the focus of the resentful stalker's embitterment and vengeance derived from organizational changes or disciplinary action that pose a threat to his or her ego or job security. The stalker may believe that he or she has been unfairly passed over in favour of the victim and may contest the perceived discrimination before various tribunals and appeals boards, with escalating harassment as the complaints are dismissed.

There has in recent years been a growing awareness and concern about workplace victimization, which in addition to stalking includes sexual harassment, physical and sexual assaults, robberies and homicide. The US Department of Justice Special Report on Workplace Violence (Warchol, 1998) found that *each year* between 1992 and 1996 over two million US residents were victims of violent crime while at work. This encompassed 1.5 million simple assaults, 51 000 rapes and other sexual assaults, an estimated 84 000 robberies and over 1000 workplace homicides. Around 40% of victims of nonfatal workplace violence knew the perpetrator, particularly in the case of female victims. De Becker (1997, p. 143) observed: 'The fear of violence at work is understandable because work is a place where many of us are forced to interact with people we did not choose to have in our lives'.

Workplace violence incorporates ex-intimate stalking, where (usually the husband) harasses his wife at her work or a 'date' stalker who refuses to let go pursues the object of interest at her workplace (both of these are discussed under 'Ex-intimates', above). Also, intimacy seeking and socially incompetent individuals may focus their attentions on a co-worker and react with violence to the humiliation of persistent rejection. Indeed, Simon (1996) noted that often perpetrators of workplace violence and stalking behaviours suffer major mental illness, a famous example being that of Californian software engineer Robert Farley, who became infatuated with fellow worker Laura Black. He responded to her repeated rebuttals by stalking her and, some four years later, after he had been sacked by the company where Laura still worked, he stormed his former workplace and shot seven innocent employees. Laura Black, although seriously wounded, survived.

Workplace homicide is an uncommon outcome at the extreme end of workplace violence, but is disproportionately represented by sensationalized media reports. Simon (1996) noted that disgruntlement is a frequent characteristic among workplace killers. These individuals are akin to our 'resentful' group, often possessing major grievances against their employers or fellow employees. They have a history of insubordination incidents, disciplinary action, frequent absenteeism and disputes with – and threats toward – the object or objects of resentment. The latter may find their activities and performance being monitored by the aggrieved worker, who may even maintain a dossier on them (de Becker, 1997). Such cases are notorious for erupting in violence, often precipitated by their dismissal. For these individuals, losing their job is akin to losing their lover, wife or battle with a neighbour. It signifies major rejection, and precipitates a refusal to let go.

Nearly half of all stalkers will show up at their victim's workplace. Stalking that erupts in the work setting, regardless of its origins, potentially endangers the safety of other workers, as tragically demonstrated by the Laura Black case. Victims can be reluctant to apprise employers and co-workers of their situation, through embarrassment or fear of reprisals. Ultimately, this becomes necessary as a consequence of the perpetrator's repeated advances, and to enable the victim to take appropriate defensive action and protect work colleagues. Indeed, a lack of awareness by Laura Black's co-workers led to dissemination of information about Black to Farley by personnel (the stalker asking a friend in personnel to give him Black's birthdate so he could surprise her; while the worker accessed her computer file, Farley leaned over and memorized Black's home address; Emerson et al., 1998). Some victims complain that their approaches to supervisors are ignored, as illustrated in the case vignette below. Increasingly however, managers and supervisors within larger organizations are addressing deficiencies in knowledge and safety practices that have in the past proved very costly.

Case example

Mr W, a 27-year-old married journalist, presented to our clinic after being stalked for approximately six months by Ms Z, a 39-year-old unmarried female clerk who worked in the same building. He had transferred from a country posting eight months earlier and recalls Ms Z approaching him soon after his arrival and commenting that he resembled her favourite TV star (a likeness that neither he nor we could see). A week later, photocopied posters of the TV star appeared around the walls at work. Mr W dismissed this as a childish joke on his co-worker's part, but over the ensuing weeks and months he was bombarded with hang-up phone calls, which rotated between his work number, his home phone, his mobile phone and even his wife's work phone, at one time receiving 400 calls over a 45-minute period.

Mr W then received a series of anonymous faxed messages, usually movie or book reviews, and on one occasion he received movie tickets through the departmental mail. These were accompanied by a none too subtle handwritten message that read: 'To the guy with the movie star looks – come join me at a movie soon' which was signed 'your BIGGEST fan'.

Convinced that Ms Z was responsible, Mr W confronted her but she laughed and denied any involvement. She none the less continued to visit his floor and hover near his work station, on the pretext of delivering legitimate messages to co-workers. Mr W threatened to complain to management but she seemed unfazed. After months of harassment he finally approached his supervisor, who 'seemed to think it was a bit of a joke'. The victim subsequently intercepted a rumour that he and Ms Z were having an affair! Apparently his work colleagues had accepted this at face value, despite the unlikely nature of the union. That same day, a taxi cab arrived at his home address, ordered in his wife's name. His wife contacted him and demanded to know 'precisely what was going on between me and that woman.' His explanation was met with scepticism and, devastated at the effect of the false rumours upon his reputation and marriage and alarmed that Ms Z had managed to access his personal file including his residential address, Mr W again approached his employer, threatening him with a lawsuit unless *appropriate disciplinary action was taken.*

Prompt action did ensue on this occasion, an investigation revealing that Ms Z had indeed made many calls from her work extension to Mr W and his wife. When confronted, she admitted her activities and conceded there had been no affair, as much, she lamented, as she'd have liked one. Mr W subsequently learnt that, over the 18-year-period Ms Z had worked there, no fewer than four other male employees had been subjected to similar harassment. While on this occasion, at his insistence, definitive action was taken (Ms Z was suspended pending the outcome of criminal proceedings on charges of stalking), disillusionment with the unassertive management style of his employers and the development of disabling anxiety symptoms forced Mr W to abandon his chosen career.

Strangers

Victims in this category are not aware of any prior contact with the stalker. The stalker's very strangeness creates confusion and alarm. Most commonly they are pursued by intimacy-seeking or incompetent individuals, either of whom may admire the victim from afar for some time before subjecting their love interest to more overt forms of harassment. On occasion the stalker's identity is initially concealed from the victim and is presumed to be a stranger, but later when the stalker chooses to shed his or her anonymity (or has no choice but to do so in order to seek greater proximity to the object of interest) he or she may actually be known to the victim.

Intimacy seekers generally select their victim on the basis of his or her elevated social status or their prominence in the stalker's environment (see Chapter 7). A socialite was pursued over a two-year period by a 30-year-old male with an untreated schizophrenic illness and secondary erotomanic delusions. He believed that he was secretly engaged to the attractive young woman whose picture frequently appeared in the social pages of the local newspaper. He wrote regularly to his imagined lover and occasionally watched her at public events, but when he finally approached her at a charity dinner he was unceremoniously evicted. Fearful that she was being held captive by her minders and prevented from joining her faithful suitor, he returned to the dinner armed with knives and 'prepared to fight'. He was easily overpowered and conveyed to a psychiatric hospital for treatment, his victim commenting: 'He sent a few letters but I thought he was a pretty harmless, pathetic kind of guy . . . I don't know what it was with *me* – I'd never seen him before in my life. . .'.

While psychotic, as opposed to personality disordered, intimacy seekers may have a lower incidence of violence toward their love object, they are as likely as other stalkers to make threats and they are among the most persistent of stalkers (Mullen et al., 1999). Occasionally these stalkers will react with extreme violence to their victim's repeated rebuffs (Mullen & Pathé, 1994a).

Those who fall victim to unfamiliar incompetent stalkers find that, typically by virtue of physical attractiveness and being in the wrong place at the wrong time, they are subsequently subjected to repeated approaches and other unwanted intrusions from a (typically) unprepossessing individual of usually limited endowment who is unnervingly impervious to rejection. Victims report crude attempts to court them, often receiving gifts such as flowers and soft toys, especially on occasions such as birthdays and St Valentine's day. In this group, victims may describe feelings of surprise and even flattery when first approached. In these circumstances they may reply with a polite and often ambiguous response, which is perceived by the stalker as encouragement. At times victims give in to their stalker's persistence, dating them on one or more occasions, perhaps out of naïve curiosity but more often in the misguided hope that their unwanted suitor will then desist. This response does indeed gratify the stalker's wishes – to have, and hold onto, a relationship – and reinforces the pursuit.

The sexually predatory stalker frequently targets strangers. The victim is an adult female in the majority of cases but neither children nor men have escaped the attentions of this group of stalkers. Commonly, victims report a shorter duration of pursuit relative to their counterparts in other victim categories, although their stalker's involvement often pre-dates the victim's awareness of their interest. This group is subject to a range of sexually abusive behaviours, from obscene phone calls to rape and even sexual murder, as detailed in Chapter 6. The following case illustrates the overlapping nature of the classificatory system, demonstrating both stranger and workplace stalking with predatory and incompetent elements.

Case example

Mr F was a 22-year-old man of Greek immigrant parents who was referred to our clinic by the Court for a pre-sentence psychiatric assessment. He had been convicted of stalking a 19-year-old shop assistant and misuse of telecommunications equipment. He presented as a rather immature and shy man with limited verbal skills but he was reasonably forthcoming at interview, expressing some guilt for his actions which he summed up as 'stupid . . . it was really dumb'.

It transpired that one day almost a year previously Mr F had been browsing for jeans in a clothing shop near the home he shared with his parents. He was approached by the sales assistant, an attractive woman who greeted him with a friendly smile and offered to help him find his correct size. As he tried the jeans on he envisioned the young woman as his girlfriend and felt highly sexually aroused. He wanted to ask the shop assistant out but lacked the confidence; he instead put the jeans aside, ostensibly to further contemplate the purchase, but with the actual intention of returning to speak with the girl of his dreams.

Mr F claimed to have made multiple further attempts to engage this woman but simply felt too awkward to proceed to ask her out on a date. Instead, he hovered outside the shop, mostly out of sight, trying to catch glimpses of her at work. He admitted also to following her to her car at the end of her shift and to watching her and a group of females as they lunched at a nearby shopping mall. He became preoccupied with her, and she became the focus of his sexual fantasies. One day, he called her anonymously from a pay phone opposite the shop, but was paralysed with anxiety and said nothing. However, on the second occasion a day later he asked her about the lingerie she was wearing, proceeding to make a number of lewd suggestions before she hung up. He made a further eight calls, all obscene, before the police intercepted.

Mr F was the youngest of a sibship of three brothers. Both brothers were substantially older and had long before married and moved out of home. Mr F considered himself a loner who had struggled at school, leaving during Year 10 [age 15–16 years] to do a printing apprenticeship. He regarded himself as heterosexual but had never had a girlfriend and remained a virgin, blaming his shyness and lack of social opportunities. Mr F's parents were concerned about their son's social isolation and had arranged on a number of occasions for him to meet the daughters of friends but Mr F was never comfortable about pursuing these. By Mr F's account his parents were caring people who both now suffered major ill-health and wanted to see Mr F 'settled with his own family' before they died. Mr F had no record of prior convictions but admitted previously following and monitoring other attractive women, though always, he believed, without their knowledge. He denied making obscene calls in the past and specifically denied paraphilias and other sexually offensive activities. He was not a substance abuser, although he was inclined to drink excessively on the infrequent occasions he ventured out socially. He said this gave him a little more confidence around people.

Mental state examination did not reveal any major mood disorder or psychotic features. Intelligence testing demonstrated an IQ in the low–average range. Mr F said he had not returned to the clothing shop since his arrest, nor had he made any attempt to further contact his victim. He recognized that his actions would have had a negative impact on her, even though she was probably unaware of the full extent of the stalking behaviours. He claimed he no longer fantasized about the woman, finding his arrest and court appearance sufficiently aversive to extinguish these feelings for her. He agreed to participate in a group programme that provided training in social and intimacy skills, and education in human sexuality.

Victims may also fall prey to an unknown stalker whose actions are motivated by resentment. The victim may well have done nothing specific to provoke the harassment but rather is selected as a representative of a particular group or class detested by the stalker. For some victims this may be only that they epitomize success in life. One female executive found herself the recipient of threatening phone calls and letters as well as having her gleaming new sports car scratched and scrawled with abusive graffiti. She was eventually confronted with the heretofore anonymous persecutor in the driveway of her home. The stalker, an unemployed young man, bitterly accused her of knowing nothing of hardship and profiting from the misery of the disadvantaged. This same man, who had been retrenched from his job two years earlier, had previously made threats to a prominent wealthy businessman, for which he still faced charges.

While the choice of target may not always be clear to the victim of a resentful stranger there is much less confusion about the stalker's feelings toward them. As their name suggests, these individuals are embittered and aggrieved and it is their intention to induce fear and distress in the object of their unwanted intrusions. Like those stalked by ex-intimates, victims in this category are subject to a range of behaviours, including being threatened and assaulted. It is of little comfort to victims that progression to full-blown assault occurs infrequently, the stalker preferring to intentionally create a climate of fear over a protracted period (see Chapter 5). Unfortunately for some victims the harassment persists or even escalates in response to legal intervention, one woman receiving death threats from her imprisoned stalker on his illegally obtained mobile phone! The woman had once worked for a betting agency with whom her stalker had a longstanding vendetta. One day he entered her office drunk and verbally abusive and she called the police, who ejected him. Outraged and humiliated, he had since focussed his hostilities on her, culminating in what the victim believed would be her two-month reprieve as he served a prison sentence for stalking and threats to kill. The prisoner was unrepentant and righteously indignant when embarrassed prison officials removed the contraband. The incident had enormous implications for the victim's well-being, shattering her confidence and trust in the criminal justice system and her capacity to ever feel safe.

The famous

These victims are most often encountered through radio, television and film but may also include politicians, royalty, sports champions and other prominent public figures. Their stalkers are drawn from the socially incompetent, morbidly infatuated, erotomanic, and the resentful. Just as celebrity stalkers not uncommonly target, concomitantly or sequentially, a number of celebrities, high-profile victims may well have to contend with more than one stalker.

Contemporary examples abound, some of whom are noted in other chapters. Indeed, in his intriguing account of celebrity stalkers and assassins, Gavin de Becker (1997), Los Angeles security adviser, noted that the phenomenon is now commonplace among celebrities, although only a small proportion of these events are ever reported in the media. It has even become a source of black humour in celebrity circles that one has not attained true fame unless one has his or her own stalker! Many place much of the blame for this malediction on the evolution of the media age.

Performers, politicians, and sports figures have long been admired and even loved, but that love used to be contained and distant . . . It was, emotionally speaking, a one-way street, because feelings could be displayed to the public figure only as part of an acceptable function, like voting, sending letters, or seeing a show . . . [Fans] didn't seek to make themselves known personally to performers . . . Before the advent of mass media, a young girl might have admired a performer from afar, and it would have been acceptable if she pursued the performer to his home, or if she had to be restrained by police. It would not have been acceptable to skip school in order to wait for hours outside a hotel and then try to tear pieces of clothing from the passing star. (de Becker 1997, pp. 232–3).

Many individuals who pursue celebrity figures share backgrounds that are remarkable for their lack of intimacy. Some harbour delusional beliefs that they have an intimate relationship with their victim (e.g. the multiply-stalked American talk show host David Letterman was harassed for a decade by a woman who insisted that she was his wife), while others understand that their love for the victim is not (yet) reciprocated. Violence occurs uncommonly, its incidence, again, being disproportionately reported in the mass media. Attacks on the victim are more likely in the face of persistent rejection or other precipitants, when the stalker finally realizes the hopelessness of the quest, or in those cases where the celebrity is the object of animosity rather than affection. For example, actress and singer Olivia Newton-John was pursued at one time by a psychotic man who vowed to kill her because he believed her to be an impostor, and the 1993 knife attack on tennis player Monica Seles was intended to eliminate her from the tennis circuit so that her assailant Günter Parche could ensure the success of her opponent Steffi Graf, whom he had idolized for years. It was reported that after his arrest Parche told police: 'Seles had no right to be the world's top player. That was Steffi's place. I love her' (Writer & Blackman, 1993). Leaders and public officials can expect to be pursued more often by those with grievances and resentments.

The media can promote stalking of public figures by its reporting of these cases, glamourizing them and fulfilling the stalker's dreams of a relationship of sorts with their victim. The attention accorded to these individuals, especially those who ultimately become assassins, may fulfil one of the stalker's objectives: to achieve fame, or at least notoriety, their behaviour culminating in the biggest and most important day of their life. Forensic psychiatrist Park Dietz observed: 'In their quest for attention and identity, these individuals go "to the people who have the most identity to spare: famous people"' (cited in de Becker 1997, pp. 259–60).

Protection of celebrity victims has become an industry in its own right, especially in parts of the world such as Los Angeles where fame is concentrated. Increasingly, the famous forward inappropriate communications for professional evaluation and can be sheltered from much of the harassment. There is evidence that stalkers can be thwarted by the inaccessability of their victim. Robert Bardo, the stalker who ultimately murdered Rebecca Schaeffer, was known to have stalked several famous people, but gave up on these because they were *less accessible* than the young actress. In Bardo's view at least, if stars 'have security and they have bodyguards, it makes you look at that celebrity different and makes a person like me stand back. It kind of stands against this hope of a romantic relationship' (de Becker, 1997, p. 242).

Unusual victims

The circumstances underlying the selection of some victims may be highly unusual. A woman who sought our assistance recounted a relatively brief but intense campaign of harassment, being subjected to repeated abusive phone calls, angry approaches in public and arson attacks on her property. Her stalker had a long history of fanatical pursuit of public figures; however, it transpired that the victim had herself stalked a local media figure and had been threatened with a court injunction. It was when her stalking activities intruded upon his stalking behaviours that she found herself on the receiving end of merciless harassment. She subsequently abandoned her pursuit of the contested celebrity. Interestingly, this decision to abandon her obsession with the celebrity appeared to be based as much on a whole new appreciation of the impact of her unwanted contact and communications as her fears for her personal safety should she again encroach on this man's territory. Thus, experiencing stalking through a victim's eyes proved to be an effective, albeit highly unusual, remedy for stalking (her stalker subsequently responding to the more conventional approach of legal sanctions). Robert Bardo experienced a similar role reversal after his incarceration for Rebecca Schaeffer's murder: 'All the fame that I have achieved from this [celebrity murder] results in me getting death threats and harassment. The media says things about me that aren't even true. I have no control over them invading my privacy, bringing up my case over and over again on TV so they can make money off it . . .' (de Becker, 1997, p. 241). Now apparently sympathetic to the plight of the famous, he wants to be regarded as the 'anti-assassin', offering advice to the stars in the hope that they may avoid harassment and harm (de Becker, 1997).

Notorious prisoners may also attract adoring fans whose behaviours can constitute stalking. An armed robber now detained in a maximum security prison who received considerable media exposure as a consequence of his multiple prison escapes has been inundated with letters – some containing nude photographs – from adoring young men and infatuated women. One flashed her genitals at the prisoner during a noncontact visit and, although she has been banned from further visits, continues to write him letters and declare her love for him. The attentions are such that this inglorious victim has now appealed through his lawyer for the 'hero worship' to stop (*The Sunday Mail*, 14 March 1999, p. 6).

Rarely, noncelebrities may be targeted by multiple stalkers, either concurrently or (more often) sequentially. While individuals who make false allegations of being stalked may assert that they have attracted multiple stalkers (see Chapter 11), there do appear to be genuine cases who, by virtue of a high-risk occupation, a proclivity to choose high risk partners, exceptional physical attributes or sheer bad luck, may find themselves re-victimized on one or more occasions. Tjaden & Thoennes (1998) found that 9% of female and 8% of male victims claimed to have been stalked by two different individuals, and 1% of female and 2% of male victims reported being pursued by three different stalkers.

The impact of stalking on victims

Helen Razer, an Australian radio broadcaster and comedienne, was stalked by a man with the delusional belief that she was his wife. Over several months, Ms Razer received a stream of disturbing letters and threatening telephone calls, was followed around town by her assailant and was approached on several occasions at her workplace during her live radio broadcasts. Her stalker had to be repeatedly ejected by her co-host. Ms Razer obtained a two-year restraining order against the man prohibiting any further contact with her, but felt so terrorized by the experience and unsupported by many with whom she worked that she suspended her successful broadcasting career. The radio host described severe panic attacks and bouts of depression as a consequence of the stalking, and she often felt unable to leave the house or talk to others. She remarked:

> I never wanted to turn into one of those paranoid, home-invasional . . . type of people, but I have, and it's sad to be so paranoid. Being stalked would shake anyone. It depends on the individual's reaction but I just felt incapable of defending myself and I don't know why. (Cooper, 1998).

As noted earlier, the clinical and scholarly literature on stalking initially focussed on the characteristics and motivations of the perpetrators, with the subsequent emergence of epidemiological studies identifying and characterizing the potential victims of this crime. However, studies focussing on the impact of stalking on those targeted are a relatively recent development.

Unlike other criminal offences, stalking is distinguished by its repetition and persistence. The stalking victim is usually exposed to multiple forms of harassment, often involving threatening and traumatic incidents, the consequence of which may be chronic fear and apprehension. Stalking characteristically produces in the victim hypervigilance and a pervasive sense of mistrust in others. Although in some instances this suspicion and caution are entirely appropriate, they can alienate victims from their usual and formerly valuable sources of support, leading to social isolation. Even the most robust of intimate relationships and friendships can be severely tested by the persistent intrusions of a stalker, together with the victim's reaction to such activities. The victim may be further isolated by virtue of the stalker's effect on their occupational functioning, leading in some cases to the destruction of the victim's career.

The psychological responses of victims of stalking have much in common with victims of other traumas, both human-derived and natural. For victims of single, violent crimes, an initial acute stress disorder is common; this may or may not give rise over time to the development of stress-related symptoms currently conceptualized most frequently as posttraumatic stress disorder (PTSD). These stress-related syndromes may also be associated with conditions such as depression, anxiety disorders and psychoactive substance abuse/dependence (Bisson & Shepherd, 1995). Research on the psychological effects of violent crime has focussed particularly on the sequelae of sexual assaults on females. PTSD has been found in up to 80% of rape victims (Breslau et al., 1991); Lopez et al. (1992) reported that 37.5% of their survey sample of 436 rape victims met criteria for chronic PTSD and 71% suffered depressive disorders.

The threat and uncertainty following the aftermath of a nuclear accident at

Three Mile Island (TMI) in the USA in 1979 provided an opportunity to evaluate the psychological impact of a *protracted* stress situation not simply confined to the immediate period after the disaster itself was terminated (Baum et al., 1983). Research from the TMI disaster found that the 'intensity and duration of stressors are necessary but insufficient to explain the persistence and dysfunction associated with stress' (Baum et al., 1993, p. 278). Davidson & Baum (1986) noted that while the original environmental mishap at TMI 'may not have been as intense or gruesome as natural disasters or combat, the *continuation of sources of threat* at TMI may have compensated by generating lasting consequences there' (ibid., p. 306, italics added). This research provides evidence that adverse effects on functioning can occur if a person remains for an extended period in a situation where he or she feels under threat (Baum et al., 1983). It has been proposed by Baum and colleagues (1993, p. 279) that 'events involving loss of control and violation of expectations for control have different effects than do events that remind us of forces over which control was never expected', such as earthquakes and other ungovernable natural forces. Trauma that involves loss of control further appears to generate more persistent disquiet than other stressors. Stress-resistance research has also shown a central role for social support, effective coping strategies and positive personality characteristics in stress-resistance and the maintenance of psychological health: 'Under high stressors, adaptive personality characteristics and family support function prospectively as coping resources' (Holahan & Moos, 1991, p. 36).

Stalking possesses many of the features that may produce chronic stress reactions and related psychological sequelae. Stalking victims are subject to persistent, repetitive trauma, as opposed to most other victims of crime and victims of other isolated traumatic events. Not only do a stalker's repeated intrusions represent a loss of control for the victim but the often ineffectual response of the criminal justice system and other helping agencies violates the stalking victim's assumptions of living in a fair and safe society and crushes their expectations of regaining control. These victims live in a state of persistent threat with associated symptoms that may far outlive the actual duration of the harassment. Furthermore, as noted earlier, the social supports that would ordinarily be expected for crime victims may be compromised by the very nature of the victimization and resultant mistrust and fear.

Although there is no published research examining the repercussions of stalking within a random, population-based sample, the survey by Pathé & Mullen (1997) of 100 self-selected stalking victims generated a number of interesting findings. Here we expand on some of the details in this study. Apart from the nonrandom nature of this sample and the subjectivity of the respondents' evaluations of the effects of their stalking experiences, this study was also limited by its lack of information on the premorbid functioning of the victims. It is recognized that variables other than the nature and magnitude of the stressor itself can influence the psychological outcome for trauma victims. Factors such as personal and family psychiatric history, poor social supports and high 'neuroticism' have all been associated with increased rates of PTSD (Bisson & Shepherd, 1995).

Virtually all 100 victims reported that the stalking had a deleterious effect on their psychological, social and/or occupational functioning. Ninety-four per cent reported major lifestyle changes and modification of their daily activities in direct response to being stalked, most often involving avoidance of any places where the stalker might be and taking additional (and frequently expensive) security measures; these included the installation of motion sensor exterior lighting and house alarms, and obtaining unlisted telephone numbers and post office box mailing addresses. Several victims changed or modified their cars, one tinting his windows so that his stalker, who persistently and brazenly followed and abused him in traffic, at least could not make eye contact. Many altered their driving habits, taking long, circuitous routes to avoid being followed home and constantly checked their rear vision mirrors for any signs of their pursuer. Curtailment of social activities was reported by 70% of victims, many attempting to circumvent any contact with their stalker. Often victims reported losing friendships due to declining invitations to functions where known associates of the stalker may have been. Although, as noted earlier, intimate relationships often suffer under the burden of the stalker's involvement, not all deteriorate. One victim in this series married precipitously and immediately fell pregnant because, she candidly reasoned, having a baby would legitimize her need to stay at home and would provide her with company!

Over half of the victims reported a decrease or a cessation of work or school attendance, in some instances attributing the loss of employment to the stalker's incessant telephone calls or other disruptions at the victim's workplace, including threats to harm co-workers or employers, and absenteeism through attendances at court or medical appointments. Over a third of the victims felt compelled to change their workplace, school or career as a direct result of the stalking, and some 40% relocated their residence, some of these on two or more occasions. A handful of victims changed their names by deed poll to avoid, or at least impede, detection by their stalker. Such was the level of fear and loss of faith in the judicial system to protect them that several victims relocated to a different state or migrated to another country at enormous financial and personal cost.

With few exceptions, victims in this study described deterioration in their mental and/or physical health as a consequence of their harassment. Many had entertained aggressive thoughts toward their perpetrator (admitted by 65%), the desire to retaliate against their assailant being barely contained in several cases. Over 75% of victims reported feeling powerless in the face of repeated intrusions and a quarter of the victims seriously considered or actually attempted suicide at some point during their ordeal. Many also reported guilt feelings, especially in relation to their perceived poor choice of partners (which, as noted earlier, family and law enforcement agencies may have reinforced). Over 80% of the sample reported increased anxiety and arousal as a consequence of the stalking, most often manifesting as 'jumpiness', panic attacks, hypervigilance and 'shakes'. Three-quarters reported chronic sleep disturbance, largely due to nightmares and hyperarousal, although many were kept awake by their stalkers' telephone calls or lay awake listening for any intrusions. Nearly half the sample reported appetite disturbance, with most experiencing some weight loss, though several victims purposefully gained large amounts of weight in futile attempts to diminish their attractiveness to their stalkers. One former fitness fanatic became morbidly obese as a consequence of being housebound with fear. Uncharacteristic nausea was experienced by a third of victims (often triggered by having to attend work or other venues associated with the stalking). Fifty per cent acknowledged excessive tiredness, weakness and headaches. Almost 25% of victims reported an increase in their alcohol and/or cigarette consumption as a result of their pursuit and harassment, these harmful substances frequently being employed to 'self-medicate' intolerable symptoms of stress and anxiety. Several subjects reported a worsening in pre-existing physical conditions, such as psoriasis, peptic ulcers, ulcerative colitis and asthma attacks. One victim experienced a miscarriage that she attributed to the stress of being stalked. Another delivered a premature, low birth weight baby as a consequence, she believed, of stress and (stalking-induced) excessive alcohol consumption prenatally.

The majority of victims in this study reported experiencing one or more symptoms of PTSD. According to DSM-IV (American Psychiatric Association, 1994), the essential feature of this disorder is the development of anxiety and avoidance symptoms that emerge following exposure to a traumatic stressor. The traumatic stressor must involve the direct experience, or witnessing, of an event that threatens to, or actually causes, death or serious injury or a threat to one's physical integrity. The person's immediate response to the stressor must involve intense fear, helplessness or horror. Additionally, the core diagnostic features of PTSD require symptoms that can be categorized into three clusters: (1) the re-experiencing of the traumatic event (through intense and intrusive thoughts, images, perceptions or dreams); (2) persistent and effortful avoidance of stimuli associated with, or resembling, the trauma, and a numbing of general responsiveness (characterized by feelings of detachment or estrangement from others, or a sense of a foreshortened future); and (3) symptoms of excess arousal, such as sleep disturbance, hypervigilance, difficulty concentrating or an exaggerated startle response.

Of these 100 victims, 55% reported intrusive recollections or flashbacks of the stalking that were recurrent and distressing, often being triggered by everyday occurrences such as the telephone ringing, an unexpected knock on the door, or seeing cars of a particular make or colour reminiscent of that driven by the stalker. A further 38% of victims described avoidance or numbing of responses, particularly feelings of detachment from others. Only a third of the victims in this study, however, met the full diagnostic criteria for PTSD according to DSM-IV. An additional 20% met most of the elements for the diagnosis, failing only to meet the criteria of a necessary stressor that involved *actual or threatened physical harm or a threat to one's physical integrity*. The majority of victims who met the criteria for PTSD in the study were female, consistent with the findings from epidemiological studies that suggest that women are at least two to four times more likely to develop this syndrome than men (Kessler et al., 1995; Breslau et al., 1998). The symptoms of PTSD were more likely to emerge in those victims who reported following, as opposed to other forms of harassment, and among those exposed to violence. This diagnosis was also more likely in those subjects who shared a prior intimate relationship with their stalker, who concomitantly were exposed to a greater likelihood of physical violence and also were more likely to be female.

The constellation of symptoms that comprise the diagnosis of PTSD – avoidance, intrusive memories, numbing of responses and excessive arousal – captures well the psychological sequelae of stalking. As a diagnostic entity, PTSD also valuably emphasizes the chronic nature of mental disorder or disturbance that can be produced by exposure to traumatic stressors. However, the current conceptualization of posttraumatic stress by the American Psychiatric Association is somewhat restrictive in that it allows for psychological decompensation following only a discrete or relatively circumscribed traumatic event that threatens or actually harms one's physical integrity. This conceptualization fails to acknowledge the psychological distress produced by prolonged trauma and repeated victimization, as in stalking, which, although not necessarily involving explicit threats to one's *physical* being, is clearly no less damaging to the victim's mental health.

This study provides a sobering account of the distress and disruption wrought in the lives of victims as a consequence of being stalked. Although the impact of stalking varied among victims, reflecting differences both in the nature of the stalking experiences, the availability of support structures, the effectiveness or otherwise of legal interventions, and perhaps (although it was not measured) the resilience or vulnerability of the victims themselves, no victim was left unscathed by their experience, with all reporting changes that in some cases amounted to profound deterioration in functioning. Contrary to popular assumptions, the accompaniment of violence with stalking was not a necessary prerequisite for deleterious effects in the victim, the majority of subjects reporting significant and usually chronic fear in the absence of any incidents of physical assault, although for many fear was a response to the threat of imminent physical violence. Instead, the menace and persistent intrusions that came to dominate the victim's life, the often incomprehensible motives of stalkers and the unpredictable nature of the behaviour itself were powerful determinants of the observed morbidity. Ironically, several victims commented that a physical assault might have been *preferable* to chronic, less tangible psychological torment; certainly, this might have provoked a more assertive and sympathetic response from helping agencies.

The study by Hall (1998) also examined the impact of stalking on the lifestyle and daily functioning of her 145 self-defined victims, noting that several victims moved residence, changed jobs or changed their surnames in attempts to elude their pursuers. Others altered their physical appearance in the hope that their stalkers would not recognize them or cease to be attracted to them, one woman going to the extreme of surgical breast reduction. The study did not systematically address the psychological impact of stalking, although 80% of victims agreed that their personality had changed as a consequence of their harassment, most victims noting that they had become less friendly and outgoing, and conversely more cautious, paranoid, easily frightened, aggressive and introverted. Many female victims responded that they were less trusting of men and increasingly suspicious of other people's motives, leading to their retreat from normal activities. Other victims spoke of chronic apprehension and distress, often persisting long after the stalking had ceased, together with the omnipresent fear that the stalking would recommence at any time. As one victim explained: 'His last contact was two years ago, but part of me is still afraid of him and when he'll pop up again. Logically I know he won't, but sometimes it still scares me' (Hall, 1998, p. 135).

In Jason et al.'s (1984) survey, the majority of subjects perceived the male stalker's behaviour as threatening and disturbing. Thirty-two per cent experienced fear, anxiety or depression. Physical ailments such as abdominal pain, eating disorders and nervous tics were reported by 18% of the cohort and 16% experienced a loss of trust in others. Over half the subjects talked to a friend, family member or a therapist, 34% took legal action and 10% made 'environmental changes', such as moving address or changing their phone number. Eight per cent said they became 'mean or distant'. Interestingly, as many as 48% claimed no psychological or physical problems as a consequence of their harassment, and a third of cases did not make any adjustments to their lifestyle, nor did they acknowledge seeking the help of a friend or professional. This study was conducted prior to the introduction of the term 'stalking' and at a time when there was a limited awareness of the phenomenon. The public interest surrounding the 'harassment' of actress Jodie Foster by John Hinckley was in fact a catalyst for the research. None the less, the methods of harassment and their reported impact were similar in nature to those described in the stalking studies that emerged a decade later. The lower incidence of disorder and disruption that is apparent in this group of victims compared with subsequent studies may reflect the diminished awareness in this pre-'stalking' era of the potential seriousness of the phenomenon ('ignorance is bliss') or the acceptability of the victim's experience, the size and selective nature of the sample or a comparatively less severe pattern of harassment.

Summary

Victims of stalking typically describe feelings of violation, a profound sense of loss of control over their lives and a pervasive mistrust of others. They commonly employ terms such as 'emotional rape' and 'psychological terrorism' in defining their ordeal. The effects of stalking are often experienced long after the stalker has withdrawn, with a residue of ongoing fear and vulnerability characteristic of most stalking victims' stress response. Given the prevalence of stalking behaviours within our community and the extent of damage they leave in their wake, the plight of the stalking victim must be recognized as a legitimate concern for mental health practitioners and the criminal justice system. But the problem of stalking must also be acknowledged as a legitimate concern for society as a whole, not only because of the considerable cost of supporting victims who can no longer work and who may have long-term health care needs but because virtually every one of us is a potential victim of stalking, be they male or female, adult or child, famous or mediocre, straight or gay, black or white, of whatever religion, executive or unemployed, model citizen or convicted felon. As we have found, even *stalkers* can fall victim to other stalkers. In Chapter 13 we present strategies and interventions that aim to minimize the chances of falling victim to a stalker and the personal and societal cost to those who do.

4

Classifying stalkers

Introduction

Classifications should not simply facilitate communication by giving names to items in a previously undistinguished landscape but should articulate relationships between conceptually similar groups as well as tell us something about what can be expected of each class. Classifications are in part creatures of convenience, which emerge within particular discourses and reflect not only the qualities of the things being classified but also the imperatives that operate in those discourses. In medicine, for example, classifications are generally diagnostic, being constructed on the basis of cause, course, outcome and, where possible, treatment. Diagnosis is used as a guide to prognosis and management. Diagnostic systems are usually subservient to those ends rather than to the purely theoretical goal of establishing mutually exclusive sets where membership in a given set, or class, is absolute with no room for vagueness or ambiguity. In any practical pursuit, such as those in which mental health professionals engage, classifications should serve the goals of the professional's clinical activities, not just the purer theoretical aims of the sciences that they mediate. Classifications of stalkers are likely to vary according to the needs of the group seeking to articulate the classification. For example, law enforcement officers, mental health professionals and advocates for the victims of domestic violence, all have legitimate concerns with stalking and stalkers; thus they have each evolved classifications that both further their ends and can be readily reconciled with the technical languages they habitually employ. Even within the mental health professions the classification of stalkers has been subject to differing priorities arising from the particular goals and theoretical commitments of the specific professional group or individual.

This chapter examines a number of classifications that have divided the universe of stalking into separate constellations or types of stalker and attempts to examine the assumptions and imperatives underlying such divisions. Finally, a multi-axial classification is outlined which we have found to be helpful in the clinical evaluation and subsequent management of those who stalk. This latter classification incorporates first a typology, secondly the victim characteristics and thirdly the stalker's mental health status. The typology is based primarily on the stalker's motivations and the context in which the stalking emerged. The classification as a whole aspires to provide a guide to the likely course and duration of the harassment, to the risks of escalation to assaultive behaviours and above all to the most effective strategies to end the stalking.

Stalking, as already discussed, emerged with its current meaning first as a convenient media term for the persistent pursuit of the famous. This was subsequently extended, particularly by advocates in the area of domestic violence, to the persistent pursuit of ex-partners (initially identified exclusively as women). Stalking was then further metamorphosed into a specific form of offending before finally being constructed by mental health professionals and behavioural scientists as a particular form of deviant behaviour.

Classifying stalking as a form of domestic violence

Those concerned with stalking as an integral part of violence against women have constructed the phenomenon specifically in those terms (Coleman, 1997; Australian Bureau of Statistics, 1996). Walker & Meloy (1998) claimed that stalking was quite simply the name given to a combination of activities that batterers indulge in to force their female partners to remain in a relationship. In short, stalking is constructed as a strategy of intimidation and control used by men within the realm of domestic violence. The focus of any subsequent classification is on the nature and extent of intimidation and on how best to predict, and thus hopefully prevent, the risks of escalation to even more serious, or possibly murderous, violence. The focus on domestic violence as the context and corollary of stalking focusses predominantly, if not always exclusively, on women as victims and men as perpetrators (Burgess et al., 1997). Sonkin (1997, cited in Walker & Meloy, 1998) differentiates between the ex-partner who is having problems relinquishing a relationship and the angry, vindictive, controlling and potentially violent stalker. Given that the priorities in work with victims of domestic violence must be the protection of victims it is entirely appropriate to deconstruct stalking into a series of acts of varying actual and implied threat (Sonkin, 1997, cited in Walker & Meloy, 1998). This approach may well be optimal in the arena for which it has been developed but obviously for those concerned with stalking in all its many and varied manifestations it is too restrictive and focussed.

Erotomanics, love obsessionals and simple obsessionals

Zona et al. (1993) were the first to advance a classification of stalkers. Their work is considered in detail because they can claim precedence and because of the continuing influence of their conceptualizations on researchers and practitioners in the field. They based their proposed typology on a review of 74 case files processed by the Los Angeles Police Department's Threat Management Unit (TMU), which was later augmented with a further 126 cases (Zona et al., 1993, 1996, 1998). The TMU was the first unit of its kind established specifically to investigate the behaviour of people said to demonstrate what they labelled 'an obsessional or abnormal long term pattern of threat or harassment'. The TMU's establishment was prompted by the high proportion of entertainment figures within the Los Angeles area attracting the unwanted attentions of stalkers. On the basis of the nature of the subjects' assumed preoccupation and prior relationships with their victims, the authors identified three groups of stalkers who they termed the erotomanic, the love obsessional and the simple obsessional.

The erotomanic group in the original publication consisted of seven subjects (six females) who met the DSM-III-R criteria for Delusional (Paranoid) Disorder, Erotomanic Type (American Psychiatric Association, 1987). This grouping encompassed only those subjects who were absolutely convinced that they were loved by those whom they were stalking. None of these subjects had a prior relationship with their victim and as a group they focussed their amorous attentions almost exclusively upon those in the entertainment industry. Those they termed the love obsessionals ($n = 32$), like the erotomanic grouping, consisted to some extent of those who harboured delusions that he or she was loved by their victim. In contrast to the erotomanic type, however, this group's delusions arose secondarily as part of a more extensive psychotic illness (most frequently schizophrenia or bipolar disorder), rather than manifesting as a pure or primary delusional syndrome. Also included in the love obsessional group were those who were said to show an intense infatuation with the object of their unwanted attentions but not to claim that their love was reciprocated. Unlike the erotomanic grouping, the majority of love obsessionals were male. Both the erotomanic and the love obsessional categories were reported to share a common fascination with media figures, frequently choosing young female 'bombshells' as the targets of their ardent affections. Neither the erotomanic nor the love obsessional groups had had a prior relationship with their victim. It was on this basis of a lack of a prior relationship that the love obsessional grouping was separated from the final group, the simple obsessionals ($n = 35$). The simple obsessional group were reported to have pursued victims with whom they had had previous contact. Their victims were typically ex-intimate partners, but included neighbours, casual acquaintances, workmates and professional contacts. Males and females were equally represented among stalkers in this grouping and they had usually commenced their pursuit after a relationship had 'gone sour'. It appears, however, that this group also encompassed individuals who stalked in revenge for perceived mistreatment, and whose motivations were primarily the extraction of retribution for injustices that they believed had been inflicted upon them.

On the basis of their classification, Zona and colleagues (1993, 1998) attempted to delineate the features that characterized the three postulated groupings. The groups did not differ according to demographic characteristics, most subjects being single and in their mid thirties. They also tended to share a lack of social competency and a paucity of prior intimate relationships. Only seven subjects in the entire sample were known to have been married previously. The duration and means of establishing and maintaining contact with the victims was reported to vary according to which group they belonged to. The erotomanic subjects maintained contact with their victims for almost twice the duration of the love obsessed (nineteen months on average compared to ten months) and four times that of simple obsessionals (five months). Interestingly, however, both the erotomanics and the love obsessionals remained fixated on their victims for substantially longer periods than their overt pursuit suggested (ten to twelve years on average). The authors speculated as to whether medication may have restrained the progression from fantasy to pursuit among these subjects, or whether they retained sufficient insight to cease their obvious pursuit in the face of negative feedback or legal consequences. The erotomanic and love obsessional groups were reported to typically correspond with their victims via letters and cards,. Simple obsessionals preferred direct contact by means of telephone calls or face-to-face confrontations. The subjects in the erotomanic grouping also approached the homes of their victims more often than the other groups, although they apparently rarely sought face-to-face contact with the victim. The authors suggest that such intimate contact would have been likely to demystify their idealized love, reducing it from the special and wondrous to the 'ordinary and banal' (Zona et al., 1993, p. 901). The simple obsessional and erotomanic groupings reportedly frequently threatened their victims (65% and 57%, respectively), although none was known to have physically harmed their victim. In the simple obsessional group seven of the thirty-five were reported to have been violent, either damaging their victim's property (five) or assaulting the victim (two). The incidence of violence in this sample was low, prompting the authors to suggest that the risk of violence associated with stalking may be minimal.

Zona and colleagues (1993, 1998) used a medical approach to classification, drawing on the existing definitions of 'delusional disorder, erotomanic type' for one group and attempting to extend existing notions of obsessive and compulsive behaviours to create their other two groups. It should perhaps be noted, however, that the information on which they based their groupings was provided in many instances primarily, or exclusively, by the victims. The complainant to the police may well have been unaware of their pursuer's current and past mental health status. Although by definition all erotomanics had a major mental illness, only 40%

of subjects in both the love and simple obsessional groups could be assigned a DSM diagnosis. The diagnoses were predominantly Axis I disorders in the former grouping (e.g. schizophrenia, affective disorders, substance abuse) and Axis II personality disorders in the latter. These diagnostic ascriptions were tentative at best and almost certainly an underestimation of the actual incidence of mental illness, or character anomaly, in their subjects. As victims, rather than the stalkers themselves, were the main sources of information for the study, there were unavoidable gaps in much of the data, especially in relation to the motivations of the perpetrators.

Zona and colleagues (1993, 1998) approach the classification of stalking from the dual perspectives of psychiatry and law enforcement. The subjects of their studies were drawn particularly from the stalkers of the rich and famous. These authors clearly recognized that stalking was not confined to the harassment of celebrities, although they had perforce to focus to a significant degree on those who stalk people with whom they have had no, or only the slightest, of relationships and who are engaged in establishing or asserting a fantasized relationship. This contrasts with subjects who stalk those in the domestic violence field, individuals, almost exclusively male, who are bent on controlling, retaining, regaining or frankly terrorizing their present or former partner. The commitments of the researchers and the use to which they intend to put their classification inevitably, and quite properly, directs the nature of the classification produced.

Zona et al. in their 1998 paper made their nosological commitments quite clear. They stated first that any understanding of a stalker's behaviour must be in terms of a more fundamental psychiatric or psychological process. Secondly, they assert that, although a review of DSM-IV (American Psychiatric Association, 1994) fails to reveal any syndrome or disorder pathognomonic of stalking, nevertheless stalking must be put into the diagnostic framework that DSM provides. It is not entirely clear to those of us whose working lives are not so defined by the words of DSM-IV why these workers should voluntarily constrain themselves in this manner but, for whatever reason, they chose to do so. The law enforcement perspective in the group also directed the typologies of stalkers, giving an understandably high priority to an approach that offered guidance on the 'dangerousness in stalking perpetrators'.

The erotomanic group is the key to Zona and colleagues' classification. The defining characteristics of this group are taken directly from the DSM (III-R and IV) and provide a clear link to the diagnostic framework of contemporary psychiatry. The expert committees of the American Psychiatric Association have taken their criteria for erotomania from the work of de Clérambault, which is discussed at length in Chapter 8. This provides a narrow and arguably impoverished construction of the pathologies of love. To compensate for the restrictive nature of DSM-IV's erotomania, Zona and colleagues (1993, 1998) constructed the love obsessional category, who may, or may not, have a psychiatric illness such as schizophrenia. All love obsessionals share the characteristic of fixing their amorous attentions on strangers or casual acquaintances with whom no real intimacy exists. This solution to the problem of the narrowness of current DSM notions of erotomanias is similar to that of Mullen & Pathé (1994a), who suggested that morbid infatuations be included in erotomanias but they went further in using the increasing knowledge about this group of stalkers to challenge the coherence of the current DSM-IV construction.

The final element in the trinity is the simple obsessional grouping, which contains a mixed group of individuals who had all had a prior relationship with the victim of their stalking, but this relationship can include ex-partners, workplace contacts, professional relationships and even neighbours and casual acquaintances. This group can be motivated by amorous motives, desire for conciliation, the wish for revenge or even to terrorize. It is this somewhat disparate group who Zona et al. (1993, 1998) reported as presenting the greatest risk of violence to the victim.

The problems created by the use of the term obsessional in two of the three categories is discussed later when we consider the equally influential work of Reid Meloy.

Some other classifications

The classification proposed by Harmon et al. (1995) distinguished stalkers first on the basis of the attachment between the perpetrator and the object of his or her attention and secondly on the nature of the prior relationship. The authors reviewed the case files of subjects who had been referred to the Forensic Psychiatry Clinic of the Criminal and Supreme Courts of New York following charges of criminal harassment or menacing. Forty-eight subjects exhibited the type of repetitive intrusions and communications associated with stalking. The author's first axis related to the nature of the attachment between the subject and the object of their attention (either 'affectionate/amorous' or 'persecutory/angry') and the second axis described the nature of the prior relationship (personal, professional, employment, media, acquaintance, none or unknown).

The majority of stalkers in this sample exhibited what the authors describe as an affectionate/amorous attachment to their victims ($n = 30$). Diagnostically, these stalkers consisted predominantly of patients with erotomanic features, although subjects with narcissistic and paranoid personality traits who stalked ex-intimate partners were also represented. Those with an amorous attachment were said to not infrequently victimize third parties who had been perceived to be attempting to foil the budding relationship between the stalker and the object of their affection. In one example, provided by Harmon et al. (1995), a 39-year-old woman with erotomania formed an amorous attachment to a veterinarian, believing that they had had prior sexual liaisons. She flooded the unsuspecting vet with more than 500 telephone calls and threatening letters, later harassing his staff and family, whom she perceived as obstructing their imagined love. This woman was particularly aggrieved by the veterinarian's secretary, who she believed was having an affair with the object of her disordered love. She approached the surgery on one occasion and lunged at the vet and his secretary with a knife, though fortunately failed to inflict any serious harm. She had been arrested five times for this ongoing harassment, which had persisted for over eight years.

Though all subjects within the affectionate/amorous division commenced their pursuit with romantic if not frankly sexual intentions, their emotions were described as on occasion turning to anger and persecution when rejection occurred. This was illustrated in another case history of a man who had been referred to the clinic on eleven occasions. For over ten years this 47-year-old had stalked and harassed a well-known singer. He claimed that she was once a passenger in his taxi, that they had had sex, and that the woman had put a hex on him that forced him to pursue her (Harmon et al., 1995).

Stalking among those in the persecutory/angry category ($n = 15$) were reported as typically emerging following a real or imagined mistreatment or injury, and often occurred in the context of a business or professional relationship. The objects of attention for these subjects were not only individuals, but frequently large institutions that placed multiple victims at risk of harassment or violence. One example provided was of a 59-year-old man who had indiscriminately stalked various solicitors and associated staff from a law firm that had unsuccessfully represented him nearly two decades earlier. The stalkers in the persecutory/angry grouping covered a more diverse spectrum in terms of their psychiatric diagnoses than the amorous group encompassing not only those with delusional illnesses, but often mood or adjustment disorders and personality disorders. One particular stalker, a former professional basketball player, indicated as characteristic of this group, was described as narcissistic. He reportedly had harassed and intimidated his former girlfriend through repeated offensive telephone calls. Referred to the court clinic, he claimed that he did not need psychiatric evaluation or treatment, nor could he understand why making such telephone calls was inappropriate, let alone criminal.

The classification proposed by Harmon and colleagues (1995) provides a meaningful framework from which to approach the motivations of stalkers and the nature of their attachment to their victim. It unfortunately did little to distinguish the pursuit characteristics of subjects. Though the subjects in the affectionate/amorous category were more likely to be single, the groups did not differ in age, gender, ethnicity, education, criminal charges or psychiatric diagnoses. Furthermore, subjects in both groups showed the same propensity for seeking physical contact with their victims and making threats of violence, although there was a greater association between threats and actual assault in the amorous group. It is further limited in that, not infrequently in practice, stalkers fluctuate between angry, vengeful intentions and largely benign intentions. Harmon and colleagues (1995) recognize that an initially amorous attachment may evolve into anger as a result of what is regarded as betrayal or rejection. This does not, however, deal with the fundamental ambivalence that can characterize stalkers' intentions and feelings from the very outset. The rejected partner may therefore begin by seeking reconciliation then, prompted by jealousy or further rejection, become vindictive before, at a later stage, trying once more for reconciliation. Similarly the amorous when repeatedly rejected may move from hopeful love to rage. Even the dismissed employee may have very complex feelings and intentions toward those on whom they focus their unwanted attentions. That being said, the broadening and separation of the nature of prior contact between stalkers and their victims, acknowledging that stalking occurs in a variety of social and occupational contexts, not just domestic relationships or celebrities, was an important step forward in the study of stalking. The small sample size in the initial study prohibited any examination of differences in the nature and course of pursuit among these distinct groups. In a subsequent analysis of 175 subjects identified from the same clinic, Harmon et al. (1998) provided a detailed analysis of the predictors of future violence in this population of stalkers. This important contribution is dealt with in detail in Chapter 12.

The typology of Kienlen et al. (1997) divided stalkers into two groups simply on the basis of whether they were, or were not, psychotic. The study examined the records of 25 subjects who were referred for pretrial mental evaluations in the context of criminal charges related to stalking. A third of the subjects were classed as being psychotic (two subjects with schizophrenia, one delusional disorder with erotomanic features, four with psychotic disorder not otherwise specified and one subject with bipolar disorder). Most of these psychotic stalkers were reported to have experienced delusions of persecution and grandiosity, rather than erotomania. For example, one subject (with the misidentification syndrome of Capgras) stalked a woman who he mistakenly believed was his estranged wife against whom he harboured animosity. Another stalker was reported to have persistently followed a former girlfriend whom he believed had cast a spell on him. The remaining seventeen subjects were judged to be nonpsychotic at the time of evaluation, a range of disorders being reported, including mood disorder, alcohol or other substance abuse and personality disorder, usually of the antisocial, dependent or narcissistic variety.

Several differences were noted in the patterns of pursuit employed by the psychotic and nonpsychotic groups. Psychotic stalkers were more likely to visit the homes of their victims, but were somewhat less inclined to send letters or keep their victims under surveillance. Nonpsychotic stalkers more often verbally threatened and also were at higher risk of perpetrating an assault. One nonpsychotic stalker was reported to have eventually kidnapped his ex-partner at gunpoint, at which point he melodramatically informed her that he could no longer live without her and asked her to end his misery by stabbing him in the heart with a knife. She chose not to seize the opportunity. In contrast, only one psychotic stalker assaulted his victim (a parent). Nearly 50% of the nonpsychotic group possessed a weapon at the time of the stalking (seven had a firearm and one a knife), compared to only one psychotic stalker, who brandished a metal pipe obtained in the course of damaging the victim's property. The authors concluded on the basis of these findings that, not only do the nonpsychotic show a greater propensity for violence than the psychotic, they are more calculating and resourceful in their use of such violence. This classification was developed to serve the purposes of mental health professionals preparing court evaluations and it reflects the imperatives of those purposes. Employing a simple dichotomy between psychotic and nonpsychotic is certainly parsimonious and has an appeal both to mental health professionals, where the division has potential management implications, and to lawyers where it has some relevance to issues of criminal responsibility. The problem with the classification is that it cuts across issues of both stalker motivation and choice of victim, which can be critical for prediction of the nature and dimension of stalking and the risks of escalation to violence. Conversely the psychotic/nonpsychotic division can claim sufficient utility to be considered a candidate for constituting one axis in a more complex classification.

Schwartz-Watts and colleagues conducted a study comparing stalkers to other violent offenders (Schwartz-Watts et al. 1997). They also examined differences between violent and nonviolent stalkers (Schwartz-Watts & Morgan, 1998). Their initial study (1997) compared the records of eighteen males charged with stalking in the state of South Carolina who had been evaluated pretrial, with a group of offenders randomly matched for age, sex and whether violence accompanied the crime. In their second study the authors compared the medical records of forty-two pretrial detainees charged with stalking, who were divided on the basis of whether their stalking involved violence ($n = 20$) or not ($n = 22$). The groups did not differ significantly on age, sex, marital status, education, substance abuse history, Axis I diagnosis or organicity. Violent stalkers were reported to be more likely to have had a prior intimate relationship with the victim. The attempt to distinguish stalkers on the basis of their risks of future violence is critical but it may be that it is better regarded as a measure of the adequacy of any proposed classification rather than contributing a classification in and of itself.

Wright and colleagues (1996), who are affiliated to the Federal Bureau of

Investigation (FBI), advanced a preliminary classification of stalkers on the basis of thirty reports that were provided, in the main, by victims. These stalking victims were asked to describe aspects of their experience using a standardized forty-eight item Stalking Incident Checklist. On the basis of their responses, the authors formulated a typology of stalkers related to the nature of the relationship between the victim and stalker (domestic or nondomestic), the content of the communications (nondelusional or delusional), the level of risk to the victim in terms of aggression (low, medium, high), the motive of the stalker (infatuation, possession, anger/retaliation, other) and the outcome of the case for the stalker (legal, suicide, psychiatric, other). Under this classification, fourteen subjects were classed as nondomestic stalkers (predominantly nondelusional/organized) and sixteen as domestic stalkers (all but one nondelusional). Domestic stalkers under this system were not only intimate partners and family members but could include workmates. Twelve stalkers were deemed to be motivated by anger or the desire for retaliation, ten were motivated by possessiveness, six by infatuation and for two the motivation was not specified. Seven committed suicide (an extraordinary mortality rate of over 20%) and only four were given psychiatric help (mostly committed by the courts on the grounds of insanity). This is a highly selected group evidenced not only by the high rate of suicide but also by six of the thirty instances of stalking culminating in murder. (It is not clear in these cases when or by whom the victim forty-eight-item checklist was completed). The elements of the classification have face validity but the small size and peculiar nature of the sample make generalization to more mundane groups of stalkers problematic.

De Becker, who also approaches stalking from a law enforcement perspective, has classified stalkers on the basis of motivation dividing stalkers into the attachment-seekers, the identity-seekers, the rejection-based and the delusion-based (cited in Orion, 1997). The delusion-based group, from a mental health perspective, tells us about the psychopathological nature of the beliefs, not their motivation, although the phrase 'delusionally motivated' has currency and is presumably what de Becker had in mind. Stalkers in the attachment-based group wish to establish a relationship with the victim, while recognizing that none exists; the example offered was John Hinckley. Identity seekers pursue the object of their attention as a means to achieve some other end, typically attention or fame themselves; here the example suggested was Mark Chapman, who killed singer John Lennon to become famous. The rejection-based stalkers pursue targets who have spurned them in some way, seeking to reverse or revenge the rejection. This latter group need not necessarily be ex-intimate partners but can include workmates and estranged friends. The delusion-based stalkers have a major mental illness in which delusions, or other erroneous beliefs, drive their pursuits. De Becker argued that the rejection based and identity seekers pose the greatest threat of violence. This classification has considerable appeal but to date has not been elaborated to any extent in the available literature.

Classification employed in this book

Mullen et al. (1999) proposed a classification that at least aspires to be multi-axial. The primary axis was a typology related mainly to the stalker's predominant motivation and the context in which the stalking emerged. The nature of the prior relationship with the victim and the psychiatric diagnosis formed the other two axes (for details of this typology, see Chapters 5, 6 and 7).

This classification emerged from the authors' experience with stalkers who were personally assessed in a clinic that had a known interest in stalkers. The courts referred the majority of cases, although there were also significant numbers referred from other health professionals and even three who self-referred, contacting the clinic after learning of its existence in the media. In most cases the clinic was charged initially with providing reports to the courts for the purposes of sentence and disposal. In those referred from health professionals and a number of those initially referred for court reports, however, the clinic became involved in the long-term management of the case. The clinic also provided services for stalking victims, which may have further influenced the approach to classification. In common with forensic mental health services in the UK, northern Europe and Canada, but in contrast to those in much of the USA, the clinic provided both assessment and treatment facilities. The classification had therefore to serve both forensic and mental health purposes and was generated by direct experience with stalkers both in the role of providing court-mandated assessments and as treating clinicians.

The primary types proposed were the rejected, the intimacy seekers, the resentful, the predatory and the incompetent. This typology attempts to capture the function of the behaviour for the stalker. What are the stalkers' purposes in pursuing this particular course of action and what needs and desires are being satisfied? The stalking behaviours have a meaning for the stalker which relates in some way to their goals. Equally, for the stalker to persist in such apparently destructive behaviours there must be results from their actions that are sufficiently rewarding to maintain the behaviour. The context in which the stalking arises is also of relevance, given its relationship to the stalkers' likely aims and their manner of advancing those aims. These variables are relevant whether or not they reflect judgements that are distorted or even delusional. The intimacy seekers are responding to loneliness by attempting to establish a close relationship. The rejected are responding to an unwelcome end to a close relationship by actions intended to lead to reconciliation or extract reparation, or both. The resentful are responding to a perceived insult or injury by actions aimed not just at revenge but at vindication. The predatory are pursuing their desires for sexual gratification and control both in and through the stalking. The incompetents are would-be suitors seeking a partner by methods likely to be at best counterproductive and at worst terrifying for their target.

The second axis related to the relationship to the victims, who were separated into ex-intimate partners, professional contacts, work-related contacts, casual acquaintances and friends, the famous, and strangers who had had no contact prior to the onset of the stalking. The clinic is situated in Melbourne, Australia and, unlike California or even New York, stars of stage, screen or radio are few and far between. In fact two of the only three victims with a claim to be celebrities were radio chat show hosts. In passing it is worth noting that radio personalities may be peculiarly vulnerable to stalking. This could be because they tend to engage directly with audiences via phone-ins and many seem to cultivate a style intended to give an appearance of direct, personal and in some ways intimate communication with the audience. The trials and tribulations of the seductive radio disc jockey who attracts an erotomanic stalker is brilliantly portrayed in the film *Play Misty for Me*, in which Clint Eastwood both starred and directed.

The final axis was related to psychiatric status, with a simplified division into a psychotic group incorporating schizophrenia, delusional disorders, affective psychosis and organic psychosis, the nonpsychotic grouping being predominantly personality disorders, with a lesser number of depressive and anxiety disorders. Substance abuse was usually a qualifier of the diagnosis, being a primary diagnosis in only a handful of cases. Nobody failed to acquire a diagnosis of at least personality disorder or substance abuse, not because of a low threshold for the recognition of mental disorders, but because of the high level of manifest psychopathology in this population.

The typology alone, and when taken together with the prior relationship and the psychiatric diagnosis, enabled predictions to be made about the duration of the stalking, the nature of the stalking behaviours, the risks of threatening and violent behaviour and to some extent the response to management strategies (Mullen et al., 1999). Table 4.1 sets out a number of the variables significantly associated with the typology of stalking in 168 stalkers. This expands on the data already published by Mullen et al. (1999).

The rejected grouping used the widest range of stalking behaviours, often following, repeatedly approaching, telephoning, letter-writing and leaving notes. In contrast, the predatory stalkers concentrated almost exclusively on furtively following and maintaining surveillance, never sending letters and rarely phoning or openly approaching the victim. Intimacy seekers were the most prolific of letter writers and they also excelled all other groups in the sending of unsolicited gifts and other forms of material. The duration of stalking was by far the longest in the

Table 4.1. Characteristics of stalkers and stalking behaviour according to typology

Variable	Stalking typology					Significance
	Rejected ($n=58$)	Intimacy seekers ($n=54$)	Incompetent ($n=24$)	Resentful ($n=24$)	Predator ($n=8$)	
Male	82%	72%	81%	75%	100%	0.43
Age (mean/SD)	38.1 (11.3)	38.2 (11.4)	34.8 (9.5)	39.1 (11.2)	29.7 (7.4)	0.21
Currently partnered	14%	10%	24%	25%	14%	0.39
Currently employed	75%	42%	59%	62%	62%	**0.01**
Stalking duration in months (mean/SD)	38.3 (47.7)	34.9 (41.7)	14.3 (12.9)	13.8 (11.2)	8.8 (11.5)	**0.01**
Number of harassment methods (mean/SD)	5.1 (1.5)	3.9 (1.6)	3.4 (1.2)	4.1 (1.5)	3.0 (0.9)	**0.000**
Substance abuse	29%	23%	16%	32%	14%	0.66
Prior criminal convictions	51%	31%	26%	48%	86%	**0.02**

Notes:
SD, standard deviation.
Bold type indicates statistical significance.

rejected and intimacy seekers and shortest, as might be expected, in the predatory stalkers.

The diagnostic variables were collapsed into a psychotic group (schizophrenia, delusional disorders, affective psychosis and organic psychosis) and a nonpsychotic group (predominantly personality disorders). The psychotic subjects were particularly likely to send unsolicited materials and the nonpsychotic to follow and maintain surveillance. The psychotic and nonpsychotic were equally likely to threaten but the nonpsychotic were twice as likely as the psychotic to proceed to assault.

The best predictor of stalking duration was the typology. Assaultiveness was also predicted best by typology, which, when combined with substance abuse and a history of prior convictions (irrespective of their nature), accounted for most of the explained variance (see Chapter 12).

The typology was of value in deciding on management strategy, as was the psychotic/nonpsychotic dichotomy. Intimacy seekers, many of whom had psychotic disorders, were largely impervious to judicial sanctions, often regarding court appearances, and even imprisonment, as the price to be paid for the pursuit of a true love. On the other hand, this group's stalking was often driven by a potentially treatable psychiatric disorder and the most expeditious manner of ending the stalking was to ensure appropriate mental health treatment. In contrast the rejected were in many cases responsive to threats, or the reality of judicial sanctions. In this group were many individuals who, if the price of continuing to harass was high enough, could desist. Given, however, that there are significant levels of psychopathology, albeit usually characterological, in most rejected stalkers, there can be an important role for therapeutic interventions in preventing a relapse into the stalking behaviours. The incompetent type can usually be persuaded to abandon the pursuit of their current victim with relative ease, but the challenge is to prevent them moving on to harass some new victim who catches their fancy. The predatory are drawn from the ranks of the paraphilics and management of their sexual deviance is central to the prevention of a recurrence in their stalking behaviours (for further discussion, see Chapter 15).

Conclusions

No generally accepted approach to classifying stalkers has yet emerged. A number of different typologies and groupings have been advanced that are the product of the particular experiences, theoretical commitments and practical needs of the groups who proposed the classifications. The division advanced by Zona and colleagues (1993, 1998) has been to date the most influential but is not ideal as it tends to be overly restrictive and is marred by too blind an adherence to the current dictates of the DSM. At this stage in the development of knowledge about stalking it is probably safe to say that the best classification to use is the one that best serves your needs. Our system of classification, which has been outlined above, works for us but this is in a context of mental health professionals who, though they assess and treat a wide range of stalkers, have no role in law enforcement and whose contact with the courts is as advisers on therapeutic options, with issues of competency rarely if ever raised.

As the knowledge and experience about stalkers and their behaviours, motivations and tragedectories increases, so classifications will become more firmly based in the realities of the stalking phenomena. Until then, doubtless differing constructions, typologies and would-be classifications will contend for attention and that inevitably elusive pre-eminence.

5

The rejected stalker and the resentful

The rejected stalker

Clinical features

One of the commonest forms of stalking is that which emerges in the context of the breakdown of a close relationship. Typically the rejected partner begins to stalk after their partner has attempted to end the relationship, or indicated that he or she intends to end the relationship. The overt aim of the stalking is either to attain a reconciliation or to exact revenge for the rejection. In practice the stalker not infrequently entertains a mixture of both of these goals, the dominant motivation shifting with circumstances and the ex-partner's responses. The usual relationship to give rise, at its dissolution, to stalking is an intimate sexual partnership, but the breakdown of any close relationship in which the rejected partner has invested emotional energy can usher in stalking. In our own experience we have seen stalking emerge following rifts between close friends, parents and their children, long-term work and business partnerships and even therapists and their clients (patients). The essential elements are the stalker's sense of having had his or her rights and prerogatives violated by the unilateral attempt to sever the relationship, combined, to a greater or lesser extent, with a sense of loss at the end of an important relationship. The rage at rejection is often augmented by distress at the perceived unfairness or humiliating nature of the rejection. The sense of loss may be heightened by the stalker's awareness that for them the lost relationship may be irreplaceable.

The rejected can be among the most persistent and intrusive of stalkers. Once established, their pattern of harassment is very difficult to alter. It is not always immediately obvious why these men and women continue so tenaciously to pursue their erstwhile partner. Those who claim to be hoping for a reconciliation and restitution of the relationship will usually admit, if confronted, that constant intrusions and threats are hardly likely to encourage their previous partner to restore the relationship. And yet they persist. Those pursuing some form of retribution (or, as they see it, justice) will often wax lyrical about how dreadful their ex-partner was and how the relationship had been absolute purgatory. Yet they are unwilling to walk away from a partnership they declare to have been a burden bereft of satisfactions. The stalking, in practice, traps both the stalker and the victim in a continuing relationship. For those stalkers who cannot abandon the hope of restoring the relationship the harassment at least provides some semblance of a connectedness to the lost partner. For the rejected stalker who is predominantly angry and vengeful the stalking seems again aimed in part at continuing a relationship in which, for all their raging, they remain enmeshed. The stalking in a sense is a continuation of a relationship, the loss of which is too threatening, or to which they remain bound by unresolved emotions and desires, made all the more compelling by their ambivalent nature.

The rejected are predominantly males. In our own series nearly 90% of those who fell into this typology were males. In epidemiological studies most of those pursued by ex-partners, were predominantly women stalked by men (see Chapter 2).

Relationship to other classifications

Meloy (1999) described the 'modal stalking victim' as a woman, younger than her pursuer, with whom she has had a prior sexually intimate relationship. The simple obsessional category of Zona and colleagues (1993, 1998), typified by a male who has been rejected pursuing a woman with whom he has had a sexual relationship, overlaps to an extent with this rejected typology. Similarly, those who are defined simply by the victim being an ex-partner are almost coextensive with this rejected group. The only exceptions are those who are stalking an ex-intimate with whom the relationship has not been sexual but a close friendship or family tie. Mullen et al. (1999) included in the rejected typology two individuals stalking their estranged mothers, six pursuing people with whom they had had a close but nonsexual relationship, and three where the victim had previously worked closely with the stalker and had formed close bonds.

The rejected typology contains a number of individuals with personality disorders predominantly of the dependent and narcissistic type. The jealous and suspicious who tend to fall diagnostically into the paranoid disorders are also well represented among the rejected stalkers.

A number of the rejected stalkers fit into one of the variants of the obsessional follower described by Meloy (1992; Meloy & Gothard, 1995). Meloy (1999, p. 88) described obsessional followers as socially isolated and characterologically narcissistic individuals in whom 'rejection stimulates shame and humiliation . . . which is quickly defended against with rage – not anger – toward what Kohut would view as a self-object and Kernberg would see as a part object'. Meloy (1999, p. 89) argued that such individuals when rejected defend themselves against feelings of abandonment by rage and devaluation, which in turn 'fuel the pursuit of the object to hurt, injure, control, damage or destroy him or her'. Meloy (1998a, 1999) considered that the most disturbing aspect of stalking is that the aggressive and destructive pursuit restores the narcissistic fantasies of entitlement and rectitude.

Personality characteristics

Narcissistic traits were evident in a number of our rejected stalkers, although this psychopathology was not perhaps as 'rampant' as Meloy (1998a) described among obsessional followers (Meloy, 1998a). One particularly startling example was provided by a man who had been repeatedly phoning and following a younger woman with whom he had had a relatively brief sexual relationship, lasting a matter of weeks. This man spent a lengthy period at the onset of the interview explaining how his victim was unattractive, stupid, had no dress sense and was without wit or charm. When asked why he was bothering to pursue a lady so bereft of positive qualities he offered that she had left him but that he had determined that they should again go out together. In response perhaps to the interviewer's puzzlement he went on to explain: it was obvious a woman like that didn't walk out on a man like *him*, but that when the relationship was restored he would of course leave *her*.

An intense sense of humiliation created when one partner unilaterally ends a relationship is not confined to the obviously narcissistic. The end of a relationship can be particularly provoking when not only the expectations of the rejected party are thwarted but they also feel publicly humiliated. One young woman, from a traditionally southern European family, had been engaged for some time to a somewhat older man from a very different cultural background. He ended the relationship on the grounds that their interests and aspirations were too divergent to sustain a permanent relationship. For him it was a rational decision politely communicated and realized as gently as possible. For her it was a gross and very public insult delivered in the face of her family and friends. The other problem for her was that from her perspective, and from her family's perspective, they were already irredeemably committed. Ending the relationship was unthinkable. She pursued this man over several months, initially with entreaties and pleas that were to her increasingly humiliating. Finally she responded with spectacular fury. She destroyed his flat, trashed his car, totally disrupted his work and repeatedly embarrassed him in public. When seen in our clinic she was a demonstrative young woman, perhaps somewhat lacking in self-esteem but certainly not someone lacking close social contacts, or given to overestimating her own qualities or capacities. She had a defined set of aims in pursuing this man. She was determined to 'get him back'. Equally, she was determined he would pay for the shame he had brought on her. In this case it was fear of imminent legal sanctions that played the greatest role in bringing her campaign to an end. That, and seeing her ex-lover in tears as he contemplated the wreckage of his treasured old MG sports car.

The commonest features we encounter among rejected stalkers are not narcissistic but those of overdependence. This overdependence is often combined with poor social skills and a resulting impoverished social network. These individuals have usually invested all their hopes and expectations in the relationship. They tend to have difficulty establishing relationships of any kind let alone intimate liaisons. Realistically they often express the fear that this may be their one and only chance for intimacy. Their reaction to the rejection has more to do with disbelief and desperation than it has with shame or rage. For many of these individuals there is no-one to be shamed in front of, except their partner. The early stages of the stalking tend to combine pleas for reconciliation with activities aimed at continuing the relationship as if no rift had occurred. One of our patients would contrive to turn up at work to drive his ex-partner home. He also repeatedly appeared at social and sporting venues attempting to escort her as he had in the past. He acknowledged that he hoped, if he persisted, the separation would simply go away. This type of appeal, however pathetic, tends eventually to generate increasingly emphatic and irritable demands from the ex-partner for a halt. These repeated rejections usually eventually either drive the overly dependent ex-partner away (in which case no further stalking occurs) or it produces anger and escalation. The following case illustrates some of these points.

Case example

Mrs P was referred by a magistrate following her conviction for breaching a restraining order. Mrs P, a 39-year old secretary, was unable to accept her banker husband's decision some twelve months earlier to end their marriage. She had repeatedly approached him at his workplace and his rented flat, pleading with him to reconsider. Mr P steadfastly rejected her advances but she did not, as he had hoped, 'eventually get the message'. Indeed, after bluntly informing his wife that she bored him and that they should never have married, Mrs P's efforts intensified. She phoned him over twenty times a day on his mobile phone and work extension, sent multiple letters to his office and home address, and often refused to leave his work premises. Tearful demands that he return now alternated with angry recriminations and vengeful attempts to embarrass him in front of his friends, co-workers and customers. Having sacrificed her job in the full-time pursuit of her husband, Mrs P made constant demands on him for money and insisted that he continue to support her in ways expected of a husband; this included washing her car and paying all her bills.

After ten months of harassment, desperate for some reprieve and fearful of losing his own job, Mr P obtained a restraining order. His estranged wife was enraged, and refused to acknowledge the order's existence. She persisted in her uninvited visitations, letters and phone calls, and began sitting in her car outside his flat, castigating him whenever he appeared. During this time, Mr P made repeated efforts to reason with her, avoiding any refutation of a future together because his earlier candour had failed; he also felt guilty and did not want to hurt her further.

One evening, Mr P arrived home late from work to find a brick had been hurled through his front window. Panicked, Mr P advised the police of the continuing breaches and property damage. He described Mrs P as an immature woman with poor self-esteem and jealous tendencies.

It was only after multiple court appearances and an actual assault upon Mr P outside his workplace that Mrs P was referred for psychiatric evaluation. The magistrate was reluctant to imprison the otherwise law-abiding defendant and handed down a community-based disposition with a condition that she undergo psychiatric assessment and treatment. She was a most unwilling participant, insisting that her husband was the one who needed a psychiatrist, to make him accept that his place was with her. She gave a history of growing up in a large Catholic family with three older sisters, all of whom were happily married and successful in their chosen careers. She had always regarded herself as the unattractive sibling. She met her future husband through a friend and he seemed to show an interest in her, so 'I chased him till he eventually gave in and we started hanging out together'. Convinced that this was her only opportunity for wedded bliss and babies, Mrs P mounted a dedicated campaign to win Mr P's hand in marriage, to which he succumbed after two years. When subsequently interviewed, Mrs P's parents indicated their early reservations about their daughter's choice of partner, regarding him as irresponsible and 'a bit of a womaniser'; they described him as 'the unhappiest groom we've ever seen', which was borne out by some of the wedding photographs, an observation to which Mrs P seemed oblivious.

Mrs P had no prior relationships and was a virgin when she began dating her husband. Her feelings of unattractiveness were more subjective than real, although her inferiority in relation to her sisters was reinforced by a weight problem and her reduced capacity to spend money on her appearance. She was a doting aunt to her two sisters' young children, but one sister had limited Mrs P's contact with the children because 'she was becoming too attached'. Mrs P had no prior contact with psychiatric services, her mother describing her as a rather clingy, sensitive child who was none the less devoted to family and a staunch Catholic. Since the separation, however, Mrs P had refused to join in family celebrations because her husband did not escort her, and she was furious if friends and family sent her invitations or cards which did not acknowledge Mr P.

Mrs P was frequently tearful throughout the initial and subsequent interviews, angrily devaluing her husband then describing him in idealized terms. She would not hear of the option of 'starting afresh', insisting that he was her husband and the only one she would ever be with. There was simply no question of another man. She could acknowledge her underlying fears that she was not good enough to attract another man, and that she was 'running out of time' (to start a family with anybody else). She also refused to accept, on religious grounds, that the marriage could be over, insisting that their commitment was life-long. She dismissed her estranged husband's right to privacy and freedom from harassment, stating that she had no respect for a law designed to prevent her from pursuing what was rightfully and legally hers, and insisting that Mr P's breach of his vows and the laws of the Church were a far more serious transgression. She alluded to ending her life if it did not include her husband, but there was no evidence at this time of a depressive disorder and she indicated that her religion prevented her from any earnest contemplation of suicide. She was aghast at the suggestion that she could physically harm her husband and similarly denied that she would hurt any of his future girlfriends (the mere suggestion of these evoking considerable distress) but she felt she would be quite justified in slashing their tyres.

Regular sessions were scheduled with Mrs P in an attempt to shift her rigid and maladaptive beliefs in relation to the marriage, Mr P, her own self-image and her prospects for the future. In addition, the legal sanctions in event of her continued disregard for the restraining order were repeatedly emphasized. Unfortunately, after some initial diminution in stalking activities, she persisted in breaching the order, maintaining that her husband alone was in control of the legal outcome, since his return to her and removal of the order were in his hands. Unfortunately, Mr P did have some influence over events in that he tended to accede to her demands to meet and frequently spoke with her when she phoned him at work. While these were understandable efforts on his part to appeal to reason and discourage further approaches, they served only to reinforce contact, strengthen her dependence on him and offer hope of future reconciliation. Further, Mr P was inconsistent in his enforcement of the order, leaving her perplexed and angry about her ability to visit him and receive a hug on one day, and being shouted off his property and arrested on another. A lack of consistency plagued this case at virtually every juncture, with a reluctance on the part of police to charge her, and bending the rules when she was held in the police cells by allowing her regular cigarettes and sympathetic chats with police. While some may have identified with her situation and possibly blamed her husband's conduct, they effectively protected her from the stark consequences of her illegal behaviours and any disincentive to persist in these.

Eighteen months after their separation, Mr P filed for divorce. Mrs P strenuously opposed this but assented in the Family Court, abusing Mr P, the lawyers and the presiding judge. She was in fact removed from the court, screaming that the divorce papers were meaningless and that she would never recognize them. Appearing only weeks later in the magistrates' court, on this occasion answering stalking charges, she berated the magistrate who referred to Mr P as her 'ex-husband' and Mrs P as 'Ms P'. Exasperated, the magistrate sentenced her to one month in prison.

Mrs P's prison experience proved very different from that of the police cells. She was bullied by other inmates and found the prison officers less than sympathetic. Her access to cigarettes was much less predictable, and she was often forced to exchange these for protection. She felt angry toward Mr P for her predicament, but came to see that she alone had the power to avoid any further punishment on this scale. She spoke regularly with the prison chaplain, who reinforced the finality of the divorce. Upon her release, Mrs P moved into a Church-run women's hostel and participated in paid charity work.

Mrs P also continued in therapy on a voluntary basis. Her anger towards her ex-husband persisted, albeit at a diminished and less destructive level. In a face-saving reversal, she said that she 'would never take the creep back', given his failure to support her through her traumatic prison ordeal. She admitted to occasionally driving down his street, curious about his social life, but there were no other breaches of the restraining order. With time and some notable improvement in her self-confidence, helped in large part by her work, Mrs P began dating a man she met through her charity work. She has developed a good deal of insight into her dependent temperament and is striving to avoid the relationship mistakes of the past. Her boyfriend, himself a rather immature individual, is aware of her stalking proclivities and accompanies her to therapy sessions whenever conflicts arise. Mrs P recently heard through a mutual friend that her ex-husband is living with a woman who is vaguely known to Mrs P. She feels 'they deserve each other'. Mr P (now engaged) has moved from his former residence and his ex-wife has shown no interest in locating his whereabouts.

Jealousy

Jealousy and possessiveness are prominent characteristics of some rejected stalkers. Typically, jealousy and excessive possessiveness manifests in the early stages of a relationship and become an ongoing theme. A number of rejected stalkers acknowledged they had been intensely jealous and that this had marred their relationships prior to the separation. A number of victims of stalking by ex-partners described, whilst still in the relationship, long histories of being subjected to cross-questioning, accusations and being checked up on. In effect some of these people were being stalked by jealous partners even before the relationship was terminated. Jealousy emerges in the context of a fear that a relationship is threatened (White & Mullen, 1989). It is, however, not only a cry of pain at threatened loss and disappointed hope but a way of keeping alive a failing relationship (Mullen, 1990, 1991). Jealousy intensifies the concern and increases the contact which the jealous person has with the suspected partner. Proust (1980/1913–22) suggested that jealousy's only virtue was that it stimulated a curiosity about their partner in the most unimaginative of men. The augmented curiosity and associated incursions are, however, rarely regarded positively by the object of suspicion.

Jealousy that continues to plague the individual even after a separation has occurred is fertile ground for stalking. Jealousy asserts a continuing entitlement not just to the relationship but to fidelity. Jealousy is nothing if not curious and intrusive (Lagache, 1947; Tallenbach, 1974). Jealousy, like stalking itself, attempts to sustain a relationship by maintaining contact through intrusion, through demands and through fantasy (Mullen, 1990). Jealousy is also productive of self-righteousness, based as it is on an accusation of infidelity and a claim to have been a victim of the other's ill-directed concupiscence. Entitlement with a self-righteous pursuit of those claims bred in jealousy all too easily feeds into the stalkers' conviction that their harassments are justified.

A piece of human behaviour such as stalking, as has already been emphasized, can be the end product of a wide range of psychological states interacting with differing circumstances. In our experience the rejected stalker, far from always conforming to the psychological profile of the obsessional follower, as advanced by Meloy (1999), is at least as likely to be a vulnerable, dependent individual clinging desperately to a lost relationship. We also encounter possessive, jealous individuals who refuse to accept that as far as the relationship is concerned separation equates to termination. In most cases the stalking is for the individual a unique form of deviance arising from a very specific set of circumstances that are experienced by the stalker as provoking, and in many cases as justifying, their behaviour. There may well be in this, or prior relationships, histories of possessiveness, jealousy, clinging dependence, insensitivity to the needs and feelings of the partner and even frank domestic violence. It is less common to obtain accounts of actual stalking in either this or preceding relationships. Occasionally, however, the stalking is part of a recurrent pattern of responses to failed relationships. These 'serial stalkers' often have marked narcissistic traits and certainly are prone to respond to rejection with rage. The following case describes such a 'serial stalker'.

Case example

Mr T was referred by the courts for a pre-sentence psychiatric report, having been convicted of stalking his ex-fiancée. This 42-year-old computer salesman had a series of failed relationships characterized by stalking.

As a 17-year-old student, Mr T dated a popular girl in his class but 'she couldn't hack it because I wasn't a virgin and she was'. She apparently resisted his demands for a sexual relationship (which would in fact have been his first). Angry at her rejection of him, Mr T responded by spreading rumours around school that she was a whore. He also despatched five taxis and a pizza delivery to her parents' home late one night.

Mr T's encounters with women were short lived over the next few years. He dropped out of a computer science course at university during his second semester, claiming that he was too advanced for the rest of the class. He found work for a time with his father in his printing business but found the work tedious, arguing constantly with his father, whose lack of ambition he had long deplored. An uncle offered Mr T a sales position in his used-car business, where Mr T began dating the secretary. By his account, this woman was very attractive and he felt constantly jealous of the attentions paid to her by other men. He spent increasing periods with her, forbidding her to go out without him, and three months after meeting her proposed marriage. He claims he was sure she would be 'good wife material and make beautiful babies'. She declined, but the two continued to see each other for several more months before an angry confrontation – prompted by her renewed interest in a former boyfriend – persuaded her to end the relationship. Incensed, Mr T made a series of anonymous, threatening and hang-up calls to the woman and created such enmity at her workplace that she was compelled to resign. On one occasion, he pushed her against a filing cabinet but her employer – Mr T's uncle – dismissed her allegation. He none the less fired

Mr T a short time later for being a 'disruptive influence' in the office, after the replacement secretary had accused Mr T of sexual harassment.

At age 27 Mr T, working again for his father, befriended a 22-year-old customer. She initially resisted his requests to go out but she relented after he besieged her with gifts of flowers and customized, romantic cards. The courtship was, by his account, a 'perfect' one, though it was equally characterized by jealousy and controlling behaviour on his part. After a year the couple married, against the wishes of the woman's parents, who described Mr T as 'arrogant and sleazy'. The marriage quickly deteriorated, Mr T refusing to allow his wife to continue her work at the beauty counter of a department store, despite their financial difficulties. He felt aggrieved when she questioned his right to go out with male friends and spend money on drinks, 'girlie shows' and gambling, further antagonizing her by increasing the frequency of his outings. One day he discovered she was taking birth control pills despite his rigid insistence on starting a family without delay; an argument ensued during which he almost strangled her. She escaped to her parents' home and they called the police. Mr T denied the assault and no charges ensued, though he was quite forthcoming about his actions when seen years later at our clinic, regarding his behaviour as justified under the circumstances ('well, she lied . . . that's hardly any basis for a marriage . . .').

Mr T's wife never returned, despite his repeated approaches to the parental home pleading for a reconciliation. He sent her bouquets of flowers, cards and long letters asserting his undying love. Often, he waited in his car outside the house, being chased on one occasion by his furious father-in-law. Mrs T was encouraged to take out a restraining order, the complainant responding with self-righteous indignation. He made repeated phone calls through the night, hanging up on his in-laws and execrating his estranged wife. His behaviour became increasingly vengeful. He spray-painted maledictory messages over his in-laws' fence. He printed flyers detailing his estranged wife's sexual habits and distributed these to all her neighbours. He severed the fuel line in his father-in-law's car and punctured his wife's tyres with a screw driver. He even removed all the clothes from their washing line and stuffed them in the compost bin. Ultimately, Mr T's intrusions were photographed by a vigilant neighbour and he was charged on multiple counts of trespass, criminal damage, threats to kill, misuse of telecommunications and breaches of the restraining order (there being no offence of stalking at that time). His conviction resulted in a good behaviour bond. His wife divorced him, prompting further attempts at contact, but during a subsequent appearance before a magistrate he was threatened with imprisonment and the stalking subsided.

Almost a year later, Mr T found work with a computer software company. Soon after, unbeknown to his employer, he was convicted of indecently assaulting a woman at a nightclub, having squeezed her breasts in the process of asking her for a date. He received a community-based order with a condition that he undergo psychological assessment. The clinical psychologist found him to be a 'narcissistic, antisocial individual with strongly misogynistic beliefs and little appreciation for the rights of others'. It was recommended that he receive counselling but he did not comply and the recommendations were not enforced, possibly because the (female) correctional officer supervising his order did not feel it was worth the argument.

While still on the community order Mr T befriended one of his clients, a fashion buyer.

She too was a divorcee, and initially rejected his advances because she did not feel ready for another relationship. Mr T, typically impervious to such extenuations, invited her for 'just a coffee', which she accepted with some hesitation. Further coffee dates ensued, then other outings and a more intimate relationship. The pattern of this relationship was remarkably similar to those which preceded it, the woman agreeing to marriage some eight months later. She, however, insisted upon a lengthy engagement, during which time Mr T's controlling, possessive ways became increasingly apparent. When his fiancée attempted to extricate herself from the relationship, Mr T threatened to ruin her reputation and career. He emailed offensive messages to her, and sent faxes to her workplace falsely alleging her sexual misconduct and dishonesty; these were read by a number of her staff, as intended. One day, Mr T arrived at the woman's apartment and demanded she let him in to 'talk'. She reluctantly agreed, because his shouting and accusations were disturbing the neighbours. Inside, he pressed her against the kitchen sink and began fondling her breasts and forcibly kissing her. She screamed, alerting the man in the adjacent apartment who came to her door to investigate. A surly Mr T departed immediately, promising to return. The woman changed her locks, installed a security door, obtained a duress alarm and notified the police. Despite his community order and an official record of similar harassment, their only action was to recommend that she apply for a restraining order.

A fortnight and numerous hang-up phone calls later, and prior to the granting of an interim protective order, the victim received a letter from Mr T's solicitor, demanding that she repay the $10 000 allegedly owed to his client. The woman sought legal advice of her own in dealing with the patently untrue claim, fearful that Mr T was plausible enough to succeed in any subsequent action. In actual fact Mr T owed his victim money (having kept some of her antique furniture) and he eventually abandoned his claim, but not until his ex-lover had forfeited several thousand dollars in solicitor's fees.

Although Mr T refrained from sending faxes and emails after the restraining order was in place and he desisted from phoning her when he learned her calls were being traced, he continued to hover around her neighbourhood and intermittently tailed her car. The victim distributed photographs of her stalker to her neighbours and urged them to notify the police whenever they sighted him. This culminated in Mr T's arrest one evening while using a nearby pay phone to arrange pizza deliveries to the woman's address. On this occasion he was convicted of stalking. Our pre-sentence psychiatric evaluation supported earlier conclusions that Mr T had a personality disorder with prominent narcissistic traits, with no evidence of major psychiatric illness. Not surprisingly, he was a difficult man to engage, his angry, entitled, self-righteous nature pervading sessions. He could none the less appreciate the significant consequences to him of persisting in his vengeful course.

Although his ex-fiancée reported one further suspicious episode (her mail was removed from her letter box and strewn around the front garden), Mr T denied any involvement and the harassment ceased. After five months Mr T's employers transferred him to another office interstate. He was offered a referral to an equivalent service there but this was declined.

Rejected stalkers are the type most likely to employ intimidation and assault in their pursuit of the ex-intimate. In part this is because such stalkers are more likely to be drawn from a population given to threats and violence when frustrated or threatened. A history of domestic violence in the relationships of those pursuing ex-partners, although far from universal, is not uncommon. The aggression is also encouraged by the presence of active jealousy, an emotion notorious for its connection to violence (Shepherd, 1961; Mullen, 1997). In addition, this is stalking often occurring in the context of continuing contact between stalker and victim. The mechanics and practicalities of ending relationships often draw ex-partners back into close contact. The mixed emotions, which can include guilt, induce the victims to attempt to conciliate the stalkers by seeing them and talking with them. The patterns of ex-partners lives have often established common places for leisure and work, together with common friends and acquaintances. Unless the victim abandons all the familiar and often valued connections then they risk encountering the rejected ex-partner. The greater the physical proximity and the more frequent the face-to-face encounters and confrontations the greater the risk of escalation to violence. Finally, rejected stalkers are often filled with a combination of self-righteousness and overwhelming entitlement, both states of mind conducive to threatening and potentially violent behaviours.

Characteristics and management of the rejected

In the study of Mullen et al. (1999) the rejected used the widest range of stalking behaviours of all types of stalker. They phoned, wrote, followed and loitered, typically employing most, if not all, of the available methods of intruding and harassing. Threats in this series were also reported to be issued by over 70% of the rejected. They proceeded to assault in over half of the cases.

Characteristics of the the rejected stalker

1 Pursue an ex-intimate.
2 Aim at either reconciliation, or exacting revenge for rejection, or a fluctuating mixture of both.
3 Maintain, by stalking, a relationship to the target, albeit distressing and damaging.

Diagnostically the rejected are a mixed bag, though predominantly they are drawn from the personality disordered rather than the psychotic range. A small number of the rejected have paranoid illnesses, usually with predominantly a jealous content or colouring. Far more frequent are marked characterological anomalies, dependent, narcissistic and paranoid traits being relatively common. Poor social skills and impoverished social networks were the rule rather than the exception. Substance abuse was acknowledged by nearly 30%. This usually involved alcohol, or cannabis, or both.

The rejected stalkers are not usually so disturbed and disordered that they cannot calculate their own advantage. Although caught up in the pursuit of their ex-partners, when confronted with a sufficiently high price for continuing that pursuit, in terms of criminal sanctions, many are able to stop. Relapses back into the stalking behaviour is, in our experience, reduced if not totally prevented by appropriately focussed counselling and support. They are often distressed, angry men whom the loss of the relationship has left adrift without alternative social supports or occasionally even contacts. They need help in letting go of the lost partner or other intimate. They often need to appropriately grieve that loss as part of the letting go. Then they need to acquire new social outlets and hopefully new, less conflicted relationships. The latter aim is often very difficult to attain, given both the low levels of social skills and the reluctance to again offer the level of trust necessary to form any close relationship. Substance abuse when present often contributes to, and potentially drives, stalking. When present, the management of substance abuse is essential in terminating the stalking.

There are a small number of rejected stalkers where major mental illness plays a significant role. Their disorders, as noted, often involve preoccupations or frank delusions about the partners fidelity. Managing intense or delusional jealousy is never easy and is particularly problematic when the jealousy has continued beyond the separation of the partners (for jealousy management, see White & Mullen, 1989). Depressive disorders are not in our experience usually apparent when this group of rejected stalkers are first seen but do emerge when they are able to abandon their pursuit, for with that abandonment comes for them the reality of the end of the relationship.

The resentful stalker

Clinical features

Stalking can be motivated primarily by the desire to frighten and distress the victim. This type of stalker is pursuing a vendetta because of a sense of grievance that has become focussed on the target of their unwanted attentions. The choice of the term resentful rather than vengeful for this group of stalkers is not arbitrary. The harassment itself often seems at first glance to be simply the attempt of the stalker to exact vengeance against someone who has upset them. When, however, this type of stalker was interviewed they almost invariably presented themselves not as avengers but as victims, who, in the process of defending themselves, were striking back at their oppressors. Further, in almost all of these stalkers the targets of their harassment were pictured by the stalkers as examples of the types of people who had repeatedly harassed and humiliated them over their past life. The particular choice of target, although only occasionally arbitrary, was usually someone identified as exemplifying the type of person who had previously oppressed and humiliated the stalker. The supervisor or co-worker may have evoked the stalker's indignation by a specific act which made them seem an opportune target. The stalker, however, almost always experienced a more generalized resentment against, for example, the firm, or authority or even 'the system'. It was for this reason that the resentful stalkers usually pictured themselves not as victimizing someone more vulnerable than they but, on the contrary, as being themselves victims striking back against the more powerful forces oppressing them.

We have encountered individuals who, in response to a specific insult have responded by an outburst of harassment against the individual who has offended them. These episodes usually consist of insulting phone calls, anonymous letters of the poison pen variety and even following, but they are rarely persisted with for more than a few days. These outbursts of angry vengefulness are, for the most part, in stark contrast to the persistent and calculated harassment of the typical resentful stalker. They are also highly specific and personal with regard to the victim. These vengeful harassers rarely persist for long enough to qualify as stalkers in our definition, but may certainly find themselves *prosecuted* as stalkers. Their victims will be among those identified in community surveys as having been stalked. The vengeful and the resentful form two overlapping types and some readers may find the attempt to distinguish them as at best overly pernickety and at worst futile. In part our distinction is based on theoretical as well as clinical grounds. A diversion into our view of the nature of being resentful may clarify the assumptions underpinning the construction of this type of stalker.

The nature of resentment

In English, the term resentment has come to mean simply indignation or ill will excited by an experience of injury or insult. Resentment derives from the French *ressentiment* (OED). This, in its turn, was compounded of the Latin prefix *re,* indicative of repetition or returning, and *sentire,* to feel or experience (Lewis & Short, 1879). The retention of the notion of repeated returns to the memories of the feelings and experiences associated with past injuries is central to understanding the power exerted by the emotion of resentment.

Scheler (1961/1910) provided a remarkable phenomenological exegesis of *ressentiment* (he, despite being Austrian, prefers the French word). He distinguishes between reprisal, revenge and *ressentiment*. Reprisal is an immediate retaliation for an experienced injury. Revenge is a planned retribution against those who are perceived as having injured you and its aim is to return injury for injury. Revenge focusses on the fantasies and plans for future vengeance. *Ressentiment,* like revenge, begins with the checking of an immediate retaliation in response to an injury in favour of delayed retribution. *Ressentiment,* unlike revenge, focusses on a repeated return to the remembered feelings of humiliation and powerlessness associated with the existing injury. The plans and fantasies for specific retaliation gradually merge into a less focussed sense of having been ill used. *Ressentiment,* once established, in contrast to revenge becomes separated from any specific exciting cause and attaches itself to a steadily lengthening catalogue of humiliations.

Resentment can become one of the most obsessive and enduring of emotions, often achieving a mood like scope (Solomon, 1976). Those caught up in resentment experience themselves as the innocent object of another's vindictiveness. If and when they do retaliate against an individual, or organization, chosen as the proxy for their various persecutors, they experience themselves as acting righteously. Resentment demands a limitless retribution for it is not payback for any specific act but for a multitude of hurts, made even more voluminous by their repeated and obsessive reliving. Revenge aims primarily to damage and reduce the enemy. Resentment aims primarily at bolstering the sense of power and righteousness of the resentful individual, an aim that is furthered in the process of confronting the target who has been transformed into an embodiment of oppression. Vengeful and retaliatory stalking are brief outbursts of harassment driven forward by the anger generated by a recently experienced injury. Resentful stalking, in contrast, is a lengthy campaign of harassment aimed at inducing fear in someone who has come to be the embodiment of those against whom the stalker entertains a multiplicity of grievances. The resentful stalker is not usually concerned primarily with obtaining a direct and proportional retribution for a specific injury but is after vindication and justification. The resentful stalker is a person whose resentment against an unfeeling and rejecting world preceded the event which precipitated the stalking. Their resentment is channelled into the harassment and focussed on the target. This is in contrast to reprisal and revenge, where the anger is evoked by, and largely confined to, the actions of the target.

Case examples

Mr A was in his early thirties. He had come from an apparently stable background but had received little attention from either of his parents, who were preoccupied with their own lives. He had had few friends and no long-term intimate relationships. Although well qualified in his profession he had failed to establish himself in regular employment. After a number of short-lived appointments on leaving university he had been reduced to agency work, often well below the level his qualifications should have commanded. Mr A attributed his social isolation and failure to progress occupationally to the malevolence and envy of others. He was suspicious and easily offended. He had pursued a range of complaints and grievances against previous employers and a previous landlord. He was constantly affronted by the contrast between his abject state and the undeserving success and happiness of those around him.

On the day which was to be critical for the emergence of stalking Mr A had learnt that a job application in which he had invested great hope had been unsuccessful. Later walking through the central business area a young woman had rushed in front of him causing him to step back suddenly and slip. She did not stop but, leaving him humiliatingly seated on the pavement, jumped into a new Series 7 BMW and drove away. This event, with the well-dressed attractive young woman literally stepping over him to her symbol of power and prestige, crystallized all his sense of resentment against the world. He later recalled having decided at that moment that enough was enough. He should strike back.

Mr A waited in a nearby café watching for the young woman's return. Later that day he followed her to her home. Over the next few weeks he obtained a considerable amount of information about her (all meticulously recorded and filed on his computer). He soon learnt she was not the owner of the BMW, nor even a successful young businesswoman. She was a secretary. The car was her employer's (who had left it illegally parked for her to take to the garage for a service). She was neither wealthy nor powerful. None of this, however, altered his selection of her as the embodiment of injustice. Later he was to rationalize this by referring to her many other advantages, including looks, friends, occupation, security, etc.

Mr A began a campaign of terror against this young woman that was to last over a year until he was imprisoned. The telephone was his main weapon. Repeated hang-up calls, occasional heavy breathing and occasional indirect threats such as 'I'm coming' and 'It's your turn now'. He phoned her at home, on her mobile, at work, in cafés where she lunched, at friends' houses that she visited. Obtaining a restricted access telephone number delayed him for only a couple of days whilst he managed to obtain the new number. He also sent letters, usually with blank pages, although he also enclosed an obituary column on one occasion.

The victim was devastated. The police were induced to act only after considerable pressure from her employers (she worked for a law firm). He was finally convicted not of stalking (the legislation still having not been introduced) but under a section of the laws governing the improper use of the telephone. While this man was in prison he created considerable anxiety by justifying his actions and repeatedly stating he would continue his pursuit, and making veiled death threats directed at the victim. Fortunately in the event he accepted a referral to a mental health service on release and did not return to harassing the victim. Throughout he considered he was the real victim in the case and that his arrest and imprisonment were another example of the injustice and general malevolence of the world.

This case history illustrates clearly the picture of a pre-existing resentful way of finding expression through the essentially arbitrary choice of a victim to stalk. In most cases the picture is less clear. The stalker usually begins their campaign of harassment following a perceived injury and often directs that campaign at a plausible target. The stalking appears to be primarily vengeful, even if the stalker's activities seem disproportionate and ill directed.

The next case illustrates what could be considered the other end of the spectrum of resentful stalking from that of the first case, Mr A. Here there was a perception that the target had inflected immense damage on the stalker. The pattern of behaviour seemed entirely understandable, albeit equally unacceptable. When assessed, however, Mr G revealed a pattern of resentment and hostility to the world. He had in the past energetically pursued claims and grievances against a variety of organizations and individuals. The stalking described below was the latest and most dramatic example of an established pattern of complaint and grievance.

Case example

Mr G was referred by his community corrections officer. Mr G, a 34-year-old invalid pensioner, had been stalking his former general practitioner, Dr N, for nearly two years. The stalking had been precipitated by the death of his wife, for which he blamed Dr N.

Mr and Mrs G had been Dr N's patients for over five years. A routine cervical smear performed by Dr N on Mrs G was abnormal but Dr N was unable to communicate the result to her patient because she and Mr G had moved to another town and had not left a forwarding address. When Mrs G finally presented to another doctor her cervical carcinoma was well advanced and she eventually succumbed to the disease.

Mr G was devastated. He initially sought redress through legal channels but the courts could not find Dr N liable because she had made all reasonable efforts to locate her patient and Mrs G had failed to phone for the results as advised. The State Medical Board investigated the matter also but concurred with the court findings. Mr G was infuriated, claiming the courts and the Medical Board were involved in a 'cover-up'. He insisted that Dr N had received preferential treatment because she was a professional from a privileged background, whilst he and his wife were not. He was determined that she should be made to 'pay'.

Mr G moved back to the town in which Dr N practised. He made repeated phone calls to her surgery, berating the hapless doctor for her negligence and promising he would destroy her 'undeserved' good name. He added also that he intended to make her suffer in a 'long and drawn out' fashion, as did his wife. Dr N, distressed at Mrs G's unnecessary demise, the subsequent legal enquiries and now Mr G's angry threats, refused to take any further calls. Undeterred, Mr G visited Dr N's surgery on repeated occasions, publicly berating her. He made a range of malicious allegations, claiming the doctor's involvement in illegal practices such as euthanasia and abortions, that she was a narcotic addict, and that her medical licence had been suspended. He also informed the waiting room of alarmed patients that Dr N had murdered his wife. After several such visits, Dr N's receptionist, fearful and on the verge of resigning, called the police. They escorted Mr G from the property and advised Dr N to seek a restraining order.

Mr G refrained from any further calls to the surgery but located the doctor's home address through the electoral roll ('I didn't have any trouble finding her'). The victim received an assortment of newspaper cuttings, delivered to her door, which referred to 'bad' doctors who had been deregistered; scrawled across these were accusations that Dr N had avoided similar treatment by 'sleeping with the judge and the chairman [of the Medical Board]'. He dropped a dead rat in her letterbox with the attached message: 'This is all you're safe to practise on', and photos of a cemetery with her name on all the headstones. Her car was badly vandalized on multiple occasions, both outside the surgery and in the carport of her home.

Mr G then began to make appearances at the local hospital where Dr N did her rounds, watching her menacingly and informing the nurses and patients that he was a representative from the office of the Health Commissioner investigating a complaint against the doctor. Dr N again reported these activities to the police who charged Mr G with stalking. He was convicted and fined. Incensed, Mr G (who had represented himself in court, confident he would be vindicated) intensified his campaign. He denounced the criminal justice system, appalled that the well-paid doctor who had 'murdered' his wife escaped scot-free while he – the grieving pensioner husband – was now expected to pay. The phone calls resumed with a vengeance, Mr G threatening the doctor's life and that of her young family. He was promptly returned to court, on this occasion accepting legal representation, and was sentenced to a community disposition with a condition that he undergo psychiatric assessment and treatment.

Mr G was surly and resentful on presentation to our clinic. He was very bitter toward the 'establishment' and the medical profession in particular. It transpired that he had a long history of dissatisfaction, not only with doctors but with a variety of other agencies.

The oldest of three boys, Mr G described a difficult and deprived childhood. His father left when Mr G was eight years old and they never re-established contact despite learning some years later that his father had won the lottery and remarried. His mother was chronically depressed and Mr G assumed responsibility for the care of his younger siblings. When Mr G was 12 years old, the youngest brother was hit by a neighbour's car while riding his bicycle on the road outside their home. Mr G, who witnessed the accident, was distraught when the doctors at the emergency department were unable to save his brother. With news of the death came a further deterioration in his mother's condition, necessitating her admission to a psychiatric institution. Mr G and his surviving brother stayed with an uncle, visiting their mother infrequently. Mr G was subsequently informed, weeks before his sixteenth birthday, that his mother had died from an 'unknown' cause.

Mr G was an average scholar who left school at 15 (following his mother's death) to pursue an apprenticeship as a boilermaker. He was a good worker, and was thrilled to have money to spend for the first time in his life. Then, late one night when returning home from a dance, his car swerved to avoid a cyclist and hit an embankment. Mr G sustained several fractured vertebrae and spent some weeks in hospital. Although he made a good recovery he was no longer able to work as a consequence of chronic back pain. He did the rounds of various doctors, angry that they could not offer more effective treatment, and was ultimately placed on an invalid pension.

Mr G met his wife at a local council rally when he was 26 and they married a few years later. He described the relationship as a very happy one, although money was short. They had few friends and no real social life but found immense comfort and mutual support in each other's company. He was quite depressed after his motor vehicle accident but refused counselling, ever mindful of his mother's experience of psychiatry. He denied any other contact with mental health services. At the initial interview, he was noted to be an angry resentful man who regarded his behaviour toward Dr N as entirely justified. He felt cruelly wronged and abandoned by the 'system'. He characterized himself as a battler for justice who stood up against the privileged and the powerful on behalf of all victims. He was determined that Dr N should pay (for his wife's death, but also, it seemed for all the other losses he had endured in his life as a consequence of the perceived slights, rejections and humiliations). His mood was neither depressed nor elevated and there was no evidence of a psychotic illness. He did not demonstrate any conviction in the scandalous allegations he had levelled at Dr N, these being intended solely to hurt her ('because nobody else will').

Mr G has been seeing a social worker to address his many losses, including his own health, and his associated feelings of guilt, helplessness and abandonment. While he is not admitting any reduction in the anger he feels towards the 'privileged' Dr N, there is no indication of any ongoing stalking activities. He has indicated a willingness to continue counselling on a voluntary basis when his community correctional order expires.

Characteristics and management

In our series of stalkers there were sixteen who fitted the category of resentful (Mullen et al., 1999). Eight had selected a target almost at random as a representative of an organization or group by whom they felt aggrieved. The other eight pursued vendettas against people who they perceived as having very specifically and particularly injured them, but even here they usually evinced a generally resentful attitude to the world. Interestingly, the resentful group, although the most likely type of stalker to threaten, were one of the least likely to proceed to an actual assault. This paradox appears to be accounted for by the calculating nature of the resentful stalker's harassment, which is aimed at creating maximum distress to the target with minimum risk to the stalker.

Characteristics of the the resentful stalker

1 The stalking behaviours are intended to cause fear and apprehension in their target.
2 The stalking emerges out of a desire for retribution against an individual, whom the stalker believes has personally, or as a member of some group or organization, harmed them.
3 The resentful stalkers usually gain a satisfying sense of power and control from their harassment of the target.
4 The resentful stalkers almost invariably feel justified in their actions and present themselves as victims fighting back against overwhelming odds.

Resentful stalkers share a number of features with the Querulants, who are morbid and abnormally persistent claimants. Both are pursuing a wide agenda of personal vindication and retribution through the medium of a specific grievance. A number of our resentful stalkers were at the same time pursuing complex claims and litigations that were not necessarily connected to the grievances motivating the stalking.

Treating the resentful group has presented formidable problems. They evince considerable self-righteousness and are difficult to engage in treatment. Attempts to compel their compliance with any therapeutic programme tends to inflame their sense of being victimized. This group is not usually caught up in a frank paranoid disorder but are usually able to calculate their own advantage. Confronted with legal sanctions they will often withdraw from the stalking. At this point therapy may become a more viable option. To some extent the efficacy of legal sanctions depends on how firmly established the pattern of harassment has become. In the relatively early stages, court orders and suspended sentences, even the threat of prosecution can be effective in terminating the harassment. Once well established, however, the resentful stalker has often invested so much of their sense of self, and have so succeeded in persuading themselves of the justice and righteousness of their actions, that withdrawal without total loss of face has become virtually impossible. It is in these latter individuals that a picture close to, if not identical with, that of a delusional disorder is apparent. Among the resentful stalkers tend to be found those with paranoid personalities or even frank paranoid illness. As noted above it is the Querulant type of paranoid disorder that predominates.

6

The predatory stalker

Introduction

> Norman discovered the film maker's address by buying a tourist map of stars' homes. He spent a month watching the mansion . . . He went to the gates at least four times and was finally arrested as he tried to run from private security guards . . . Norman boasted to police that he wanted to rape Spielberg while the director's wife . . . watched . . . [He] kept diaries about Spielberg's films and family, stockpiled sex toys and made repeated attempts to break into the director's sprawling estate . . . [When Norman was arrested] he was carrying a 'rape kit' containing a knife blade, razor blades, tape and handcuffs . . . Police also discovered a book with a shopping list of tools they say Norman planned to use on Spielberg, including three eye masks, three sets of handcuffs, four pairs of nipple clips and three dog collars.
>
> Australian newspaper reports from the June 1998 trial of Jonathan Norman, who stalked American film director Steven Spielberg. He is now serving a twenty-five year sentence.

The predatory stalker's behaviours are a means to an end, and that end is an attack, usually sexual, on the victim. The predatory stalker prepares for and anticipates the attack in the process of following and observing the victim. The behaviour of the predatory stalker is, however, seldom entirely instrumental. This group is selected in part from the ranks of those who delight in the sense of control and power that accrues from watching and planning an assault on the target. In contrast to the resentful stalker, for whom harassment is designed to inflict fear and distress, predatory stalkers seem to derive excitement from the surreptitious observation of their victim. Often there is no manifest intent to disturb or even alert the victim to his or her emerging fate. The victims of the predatory stalker frequently live in ignorance of the destiny their stalker is preparing for them.

Predatory stalkers constitute a small but salient subset of stalkers, who have been disproportionately represented, in their most ostentatious and dramatic forms, in fictional portrayals of stalking. For predators such as Jonathan Norman, the stalking activities are the prelude to sexual attack, but in addition these behaviours may in themselves be sexually exciting, providing an erotic gratification from the sense of power over the victim and, in some instances, their capacity to humiliate them by unwanted intrusions and the arousal of fear.

Clinical characteristics

The predatory stalker shares features in common with stalkers for whom sexual gratification is not the predominant motivator. For example, those with sexually aberrant behaviours often share the socially incompetent stalker's interpersonal inadequacies, feelings of sexual inferiority and pervasive sense of failure. Unlike other categories of stalker, however, the predator is more gender specific. With few exceptions, sexually deviant and sexually predatory behaviours are the domain of men. Their human prey, on the other hand, may be male or female, adults or children.

In the sexually perverse, poor self-esteem and low self-efficacy in social relationships are commonly encountered and are often accompanied by deficits in sexual knowledge, intimacy and courting skills (Finkelhor, 1984; Hall, 1989). Panton (1978) observed that 'child molesters tended to be anxious, inadequate individuals who felt insecure in their associations with others and who expected rejection and failure in adult heterosexual advances'. Wilson & Cox (1983) concurred, noting that the paedophiles in their study were 'more likely to be shy, sensitive, lonely, depressed, and humourless'. Hall (1989, p. 141) noted that 'paedophiles often report that they feel inadequate in adult situations. They fear rejection from adults and avoid situations in which the rejection might be forthcoming . . . By avoiding adult situations, they miss the opportunity to gain experiences in interpreting the non-verbal and other social cues needed to form and maintain successful adult relationships'. Indeed, McConaghy (1993) believed that for sex offenders in general it is these difficulties in interpreting the social cues, rather than a lack of social skills per se that predispose them to seek inappropriate and nonthreatening sexual objects. MacCulloch et al. (1983) found similar deficiencies in their cohort of sexual sadists, all of whom experienced general difficulties in social relationships from an early age: 'These developed after puberty into a problem of relating sexually to their preferred sex, commonly epitomised by an inability to make any sort of appropriate approach.' Many stalkers share similar deficits, which in these individuals appear to play a pivotal role in the evolution of stalking. Accordingly, it is reasonable to expect that some stalking behaviours may feature in the repertoire of the sexually deviant and this is likely to have been the case long before stalking was ever recognized as a discrete phenomenon.

Lindsay and colleagues (1998) reported two cases of intellectually disabled sex offenders who stalked. One made frequent direct approaches to his female victim at her home over a six-month period, requesting that she have sex with him and exposing his genitals to her. The other became enamoured of a female supervisor at his sheltered work placement, following her and becoming more persistent and abusive in response to her continued rejection of him. In this case the stalking, which included vandalizing the victim's car and that of her longstanding partner, travelling some distance to watch the victim's basketball team play, and verbal abuse, persisted for four years before the perpetrator was convicted of sexual harassment and vandalism. Both these men were in their mid twenties and their intellectual functioning was in the mildly retarded range. The first case, regarded by Lindsay et al. to be typical of their 'nuisance' category, received a two-year probation order with a requirement for treatment, while the second, categorized as 'delusional', received three years' probation with similar conditions. While intellectual disability has received scant attention in the stalking literature to date, it may be of particular relevance to the sexually motivated group of stalkers, given that up to 50% of intellectually disabled offenders have sexual convictions (Cockram et al., 1992) and the lower incidence of stable relationships and social competence generally in this population. Indeed, low intelligence is a not uncommon finding among incompetent stalkers (see Chapter 7).

Increasingly since the introduction of anti-stalking legislation, sex offenders are attracting charges of stalking, with or without more specific sexual charges. The offence of stalking can occasionally disguise that which is primarily sexual deviance. It has long been recognized that sexually illicit acts may be concealed by crimes that are overtly nonsexual, such as the would-be rapist convicted of breaking and entering (in search of a victim), the fetishist of theft (of undergarments from clothes lines) or the voyeur convicted of trespass. Hence, in a man charged with stalking a woman who is a stranger, the possibility of some wider sexual psychopathology must be considered. MacCulloch and co-workers (1983) have noted, in relation to a cohort of sexual sadists, that aggressive and sadistic fantasies may progress to 'behavioral try-outs', or enacting the fantasies in vivo: 'At varying stages of these behavioral try-outs criminal offences were committed. In this context some offences which are not overtly sadistic are as significant as overtly sadistic sexual offences because they are part of an escalating sequence of sadistic behavior which, if unchecked, can ultimately lead to loss of life.' They considered it 'extremely rare for any connection to be made between early non-sadistic offences, later sadistic offences and sexual fantasies.' There are serious risks in failing to recognize connections between stalking and sex crimes.

The characteristics of the predatory stalker

1 The stalker's gender is male.
2 Stalking behaviours are intended as preparatory to an assault, usually sexual, upon the victim.
3 The stalking is a combination of information gathering, rehearsal, intrusion through surreptitious observation, and the exercise of power.
4 The stalker's intent in most cases is not to disturb or alert the victim prior to the fantasized or planned attack.

Associated features may include:
1 The stalker often demonstrates deficiencies in self-efficacy and social relationships.
2 Stalking behaviours do not always betray their sexual origins.

Mullen et al. (1999), in a clinical study of 145 stalkers, assigned six subjects (4%) to the predatory category. Diagnostically, this group comprised predominantly paraphilias. All were men, with a mean age of thirty-two years. Half were currently employed and two had adult partners, though the quality of these relationships was dubious. The duration of stalking by predators was significantly shorter than that by other stalkers, and they had the narrowest range of harassment methods. Predatory stalkers favoured following and surveillance of their victims, phone contact being confined to those for whom their anonymous obscene calls were a source of sexual gratification. The predatory group was more likely to have prior criminal convictions, with an official record of offences, most often sexual, in the majority of cases. The incidence of threats made by the sexually motivated stalker was relatively low, with one-third threatening their victims. This was a similar proportion to the incompetent group, as opposed to 87% of resentful and 74% of rejected stalkers. However, half the predatory sample assaulted their victim. Indeed, these stalkers were *more likely in this study to assault their victims* than all other categories of stalker except the rejected. The authors noted that, unlike other groups, 'there is a troubling lack of warning of the danger as they are the least intrusive stalkers, often only glimpsed by their victims who may report fearing, but not being certain they are followed'.

Stalking in paraphilias

Paraphilias are characterized by 'arousal in response to sexual objects and situations that are not part of normative arousal-activity patterns' . The DSM-IV requires that, as a minimum:

A. Over a period of at least 6 months, recurrent, intense sexually arousing fantasies, sexual urges, or behaviours involving . . . (sexual object/situation).

B. The fantasies, sexual urges, or behaviours cause clinically significant distress or impairment in social, occupational, or other important areas of functioning.

Arousal to the objects that excite paraphiliacs can be part of normative patterns, some authorities contending that fantasies of involvement in certain 'deviant' sexual activities may be a common experience in the normal population. Not all paraphilias are proscribed legally, and as such do not constitute arrestable sex *offences*. Likewise, sex offences, including many sexual assaults, may occur in the absence of DSM-IV-defined paraphilias.

As we have earlier noted, paraphilias and nonparaphilic sexual offences may potentially manifest as stalking behaviours, although it is less likely, relative to other categories of stalker, that the predator's attentions will be as enduring or exclusively focussed on a single victim. The following case vignettes are illustrative of paraphilias associated with stalking. Some of these exhibited multiple paraphilias, a finding familiar to researchers and clinicians in this area (Abel et al., 1988). The cases are drawn from those attending our forensic mental health clinic, which provides an outpatient treatment programme for sex offenders in addition to becoming, in more recent times, a referral centre for stalkers. The vast majority of these referrals are made by the courts, adult parole board and correctional services. Those treated at the clinic tend to represent the more complex and recalcitrant end of the sexually offensive spectrum, with few enjoying stable employment or satisfactory adult relationships.

Telephone scatologia

In scatologia, also known as telephonicophilia, the arousing fantasies and sexual urges or behaviours relate to lewd phone calls. Freund (1990) regarded scatologia as an auditory analogue of voyeurism. The following case is an example of the progression from commercial telephone sex to illegal obscene calls to female victims, then to what amounted to stalking a specific victim by phone.

Case example

Mr E was a 34-year-old single male convicted of stalking a female TV host. Over a three-month period Mr E made repeated obscene calls to the woman, with whom he was besotted since he first saw her on TV twelve months previously. In addition, he sent several anonymous cards to the TV studios where the woman worked, all containing sexually explicit messages relating to his sexual fantasies about her. The woman sought police advice and, contrary to all that is known about stalking, to say nothing of common sense, she was persuaded to arrange a meeting with her stalker in a public place so that the police could apprehend him.

Mr E was startled by his victim's proposition, nervously agreeing to the face-to-face encounter. The TV host had no difficulty discerning which of the men at their rendezvous was her stalker: Mr E sat alone, staring self-consciously at his hands, visibly sweating and trembling. She approached him – herself weak with anxiety – and as soon as he had confirmed her suspicions the police swooped.

Mr E at no stage denied his criminal actions. He was ultimately sentenced to a community-based correctional order with mandated psychiatric treatment. He was a co-operative individual who expressed considerable remorse for his actions and concern for the trauma that he had inflicted on his victim. He denied any intention to make further contact, claiming he felt physically ill whenever he allowed himself to think about his actions. Initially at a loss to explain his behavior, Mr E demonstrated sufficient insight to appreciate the role that life-long interpersonal difficulties may have played. He had always been a rather insecure, unassertive person with few friends. He had been close to his mother, who had died from lung cancer two years previously. In contrast, his father was an intolerant and punitive man who criticized Mr E for his reluctance to play contact sports or to bring home a girl, sure signs that his son was a 'poofter'.

Mr E was an average scholar who completed high school and proceeded to study Arts at university. He abandoned this after his first semester because he found university life and study too stressful. He struggled to find work, having to rely upon social security payments. He rented a cramped one-bedroom flat, spending increasing periods alone, his outings dwindling along with his finances and self-esteem. Although he had two male friends from school days they drifted apart and contact with his parents was limited by geographical distance and his mother's ill-health. His only sibling – an extroverted younger sister to whom he had never felt close – had since married and moved interstate.

Mr E had always yearned for a relationship with a woman. Despite his father's accusations he regarded himself as heterosexual but felt shy and awkward in the presence of women. He acknowledged regular masturbatory fantasies involving consensual sexual acts with adult women, as well as fantasies of idealized, romantic love. Then one day he stumbled upon the telephone sex lines, finding their explicit content intensely sexually arousing. He dialled these frequently for about three weeks, until he received his quarterly phone bill, which was astronomical. Further in debt, he vowed to forgo this pastime, but it created a considerable void in his life that could not be filled by the occasional purchase of 'soft' pornographic magazines. He was unable to afford other visual erotica such as videos, strip shows or pornographic websites on the Internet.

Mr E admitted then proceeding to make random phone calls and 'talking dirty' if a female voice answered (but hanging up if the recipient was a male). He gave little thought to being discovered, sometimes redialling the same household if the response was suitably gratifying. While he had fantasized about conventional sex and romance with the TV host virtually from the first time he watched her show, he did not have her number and had no real plans to pursue her. However, one day the woman was featured in the 'celebrity homes' section of the newspaper, in which her street and suburb were revealed. Curious, he drove along the street, identifying the actual house from the picture in the news article. He then ascertained her (unlisted) home phone number by reading it off a phone bill in her mailbox.

The inevitable publicity surrounding the victim's ordeal had a profoundly aversive effect on this man's scatological activities. It was nevertheless important to address Mr E's social ineptitude in a bid to diminish his personal suffering and minimize his need for deviant outlets in the future. Self-esteem-building exercises and assertiveness training proved beneficial, as was his inclusion in a basic social skills group specifically for sex offenders. In addition, grief counselling was undertaken to assist him to deal with issues surrounding the loss of his mother. He resumed his studies and joined a university volleyball group, befriending one of the women on his team. He also plays tennis on a regular basis with his father, who was shocked by his offences but now admits his respect for his son's courageous efforts to deal with his problem.

Depending on the nature of their deviancy, predators may share the goals of other stalkers (to possess the object of attention) but attaining an intimate relationship is frequently *not* the desired end point. Mr E demonstrated this somewhat paradoxical response to his victim when she apparently submitted to his advances. With abject insight into his physical, emotional and social shortcomings, the prospect of shedding his anonymity for face-to-face contact with his beautiful and accomplished victim proved terrifying rather than sexually arousing.

Exhibitionism

In exhibitionism, the fantasies, sexual urges or behaviours pertain to exposure of one's genitals to an unsuspecting stranger. Of the sexual deviations, exhibitionism is one of the most common and it can occur in conjunction with other paraphilias such as voyeurism(Freund & Blanchard, 1986).

Case example

Mr M was a 54-year-old clerk with a thirty-year history of exhibitionism for which he had served two previous terms of imprisonment. His most recent offence attracted a charge of stalking in addition to wilful and obscene exposure. Mr M, a homosexual, became attracted to a new co-worker, a 27-year-old man. He began to fantasize about exhibiting his genitals to the man and eliciting the desired response of an invitation to mutual masturbation and fellatio. Over the ensuing six weeks Mr M, who worked on a different floor from this man, made repeated visits to the man's workstation under the guise of running errands for his boss. He also anonymously posted advertisements for gay social events and venues on the office walls, leaving some flyers on the man's desk. One day, Mr M overheard that his co-worker's motor vehicle was unserviceable and he promptly seized the opportunity to offer him a ride home, which the man unwittingly accepted. The next day Mr M posted some gay male pornographic material to that address. He followed this up with a phone call during which he admitted his feelings for the man, the object of his attention promptly terminating the call. Angry and humiliated, Mr M phoned back and threatened to 'out' the man to his family and employer if he continued to reject him, unswayed by the man's insistence that he had a girlfriend and wasn't gay. Shortly thereafter, Mr M followed his co-worker to some little-used toilets at the back of their office block and exposed his genitals as the man tried to leave. The victim fled, fearing he would be raped, and reported Mr M to his employer and the police.

Mr M was not imprisoned on this occasion, agreeing to participate in a community sex offender programme, his first experience of treatment. He was dismissed from his job and had virtually no remaining supports; his parents and only sibling were deceased and his friends were limited to a few ex-prisoners. His contacts from his regular forays to gay saunas were generally fleeting, although four years earlier he had sustained a five-month relationship with a 30-year-old man. He presented as a rather introverted individual with a depressed mood accompanied by low energy, poor appetite, weight loss, impaired sleep and suicidal ideation. He expressed contrition for his actions and was very pessimistic about his treatment prospects.

Mr M was commenced on the selective serotonin reuptake inhibitor antidepressant fluoxetine. His depression resolved over the ensuing months. It was likely also that the antidepressant's serotonergic action contributed to a reported diminution of sexual drive and improved control over his exhibitionistic urges. Cognitive behavioural techniques were introduced to promote internal controls. Seven months later he formed an intimate relationship with a 42-year-old man who has been apprised of Mr M's offending history.

Fetishism, voyeurism

In fetishism, the fantasies, urges or behaviour pertain to the use of nonliving objects such as female underwear, the objects not being limited to 'articles of female clothing used in cross-dressing . . . or devices designed for the purpose of tactile genital stimulation. . .' (American Psychiatric Association, 1994). The sexually arousing stimulus in voyeurism is the observation of an unsuspecting person who is naked, in the process of disrobing, or engaging in sexual activity.

Voyeurs or 'peeping Toms' may return repeatedly to a setting where they have had previous success, increasing the probability of being apprehended and of their behaviours being labelled as stalking. The following individual exhibits multiple paraphilias, predominantly voyeurism, fetishism and scatologia.

Case example

Mr B was a 20-year-old single farm hand who was convicted of stalking and using a telephone to harass. A pre-sentence psychiatric report noted the presence of multiple paraphilias and recommended that he be referred to our sex offender programme. He was given a two-year suspended sentence with a condition he participate in this programme.

Mr B presented initially as a rather imperious and immature young man. He was loath to discuss his offences, minimizing their seriousness and attributing blame to his victim. He revealed that he had admired a local woman from afar for more than twelve months. He was attracted to her 'pretty hair' and big breasts, and yearned to go out with her but said he lacked the courage to ask her for a date. Instead, he followed her on foot and by car on several occasions, secretly taking photographs of her, then after locating her home telephone number in the local directory he made a series of obscene calls to her. He admitted also to having stolen some items of lingerie from her clothes line, masturbating with these during and after his calls and ejaculating over the garments and the photographs. He was apprehended after his panic-stricken victim arranged for the calls to be traced.

At the age of 10 years, Mr B was cautioned by police for shoplifting (a *Penthouse* magazine). At age 17 he was apprehended and charged with two counts of trespass on separate properties in his country town and received a small fine. Shortly thereafter he was convicted of burglary and theft, receiving a further fine. A year later he pleaded guilty to one count of indecent assault after grabbing the breasts of a female acquaintance at a hotel, and one count of wilful and obscene exposure. His victims on that occasion were two adolescent females who were cycling past as he hitchhiked along a main road. Mr B had not received any prior psychiatric evaluation, although his mother had previously expressed her concern to his lawyer and the presiding magistrate, adding that he kept a large number of pornographic magazines and videos in his bedroom and that for some years items of her underwear had gone missing and she strongly suspected, despite his protestations, that he was responsible.

The available documentation supported our suspicions that all of Mr B's prior recordable offences were sexually motivated. He admitted that he had actually been peeping at women in their bedrooms when apprehended for trespassing, in one case returning repeatedly prior to being discovered. He had burgled a home, but only after his illegal entry in search of the female occupant's underwear; he admitted to ejaculating over the woman's pillow, although this was not reflected in the charges. The theft (one count) related to stealing lingerie from that victim's clothes line but Mr B confessed he had targeted many more without detection. He was more reluctant to acknowledge other instances of exposing himself, but the probability of additional victims appeared high. In addition, he alluded to dozens of obscene telephone calls that may never have been reported by his female victims, having accrued huge phone bills on his employer's phone.

Mr B was a rather solitary individual from a young age. He was a poor achiever at school, a psychological assessment in Grade 9 [age 14–15 years] indicating that he functioned in the borderline intellectual range. He left the educational system at the commencement of Grade 10, working for a short time in the local supermarket before becoming a farm hand eight months prior to the most recent offences. His employer commented that he was quite a good worker but that he tended to drink to excess and to make inappropriate sexual remarks to the farmer's 40-year-old wife and 16-year-old daughter. Mr B had never experienced a relationship with any adult but said he had had sexual intercourse with female prostitutes on about five occasions. He would have preferred this more regularly but his low wages and living circumstances precluded it. He proudly added that he often frequented peep shows when he was in town and once exceeded his allocated two minute viewing time by about two hours before the licensee discovered that his booth was faulty.

Mr B's only other major expense was alcohol. He was a regular at the local hotel and he described feeling 'cool' around the ladies when he drank. The publican begged to differ, observing that when Mr B imbibed he became obnoxious toward women, and had achieved some notoriety for his foul language and lewd acts, including the incident where he grabbed and bruised a woman's breasts. This woman had apparently been stalked by Mr B over a six-week period, receiving frequent obscene calls as well as being followed and having some items of clothing stolen from her laundry, although the police felt unable to charge him on these other matters.

Mr B is currently participating in a sex offender treatment programme, combining behavioural techniques to control deviant sexual arousal patterns, education in human sexuality, relationship skills training and victim empathy training. He in addition sees an alcohol counsellor and will be considered for anti-androgen therapy should nonpharmacological measures prove insufficient.

Paedophilia/hebephilia

The fantasies, sexual urges and/or behaviours in paedophilia involve sexual activity with a prepubescent child or children. A number of child sexual abuse cases have involved stalking behaviours, some of these culminating in murder. McCann (1995) contended that anti-stalking legislation does not meet the needs of child victims in that existing laws place emphasis on the victim's subjective sense of fear and apprehension, yet in children this will depend on their developmental stage and cognitive maturity. It was suggested that the threat perceived by adults in the child's family would be a more appropriate measure in cases where young children are stalked.

In the following example, the offender is more accurately described as a hebephile or ephebophile than as a paedophile, since his victims were postpubertal minors.

Case example

Mr S was a 36-year-old single man convicted of stalking two teenage girls. He had taken an interest in the schoolgirls in shops he frequented near a high school. He admitted to following the girls in his car on several occasions as they walked home from school. He had even driven slowly up and down the street where one of the teenagers lived. The girls became aware of Mr S's interest in them, panicking when one day he pulled up beside them and offered them a ride. When they declined he grabbed one but she managed to wriggle free. The girls then ran to the nearby police station with Mr S in hot pursuit, brazenly following them into the police carpark.

While Mr S at no time denied his activities he disputed the distress he had caused to his young victims. He acknowledged a sexual interest in the schoolgirls but insisted he was 'only looking . . . I wasn't going to hurt them'. He said that he found the immediately postpubescent female body very attractive and that many adolescent girls 'asked for it' because they wore skimpy outfits. Due to concerns that he might reoffend or interfere with the witnesses Mr S was remanded in custody and a month later sentenced to a community-based correctional order with a condition that he receive psychiatric treatment.

Mr S presented as a rather aggrieved individual who accepted little responsibility for his illegal behavior. His month in jail had been a daunting experience and he seemed genuinely perplexed by the hostility from other inmates. Indeed, he had initially refused protective custody but quickly sought refuge with other sex offenders after mainstream prisoners urinated in his apple crumble. This experience seemed instrumental in his motivation to address his sexual problems.

An only child, Mr S's parents migrated to Australia from southern Europe when he was 11 years old. He struggled with the English language and was teased mercilessly by his peers at school. He was a studious person who managed average grades, but he left school at 15 to work in a textile factory alongside his father. He had no real companions around his own age and his clumsy attempts to befriend girls failed dismally. He recalls at the age of 14 following a female classmate home because he was curious to see where she lived, believing she would make an ideal girlfriend. He returned to the address on a number of occasions on week days and weekends, hoping to see her and find the courage to ask her out but inexplicably her family moved away and he never saw her again.

When Mr S turned 18, an older male work colleague encouraged him to visit a brothel. Although he returned on many more occasions, he did not find sexual intercourse with 'mature women' particularly inspiring. Seven years after he commenced the factory job, Mr S, bored and seeking better wages, obtained temporary work with a concreter. His first job was at a secondary school, which brought him into contact with the students. There was a small group of 14- and 15-year-old girls in particular who hovered about and, in his words, flirted with him. Emboldened by his improved financial position and his 'macho' working man image, Mr S offered one of the girls money in exchange for sex. He claims she agreed, but on that one occasion only. He found the experience intensely pleasurable and thereafter regularly purchased teenage pornographic magazines, which he carefully concealed from his parents with whom he still resided. As anticipated, Mr S divulged a long history since early adulthood of loitering near schools and undetected or unreported following of teenage girls.

For many years he had taken refuge in a rich sexual fantasy life that revolved around schoolgirls, following them, controlling them and having sex with them. His tailing of teenage girls fuelled his fantasy material for later masturbation. He repeatedly denied any fantasies, urges or behaviours involving rape of minors, nor sexual attraction to males.

Mr S participates in our outpatient programme for sex offenders, which has focussed particularly on his deviant sexual arousal patterns, deficient interpersonal skills and pro-offending attitudes. Eighteen months after first presenting there has been no evidence of further stalking, but he remains a fairly solitary individual who tends to avoid adult social opportunities by working long shifts in a refrigerator factory.

Sexual masochism and sadism

In sexual sadism the source of sexual gratification is 'acts (real, not simulated) in which the psychological or physical suffering (including humiliation) of the victim is sexually exciting to the person' (American Psychiatric Association, 1994). It has been proposed that it is the wish to control another that is the primary motivating force in sadism, (MacCulloch et al., 1983), Krafft-Ebing (1986, p. 86) observed that 'mastering and possessing an absolutely defenceless human object . . . is part of sadism'. Boss (1949), in perhaps the most profound examination of the psycho-pathology of the sadist, highlighted the sadist's attempt to break through the barrier they experienced between themselves and others via a violent and imposed penetra-tion. The inflicting of pain or humiliation is substituted for the mutuality of an inti-macy they believe to be beyond their grasp. Sadistic fantasies may well be relatively common, but if they find expression in any action it is usually in choreographed per-formances with like-minded partners in sadomasochism (S&M) clubs or with pros-titutes specializing in these particular sexual theatricals. The DSM-IV definitions exclude such sadistic interests or desires from the category of a paraphilia because they are simulated, although it is difficult to imagine what else these performances constitute if it is not the deviant expression of deviant desires (however common lesser forms of such a sexual proclivity may be). There is fortunately a wide gulf between indulging in sadomasochistic fantasies, or even participating in dramatur-gical representations, and the inflicting of pain or worse on a frightened and coerced victim. This gulf is bridged by few but those who do so can be amongst the most cal-culating and vicious of sexual offenders. Serial killers are drawn predominantly from the ranks of such deviants. These fortunately rare sexual crimes are grossly overrepresented in popular media depictions of predatory stalking.

Sadism finds satisfaction in unfettered and unlimited access to the object of lust. It is in theory a one way street in which the sadist's desires have free rein over the captive and utterly compliant body of the other. It is not only about such control but also about the humiliation and degradation which emphasizes the sadist's power over the object of lust and the extent to which the other will go to satisfy the fantastic desires of the sadist. Sadism, at least in the idealized constructions of its habitués, surpasses inhibition, the partial and the constrained desires of normality in search of a transcendent erotic. Curiously sadists, at least in fantasy, often con-struct the object of their desires as both trapped and overwhelmed, whilst simulta-neously being compliant and attaining pleasure through the complete satisfaction of the sadist's desires. Perhaps this is not so curious, given that the wish to be the subject of unfettered desires is often combined with the wish to be the object of the controlling and overwhelming desire of the other – thus the interchangeability of sadism and masochism in many practitioners. Sadism, particularly when it mani-fests in adolescent boys, can be linked to curiosity, a need to penetrate all those unknown places in an exploration unhindered by the sensibilities of the other or the demands of the possible, let alone the decent.

Stalking potentially satisfies some of the sadist's erotic fantasies. The stalker intrudes on the victim, satisfying curiosity by, in a very real sense, penetrating their privacy and integrity. These stalkers are free to indulge their fantasies as they watch, follow and loiter. They learn more about the victim and in doing so attain a sense of control and power. Finally, by inducing fear and a sense of helplessness in the victim they potentially further satisfy their erotic desires. To some degree this sadistic aesthetic plays a role in a wide range of stalkers but in the predatory stalkers it is often the central motivation. The stalking feeds the sadistic fantasies and for those sadists who move from the world of their imagination to the realization of their desires stalking becomes a preparation, a rehearsal and finally a preliminary to attack.

Case example

Mr H was in his mid twenties when he presented. He had attended his local emergency room stating that he was afraid he was going to kill someone. This led to the young man being directed by a sceptical casualty officer to a duty social worker, a curious but as it turned out serendipitous choice. The social worker, recognizing the very real threat, made a referral to our forensic clinic insisting, successfully, on an immediate assessment.

Mr H had decided to seek help at the point when he was about to abduct a young woman whom he had been stalking for over six months. He had chosen a deserted house in an isolated location, acquired ties and ether, as well as having devised a plan of abduction based on a detailed knowledge of the victim's routine. It was when he realized that he was rapidly approaching the point of no return that he made the decision to seek help rather than proceed.

Mr H was a pleasant looking young man with a diffident manner and a minor speech impediment, which became more pronounced when he was stressed. His use of language and the way he articulated his dilemma suggested good intelligence, although he had only the most basic of formal education. He was an only child. His father had been a heavy drinker, intermittently violent to both his partner and Mr H. He finally left the relationship when Mr H was eight or nine years old and had had subsequently only brief and superficial contact. Following the breakdown of the marriage, Mr H's home life became even more unsettled, with frequent moves both from place to place and from his mother's care to that of his maternal grandparents. The mother had a series of relationships and his placement with the grandparents was usually dictated by the mother's need to acquiesce to the demands of her latest male partner. As a consequence Mr H was subjected to fluctuating maternal attentions with unpredictable periods when she was entirely unavailable. At school he remained socially isolated, partly as a result of temperament, partly because no sooner had he begun to settle in a school than he was moved to a new location.

Mr H left school without qualifications. He left home immediately, moving to a bedsitter in which he remained until the time of his assessment. He worked in a number of unskilled occupations, the longest being as a storeman. A year prior to his presentation he had begun attending evening classes to acquire the educational skills he lacked. As an adolescent and young adult he remained socially isolated with only casual acquaintances garnered from work contacts. He had asked women out on a number of occasions but, even when they responded favourably to his initial approaches, this had not progressed to any lasting contact let alone an intimate or even sexual relationship.

Mr H, when first seen, had an established pattern of sexual fantasy centring on bondage, rape and the penetration of a woman with a knife. It was not clear when these sadistic fantasies first emerged nor exactly when they had become the dominant images in his masturbatory practices. He initially related this transition to having acquired some three years previously a number of bondage magazines and copies of sadistic books, in particular the *Story of O*. Later it emerged that sexualised fantasies of abduction and killing had probably been present from early adolescence and that the books and magazines, at best, gave more detailed form to, and possibly encouraged a greater focus on, the sadistic daydreams.

Mr H was aware that the fantasies of abducting and raping were at least in part a reflection of his belief that he would never be able to establish and maintain a normal sexual relationship. He required no interpretation to connect the need to control a woman with his experience of multiple and unpredictable desertions by his mother. He described experiencing himself as cut off from others, particularly young women, and seeing them as removed from him by an impenetrable shield. His sadism, as is the case so often, was about the rending and tearing of barriers which he experienced as standing between him and any intimacy with the desired woman.

At a later stage Mr H recounted episodes of voyeurism in his late teens when he would follow women he found attractive, making every effort to avoid their noticing his pursuit. When he found out where they lived he would return at night and, when it was possible, attempt to observe them by peeping through windows. He was never discovered in these voyeuristic excursions. The first extended period of stalking had not, however, occurred until he began the pursuit of the woman he had been planning to abduct.

Mr H had met this woman briefly at the college of further education he attended in the evenings. He had planned originally to ask her out but so sure was he that she would reject his approaches he never progressed beyond saying hello to her on a couple of occasions. Catching sight of her in the street one day, he followed her to her home. The surreptitious following gave him exactly the sense of power and control over her that was absent in his contemplation of the more usual approach of asking her for a date. He began loitering in the vicinity of her house at night and taking opportunities to observe her, for example on the train to work in the morning and when she went for lunch with work colleagues. A pattern of following and observing developed, during which he elaborated increasingly complex fantasies of rape and murder. This continued with fluctuating intensity over a period of nearly a year. He had assumed that he had managed to track his victim without her observing his presence but a few weeks earlier she had walked over to him at the train station and loudly accused him of following her, saying that if he did not stop she would call the police. Her angry accusations attracted considerable attention from those around them on the platform and Mr H believed, probably correctly, that she was arousing the sympathy of the onlookers. He fled.

Following this humiliating public exposure Mr H became afraid to engage in any obvious stalking and confined himself to observing her house in the dead of night. His sadistic sexual fantasies about her were now augmented by a sense of righteous indignation at the manner in which she had publicly upbraided him. He concluded that the only way forward was for him to put into practice his fantasies of abduction. On completion of this dreadful project he was intending also to end his own life by hanging. Fortunately, before putting these plans into action, a moment of insight into the awful nature of this carefully prepared murder–suicide enabled him to seek help.

When initially assessed Mr H was actively suicidal, having now resolved to kill himself rather than abandon himself to his murderous project. It was apparent that he had had significant depressive symptoms for some considerable time and that in part the increasing insistence of his sadistic fantasy life reflected an increasing hopelessness about himself and his current existence. His initial management focussed on treatment of the depressive symptoms with a postponement of the fuller exploration of his sexual deviance and social and interpersonal difficulties. Mr H's commitment to avoid slipping back into a murderous state of mind led to an enthusiastic engagement in treatment. He attended both for counselling and for treatment of his depressive symptoms. He also continued contact with the social worker who had originally assessed him assiduously, following all her suggestions with regard to changing his work to enable greater interpersonal contact, joining a sports club and actively developing social contacts when opportunities arose. Retrospectively, it was clear the planned abduction and associated panic that had led him to the emergency room was a watershed in this man's life.

To revive a word from the dead language of psychoanalysis, sadistic behaviours are overdetermined. In Mr H's case, sadism was a response in varying degrees to a frustrated sexuality, a lack of intimacy, social alienation and the powerlessness of a devalued and abused childhood. Taking out of the equation even the social isolation made the resort to actual sexual violence less probable.

Paraphilic asphyxia (asphyxiophilia)

Sexual excitement is produced, or enhanced, in certain individuals by a degree of asphyxia. Central to the practices surrounding erotic asphyxia is the production of a degree of cerebral hypoxia, usually by mechanical constriction of the carotid arteries in the neck but also by chemical means (usually involving inhalation of toxic gases) or the obstruction of breathing (Hazelwood et al., 1989). Various forms of auto-erotic asphyxia are the commonest manifestation of this curious and potentially lethal sexual practice. In auto-erotic asphyxia, sexual excitement during masturbation is augmented by ligatures around the neck or by restrictions to breathing such as plastic bags over the head. Asphyxia also forms part of the sexual activities of some practitioners of bondage or other sadomasochistic pursuits. In these situations the erotic element is usually the experiencing of the effects of cerebral anoxia, but for a small group sexual excitement is produced by asphyxiating their partner. The erotic triggers for those who are excited by inducing, or witnessing, asphyxia are around control, the helplessness of the partially asphyxiated 'partner' and the appearance of total abandonment. Like any deviant or paraphilic practice, erotic asphyxia can form part of an individual's sexual repertoire or become virtually the exclusive expression of their sexuality.

A rare variant of erotic asphyxia is sexual excitation both at the sight of someone being asphyxiated by drowning and at the sight of a drowned corpse. The drowned body as a provocation to sexual excitement for these individuals is not primarily necrophilic but connected to the fantasizing of the process of drowning. The following is an extract from a young man's account of this condition, which was published in full by Money (1988). The subject is referring to the drowning murder of a woman on a popular TV police drama:

Now it never ceases to amaze me that drownings of girls are the longest murders that they do on T.V. A shooting of a girl isn't much, and neither is a stabbing (for me, psycho and slasher films don't count), but a drowning of a girl has more camera angles and lots more shots. It takes longer to drown a girl, and they have special music for the scene too, usually thrilling types of music that are supposed to be exciting, and maybe it is supposed to be scary, but I know one thing, that whole thing has fucked up my life for the past two weeks now. I keep seeing the vision of the murder over and over and over in my mind, over and over and over again. Orgasm after orgasm. For days and days. If only I could have taped it and watched it over and over again. In filming a girl drowning, a lot of the extra footage is not even used. I wish I could get hold of that extra footage of her drowning . . . (Money, 1988, pp. 164–167)

The following case shared similar fantasies, led to stalking and was complicated by alcoholic brain damage with an organic delusional disorder of erotomanic type:

Case example

Mr U was a 44-year-old invalid pensioner referred to us by his defence lawyer after he was remanded in custody on charges of stalking. His history of violence was noted, including his discharge from the army after threatening the life of another soldier, serious assaults upon his wife (using a knife on one occasion) and numerous pub fights.

Mr U became enamoured of a teacher at an adult literacy course, claiming it was 'love at first sight'. He described her in detail, believing her to be the most beautiful woman he had ever seen. He had gathered considerable information about her, including her address, the addresses of immediate members of her family and her usual movements.

Over the six months since his first contact with his teacher, Mr U took every opportunity to see her and to talk to her. He said that at the time he was convinced that she reciprocated his feelings and was in love with him. He claimed this affection was revealed by her waving to him, talking to him and smiling at him. He made a number of attempts to follow her and phoned both her and her family. One evening after consuming a large quantity of alcohol, he approached her in her office, expressed his affection and was politely but firmly rejected. He became angry, threatened her and pushed her against a wall. Subsequently he phoned both her mother and her sister and made death threats. He also went to the sister's address looking for her and it was then that the police were phoned and he was arrested.

Mr U acknowledged his violent past, understanding this to be a major factor in his wife's decision to leave him two years previously. He conceded also that he had a long history of problem drinking. This was supported by documented evidence of global cognitive impairment with a recent computerized tomography scan demonstrating mild atrophy of the cerebral cortex.

In addition, exploration of his sexual development and fantasies revealed his longstanding propensity to indulge in fantasies of drowning women. He described feeling sexually aroused by visions of women drowning but also by visions of dead women floating and even decomposing in the water. Chillingly, he admitted to entertaining such fantasies in relationships, both to women he had known in the past and most particularly to the teacher that he recently stalked. He had on occasions planned in detail how he could either drown someone or kill a woman and place her body in the water. Despite his years of alcohol excess he reported normal sexual functioning.

While in custody, Mr U received psychiatric treatment in the form of depot injections of the antipsychotic medication flupenthixol. When released two months later on a community-based correctional order he agreed to attend our clinic, although there was no legal imperative to do so. Mr U was placed in supported accommodation with regular input from prison postrelease outreach services. He has lost interest in drinking since his stint in prison and involves himself on a voluntary basis with a welfare agency sorting clothing donations. His erotomanic delusions have responded favourably to the antipsychotic medication and he has not been in further contact with his victim. He is quite frank about the continuation of his bizarre sexual fantasies but asserts that they have diminished substantially in frequency and intensity and he has not experienced any strong urges to act on them. Basic behavioural strategies have assisted in this regard, together with support and efforts to improve his living skills. It is recognized that Mr U will require close supervision over an extended period and at the present time he can accept the necessity for this.

Management of the predatory stalker

A major finding emerging from our present state of knowledge of predatory stalkers is their high potential for sexual assaultiveness, which may occur in the absence of prior warning. Furthermore, as a group, these stalkers show a tendency for shorter periods of pursuit, commonly terminated by arrest or sexual attack. When sexually motivated stalkers are apprehended they may be charged with sexual offences alone or in addition to charges of stalking, but the latter may be brought without reference to the crucial underlying sexual pathology. The predatory group highlights the perils of approaching stalking as an homogeneous entity, with an exclusive focus on the harassing behaviours to the neglect of their context and driving force.

Although only a small subset of stalkers, it is imperative, given their potential to pursue multiple victims and their sexual assaultiveness, that this group of stalkers be recognized and appropriately treated. The avoidance of treatment programmes that typifies sex offenders in general as well as issues of dangerousness and recidivism dictates that the success of any treatment is likely to depend on the appropriate mix of legal sanctions and therapeutic interventions. While it is generally recognized that the insistent and compulsory nature of paraphilic behaviours respond poorly to incarceration, imprisonment may prove the only realistic dispositional option for serious recidivist offenders. Ideally, these individuals should be included in prison sex offender treatment programmes with continuation of treatment upon release, preferably as a condition of any parole order. It is useful to draw on the combined resources of supervising community correctional and specialist forensic mental health services in the management of these challenging cases. This co-operative approach has equal merit in the treatment of offenders who receive a community-based disposition.

While it is beyond the scope of this book to detail current treatment approaches for sexually deviant and offensive behaviours, it should be noted that a comprehensive approach addressing both offence-specific and offence-related factors is most likely to succeed in reducing recidivism. Lindsay and colleagues (1998) suggested that cognitive therapy that is group, rather than individual, based may be more efficacious in the intellectually disabled sexual predator, with the constructive application of group pressure to highlight cognitive distortions and facilitate attitudinal change, in addition to providing important opportunities to develop interpersonal skills. Predatory stalkers commonly share with their nonsexually deviant counterparts a lonely and socially inept existence, with a paucity of meaningful adult relationships. These deficiencies pose a significant therapeutic challenge, but life skills training combined with cognitive behavioural and pharmacological therapies specifically directed at the sexual aberration offer hope to the sexually deviant stalker and a reprieve for his victims.

7

Intimacy seekers and incompetent suitors

Introduction

The intimacy seekers and the incompetent suitors are, in combination, among the most numerous and persistent of stalkers. Both groups are attempting to establish a relationship with the object of their unwanted attentions. They pursue acquaintances and strangers on whom they have focussed their interest. It is usually among these two types of stalker that the 'star stalkers' who pursue the famous are to be found. Although there are similarities between the intimacy seekers and the incompetent suitors with regard both to their behaviours and to the factors that predispose to their embarking on stalking, we argue below there are sufficient differences to distinguish between the two types.

Those who view stalking primarily in the context of violence against women, often emphasize that those who stalk a hoped-for partner are showing insensitivity and the desire to dominate rather than necessarily being psychiatrically disturbed, let alone pursuing some misguided quest for love. Emerson et al. (1998) clearly articulated the view that such stalking is a product of social pathology, not individual psychopathology. They argued that the behaviour arises from a one-sided attempted to create a relationship which ignores the legitimate interests and rights of the object of these unwanted attentions. Emerson et al. (1998) were forthright in their opposition to pathologising the stalker. They wrote, 'conceptualizing stalking as a result of mental imbalance obscures the relationship bases of many stalkings, and makes the intricate social processes of stalking secondary to the stalkers' individual psychopathology' (Emerson et al., 1998, p. 290).

There is considerable merit in the notion that some stalking behaviours are the product of the insensitive, inept and grossly overconfident actions of individuals who cannot conceive that their approaches would generate anything less than reciprocal interest. In both the community surveys from Australia and the USA (Australian Bureau of Statistics, 1996; Tjaden & Thoennes, 1998) there were substantial numbers of women, and to a lesser extent men, who were pursued by acquaintances or strangers. A significant proportion of these victims believed their pursuer was intent on establishing a relationship. Certainly in the survey of Tjaden

& Thoennes (1998) many of these particular victims considered the stalker's primary aim was to exert control over them or to gain their approval and attention. In contrast, studies based on clinical or court-referred samples emphasize that among stalkers intent on pursuing the establishment of a relationship there are high levels of psychopathology, including psychotic conditions such as erotomania. The differences in part reflect the fact that community surveys have access only to the assumptions of the victim about the intentions and state of mind of the stalker. It is also a product of the skewed nature of clinic and court samples that overrepresents the more persistent and outrageous forms of stalking. It is usually necessary to attract considerable attention before being brought to courts, clinics or hospitals. We may speculate that the attitudes of certain males in our society to women or men that they 'fancy' are conducive to behaviours which unreasonably intrude on those they wish to attract, and their actions, intentionally or not, arouse fear. As knowledge of the commoner and less dramatic variants of stalking improves so it is likely our knowledge will increase of those attitudes and states of mind more closely approximating to the normal (statistically that is) but capable of sustaining stalking behaviours. This will almost certainly include those attempting to establish a relationship whose behaviour is reprehensible but who have no psychiatric disorder or gross personality deviations.

In part we have attempted to accommodate the awkward, insensitive and pushy would-be suitors into the category of the incompetent. The intimacy seekers we conceptualize are stalkers who are bent on establishing or asserting a loving or otherwise intimate, relationship with the target. The intimacy seekers not infrequently have serious mental disorders. It may be that, given that the intimacy seekers and the incompetent suitors are both attempting to establish a relationship with a stranger or acquaintance, they should be considered as a single type. The differentiation we attempt to advance is based on the manner in which the stalkers regard their target and the expectations and hopes they have invested in the realization of a relationship with them.

Intimacy seekers

Clinical features

The intimacy seekers nearly all share, as a group, the aim of establishing a loving relationship with the object of their unwanted attentions. The occasional intimacy seeker claims that a close friendship or a supportive and nurturing relationship is their goal, not romance, but even here amorous, if not frankly erotic, overtones are often painfully obvious to all but the stalker. All those in the intimacy seeker typology have common aims and a similarly disruptive and counterproductive manner of pursuing those aims. The individual psychopathology that sustains them, however, covers a wide spectrum from the severe mental illness of schizophrenia to the character anomalies of the narcissistic personality disorders. Those driven by frankly delusional beliefs about the nature of the supposed relationship are usually considered to fit into the category of erotomania. It is in the psychiatric literature about erotomania that some of the richest clinical accounts, and speculation, about those who stalk are currently to be found (see Chapter 8). Erotomania is used by Zona et al. (1993) to describe a category of stalkers. This could produce confusion. Erotomania is employed here in its traditional usage to delineate a delusional disorder. Chapter 8 concerns mental disorders, a common feature of which is stalking. This chapter is about a type of stalker, one disorder from which he or she may suffer being erotomania.

The intimacy seeker believes the object of their attentions is uniquely placed to satisfy their desires. They endow their target with qualities that make them an ideal partner. It is love that involves endowing the beloved with the special qualities of desirability and excellence. The typology of intimacy seekers is a category of lovers. Intimacy seekers are not would-be lovers, nor aspirants to a relationship, but those who already love. A proportion of intimacy seekers are already convinced that their love is returned, all the evidence to the contrary notwithstanding. The nature of the love may occasionally not be romantic, but be maternal, fraternal or the child's love of an idealized parent, but it is love. The intimacy seeker is obsessed with the target (we use obsessed here in its nontechnical sense of being intensely preoccupied). Or to be more precise they are obsessed with their fantasies about the object of their attentions. Their deepest feelings have been engaged in the hoped for or imagined relationship. The motivation of the intimacy seekers is to enable their love to find expression in an intimate relationship.

The characteristics of intimacy seekers

1 They have a desire to realize a relationship with the person who has engaged their affections or who they believe already loves them.
2 They persist with their approaches and communications oblivious or indifferent to the target's negative responses.
3 They endow their target with uniquely desirable personal qualities.
4 They are convinced that their quest will culminate in an intimate relationship with the target.
5 They usually live a life bereft of intimacy and the apprehended relationship and the pursuit of the target offers a solution to that isolation.
6 The desired attachment is usually romantic but can be parental, filial or close friendship.

Mullen and colleagues (1999), in their study of stalkers, classified a third of their 145 stalkers as intimacy seekers. This group contained a higher proportion of severely mentally disordered individuals than any of the other typologies. Over half had delusions that the individual they were pursuing was in love with them. This deluded group, despite all the evidence to the contrary, were convinced that the objects of their affections were encouraging their approaches and responding to them in a loving manner. These intimacy seekers with frank erotomanic delusions included five subjects with schizophrenia, two with mania and twenty with delusional disorders. The remaining twenty-two subjects placed in this study in the intimacy seekers typology also had significant psychopathology. Fifteen exhibited what these authors termed 'morbid infatuations' (see Chapter 8) and the remaining seven had sufficient character disturbance to sustain an unequivocal diagnosis of personality disorder that was usually of the narcissistic type.

The intimacy seekers were amongst the most persistent of stalkers, continuing to harass for longer than any other type except the rejected who were similarly persistent (see Table 4.1). The intimacy seekers were predominantly an isolated group of people who in most cases lived lives bereft of close friendships let alone intimates. The relationship they sought often promised a solution to the central dilemma of their life: that of loneliness and the lack of either emotional or physical closeness to another person. The persistence of their pursuit reflected the centrality the longed-for relationship had come to occupy in their lives.

The intimacy seekers search for, and find, a solution to their lives' lack of intimacy in the pursuit of someone to whom they have attached their affections. The intimacy seekers in our initial analysis (Mullen et al., 1999) were almost all living alone and few had ever had a partner at any time in their lives. Loneliness is common and stalking fortunately far less common, so the lack of intimate attachments is not likely to be in itself sufficient to evoke stalking behaviours. To create and sustain an attachment to someone who is actively rejecting or indifferent requires a capacity to either reinterpret the negative responses of the loved one as encouraging, or at the least not rejecting. This capacity can be a product of a disordered state of mind that invests the world with meanings derived from the individual's convictions rather than reality. Thus in erotomanic delusions any response, however negative, from the loved one is interpreted as encouragement. In the totally self-absorbed egoist may be found a similar imperviousness to reality and insistence on the world being as they desire. The intimacy seekers have usually invested so much of themselves, and so many of their hopes for the future, in the apprehended relationship that they vigorously defend themselves against any challenges to their vision of the supposed relationship.

Intimacy seekers are a remarkably persistent type of stalker, on average pursuing their victim for over three years (Mullen et al., 1999); despite repeated rebuffs and the manifest failure of their quest they abide. In part this reflects an intense sense of entitlement. They do not simply wish for a particular relationship – they believe that they are *entitled* to that relationship. Not infrequently one hears from intimacy seekers words to the effect that their target owes them love, or owes them a response. This supposed debt is for some of these stalkers justified in terms of all they have sacrificed and 'done' for the target. The consistent harassment is reconstructed as services rendered and as loving attentions rendered that call out for reciprocal responses. The persistence also reflects the gratification intimacy seekers obtain from their pursuit and hopes irrespective of signs of success. It is better to love and hope for love, however vainly, than to live an existence bereft of even the distant expectation of love.

The intimacy seekers tend to favour less immediately intrusive forms of communication, frequently employing letters (75%) and the telephone (75%). Unsolicited gifts (57%) are not infrequent. They are less likely to follow and maintain surveillance of their target than the rejected (85%) and the incompetent (75%). The intimacy seekers are often shy isolated people and this influences to some extent their stalking. Nevertheless following and surveillance does occur (60%).

The intimacy seekers are in their eyes pursuing a course of conduct aimed at establishing an intimate relationship. As one would expect from this situation, declarations of love, invitations to meetings and the giving of keepsakes are common. The rebuffs, rejections or plain indifference with which such communications are received are usually ignored by the intimacy seekers or reframed in a positive light. Occasionally, however, frustration or a rejection that penetrates the stalker's defences will evoke threats and even occasional violence. Similarly, direct approaches that evoke distress or anger from the object of the stalker's attentions may occasionally be the trigger to threatening or even violent behaviour. This aggression can be directed either at the victim or at some third party believed to stand between the intimacy seeker and their beloved. As is discussed in Chapter 8 on erotomania, the intimacy seeker who deludedly believes a relationship already exists with the target may become jealous over what, from their peculiar perspective, is seen as infidelity.

Many intimacy seekers, we believe, fall into the established categories of erotomania, including both those with delusional disorder, erotomanic type, and those with erotomanic delusions secondary to some other psychotic process such as schizophrenia. The residual group of intimacy seekers that remains following the removal of those who fall into the currently favoured definitions of erotomanic disorders are predominantly what we have previously terms morbid infatuations (Mullen & Pathé, 1994a,b). The erotomanias and the morbid infatuations are dealt with in detail in the next chapter. Here we confine the account of intimacy seekers to those whose attachments are not to those with whom they wish to establish primarily a romantic or erotic relationship but from whom they seek an intimacy akin to that of parent/child or close friendships. Perfectly normal and reciprocal intimate relationships can incorporate complex mixtures of attachments redolent of dependency, parenting and friendship as well as the romantic. It is perhaps not therefore to be wondered at that the abnormal attachments of intimacy seekers can incorporate similarly complex needs and hopes. The following case exemplifies such a mixture with the desire for a mothering and caring relationship in which the erotic played at best a secondary role.

Case example

Mr D was referred for a court assessment following a conviction for stalking. He was at the time 32 years old. He had grown up an only child in a disorganized home. His mother, who was the sole parent, was often absent for long periods. He was cared for during her absences by a mixture of relatives, paid child carers and occasionally placed in children's homes. Frequent changes of school severely disrupted his education and despite having a measured IQ in the superior range he acquired no academic qualification. Solitary and often bullied at school, he grew up into an isolated man with no close friends and no social or group activities.

Mr D had worked in semi-skilled occupations but became bored and left most jobs after a few months. He had started courses in computing but despite excellent grades had withdrawn on each occasion because of the strain of interacting with fellow students and teachers. He had had a few years previously an extended sexual relationship with a woman considerably older than himself who appears to have made few, if any, emotional demands upon him. Mr D had been out of work for over five years when first seen at the clinic. He lived on Social Security, renting a room in a boarding house and spending much of his days reading in a local library. Although physically fit he was prone to concerns over his health. His hypochondriacal tendencies were fed by his reading and expressed in repeated presentations at the surgeries of general practitioners.

Two years earlier, on his travels around medical surgeries, Mr D had consulted a female doctor. This particular practitioner had perhaps taken a more careful history, perhaps been more empathic, perhaps recognized both the distress and the untapped potential in her patient. For whatever reason, unlike prior consultations, on this occasion Mr D felt understood and cared about. He returned to the doctor the following week. She made regular weekly appointments during which she began an entirely appropriate exploration of the factors underlying Mr D's preoccupations with ill health. Mr D began presenting at the surgery between scheduled appointments. The doctor firmly discouraged this but he persisted. Mr D began phoning both the surgery and the doctor's emergency numbers with increasing frequency. She struggled to control this by offering a scheduled ten minutes to phone her between appointments but without success. The doctor began to be troubled by the frequency with which she encountered Mr D when out shopping and when out with her family and friends. Although initially inclined to attribute these meetings to chance she soon realized that their frequency suggested Mr D was putting himself deliberately in her way. The doctor did not confront Mr D but when he next attended told him she could no longer see him and had arranged for him to be followed up by her partner. He became distressed and talked of suicide. She relented and made a further appointment for him to see her. The intrusions seemed to decrease. She no longer encountered him away from the surgery and he phoned only occasionally between appointments. This continued for a number of weeks. The situation, she thought, had been normalized until returning home late one night she saw Mr D in her car headlights lurking in the next door neighbour's garden. The following night her husband found him again outside of the house. Mr D ran away when approached.

The doctor, not surprisingly, became alarmed. She wrote a letter to Mr D saying she could no longer see him and asking him to stay away from her. She did offer to arrange for him to be seen at another practice. Perhaps less wisely, at this stage, she also offered to arrange for him to see a psychiatrist. What followed was a barrage of phone calls, letters and approaches both to the surgery and her home. A court order was obtained restraining him from contacting or approaching the doctor. This was ignored. Visits from the police produced no amelioration in the harassment and finally Mr D was prosecuted for stalking.

Mr D when interviewed spoke glowingly of the doctor. He admitted anger when she had taken out the court order against him but claimed to understand how she might have been made fearful by his repeated intrusions. He said she had been the only doctor who had ever really listened to him and who had understood him. He said he knew she had cared about him and he was convinced that she, and only she, could effectively treat him. He denied any romantic or erotic interest in her, although with no prompting he provided a eulogy on her good looks and vivacious personality. He said he needed her care and her medical skills. At a later session he talked of her as the ideal friend. On yet another occasion he spoke of her as the perfect mother, contrasting the way his mother treated him with how he believed the doctor mothered her children.

Mr D continued to attempt to contact the doctor, occasionally using imaginative approaches such as through the State's Health Commissioner, the Medical Board and the Ombudsman, pursuing a claim that she was obliged to complete the course of treatment on which they had embarked. Eventually he accepted counselling from a male psychologist with whom he formed a good therapeutic relationship. He has not to date attempted to overstep the bounds of this professional relationship.

Mr D's excessive attachment grew out of a situation of profound loneliness. He created around the doctor a fantasy of the perfect physician who would rescue him from his physical and mental ills. (Although the doctor behaved appropriately throughout, it is possible the rescue fantasies were not confined to the patient.) Mr D also described elaborate fantasies of moving in to live with the doctor, not as a lover but as a child to be cared for by her and her husband. She was for him the only person who could help him. She was irreplaceable and the embodiment of all the medical and maternal virtues. She was to be his saviour and no substitute would be accepted. He ruminated about her for hours on end and at the height of his infatuation she dominated his every thought.

In the next chapter a number of further case examples of intimacy seekers are provided. These cases detail erotomanic attachments that have sustained stalking.

Management

The management of many intimacy seekers revolves around the effective treatment of the mental disorder that underlies the stalking. This group are usually impervious to judicial sanctions. Restriction orders, other court orders, even suspended sentences are usually viewed as challenges to be overcome rather than as deterrents. If imprisoned, intimacy seekers are more likely to view their confinement as a test of their devotion rather than a punishment. They often take pride in not being diverted by impediments such as legal restrictions.

Incompetent suitors

Clinical features

The stalkers who fall into the incompetent typology cover a wide range of individuals, many of whose behaviours and attitudes differ only in a minor, albeit critical, degree from the mass of their fellow citizens. Incompetent suitors are all, to some extent, impaired in their social skills and most particularly in their courting skills. In some the impairment would seem to be closer to a wilful ignorance, or cavalier indifference, than any actual deficit in social knowledge and aptitude. At one end of the spectrum of incompetent suitors we have the intellectually limited and socially severely impaired, who pursue those who attract their romantic interest with a gaucheness and insensitivity born of profound interpersonal incapacity. At the other extreme are individuals approximating to a feminist's caricature of a typical male; an assertive, overbearing, insensitive egoist who cannot conceive that every woman is not simply waiting to fall into their arms. (In practice the incompetent type of stalker of all varieties can be female as well as male and they can target men as well as women.)

The incompetent suitor usually harasses any particular victim for relatively brief periods, having the lowest average duration for stalking of any type. They are, however, the group with the highest recidivism rate in terms of embarking on a course of stalking targeting a new victim. The incompetent type usually favour direct approaches to forms of communication such as those involving letter writing. The behaviour of the incompetent type of stalker can be caricatured as that of the inept suitor who fails to abide by the basic social rules governing courting rituals.

The characteristics of the incompetent suitor

1 They possess a sense of entitlement to a relationship with an individual who has attracted their interest.
2 They are indifferent to, or uninterested in, the target's preferences in the matter.
3 They are unable, or unwilling, to appreciate the negative responses to their communications and approaches.
4 They initiate persistent inept attempts to begin a relationship with the target.

The two cases of stalkers with intellectual disabilities reported by Lindsay et al. (1998) in the previous chapter are also illustrative of incompetent suitors. Both cases made crude and sexually explicit approaches to women to whom they were attracted and persisted in repeatedly approaching and propositioning these women despite clear indications that the attentions were unwanted. Underlying these incompetent attempts to establish a relationship were reported assumptions about what constituted appropriate courting, such as staring at women being a good way of showing that you are attracted to them, and that the victims had encouraged their approaches by smiling and laughing with them.

Stalking is not the product simply of ineptitude in approaching those to whom the stalker is attracted. Stalking involves repeated and persistent intrusions and the social incompetence needs to be combined with either a sense of entitlement or some attitude conducive to repeatedly inflicting unwanted contact on another.

Case example

One of the men seen in our clinic was severely disabled by a lack of appropriate social skills. He was of good intelligence but had had lifelong problems interacting with others. There were elements in his history suggestive of Asperser's syndrome, with an obsessive interest in train timetables dating from early childhood and a fascination with watching the flickering of flames. This man had never had any close relationships. He had, however, held a job for several years involving detailed but repetitive tasks. His peculiarities had been tolerated by fellow workers until he kept approaching a young female co-worker and inviting her out. Despite her firm refusals he continued to repeat his request and took to following her home and standing outside her house. He finally lost his job because of his refusal, or inability, to curb the harassment of this woman. Interestingly, once he stopped going to work he made no further attempts to approach this particular young woman. No legal proceedings were instituted. Some time later he began to attend discos. This was on the advice of a man of his own age who he remembered from school and who he had approached in the street to ask how to find a girlfriend. His technique in the disco was to stand in front of any woman who took his fancy and ask her to dance. Given his unprepossessing appearance (he dressed in a peculiar manner with cardigan, wool shirt and baggy trousers reminiscent of the 1950s) his offer was always declined. This led to his following the young woman around the room either repeating his request or demanding an explanation for the refusal. After repeating this performance a few times he was invariably ejected from the venue and was soon permanently banned from these establishments.

He was referred to the clinic after repeatedly approaching and pestering a young woman at a local train station with requests for a date. He had harassed this woman on a daily basis for several months before finally being arrested and charged. When seen, he expressed considerable anger at being forced to come for assessment. He made clear his view that he had done nothing wrong and had as much right as any man to have a girlfriend. He believed the fault, if fault there was, lay in the persistent refusal of those he had chosen to approach to accept his offers of a date. When he had finished venting his irritation he suddenly demanded of the interviewer how he managed to 'get dates'. In response to the demur that such activities were long in the past he leaned over the desk, grabbed the interviewer by the lapels and forcefully repeated his request to be told 'how to do it'.

It emerged later in therapy with this man that in the months prior to referral he had been planning to abduct a young woman and keep her imprisoned as his girlfriend. He had read, *The Collector*, written by John Fowles, and decided that this might offer a more successful way of obtaining a girlfriend for his long-term use.

This case illustrated the ineptitude, the sense of entitlement and the utter disregard of the other's wishes and feelings. To relate for this man was to own and to acquire the use of. Those he approached were devoid of qualities other than being to him attractive. Their individuality, like their personal preferences, were of no interest to him.

This is an extreme example produced by profound disturbance in this man's capacity to understand other people as autonomous beings whose interests should be respected. The vast majority of the incompetent type are, as noted earlier, men and women without gross or obvious psychopathology. We suspect that many of those who in community surveys report stalking experiences when strangers or distant acquaintances pursue and harass them are falling victim to the incompetent type of stalker. Most such perpetrators are never assessed, given that these events are often relatively short lived and even if more extended rarely lead to prosecution. When we see such individuals in our clinic it is usually because they have come to notice for other reasons.

Case example

In one instance a man in his thirties was referred for reports following a guilty plea to criminal damage. He had vandalized the car of a young woman who worked as one of the bar staff in a large hotel much frequented by young singles. He had not had any prior convictions. He was a man of good intelligence who worked in a skilled occupation earning high wages. A long-term relationship had ended some months earlier. He had begun going to a local hotel with a reputation as a meeting place for singles. His approaches to various women had been unsuccessful. This may have been because he was ten or fifteen years older than most of the customers. He had noticed a young woman, tending the bar, with whom he had had a number of brief conversations. He formed the opinion that she was attracted to him. He invited her out. She laughed off the invitation. He asked her again a few days later and she made an excuse about hotel policy. Failing to see this as a polite brush off he phoned her at work the next night to repeat his invitation. This time she was even clearer in her rejection of the offer. Later that night after he had uncharacteristically consumed a considerable quantity of alcohol he phoned her again. On the second occasion he acknowledged that he was 'out of order' and made a number of crude suggestions.

Somewhat chastened, he returned to the hotel the next night, to apologize, he claimed. She avoided coming near him but he was adamant that she kept looking over in his direction, giving him encouraging and inviting glances. He began phoning her repeatedly to apologize and ask her out. She stopped taking the calls and he was asked to stop phoning. He came once more to the hotel demanding to see her. There was a confrontation with other staff and he was ejected. Later that night he vandalized her car. He admitted he knew which car was hers as he had watched her leave work on a number of occasions.

When seen in the clinic he was apologetic about both the damage to the car (he had made full financial restitution) and the one obscene call he had made when intoxicated. He insisted, however, that she had fancied him and led him on. He saw himself as more victim than victimizer. He had read her statement about the fear and distress his behaviour had caused her, but the only part of the statement that seemed to have impacted on him was her reference to his being middle aged and fat (he was particularly proud of his gym-sculpted biceps).

This combination of an assertive insensitivity with a narcissistic assumption that any approach from them will be bound to be welcome is, we suspect, a relatively common accompaniment of stalking behaviour in the community. Although commoner among men, it is not gender specific.

Case example

A further example of what we would regard as an incompetent stalker was referred to our clinic by a private psychiatrist. The patient, a man in his early twenties, had been taken to the psychiatrist by his mother, who had been alarmed after hearing from him that he had been banned from one of the university computer laboratories because he had been accused of sexual harassment.

This young man had always been shy and awkward with few friends. He was of high intelligence, with a facility for maths and computers. He had successfully completed his degree in computer studies and was now finishing off a Master's. He had had, when younger, a number of nonsexual relationships with girls of his own age, usually arranged by his somewhat omnipresent mother and her friends. (He came from an ethnic background where encouraged if not frankly arranged marriages were still far from rare.) He still lived at home.

His only outlets related to the social were via the Internet. As part of his course he was in a tutorial with a female lecturer to whom he became increasingly attracted.

He began to email her between tutorials with what were initially work-related questions. Later he asked her via the Internet for a date. She declined and to save his feelings cited university policy on relations between staff members and their students. This he took as encouragement and he made a couple of direct approaches to her in person. She again politely put him off. From this point he began a campaign that was initially entirely to persuade her to go out with him but became increasingly contaminated by angry and vengeful acts precipitated by what he regarded as her recalcitrance. He sent her numerous emails, many with spurious and misleading provenance. He hacked into her computer and initially rearranged her files and later deleted some of her work in progress. He left frankly obscene material downloaded from the Internet in her email.

When seen at the clinic, he continued to insist that the victim wanted a relationship with him because he was her cleverest student. He claimed that she was playing 'hard to get' to stimulate him to increasingly 'clever' ways of communicating with her. To the man's credit he became appropriately distressed when he was confronted with a copy of the victim's statement about how frightened and how violated she had been made to feel by his actions. He was persuaded to stop his pursuit, in part one hopes from a glimmering of empathy for the victim, but one suspects because it became clear that to persist would have ended his university career.

Management

Managing incompetent suitors is far from easy. They respond relatively readily by stopping their stalking activities to either judicial sanctions or counselling. The challenge is to prevent them reverting to stalking when next their attention is captured by what they regard as a potential partner. They often need to improve their social skills but such improvements are not easily obtained. They need to acquire greater empathy and concern for those they harass but victim empathy is not easy to instil. Some need to grow up, some just need to understand the nature and importance of culturally appropriate courting rituals. Not a few are improved if their substance abuse is curbed (although they often argue that this takes away their only social skill). As always, the closer someone is to the normal range psychologically and behaviourally the more difficult it can be for mental health professionals to assist in that change.

Intimacy seekers versus incompetent suitors

At the core of the incompetent's stalking is their need for a relationship. At the core of the intimacy seeker's stalking is their fantasy of love and quest for fulfilment. These two types of stalker share a sense of entitlement; they share a self-centred approach that invests their needs with absolute primacy and they share a blindness to the real wishes of the person unfortunate enough to have attracted their attention. There is a world of difference, however, between, on the one hand, believing that as a result of true love you have embarked on the most important activity in your life and, on the other, believing that someone should go out with you on a date. Given that no relationship has existed, and that to even a casual observer no relationship seems likely to emerge, it is probable that the judgements of the intimacy seekers are even more radically disturbed than the judgements of the incompetent suitor. There is a wide spectrum of levels of disjunction between the real situation and the situation supposed by the stalker to pertain. At one extreme lie those with an absolute conviction that the target is in love with them, despite no actions or communications from the supposed lover that would reasonably sustain such a belief. At the other end of the spectrum is an assertion by the stalker of the right to begin a relationship with someone irrespective of their expressed inclinations. In between are those stalkers who, although they believe they love the target of their attentions, know their feelings are not shared but with varying levels of conviction believe eventually their love will be reciprocated. The incompetent suitors are like any aspirant to a relationship in terms of what they desire and how they perceive the object of their attentions. What differentiates them is the manner in which they push their claims and the importunate and self-centred nature of those claims. Incompetent suitors differ from the majority of those wanting a relationship in relatively minor, albeit important, ways. They are usually essentially normal people disabled by such matters as poor social skills, over inflated egos and interpersonal insensitivity. As expected, the level of psychopathology found in intimacy seekers is far greater than in the incompetent. The incompetent verge on normal. It is probable that the incompetents will be far more numerous in those stalking other members of the community in search of a relationship. On the other hand, given the selection processes currently operating, those reaching the courts and mental health clinics are more likely to be intimacy seekers.

The erotomanias and the morbid infatuations

Introduction

The emergence of stalking as a distinct category of behaviour brought the topic of erotomania into the clinical limelight. The new found prominence of a syndrome that has previously languished among the uncommon, not to say obscure, psychiatric syndromes, highlighted the inadequacy as well as the utilities of what had been a venerable, if little used, conceptualization. A detailed account of erotomania and its variants is now provided, in part because such disorders are the origin of many intimacy seeker's behaviour and in part because it still provides the richest source of clinical literature relating to stalking.

Currently the erotomanias tend to be viewed as conditions characterized by a delusional system that centres on the belief that the sufferer is the object of the love of another. The erotomanias are considered to exist either as primary (pure) or secondary (symptomatic) conditions. The primary erotomanias are a monodelusional state unaccompanied by other severe disturbances of mental state such as hallucinations. The secondary erotomanias involve a delusional system arising in the context of a pre-existing psychotic condition, for example schizophrenia. To a greater or lesser extent each of the elements that constitute this conceptualization are under challenge. The exclusive emphasis on a delusional belief in being loved, which excludes pathological infatuation, has been questioned (Stone, 1984; Mullen & Pathé, 1994a). The very existence of a primary erotomania has been questioned by those who regard this condition as always a symptom of some more widespread psychotic disturbance (Ellis & Mellsop, 1985). Finally, confining erotomania to delusional disorders has been questioned, a questioning that has become more insistent as mental health professionals struggle to conceptualize the psychopathology of stalkers (Meloy, 1989; Mullen & Pathé, 1994b; Zona 1993).

A history of erotomania

Esquirol (1965/1845) coined the term erotic monomania, which he later conflated to erotomania. He described erotomania as characterized by an exaggerated and irrational sentimental attachment, usually to someone who in reality has little or no relationship to the sufferer. He held the erotomanic was 'the sport of his imagination' (ibid., p. 335) and the condition 'an exaggeration to the extreme limit of the amorous passions' (ibid., p. 339). Esquirol makes a clear link between the more exuberant expressions of love in the nondisordered and the amorous sentiments of the erotomanic, which are distinguished in degree rather than in kind. Among those he includes in, or on the borders of, 'erotic delirium' are Aristotle 'who burns incense to his wife' (Esquirol, 1965/1845, p. 341), Tasso who pined for his lover for fourteen years, Héloïse and Abailard (where erotomania associates to religious sentiments) and Cervantes' character Don Quixote. These are all instances where love may well have been taken to extremes but other than the fictional Don Quixote they did not need to create a fantasy, let alone a delusion, that their love was returned. It is, however, unnecessary to burden this early nineteenth century descriptive psychiatrist with a modern nosological framework. Esquirol, although he writes of erotomania as an exaggeration of the normal passion of love, also places it in the category of monomanias, which are, one suspects, intended to constitute a distinct pathological category.

The monomanias also included pyromania, homicidal mania, religious mania and reasoning mania. Central to the notion is that the sufferer feels, reasons and acts as does the rest of the world except upon a single point. This, for Esquirol, did not rule out the possibility of hallucinations and illusions related specifically to the defining morbid beliefs. Esquirol (1965/1845) also makes a special point of the ability of some monomaniacs to persuade others of the truth of their beliefs. Esquirol includes as an example of a monomaniac William Miller, who in the America of the 1840s preached the end of the world, persuading considerable numbers to join him in awaiting the world's destruction. When the end failed to arrive on time, this led not to disillusionment in Miller, nor to a loss of faith in him by his followers, but to a recalculation of Doomsday's date.

The capacity of some monomaniacs to persuade others of the force of their ideas can be of considerable relevance. Not a few erotomanics convince others, including on occasion the courts, that they are telling the truth and that the victims of their attentions are attempting to deny their previous commitments and avowals. An erotomanic journalist who stalked a New Zealand surgeon, when finally charged and brought to court, persuaded the judge that she was the injured party rejected by an unfeeling ex-lover (Brenner, 1991). The judge went so far as to indicate to the accused woman that he had sympathy for her plight and made abundantly clear his disdain for what he mistakenly assumed was a philandering doctor who had driven the poor woman to such desperation and despair. Poetic justice asserted itself and the lady over subsequent weeks transferred her affections from medical practitioner to jurist and began making amorous approaches to the judge.

The judge soon found himself on the wrong end of stalking. When he resorted in his turn to the law for protection the woman found herself imprisoned rather than the object of further judicial sympathy. In one of our cases a man with an erotomanic fixation on an adolescent girl who lived near to him persuaded his elderly parents that he was finally to be married. The parents had made various arrangements for the expected nuptials and were righteously indignant when the police came round investigating the claims by the supposed fiancée that she was being stalked. Even more impressive was another of our patients who, following his killing of a young woman prominent in the entertainment industry, persuaded police, examining psychiatrists and the court at the initial hearing that he had killed her because of her infidelity. His account of their having had a romance lasting many months was only challenged quite late in the hearing when the evidence of her family and friends made clear she had never had any contact with this man outside of his fantasies.

Esquirol's nine case examples of erotomania are a mixed bag. There are two women and a man who are infatuated and convinced that their love is returned by the object of their affections; two women and a man who are so absorbed in their love for someone who is unavailable that they pine, and in one case die; two elderly women infatuated with younger men, although it is unclear whether they believe their feelings to be reciprocated; and finally one young woman deserted by her erstwhile love who continues to be overwhelmed by melancholy and preoccupied with the lost partner. The cases, like the text, suggest Esquirol is taking a broad view of the precise manner in which the abnormally exaggerated sentiments of love manifest. Equally clear is the description in several of the cases of what we would now term stalking, with repeated following, loitering outside the house of the fantasized lover and sending of frequent letters.

It is worth resurrecting one of Esquirol's case studies, albeit in much abbreviated form:

Case study

An unattached 36-year-old man of melancholy disposition and unprepossessing appearance conceived a passion for a beautiful actress. He made numerous attempts to communicate with her and approached her repeatedly. He followed her and loitered outside both the theatre and her home. She made clear her lack of interest and he was warned off by the lady's husband and fellow actors, but despite all he continued to pursue her. He watched her nightly at the theatre and became convinced that she gave him encouragement by looking in his direction and by her 'flushed and shining face'. He began to pursue her whenever she appeared in public and chased after her when she left Paris for the country. He was assaulted on a number of occasions by the lady's friends and husband, with on one occasion sufficient ferocity to lead to his hospitalization, but he still was not discouraged. He was convinced that she was being forcibly prevented from either speaking to him or responding to his overtures. He spent his whole income on the pursuit of the lady and most of his waking hours were taken up with the quest. Esquirol, with a brutal directness lost to modern practitioners, put the following question to the man. 'How could you believe she loves you . . . you have nothing engaging about you . . . you [are] not handsome . . . you possess neither rank or fortune.' His reported response was: 'All that is true, but love does not reason, and I have seen too much to leave me in doubt that I am loved.' (After Esquirol, 1965/1845, pp. 337–9).

This is a clear account of an individual who stalked, in our modern sense, and who laboured under the conviction that his love was reciprocated, despite ample evidence, apparent to the outside observer, that there were no grounds for such hopes.

The term erotomania came to be used in three distinct ways during the nineteenth century. In addition to the erotomania described by Esquirol there was the long-established category of the love melancholies, in which a wide range of symptoms, including, but not restricted to, those we would recognize as depression, were attributed to sentimental or erotic attractions that had either been unrequited or indulged in excessively (Burton, 1621; Harvey, 1672 (quoted in Hunter & McAlpine, 1963)). There were also the Erotic Manias (also known as nymphomania and satyriasis), which were described vividly by Isaac Ray (1839, pp. 192–3) as 'states of the most unbridled excitement, filling the mind with a crowd of voluptuous images, and ever hurrying its victim to acts of the grossest licentiousness'. This enviable form of erotic disorder was also on occasion extended to incorporate those sexual behaviours we now pusillanimously refer to as the paraphilias (Macpherson, 1889). Esquirol (1965, p. 335) was at pains to distinguish such nymphomania and satyriasis, with their 'evil' origins in the 'organs of reproduction whose irritation reacts upon the brain', from the amorous sentiments of his erotomania. Love melancholy, however, appears, at least in the case examples, to be incorporated into Esquirol's concept of erotomania. Contemporary writers who seek, and find, the origins of erotomania in the writings of classical Greece and Rome are usually annexing descriptions of love melancholy to erotomania (Enoch & Trethowan, 1979).

Krafft-Ebing (1904/1879), who preferred the term erotic paranoia to erotomania, wrote 'the nucleus of the whole malady is the delusion of being distinguished and loved by a person of the opposite sex who regularly belongs to one of the higher classes of society . . . the love, as should be emphasized [is] romantic, enthusiastic, but absolutely platonic' (ibid., p 408). Kraepelin (1921/1913), who also places erotomania firmly among the paranoias, gives the following pre-eminent clinical description:

the patient perceives that a person of the other sex distinguished really or presumedly by high position is kindly disposed to him . . . an intercepted glance, a chance meeting . . . let this hidden love become certainty to the patient . . . Very soon every chance occurrence, clothing meetings, reading, conversation acquire for the patient a relation to his imagined adventure . . . the whole colouring of the love is visionary and romantic . . . finally the patient resolves on further steps. He promenades before the window of the adored one, sends letters . . . but [if] things take an unfavourable turn the loved one can become the enemy and the persecutor of the patient'. (Kraepelin, 1921, pp. 245–9)

Kraepelin's English contemporary Hart (Hart, 1921, p. 122), seemed to imply that erotomania was specifically a malady of aged females when he wrote 'in Old Maid's Insanity an unmarried lady of considerable age, and blameless reputation, begins to complain of the undesirable attentions to which she is subjected by some male acquaintance . . . . [who she explains] is obviously anxious to marry her and persistently follows her about'. Hart proceeds to explain this 'by no means uncommon sequence of events' as follows: 'The patient's sex instincts have been allowed no normal outlet, and have finally become sternly repressed . . . the repressed instincts obtain expression, however, by the mechanism of projection' (ibid., p. 123). The unacknowledged erotic passion is, according to Hart, projected into the object of affection, who is then experienced as the unseemly and intrusive suitor.

Kretschmer (1974/1918) considered erotomania to be based on an exaggeration of those dispositions to be found in normal lovers and therefore could involve beliefs that one was loved as well as a morbidly enhanced infatuation. In total contrast, de Clérambault (1942/1921), whose name has come to be attached specifically to this syndrome, argued strongly that the term erotomania should be confined to those who believe that they are loved and who insist that the supposed lover both initiated the relationship and remains the primary pursuer. He added to existing descriptions an emphasis on a sudden explosive onset, and that the erotomanic insist that they are either responding to the other's supposed advances or have made every effort to discourage the claimed interest. De Clérambault (1942/1921) also modified the previous literature's emphasis on the love being sentimental and platonic, recognizing that overt carnal desires and clearly sexual behaviours could form part of the clinical picture.

De Clérambault (1942/1921) described two broad groups of erotomanics: the primary or pure erotomanic and the secondary or symptomatic erotomanias. His pure syndrome is a direct descendant of Esquirol's monomania, Kraft-Ebbing's erotic paranoia and Kraepelin's paranoiac megalomania, erotic type. The secondary category of de Clérambault can be regarded as elaborating the descriptions of erotic delusions which appear in Bleuler's (1950/1911) famous monograph, which established the notion of the schizophrenias. Bleuler (1950/1911) described a variety of 'erotic delusions' arising as part of schizophrenic disorders. He wrote, 'the erotic delusions consist mostly of a mixture of grandiose and persecutory ideas . . . with women it is mainly a question of marrying into a higher social class . . . the male patient believes every woman who strikes his fancy is in love with him . . . very often the beloved becomes the persecutor (or the love is complicated by jealousy) (ibid., pp. 121–2). De Clérambault (1942) recognized that it was not just the schizophrenias but that any disorder capable of generating delusions could have, as a content of those delusions, erotic fixations.

It is the French psychiatrist de Clérambault whose work has had the greatest influence on the development of contemporary psychiatry's conceptualizations of erotomania, at least in the English-speaking world (despite, or perhaps because of, his works remaining largely untranslated). Erotomania is still referred to, on occasion, as de Clérambault's Syndrome. De Clérambault deserves to be remembered for his delineation of 'Les Psychoses Passionelles' of which erotomania was but one form (Baruk, 1974; Mullen, 1997). There was in fact little originality in de Clérambault's description of erotomania itself and that which was original has not survived the test of time. De Clérambault, however, left a legacy that continues to bedevil psychiatric nosology. He firmly shifted the emphasis in erotomania to an exclusive focus on delusions in which there is an absolute and central belief that the object of the patient's disordered affections loves them and initiated the supposed relationship.

The initial re-emergence in more recent times of erotomania in the English language literature was in large part due to a number of influential reviews and reformulations (Hollender & Callahan, 1975; Seeman, 1978; Enoch & Trethowan, 1979; Segal, 1989). The most significant stimulus, at least prior to the emergence of stalking as a major issue, was, however, undoubtedly the inclusion into DSM-III-R (American Psychiatric Association, 1987) of erotomania as a specific form of delusional disorder. It is difficult to overestimate the importance of this decision by the committee compiling the DSM to revive the much maligned categories of paranoia in the form of delusional disorders. For better or for worse, and we believe it is both, the DSM has become the dictionary for contemporary mental health professionals that confers, or withdraws, legitimacy to the many and varied constructions of disordered and dysfunctional states of mind. The *impromata* of the DSM gave erotomania a new lease of life. The delusional disorder grouping revived in DSM-III-R owed much to Kraepelin's category of paranoia but the erotomania was pure de Clérambault.

Pathologies of love

The nature of love has largely been the province of poets, novelists and artists. The psychiatric and psychological literature has tended to be reductionist, suggesting love is, if not frank self-deception, merely a cover for raw sexuality or for such things as the mysterious forces of libido or a clinging form of object relationship (Bowlby, 1969; Harlow, 1974; Frijda, 1986; Buss, 1994). A scholarly literature, mainly from philosophers, has accorded love some respect as an emotional experience in and of itself (Scheler, 1954/1912; Singer, 1966, 1987; Solomon, 1980; Scruton, 1986). The infatuation of falling in love and being in love are suggested to be separable states of affairs (Fisher, 1990). Infatuation does not necessarily require encouragement or even a response from the object of these affections. In normal individuals, however, if the love fails to elicit a favourable response the would-be lover usually will eventually abandon hopes for a relationship and gradually detach their affections from the lost cause. Some sense of sadness and residual longing for the failed romance may remain but the rejected suitor is left emotionally able to seek new attachments (Baumeister & Wotman, 1992). Occasionally unrequited love in normal people may not wither but, by an act of self-abnegation, continue without the expectation, or demand, for a response (Fisher, 1990). The borderline between the banalities of broken hearts and the realms of the pathological is approached when fantasy and self-deception begin to substitute for a lack of response from the beloved. Blocked from progress into the mutuality of attraction, desire and benevolent concern, which constitutes being in love, the erotomanic turns to assertion and unfounded conviction. Theirs is not the sad acceptance of lost love but the strident claim that love is, or will be, theirs, irrespective of the apparent behaviour and stated feelings of the beloved. Love for the erotomanic is transformed from a communion with another into a lonely, idiopathic but utterly preoccupying erotic fixation. Although current definitions of erotomania allow only for a pathological state of believing one is loved, there also occur morbid infatuations and in clinical practice most pathologies of love involve a mixture of both infatuation and a belief in being loved (Mullen & Pathé, 1994a).

Pathological beliefs of being loved (erotomania)

De Clérambault's focus on a false belief of being loved in defining the psychopathology of erotomania appears to be understandable, given that he is constructing erotomania primarily as a paranoid or delusional disorder. A claim to be loved, and to have had that love revealed by specific actions and events, is usually open to falsification. The assertion that one loves another, however, is difficult to argue with, let alone declare to be false, particularly when no accompanying claim is made that the affection is returned. The falseness of the beliefs was held by many psychiatrists to be a theoretical prerequisite for that belief to be considered delusional. In practice, however, it is not so much the falsifiability of the central belief that indicates a delusional development but the reasons advanced for the belief.

[Current definitions of delusion often begin by emphasising the falseness of the belief. The inadequacy of falseness as a criterion is that we are often dealing with convictions that are either unverifiable (as, for example, many instances of jealousy) or depend on perspective and balance (as in the paranoid litigant), which places the assertions in the realm of probabilities, not truth and falsity. Clear delusions may have at their core an essentially correct evaluation of the world (as with delusional jealousy) or may depend on personalized extensions of widely accepted beliefs (that there is a God who does direct, and in various ways communicate with, his/her creations). It is from Jaspers' (1963) approach, particularly his emphasis on the way the delusion emerges and the effects on the life of the patient, that a more clinically robust understanding and recognition of delusions is to be obtained.]

In erotomania it is rarely necessary to question the object of the patient's disordered affections to establish that the supposed lover does not harbour an undying passion for the patient. For example, it hardly seemed necessary to check with the supposed lover of one of our patients when she declared that she realized he loved her when one morning in the lift at work he spoke to her about the difficulties he had had with the traffic that morning. This banal, not to say boring, conversational gambit was, the patient insisted, a declaration of love. She did not, as far as could be told, distort or elaborate what he said but she just endowed it with an utterly implausible meaning. Even in a postmodern world, an exegesis of a text consisting of an account of traffic problems in terms of an amorous declaration, seems to be stretching the prerogatives of the listener (reader) somewhat far. This woman later stated she had had her beliefs in his love actually confirmed by his angry demand that she cease writing him embarrassing and inappropriate love letters. The assumption of disorder in such patients depends in large part on the eccentric, if not bizarre, grounds on which they base their convictions of being loved, and their remarkable capacity to reinterpret even the clearest of rejections as encouragement, if not outright expressions of love. One of our patients earnestly recounted how he had approached the object of his affections in the street to declare his love and she had responded by telling him to 'fuck off' and leave her alone. When it was suggested that this might indicate that she wanted nothing to do with him he happily explained that, on the contrary, it was another hopeful indication of their developing intimacy for after all fucking was part of loving! The other elements that suggest pathology are the degree of preoccupation with the supposed lover and the extent to which these preoccupations disrupt the afflicted individual's functioning.

Pathological beliefs in being loved can be characterized as involving:

1 A conviction that they are loved, despite the supposed lover having done nothing to encourage, or sustain, that belief but on the contrary having either made clear his or her lack of interest or remaining unaware of the claimed relationship.

2 A propensity to reinterpret the words and actions of the supposed lover to maintain the belief in their supposed romance.

3 A preoccupation with the supposed love that becomes the central element in the disordered individual's existence.

These three essential criteria are often accompanied by:

4 A conviction that the claimed relationship will eventually be crowned by a permanent and loving union.

5 Repeated attempts to approach or communicate with the supposed lover (that is, in effect, to stalk them).

Pathological beliefs in being loved may be clearly delusional, as where the love is revealed in some extraordinary manner and extends to effect a wide area of the patient's experience of the world (for instance as with a patient who became convinced the telephone and postal services were in league with the Secret Service to interrupt the communications of love from the object of his affections). On occasion, however, there is a plausibility about the notion of an actual, or potential relationship, and even some acknowledgement that they could be overhopeful, or premature, in their claims for their love being reciprocated.

In the great period for descriptive psychopathology, which reached its height in the work of Jaspers (1963), delusion could arise as the product not only of process disorders, such as schizophrenia, but emerge out of developments (or as we would now call them, personality disorders) and reactions. Delusion was not a privileged indicator of psychosis and disease process, but an abnormal mental phenomenon that could arise in a variety of ways with at one end the direct disruption of brain function by, for example, a tumour, to at the other extreme the interaction of a sensitive personality with a hostile environment, as with the persecutory states associated with immigration (Ungvari & Mullen, 1997). The narrowing of concepts of delusion in psychiatry has been part of a process of constructing specific disease entities with their 'about to be discovered' neuropathologies and their already available specific treatments consisting of the pharmaceutical companies latest magic bullets. DSM-III and DSM-IV (American Psychiatric Association, 1980, 1994) are the most obvious and influential embodiment of this ideology, which dominates modern psychiatry and increasingly clinical psychology. Classical psychiatric notions of psychopathology understood disorders as arising as a result of complex interactions between developmental experiences, current social and cultural influences, personality and occasionally disease process. These ideas have largely been lost and survive only in the anaemic notion of the biopsychosocial model, to which lip service is paid more often than serious theoretical attention. The rich tapestry of human experience is cut up into pieces that are reified into specific disorders, each with its operational criteria and particular nostrum. This process of constructing specific disease categories works for other areas of medicine, why not for psychiatry? The answer is that it works for medicine, as it does for psychiatry, when one is in fact dealing with specific disease entities whose necessary, even if not sufficient, cause lies in a specific organic (biological) lesion or disease process. Just as such approaches fall down in dealing with, for example, essential hypertension, so they all too often choke on the clinical complexity of much psychiatric disorder. In the area of erotomania the occasional strengths of a categorical approach are obvious (mainly in the secondary or symptomatic erotomanias), but equally the limitations become painfully constraining in the primary or pure syndromes.

Pathological infatuations (borderline erotomania)

The definition promulgated in DSM-IV, which continues to embody the influence of de Clérambault, requires that erotomania be equated with 'a delusion that another person, usually of a higher status, is in love with the individual' (ibid., p. 765). The potential implications of such exclusivity was dramatically illustrated in the trial of John Hinkley, who in 1981 attempted to assassinate President Reagan. Hinkley had developed an intense and preoccupying infatuation with American actress Jodie Foster and had claimed that his desire to attract her attention lay behind the attack on the President. He is reported as writing 'Jodie I would abandon this idea of getting Reagan in a second if I could only win your heart' and saying 'my assassination attempt was an act of love . . . I'm sorry love has to be so painful' (Low et al., 1986; Caplan, 1987). Evidence was given at the trial to indicate that Hinkley did not have erotomania because he at no time claimed that Jodie Foster loved him or even currently reciprocated his interest. The consuming infatuation with Jodie Foster, which had led directly, through a tortured reasoning process, to his attempt to kill the President, was not considered capable of sustaining a diagnosis of delusional disorder because Hinkley made no claim that Jodie Foster had reciprocated his affections (Low et al., 1986; Goldstein, 1987; Meloy, 1989). Hinkley was eventually found insane on quite other grounds, creating such an outcry that it shook the time-honoured approach to the insanity defence to its core (Steadman et al., 1993). The question of a severe mental disorder based on a morbid infatuation, though important, was just one of the diagnostic issues in this trial where clinical experience confronted the word of DSM-III, and the word won (Stone, 1984).

The problems created by insisting on a criterion that gave absolute priority to de Clérambault's 'delusion of being loved', is further illustrated by the two following case histories (from Mullen, 1997).

Case example

A 36 year old man who when first seen had pursued a young woman with declarations of love and offers of marriage for eight years. He was the only child of an elderly couple. The father had been effectively absent from the home and the mother an intrusive and domineering presence. Socially isolated at school and with only one friend during adolescence he had nevertheless completed an apprenticeship and established with the friend a thriving business. Some months prior to his first encounter with the young woman he had gone on holiday with his friend and business partner and though the precise events were never revealed there appears to have been a confrontation with his sexuality and possibly the homosexual elements in their relationship. This led to a complete severance of contact with his only companion. He became preoccupied with the need to marry and to find a pure and virginal bride.

He began frequenting discos and clubs. One evening he encountered a 15 year old woman who he immediately recognized as his 'God chosen bride'. This recognition was based on her wearing predominantly white, and an air or emanation he discerned from observing her. He asked her to dance, she accepted. He approached her a second time but whether due to his manner or lack of terpsichoreal skill, she declined to repeat the performance. He returned to the same club the next night in the hope of seeing her but was disappointed. He eventually managed to trace her and ascertain where she lived. He sent flowers and an invitation to go out. She wrote a polite refusal. He repeated the process several times and received a response from her parents that they and their daughter wished him to cease these attentions. He began following her in the street. He would stand in a park opposite her house at night. He continued to send letters. An elder sister approached him and demanded he stop harassing the young woman. He continued. The family contacted the police and were informed no offence had been committed (this being in the days prior to anti-stalking legislation). The father and an elder brother confronted him one night as he kept vigil outside their house and threatened him. The next night he returned armed with a firearm which he brandished when approached. He was arrested.

On release from police custody, having received a noncustodial sentence, he returned to his pursuit of the young woman. By this time his business had collapsed. His every waking moment was occupied with pursuing or thoughts of the young woman. He had exhausted his financial resources in part by buying flowers and gifts (which were repeatedly returned), but also by paying for cosmetic surgery in the belief that if his receding hairline, slightly off centre nose and possibly overprominent ears were corrected she would respond to his approaches. This man's dogged pursuits of the object of his affections continued for years. He was imprisoned and committed to hospital (though not treated), but this produced only interruptions in his quest. The family moved, the young woman changed her name and she married but still he was there. When examined over these years he insisted she would one day be his wife and that they were destined for each other but he recognized she was currently frightened of him and did not, nor never had, borne him any affection. He believed her mind had been poisoned against him by her family, particularly by the sister who on one occasion he assaulted. He was convinced however that eventually she would see through these falsehoods and recognize in him her destiny.

Case example

The second case involved a man in his late forties who became infatuated with a woman of a similar age. This man was the youngest of a large family and had had a close relationship with his mother. He was apparently socially successful at school and in adolescence and in adult life had considerable success working as a salesman. He had had numerous brief heterosexual affairs. He was a heavy drinker and in later life a regular smoker of marijuana. He dressed immaculately and he had an expensive sports car even though in recent years he lacked the finances to support such an indulgence. On first meeting he radiated charm with an easy and expansive manner and an engaging verbal fluency. It became obvious however on closer acquaintance that he was vulnerable to even the slightest criticism and was prone to blame and accuse others for any reversal however minor. In the two or three years prior to his meeting the object of his affections his life had been going badly. His business had collapsed and his attempt to redress the decline through dishonest handling had resulted in a prison sentence. His substance abuse had increased. He had alienated most of his acquaintances and all of his surviving family. His boyish charm had abandoned him and he no longer had much, if any, success in finding sexual partners. The object of his affections was a senior civil servant whom he had encountered while trying to establish yet another business. Initially taken by his charm, she had gone out with him on two occasions. He claims, but she denied, they had had sexual intercourse. She had become disenchanted with him and declined further invitations. He began phoning her repeatedly at home and at work. She had her calls monitored to prevent this. He wrote numerous letters. She returned them unopened. He took to intruding on her at work. She had him barred from the building. He followed her in the street and repeatedly came to her flat. She obtained a court order restraining him from approaching her or her flat. He responded by breaking into her flat so when she returned home he had literally moved in. She called the police. He was bound over to keep the peace. He broke into her flat once more and when she attempted to call for help threatened and eventually struck her. He was imprisoned but on release took a taxi from the door of the prison to her flat. He was serving a third prison sentence when eventually assessed by our service. He made no claim that she loved him, going only as far as stating a belief that she might have been beginning to fall for him and because she was afraid of a developing relationship had stopped seeing him. He accepted she was now terrified of him because of his acknowledged inept attempts to win back her affections. He was adamant, however, that he loved her and she was the perfect partner. He was convinced he would eventually wear down her resistance and she would give him another chance. He was certain they were destined for each other. He thought about her constantly and ruminated on potential strategies to gain her love and attention.

The challenge cases such as these present to the current psychiatric orthodoxy with regard to erotomania has become more insistent with the emergence of stalking as a category of criminal offending. The courts are now turning increasingly to mental health professionals for explanations of stalking behaviours and remedies that will prevent such behaviour continuing. Among those who stalk are those who are convinced that the object of their attentions loves them. Such individuals can be comfortably accommodated in current definitions of erotomania. Equally, a group of individuals has been recognized who, although they persistently pursue the object of their affections, make no strong claims to their love being reciprocated. Such individuals have been considered to constitute a subgroup of erotomania, termed borderline erotomanics by Meloy (1989) and pathological infatuations by Mullen & Pathé (1994a). Meloy (1998a, 1999) referred to an 'extreme disorder of attachment', which involves repetitive and persistent preoccupation with the beloved and manifests in the pursuit of the object of attention. Meloy (1989) emphasized in these individuals the presence of a borderline personality disorder, or related personality traits, together with what he regarded as an obsessional attachment to the loved one. Segal (1989, 1990) also acknowledged the presence of such states, regarding them as exaggerated reactions but appearing to confine such reactions to those who have had an actual relationship and been rejected. Although Meloy (1989) derived his concept of borderline erotomania from a coherent psychodynamic theory, the acknowledged need for postulating a new subgroup of erotomania is that DSM-III and IV specify that the central feature of erotomania is that the object of the patient's attentions is believed to love the patient. Confined by the words of the manual, a new category must be created for those cases that simply do not fit. Meloy (1989, 1997) accepts the constraints on erotomania and postulates an additional and separate disorder. Mullen & Pathé (1994a) rejected the currently accepted form of words for defining erotomania and appealed to a far longer clinical and nosological tradition, which does not accept the exclusive emphasis on a morbid belief in being loved. They suggested that pathologies of love (erotomania) as well as pathological beliefs of being in love can include pathological infatuations. Pathological infatuations are characterized by:

1 There is an intense infatuation without necessarily any marked accompanying conviction that the affection is currently reciprocated.

2 The object of the infatuation has either done nothing to encourage the feelings or clearly rejected any continuing interest or concern.

3 The infatuation preoccupies the patient to the exclusion of other interests, resulting in serious disruption to his or her life.

4 The subject insists on the legitimacy and probable success of his or her quest.

These elements are usually accompanied by a persistent pursuit of the object of affection, with gradually escalating intrusiveness that often creates fear and distress in the object of these unwanted attentions.

Pathological infatuations can phenomenologically be considered delusions or overvalued ideas, the two forming a continuum, with overvalued ideas in turn merging into the more heartfelt beliefs of ordinary people. Occasionally pathological infatuations can be true obsessional phenomena.

In normal individuals periods of intense infatuation may occur (particularly in adolescents) but they usually fade when it is clear that no favourable response is to be expected from the beloved. The teenage 'crush' lacks the conviction of eventual fulfilment (although fantasies of such fulfilment are common). These infatuations act as a pleasurable embellishment to a life not yet complicated by real erotic entanglements. Adolescent crushes are often social experiences in which the absorbing interest in a particular figure in the teenage culture is shared with like-minded peers and pursued through groups and clubs. This is in stark contrast to the isolating nature of pathological infatuations. Even the adolescent's passion for some admired, although usually unavailable, figure in their immediate environment is usually shared with friends and becomes a matter for joint interest and enjoyment. Occasionally such teenage crushes do not evaporate to be replaced by actual relationships but persist into adult life. This can continue to provide a largely harmless hobby or may progress to an obsessive preoccupation, which may culminate in stalking behaviours.

One of our more curious referrals occurred when two women in their late twenties sought of their own initiative a joint assessment. They reported a shared obsessive interest in a retired schoolmaster. They had been school friends and in their early teens had confided each to the other an infatuation with one of the teachers at their school, a man who at that time would have been in his late fifties or early sixties. They had combined to gather information about this object of their nubile imaginations and by dint of enquiries, following and observing, acquired an extensive dossier on him. This not untypical teenage crush did not, however, recede before the emergence of real encounters and relationships of later adolescents. In part the crush continued because both these women were markedly shy and retiring and neither had their first boyfriend until into their twenties. It was also reinforced by becoming an important bond in their own friendship. The infatuation survived their leaving school and continued into adult life. The intensity of their shared interest in the increasingly idealized vision of this schoolmaster did not abate, although their actual and potential intrusions on his privacy became less frequent. They rationed themselves to unsigned cards at Christmas, St Valentine's Day and his birthday and to the occasional phone call in which they would hang up when he answered. Both, however, retained an image of this man as the ideal lover and both fantasized about one day being united with him. These were not unintelligent women and both were aware of the yawning gulf between their imaginings and the reality of the ageing schoolmaster. They entertained no expectations that this man returned their affections, in fact they hoped that he was unaware of their interest. The constructions they had made around this man operated as an ideal against which the men they encountered were measured. By that yardstick all actual and potential suitors were found wanting. In effect this prevented them accepting the opportunities for real relationships that had presented. They were aware that the persisting infatuation had become a bar to their establishing an actual relationship and it was for this reason they came seeking help.

In most erotomanics morbid infatuation coexists with a morbid conviction of being loved but there can be states that are virtually exclusively, either morbid beliefs in being loved or morbid infatuations.

Primary and symptomatic forms of erotomania

The erotomanias can, as indicated by de Clérambault (1942/1921), be broadly divided between those which emerge as a symptom complex within some underlying process, such as schizophrenia, and those which emerge as a pure or primary disorder.

Erotomania is encountered most often as part of a recognizable psychiatric syndrome where it forms part of the symptomatology of the underlying disorder. In theory any condition capable of giving rise to a delusional development can generate a pathology of passion. Further, obsessive–compulsive disorders can centre on a morbid infatuation or a compulsive pursuit of a supposed lover.

The features of a symptomatic (or secondary) erotomania are:

1 The erotomania owes its genesis and evolution to an underlying mental disorder that emerges prior to or contemporaneously with the erotomanic beliefs.
2 The clinical features of the underlying disorder are present alongside the erotomanic features.
3 The erotomania usually resolves as the underlying disorder resolves.

Mental health professionals are most likely to encounter pathological love as part of a wider disturbance of mental state accompanying a mental disorder such as schizophrenia. DSM-III-R listed twenty-two separate disorders that could have erotomanic delusions as one of their symptoms. Erotomania has been specifically described in association with schizophrenia (Hayes & O'Shea, 1985), affective disorders (Raskin & Sullivan, 1974; Rudden et al., 1990), schizoaffective disorders (Gillett et al., 1990) and a range of organic psychosyndromes (Lovett Doust & Christie, 1978; Drevets & Rubin, 1987; Signer and Cummings, 1987; Gaddall, 1989). The majority of symptomatic erotomanias seen in practice arise in illnesses of a schizophrenic type. Rudden et al. (1990) reported that twelve of their twenty-eight cases had schizophrenia, Mullen & Pathé (1994a) reported that, of their sixteen cases, seven had a primary diagnosis of schizophrenia and three of mania as part of a bipolar disorder. In the series of Menzies et al. (1995), of thirteen cases, nine had a primary diagnosis of schizophrenia and of Gillett et al.'s (1990) eleven cases, three had schizophrenia and four a bipolar illness.

The symptomatic erotomanias differ from those occurring as pure or primary erotomanias not only by being accompanied by the other disturbances of mental state specific to the generating disorder but also by the sufferers being more fickle in changing the object of their attentions over time and in tending to have more obviously carnal desires and intentions (Mullen & Pathé 1994a). In erotomanic syndromes occurring in manic states the preoccupations usually disperse when the mania settles but with a recurrence of the disorder the pathology of love can recur, often fixing on a new object. In the schizophrenic disorders the pathology of love tends to fluctuate with the course of the illness, again with resolution during periods of relative quiescence and a return, often with a new object, during exacerbations. One of our cases with schizophrenia had pursued six different women over a period of ten years, convinced that they loved him. His victims were selected from health staff and on one occasion a young woman he saw in the street. Erotomanic symptoms associated with the schizophrenias may be associated with a greater frequency of sexual attacks on the object of their attentions (Mullen & Pathé 1994b). The risk of assaultive behaviour in general was not, however, reported by either Menzies et al. (1995) or Mullen et al. (1999) to be significantly associated with a primary diagnosis of schizophrenia.

Typical examples of a symptomatic erotomania arising as part of a schizophrenic disorder are illustrated by the following cases.

Case example

Mr R came from a stable and caring home. He was noted from infancy to be a slower developer than his elder brother and sister and at school was identified as having learning difficulties. He was placed in a special school where he progressed educationally to the point of acquiring literacy but remained an odd, solitary child with no real friends. Soon after leaving school he showed the first signs of a psychotic illness. He was diagnosed as having a schizophrenic illness and had his first very brief admission. A week or so later he was arrested and subsequently convicted of setting a fire in an abandoned warehouse, for which he was imprisoned. He served his sentence in the prison psychiatric unit. On leaving prison he was, if anything, more socially awkward and withdrawn. He lapsed once more into a floridly psychotic state. An extended admission brought his illness into remission and he was placed in a community housing project. He lived quietly for seven years, having little contact with anyone except his community nurse and visits from his ageing parents. A new community nurse, Mrs I, was appointed at the local mental health clinic, with responsibility for encouraging greater independence and social activity among the more disabled of the clinic's patients. At about the same time as this female staff member began visiting Mr R, for reasons that escape easy explanation, Mr R's antipsychotic medication was ceased. Mr R misinterpreted Mrs I's interest and encouragement as representing a special and amorous interest in him personally. A number of months passed in which he neither gave any indications of his feelings nor sought any response from Mrs I about what he fondly believed to be her feelings. He spent an increasing amount time fantasizing about Mrs I. He obtained from the clinic a photograph in which she appeared, but this was not sufficient to satisfy his desires. He bought a camera and took photographs of Mrs I when she came to visit him at his unit. She was too surprised to object and at this stage still saw him as a disabled man who was responding to her assistance and learning to become a little more socially outgoing.

The photographs became for a time the centre of Mr R's existence. He came to believe that through the pictures a spiritual and physical contact was established between himself and Mrs I. He would masturbate gazing on the photographs and through this process he became convinced that he had impregnated Mrs I. During this period the active symptoms of Mr R's schizophrenic illness became more obvious. He was hallucinating, Mrs I's voice being prominent among the voices. The television began referring both directly and through coded messages to Mrs I's love for him and offering guarantees of their later happiness. At this point during one of her regular visits Mr R declared his love and told Mrs I that their future happiness was assured. Mrs I's response was, like so many professionals before her, a polite, 'that's very kind of you' and a gentle explanation that they had a professional not a personal relationship. She concluded by assuring him that his misunderstanding although unfortunate could now be forgotten. Mrs I in her later statements to police makes clear that she felt at the time she had dealt successfully with 'the embarrassment'. Some weeks passed with no further embarrassing outbursts from Mr R and Mrs I continued to visit. Mr R's account makes clear that he believed his overtures had been received with enthusiasm and the seal placed on their mutual love. As so often seen in these cases Mr R's account of what passed between them on that afternoon differs little from that of Mrs I's; what differs is the meanings attributed to the words and actions.

Mr R began to follow Mrs I and loitered around her house and outside the clinic when she was working there. About a month after his declaration he wrote Mrs I a letter about their love, her pregnancy and that they were now married. The letter is disorganized both in the forms of expression and the calligraphy, but its central message is clear. Mrs I discussed the letter with 'the team' at the mental health clinic and received appropriate support and the totally inappropriate advice not to worry and to work through this with Mr R. Her confronting Mr R with his inappropriate letter was understood by the increasingly psychotic Mr R as a further declaration of love. Mr R sent further letters, enclosing soiled and much used photos of Mrs I, and became a virtual fixture outside her home. Mrs I became increasingly frightened as did her two children who could not understand why there was a strange man outside their house.

Mrs I refused to continue seeing Mr R and one evening she and her husband confronted him outside their house and politely but firmly told him not to trouble them further. Far from having the desired effect, Mr R's letter writing and following intensified and he began repeatedly approaching Mrs I and making confused and occasionally lewd suggestions. She obtained a court order to prevent him contacting her. He, as is usual in such situations, ignored the order. She and her family became increasingly distressed. She wrote a letter stating that she was a married woman with no interest in him. He wrote back that she was married to him.

This continued for several months. Mr R remained untreated and, following an episode at the mental health clinic when he threatened another nurse and threw a chair across the room, he was rediagnosed as personality disordered.

The disturbances in his mental state intensified and he was now almost constantly hallucinating. He cornered Mrs I in a supermarket and demanded that she accompany him to his home as she was married to him and expecting his child. She in terror screamed at him to leave her alone and that she never wanted to see him again. On this occasion he understood that she was rejecting him. That evening he vandalized her car and sent a threatening letter. The police were involved at this point but took no effective action. A week later he broke into her home whilst she was alone and when she tried to run from his disorganized proclamations of love, he grabbed her and held her whilst he spoke at length. His communications were largely rendered incomprehensible by his excitement and disordered language, but they centred on them being husband and wife. She persuaded him to release her and ran for help to neighbours. He was finally arrested and bailed to his parents. He accepted his parent's instructions not to go out alone in exchange for their taking a letter each day to post to Mrs I. After a forensic assessment he was admitted for treatment.

Another example of a symptomatic form of erotomania is the following case.

Case example

Mr C. came from a privileged family background. He was the youngest of three children by nearly ten years. His early development was normal and at primary school he was an academically able child and, if not socially outgoing, did at least have a circle of friends. At the age of 15 years he was noted to be having more difficulties coping and rather than, as is usual at that age, increasing his social activities he was becoming more isolated and house bound. In his final year at school, despite the promise he had shown, there were indications of declining achievement. In an attempt to boost his school performance the parents engaged two tutors, one a female university student. Mr C became infatuated with the young woman tutor and began, after only a few weeks, writing love letters to her. She attempted to deal with this by polite refusal of his approaches, but when he persisted she resigned the tutoring position. He continued to write and phone and began turning up both at her flat and at the university. His pursuit escalated and she sought help from the police but this was prior to the enactment of anti-stalking legislation and they told her that there was nothing they could do. She appealed to his parents who responded initially by confronting him. He assured them that the young woman really loved him and was sending him messages of affection in ways they would not understand. The parents at this point suspected Mr C was becoming mentally disordered. They took him to their general practitioner who was reassuring. They took him to a private psychiatrist who said it was an adolescent crush. In the meantime Mr C had abandoned his studies, left school and was spending most of his waking hours either in pursuit of the young woman or in thinking about her. She in desperation confronted him and forcibly expressed her anger and dislike of him. He struck out at her, knocking her to the ground. He was charged and bailed on condition he did not approach the victim. He was taken back to court on two occasions for breach of this bail condition before the magistrate finally remanded him in custody.

When assessed in prison, perhaps due to the fright of sudden incarceration, he was willing to speak at length about his experiences and beliefs. He knew absolutely the young woman loved him. He was convinced his brain had been altered by some obscure process and he now had the capacity to read others' thoughts and was progressing to a state of divine perfection. He had a variety of bizarre beliefs about bodily change. He experienced ideas of reference, believing the radio and newspapers had hidden messages from his beloved. There were no hallucinations and at that stage his spoken and written language was unremarkable in form. He never subsequently experienced hallucinations. Over the next three years, during which time his schizophrenic disorder was largely treatment resistant, the delusional beliefs became both more extensive and more bizarre and his use of language became disorganized with neologisms, idiosyncratic use of phrases and a breakdown of the usual connections and organizing themes that render communications easily comprehensible. He retained his conviction that he was loved by his one-time tutor and that their relationship would eventually be crowned by marriage. On the first two occasions he was given leave to go home from the hospital he attempted unsuccessfully to contact the young woman.

A remission in his illness was finally obtained with one of the newer antipsychotics. He had a period of several months symptom free and was able to return home and even begin to prepare to resume his studies. Sadly he developed a blood disorder, a recognized complication of this particular drug, and the medication had to be ceased. Within weeks he had relapsed back into active illness. He developed an erotomanic fixation on the female registrar treating him at the time. Many of the beliefs, experiences and activities that had characterized his first erotomanic state were now repeated with the new object of affection. On this occasion his intrusiveness was more limited as he was hospitalized but until prevented he made ample use of letters and the phone. He succeeded in making it impossible for the young doctor to continue working in the unit. The erotomanic preoccupations were interwoven with grandiose and religious delusions often bizarre and expressed in language-disordered speech and writing.

In contrast to the symptomatic forms, the pure or primary erotomanias have the following characteristics:

1 The erotomania forms a discrete entity that initially develops unaccompanied by features of other mental disorders, such as hallucinations, passivity experiences or clear mood disorders (subsequently affective disturbances may emerge in response to the travails of unrequited love or persecutory or jealous beliefs come to complicate the picture).

2 The erotomania usually emerges suddenly, although often in an individual with pre-existing vulnerabilities of personality which tend to make them needy of love and affection, prone to misinterpret the words and actions of others and stubborn in asserting their own view of the world and in pursuing their own sense of entitlement.

3 The erotomanic preoccupation once established becomes the organizing

principle around which the sufferer's life revolves and forms a chronic fixed system of beliefs, often of delusional intensity. (On topics other than those pertaining to the supposed romance the patient remains as clear thinking, orderly and apparently rational as previously.)

4 The erotomania is fixed on a single object of affection (these are usually monogamous attachments of great fidelity).

Most recent authorities confine the primary or pure erotomania to those where the central convictions are delusional (Hollender & Callahan, 1975; Lovett Doust & Christie, 1978; Seeman, 1978; Taylor et al., 1983; Ellis & Mellsop, 1985; Munro et al., 1985; Segal, 1989; Gillett et al., 1990). There is, however, a parallel, albeit weaker, tradition of seeing pure erotomanias not as discrete psychotic disorders separated in kind from normal experiences but as being the exaggeration of the normal passion of love, which at one extreme forms a delusional disorder and at the other an intense and preoccupying infatuation that borders upon the normal.

The central features of the primary or pure pathologies of love are that they are discrete entities unaccompanied by features of other disorders. Their emergence may be usually understandably related to the patients' previous personalities and to their current personal and social situation. A provoking event can often plausibly be related to the onset. This precipitating event has been suggested to involve a 'narcissistic wound' or loss (usually of a supportive relationship) (Hollender & Callahan, 1975; Enoch & Trethowan, 1979; Evans et al., 1982). Pure pathologies of love often appear to emerge from a context of emptiness to fill a vacuum in the patients' lives. Taylor et al. (1983) noted that all their cases had led lonely and solitary existences, with no sexual partners for many years prior to the emergence of the erotomanic fixation. Segal (1989) pointed to certain common themes in the lives of these patients, which included socially empty lives, a lack of sexual contact and low socioeconomic status. Mullen & Pathé (1994a) noted that all their five cases of pure erotomania were, at the time the disorder emerged, facing a life that appeared to them bleak, unrewarding and bereft of intimacy. The erotomanic fixation can be postulated to provide at least a semblance of an intimate relationship and a route to the engagement of the loving and erotic affections of the patients. Scheler (1954/1912), in his classic study of the phenomenology of love, suggested that we do not love someone because they give us pleasure but we experience joy through loving. The act of love, even if unrequited, is itself still accompanied by a feeling of great happiness. For those whose life is empty of intimacy the rewards of even a pathological love may be considerable.

The premorbid personalities in pure cases of erotomania have variously been described as shy and awkward (Krafft-Ebing, 1904/1879), hypersensitive and self-referential (Kretschmer, 1918), proud and rebellious (de Clérambault, 1942), narcissistic (Enoch & Trethowan, 1979; Meloy, 1989), schizoid (Munro et al., 1985), lacking in confidence, suspicious and socially avoidant (Retterstøl & Opjordsmoen, 1991), and timid and withdrawn (Seeman, 1978). The features common to these various formulations are of a socially inept individual isolated from others, be it by sensitivity, suspiciousness or assumed superiority (Mullen & Pathé, 1994a). These patients tend to be described as living socially empty lives, often working in menial occupations and being, or feeling themselves to be, unattractive (de Clérambault, 1942; Hollender & Callahan, 1975; Enoch & Trethowan, 1979; Segal, 1989). The desire for a relationship in many cases is balanced by a fear of rejection or a fear of the realities of intimacy, both sexual and emotional. The following case history (from Mullen & Pathé, 1994a) illustrates a pure or primary pathology of love.

Case example

Ms Y was the only child of elderly and unsupportive parents. As a child she described herself as intensely self-conscious and easily frightened, with no close friends. Although able academically she did not enter university, opting instead for a commercial course and a position as a typist. Her husband was her first and only boyfriend. The marriage went badly from the outset and there were considerable sexual difficulties. They had few shared interests and there was little intimacy. Her work provided the only arena of social interaction. A few months prior to the onset of symptoms she lost her job due to the firm's closure.

She had poor self-esteem and acknowledged that she had always been somewhat suspicious of others and tended, when in public places, to feel that people looked at her, laughed at her behind her back, and made derogatory remarks. She was very concerned with order and cleanliness and had a number of cleaning and checking rituals.

She was referred from the courts following a breach of a restraining order and charges arising out of telephone calls to a local clergyman. Ms Y explained that she had been the object of the romantic intentions of this particular clergyman for several years. Following her first meeting with him she noted that he regularly drove past her house and waved to her. She suspected that at night he would clamber up trees behind the house to watch her as she undressed. She never actually saw him, but claimed that she knew he was there. She also reported that he began to communicate with her by barely audible blips that could be heard from the telephone, both when the receiver was in place and when she lifted the receiver. She was initially discomforted by his attentions, but gradually began to realize that they were the manifestations of a shy man in love with her. She began to return his telephone calls. She said that he always denied having made a call and she realized that this was a 'friendly game' that was meant to entice her into an increasingly profound relationship. She began to telephone more frequently, and finally declared her love. His apparent surprise and disavowal she recognized was because he was still married and would have to disentangle himself from his present encumbrances before they could be united.

The clergyman became increasingly distressed and after the failure of mediators to dissuade her from further contact he obtained a restraining order. She noted, however, that at the same time he increased his covert communications via the blips and squeaks emanating from the telephone. She kept a meticulous record of these supposed communications, which occurred anything up to 150 times a day. He obtained an unlisted number but she soon discovered the new number. The clergyman claimed that his life was now totally disrupted by her calls and her other communications.

This lady was absolutely convinced that the clergyman loved her and intended to marry her. She said that he initiated the contact and that he still remained the one more intensely in love. She had no difficulty in explaining all his words and actions, even that of taking her to court, as covert expressions of undying devotion. There were no hallucinatory phenomena, the noises from the telephone most probably being illusions. There were no other abnormalities in her mental state.

This lady responded remarkably well on a dose of 4 mg of pimozide a day. The absorption with the supposed lover rapidly decreased from a virtually total domination of her waking thoughts to an occasional consideration of the matter. She continued to assert that this man had approached her but increasingly she would both disavow any interest in him and accept that he no longer retained any interest in her. Interestingly, the relationship with her husband improved for the first time and they began to communicate and enjoy something approaching a marital relationship. Six months after commencing treatment this lady, on her own initiative, stopped the pimozide. There was a rapid return of symptoms and within a matter of weeks she was again plaguing the clergyman with letters and telephone calls. The reintroduction of the pimozide produced another gratifying resolution in her symptomatology. She remains on regular medication.

Case example

Ms L, a female aged 47, was the youngest of four children. Ms L's father was disabled as a result of a work injury and her mother was the dominant figure. Ms L was described as shy and isolated both at school and as a teenager. On leaving school she obtained a job as an accounts clerk, which she had retained until a year previously.

Her husband was her first and only boyfriend. They married when she was 22 and he was 30 years of age. He was always the dominant figure in the relationship, making all of the decisions and controlling the money. His views always prevailed, giving her no opportunity to even vent her own opinion or feelings.

Ms L was always painfully shy and self-conscious. She reported frequently feeling that people looked at her and laughed at her behind her back. At work she was occasionally overwhelmed by suspicions that others were ganging up on her and talking about her. She said she always put these fears back in control by using logic because 'I know it's not real'. She avoided social contacts outside the family. She was a well-organized individual but had no obsessional or phobic symptoms.

Four years previously she had come to 'realize' that a senior partner in the firm for which she worked entertained romantic feelings about her. She had always admired him and considered him a gentle and concerned individual. Her preoccupations with this man increased markedly after the sudden death of a younger brother who had been the person with whom she had had the closest relationship. The love crystallized following an incident when the object of her affections spoke to her one morning about the weather and the prospects for the upcoming ski season. It was this she claimed made her realize that he reciprocated her affection. She said 'I knew this meant he had strong feelings for me, because usually I am completely ignored. No one chats to me. They think I'm not intelligent enough'. Over the next few months she felt that he expressed his love in a variety of roundabout ways: clothes that he wore, the way he nodded a greeting, and the occasional exchanged good morning. It was not, she said, so much what he said but the tone of voice and the way he said it. She became interested in her appearance for the first time in many years, took up aerobics, lost 10 kg and began colouring her hair.

The object of her attentions, in a victim impact statement, said he had been aware for some years that she was infatuated with him, but this was entirely one sided and had never been encouraged. He had tried to ignore it but it became, in the last three years, increasingly intrusive. She would follow him; turn up unexpectedly; stand next to his car after work, awaiting his departure; write notes to him and phone him both at work and at home. He arranged for her to be made redundant to prevent continuing harassment at work.

Eight months prior to the admission, Ms L, while trailing the object of her affections, observed him to meet and have a drink with a senior secretary from the firm's office. Over the next week she tailed both this lady and the object of her affections. She became convinced that he was having an affair with this woman. She found herself troubled by intrusive images of her would-be lover in the arms of this other woman. She became increasingly distressed and angry. She made a number of accusatory phone calls to both the object of her affections, his wife and the secretary she supposed to have stolen his affections from her. At one point she attempted to throw herself in front of his car. She caused a major incident at his place of work by accusing him in front of a number of colleagues of having an affair and having deserted her. At this time she began to develop signs of depression with sleep disturbance, loss of appetite, self-denigratory ruminations and suicidal thoughts. Immediately prior to her admission she confronted the object of her affections with a rifle she had taken from her husband's gun cupboard. He claims she pointed it at him and threatened him, although she denies actually directing the gun at him. The gun was discharged but the circumstances are in dispute. She left to return home, where she attempted to stab herself through the heart and in fact succeeded in inflicting a serious chest wound.

On admission she acknowledged that she was still preoccupied by thoughts of her supposed lover. She believed that there would still be a reconciliation between them because he remained in love with her and she returned his affection. She acknowledged that she was still plagued by jealousy and that vivid images would intrude into her consciousness of him having intercourse with her supposed rival. She claimed no longer to be actively suicidal because she recognized that eventually this hiccup in their relationship would be sorted out and they would have a future together.

This lady was commenced on both antidepressants and 6 mg of pimozide and over the subsequent four weeks, the intensity of her preoccupations with this supposed beloved gradually decreased. She came to recognize that the relationship was now over and there was no future, given what had occurred. She still retained the belief that he had returned her affections, although she accepted that she may have been overhopeful in her expectations for the relationship. She remains on medication.

Mullen & Pathé (1994a) noted that, in all the pure syndromes in their series, the premorbid personality was marked by exquisite self-consciousness, with a tendency to refer the actions and utterances of others to themselves, usually endowing these with a denigratory or malevolent colouring. It is not difficult to extrapolate from such a tendency to the development of a pathology of love, given that all that may be required to set such a development in motion is seeing the actions and utterances of one particular person not as malevolent but as loving. These character traits may also provide some rationale for why apparently intelligent and not unattractive people are so handicapped in social and erotic relationships that they are driven into fantasy and delusion to satisfy their needs of intimacy.

The view advanced here of the pure forms of pathologies of passion being an extension of normal emotional reactions leaves problems regarding the boundary between the pathological and the morbid. The boundary issues are particularly acute in instances where there has been some form of real relationship, however fleeting, between the individual and the object of their affections. That the feelings were reciprocated at some stage makes it difficult to subsequently designate the love pathological. The other area of potential confusion is where unrequited love is pursued with such misplaced enthusiasm that it gives the mistaken impression of pathology. The following case exemplifies this latter quandary.

Case example

Ms J was a 27-year-old of borderline intelligence from a stable middle class background. She had worked as an office cleaner. She was shy and self-conscious, having little social life. Following a Christmas party she had intercourse with an office worker in his thirties who was married with children. They were both intoxicated at the time. This was her first sexual experience. She approached him subsequently but he, apparently embarrassed by the connection, rejected her with increasingly brutal directness.

Ms J believed that the man must care for her and that his actions indicated that he loved her. She was distressed and confused by his subsequent behaviour and having no basis for comparison decided that he could not mean what he said. Over the next four months she approached him repeatedly; she telephoned him frequently; she turned up at his home and followed him to his golf club. She understood that he was trying to put her off but could not accept that he had no feelings for her. Following one particularly direct and abusive rejection she became angry and vandalized his car. She still kept pestering him, hoping to reawaken his interest. He took out a restraining order. She was enraged and went to his house and in front of his wife and children accused him of destroying her life. She refused to leave. The police were called and she was committed to hospital.

The behaviour of this young woman resembles that of someone with erotomania. All her hopes and fantasies about the future became dependent on the supposed love. She was totally preoccupied with this man to the extent of neglecting her work and herself. She certainly made repeated and sustained attempts to approach the supposed lover despite increasingly insistent rejections. She did not, however, reinterpret the man's words and actions to maintain the belief in his love but simply found herself incapable of crediting his change of heart. When she finally accepted that the relationship was over she moved to anger and distress. Her behaviour was based on a misinterpretation, fostered by naïveté and sustained by a desperate hope, and though she behaved like someone with a pathological infatuation, she did not think like such an individual.

The object of affection

De Clérambault (1942/1921), following Kraepelin (1921/1913), considered that the erotomanic fixed their attentions on individuals of higher social status. This was given even greater emphasis by Segal (1989), who contrasted the physically unattractive erotomanic employed in some menial occupation with the attractive, high status, intelligent (!) object of their affections. The popular attention given to the erotomanic followers of the rich and famous has reinforced this stereotype.

Part of normal love is endowing the beloved with attractive attributes and it would be a poor suitor who could divine no claim to excellence in the object of their affections. The love of the erotomanic, being little constrained by practicalities or even plausibility, is free to fix on almost anyone, so his or her desire for excellence need not be mitigated by pragmatic considerations about likely success. In our experience, however, the objects of pathological love are almost as varied in their personal and work attributes as are the objects of normal love. The erotomanics fix their attentions on those that they find attractive and with whom they have a real, or supposed, contact. The famous, who intrude themselves, via television, radio and videos, into our homes, often creating a pseudo-intimacy, clearly become targets more frequently than most. Objects of attention are often chosen from among individuals encountered in the work environment, either through employment relationships or by being a customer or client of the service offered by the future victim (Harmon et al., 1995). At high risk are professionals, particularly health professionals, whose work not only brings them in contact with vulnerable people but often does so in a context of being helpful and concerned. In our experience, male erotomanics, like their nondisordered brothers, most often bestow their affections largely by virtue of the perceived physical attractiveness of the object of affection. Anyone can become the object of the disordered affections of the erotomanic and, although the high risk groups do have high status, they do not account for all victims. Similarly, though erotomanics are drawn from the lonely, socially incompetent and disordered, they are in our experience far from universally physically unattractive and some have attained high social status (there being a medical practitioner, an academic and a lawyer among the erotomanic stalkers known to our clinic).

Prevalence

The prevalence of erotomanic syndromes, both pure and clearly symptomatic, is unknown. Attempts to estimate how frequently these conditions are found in patient populations have been made using retrospective case note surveys (Rudden et al., 1983; Retterstøl & Opjordsmoen, 1991; Menzies et al., 1995). Retterstøl & Opjordsmoen (1991) reported an incidence of 0.3% in an inpatient population and there are estimates that between 3% and 10% of delusional disorders centre on erotomanic beliefs (Rudden et al., 1983; Menzies et al., 1995). As the profile of delusional disorders rises, erotomania is likely to be recognized and noted with increasing frequency.

Traditionally, erotomania was considered predominantly, if not exclusively, a female complaint, but recent studies indicate that it is found in men and women in roughly equal numbers, in the gay and the straight and in individuals from a range of cultural and social backgrounds (Lovett Doust & Christie, 1978; Taylor et al., 1983; Dunlop, 1988; Eminson et al., 1988).

Management and prognosis

In the symptomatic erotomanic syndromes the treatment relevant to the generating disorder is provided, augmented where appropriate with antipsychotic agents and psychotherapeutic interventions directed at the pathology of love. In the reactive (pure) syndromes the mainstay of management is antipsychotics in low to moderate dosage (e.g. pimozide 2–6 mg per day) combined with counselling and support, which both confront the cognitive distortions sustaining the erotomanic fixation and hope to move the patient to a more effective engagement with other people. This is often a protracted and frustrating process, with slow progress and frequent reverses but nevertheless real therapeutic gains are usually possible if the patient remains engaged in treatment.

The literature in general does not indicate a good response to treatment even in the symptomatic conditions. Gillett et al. (1990) suggested a poor response in their four cases with a primary diagnoses of schizophrenia and even more surprisingly a refractory erotomania in a case of mania that persisted despite effective treatment of the mood disorder. Segal (1989), on the basis of a literature review and his own experience, noted the extreme persistence of the erotic delusions, with at best some remnant of the delusion remaining in all except the rare case. These gloomy prognostications are reiterated by Leong (1994), who goes so far as to suggest courts and social policy-makers 'should not place much emphasis on psychiatry and other mental health disciplines in diminishing the erotomanic delusion' (ibid., p. 384) and seems to imply that criminal and civil sanctions may be more appropriate. One of the few long-term follow-up studies suggests a somewhat less grim outlook, with favourable outcomes in two cases, relatively favourable in one and poor or uncertain in three (Retterstrøl & Opjordsmoen, 1991). Claims for the efficacy of pimozide or other antipsychotics in the pure (reactive) syndromes have been made (Munro et al., 1985; Stein, 1986).

An abiding problem with managing these cases is the almost total lack of motivation for treatment. Those caught up in pathological love do not see themselves as ill but blessed with a romance whose only blemish is the tardiness of response in the beloved or the interference of third parties (often including the would-be therapist). The benefits of these disorders for the patient should not be forgotten, for they provide some solace for their loneliness, some support for their damaged self-esteem and some purpose to their otherwise empty existences. As Segal (1989, p. 1265) pointed out 'erotomania, if kept under control, is not an altogether negative phenomenon, since it may provide solace for a few lonely souls, who might otherwise spend their lives in unrelieved isolation and solitude', although one might question whether if indeed unrequited love is 'kept under control' it qualifies as an erotomania.

A somewhat more optimistic picture was painted by Mullen & Pathé (1994a), who considered the general therapeutic pessimism about erotomanic syndromes to be misplaced. Their experience was that the response to treatment in the symptomatic disorders reflected the nature and severity of the underlying disorder, their three cases secondary to manic illnesses making a complete recovery but those with intractable schizophrenic disorders often continuing to harbour erotomanic delusions although usually in a less florid and preoccupying form. The pure or reactive pathologies of love had a variable outcome, although four out of five either made a full recovery or showed marked amelioration of symptoms with low doses of antipsychotics and supportive psychotherapy. They emphasized the need to persist with treatment in the pure syndromes over many months before improvement can be expected.

An element worthy of emphasis in their management is improving the social supports and networks of patients with pathologies of love. Although in our experience it is rarely possible to assist these patients to find and maintain intimate relationships it has in some been possible to engage them in social activities and contacts that provide considerable support. If their lives remain bereft of human contact let alone intimacy it will be difficult to induce them to abandon the only semblance of a relationship they possess.

The widely held pessimism about the effective management of erotomanic syndromes is a self-fulfilling prophecy made prior to any substantial trials of treatment. It is particularly unfortunate at a moment when mental health professionals are likely to be increasingly asked for opinions by the courts about the appropriate disposal of stalkers driven by erotomanic preoccupations. It is probable that only effective treatment is capable of freeing the victim from pursuit and the patient from an all-encompassing preoccupation. We are failing both our patients and their victims by not using the management approaches already available and working on developing more effective therapeutic interventions.

9

Same gender stalking

Introduction

Stalking is usually conceived of as a properly heterosexual activity, with men pursuing women and women pursuing men. Instances of same gender stalking have been thought to constitute a rarity, some suggesting fewer than 1% of all cases (Meloy, 1996), but more recent studies of stalking behaviours undertaken in larger, less selective populations indicate that they are more prevalent than was formerly estimated (Tjaden & Thoennes, 1998; Mullen et al., 1999). Gender has received minimal attention in most stalking studies despite the consideration given to a range of other demographic variables with predictive potential for, say, the course of the pursuit or the likelihood of stalker violence. While it has been suggested, for instance, that females who stalk female ex-intimates may be more likely to assault their victims (National Institute of Justice, 1996) this issue has not been examined empirically.

In our clinical experience those stalked by individuals of the same gender are exposed to greater scepticism and indifference by law enforcement and other helping agencies. This is not entirely a homophobic response as it appears to be independent of the victim's sexual orientation, although the victim's stated sexual proclivities are not infrequently called into question. If indeed same gender stalking victims are more vulnerable than their opposite gender counterparts to physical attack, if their lives are no less disrupted by their stalker and if they are at least as vulnerable to the emotional sequelae experienced by their opposite gender counterparts, then it is likely that the psychological and personal safety needs of this group of crime victims are not being adequately addressed.

This chapter reviews cases of same gender stalking reported in the literature over the past sixty years, including our recent study of twenty-nine same gender stalkers and their victims. Until recently most of the information pertaining to same gender stalking was confined to media reports of same gender celebrity stalkers and the literature on erotomania. Case reports of same gender erotomanic attachments have tended to employ misleading terminology such as 'homoerotomania' or 'homosexual erotomania', implying homosexuality in the sufferer, victim or both, when in actual fact this cannot be assumed in all cases. It has been noted that erotomanic attachments are more often characterized by the idealized and spiritual than the carnal aspects of love (see Chapter 8). Consistent with this, the reported cases of same gender erotomania have not necessarily demonstrated a homosexual orientation nor indeed have their victims. For the purposes of the following review, the terms 'homoerotomania' and 'homosexual erotomania' are applied in accordance with their usage by the author(s) concerned, but they should be regarded as indicative of homosexual orientation neither in the stalkers nor in their victims.

Media reports of same gender stalking

Case reports of same gender stalking that are from time to time reported in the popular press predominantly involve celebrities and other public figures. These have included, in the USA, singer John Lennon's assassin, Mark Chapman, and more recently Jonathan Norman, who stalked film director Steven Spielberg with the stated intention of raping him (see Chapter 6). Author Stephen King was reputedly the victim of two male stalkers and actress Sharon Gless was pursued for years by a woman claiming to be in love with her; it was reported that this woman had planned to ambush and sexually assault Gless, then commit suicide (Writer & Blackman, 1993). A 46-year-old woman who pursued singer Judith Durham in Australia for over five years was sentenced to a suspended jail term for stalking. The court heard that the woman, a longstanding devotee of the former lead singer of The Seekers, sent faxes and letters, made hundreds of phone calls to Durham and her family, friends and lawyer, followed her to concerts, publicly maligned her and initiated spurious legal action against her. Three weeks before her stalking conviction, the woman repeatedly delivered doormats to the singer's home, forty-two in total, because she felt the celebrity had treated her like one (*The Age*, 20 August 1998, p. 3).

Finally, a number of personal and fictional accounts of homoerotomania have appeared in literary circles in recent years, notably psychiatrist Dr Doreen Orion's account of being stalked by a female ex-patient in *I Know You Really Love Me* (1997) and Ian McEwan's novel *Enduring Love* (1997), which portrays the plight of a man pursued by a male stranger with an erotomanic attachment to him.

Case reports of same gender erotomania

In 1937, Fretet (cited in Signer, 1989) described an alcoholic male with homoerotomania. Later, homoerotomania in a woman with a bipolar disorder was described by Bastie (1973). The latter was not exclusively homoerotomanic, having a history of hetero-erotomanic episodes also. Peterson & Davis (1985) reported the case of a man with schizophrenia and a chronic, fixed erotomanic delusion involving a man whose life he threatened when rebuffed. Signer & Isbister (1987) referred to a possible homoerotomanic episode in a schizoaffective woman, and homoerotomania in a woman with bipolar disorder and left temporal lobe epilepsy was reported by Signer & Cummings (1987).

Dunlop (1988) presented two cases of homosexual erotomania, in both cases women who 'developed passionate feelings, similar to those of a schoolgirl "crush"' toward, in one, a female hospital administrator and in the other a woman who worked in a store. The former, who had a past diagnosis of schizophrenia, repeatedly approached her victim and bombarded her with presents, including groceries, money (up to £2000) and even a set of garden furniture. In the second case, a 22-year-old woman spent much of her time purchasing goods in her victim's sales department. When she was banned from the shop she bribed strangers to go there and make further purchases from the victim on her behalf (see Chapter 10). She kept a diary that detailed her extensive and ambivalent feelings for her victim. Dunlop considered these cases to be very similar in other respects to those of heterosexual erotomania, satisfying generally accepted criteria for primary or pure erotomania. She noted also a lack of any sexual element to their amorous attraction, although Case 2 described her feelings as 'more than platonic'. The author suggested 'it is probable that these women could not have coped with more intimate contact', preferring instead this form of distant romantic worship.

Urbach and others (1992) wrote of homosexual erotomania in an adolescent, the teenager becoming aggressive toward her love objects when spurned. Meloy (1992) described a possible case of homoerotomania, an 'aggressive, hysterical, and paranoid' homosexual male who pursued, somewhat unusually, a schizophrenic man. He regularly approached his victim, haranguing him and insisting that his victim was in love with him. He would not agree to assessment or treatment.

Boast & Coid (1994) reported the first known case of 'male homosexual erotomania' in association with human immunodeficiency virus (HIV) infection. This 30-year-old homosexual man with acquired immune deficiency syndrome (AIDS)-related complex became enamoured of his volunteer support worker, who was himself homosexual. The patient modified his personal appearance to resemble the love object and made sexual advances toward him. The volunteer withdrew from the case but the patient continued to pursue him, angrily alleging that the worker had encouraged his affections. He sent bizarre letters with claims such as that their spirits had met and spoken to each other, and referred also to the writer's communications with Satan. He then left threatening messages on the victim's answering machine and ignited paraffin in the victim's letterbox, later telling him he wanted to watch him 'die in agony.' He was subsequently arrested and placed on probation with a mandate to receive psychiatric treatment. His psychotic disorder was thought to be reactive to specific stressors rather than a consequence of AIDS-related involvement of the central nervous system. Michael et al. (1996) also reported a case of homoerotomania in association with organic pathology (polycystic ovary disease), although the aetiological significance of this condition in the development of the patient's delusional disorder was similarly uncertain. This woman was bisexual and developed first 'homosexual' erotomania, in which the love object was her married female lecturer, and later 'heterosexual' erotomania involving a famous film producer. While the patient wrote letters, sent gifts and made sexual advances toward the former, there were no manifest stalking behaviours associated with the male victim, communications being limited to telepathic messages.

Cases of same gender erotomania and associated stalking behaviours have been noted in several larger series of erotomanic patients. Lovett Doust & Christie (1978) presented eight cases of erotomania, two of whom focussed their attentions on individuals of the same sex. One female developed homosexual erotomania following cortisone injections for eczema:

After the cortisone the patient became convinced that her older woman friend had developed a secret passion for her and felt it terribly urgent to be close to her. She felt that her friend was exercising a compelling power over her and was sending messages of support and encouragement during her sickness. The patient stated she did not know how these messages were conveyed, but was certain that she was receiving them and that they were being relayed by her friend. The patient was very much moved by these communications and felt that she had to respond. She would fondle her telephone at home in case it might suddenly ring and thus ensure that if the caller were really her friend she would be there to answer it. But it never did ring. Instead the patient would place calls to Vancouver in an attempt to reciprocate what she firmly believed was her friend's kind thoughts about her and respond to the love she knew her friend was feeling for her. Often the patient's calls were fruitless because no one was home when the telephone rang. On the occasions when her friend answered the telephone she would reassure the patient, telling her to rest and not to worry and certainly not to keep calling her as it seemed only to increase the patient's anxiety and must surely be very expensive. The patient was convinced that her friend's husband was inadequate. She felt that he was not only a poor provider, but also that he suffered from ill health and demanded far more of his wife's time and affection than she could spare. (Lovett Doust & Christie, 1978, p. 101)

The authors considered this case to be homosexual, while they regarded their second case, a male who manifested homoerotomanic delusions during bouts of heavy drinking, as ambisexual. Gillett and others (1990), in their postal survey of thirty-four consultant psychiatrists in the north-east of England, which requested access to the case-notes of patients demonstrating 'a delusional conviction of being in amorous communication with another person', found eleven patients, all female, who exhibited erotomanic phenomenology. One of these exhibited 'homosexual' erotomania, typically rationalizing the paradoxical responses of the woman she believed to be in love with her. This case received a diagnosis of bipolar disorder but the erotomania was noted to be refractory to treatment of the underlying mood disorder and was 'unrelated to the course of the bipolar illness'.

In dispelling the earlier notion of erotomania as a disorder of 'chaste heterosexual women' Giannini and others (1991) presented five cases of erotomania in sexually experienced women. One of these was employed as a private secretary to her victim, a wealthy married woman eight years her senior. Since there were no manifest stalking behaviours, the secretary's family dissuading her from forwarding sexually explicit letters to her employer, the older woman was apparently never aware of this homoerotomanic attachment during the two years of her secretary's employ.

Studies of stalkers and stalking victims

Harmon and colleagues (1995), in their archival study of forty-eight people charged with harassment and menacing, uncovered two cases of same gender 'obsession'. One of these, a 38-year-old woman with erotomania, targeted several women including her social worker and drug counsellor. In Zona et al.'s (1993) analysis of seventy-four case files of obsessive harassment, three of seven in the erotomanic group (one male and two females) were described either as homosexual or bisexual; three of thirty-five in their 'simple obsessional' category were described as homosexual, while two of thirty-two in their 'love obsessional' group were noted to be homosexual or bisexual.

Several recent stalking victim studies have commented on same gender stalking. Fremouw and others (1997), in their large college-based survey of stalking, found that 30% of females and 17% of males had been stalked. In what they termed 'a few' cases, subjects claimed to have been stalked by a person of the same gender. Tjaden & Thoennes (1998) found that 2% of male respondents in their study reported stalking victimization during their lifetime, 60% of whom were pursued by males. Men tended to be stalked by strangers and acquaintances who in 90% of cases were male. The researchers noted: 'There is some evidence that homosexual men are at greater risk of being stalked than heterosexual men: Stalking prevalence was significantly greater among men who had ever lived with a man as a couple compared with men who had never lived with a man as a couple.' The lifetime prevalence of stalking victimization in women in this study was 8%, with up to 6% of these reporting their stalker's gender as female. While it is noted that the majority of females were stalked by some form of intimate partner, the prior relationship in female–female stalking cases was not reported.

Hall's (1998) study of 145 self-defined stalking victims also found high rates of males stalking males. While females were with few exceptions stalked by the opposite gender, male victim respondents were almost as likely to be stalked by a male (female stalker in 52% of cases; male in 44%). In those cases in which stalker and victim had had a prior intimate relationship (57% of the total sample), males overwhelmingly targeted females (99%) while 1% of their victims were males. Thirty-three per cent of female postintimate relationship stalkers ($n = 3$) stalked females. In all, 5% of the intimate relationships that culminated in stalking were homosexual. Same sex stalking was more pronounced when victim and stalker had been prior acquaintances; of the 35% of cases in this category, 56% of males were stalked by males. Of the nine cases in which the stalker was previously unknown to the victim, same gender stalking occurred in three or 38% of females stalked by strangers and in the single case of a male stalked by a stranger. In our Australian survey of 100 stalking victims (Pathé & Mullen, 1997), 14% of the cohort experienced same gender victimization, ten of the eighty-three female victims (12%) being stalked by females, and four of the seventeen male victims (24%) stalked by males. These victim studies did not address the extent to which unwanted contact was sexually motivated.

Between 1993 and 1998 the authors collected data on twenty-nine same gender stalkers and compared them with 134 opposite gender stalkers referred to a forensic psychiatric clinic over the same period (M. Pathé et al., in submission). As this is, to our knowledge, the largest study to date of same gender stalkers, the findings will be considered here in detail.

Of the same gender group there were eighteen female and eleven male stalkers. The ages of these same gender stalkers ranged from 15 to 53 years, with a median of 38 years. Only two were in a stable intimate relationship, both of them male, while five were separated or divorced and twenty-two were single. Sexual orientation as reported by twenty-eight of the stalkers was predominantly heterosexual in 71% (sixteen female, four male), homosexual in five cases (two female, three male) and a further three, all men, declared themselves to be bisexual. Same gender stalkers were employed in fifteen cases (54%), three of whom held professional positions, eleven (39%) were unemployed, one was a student and another a housewife. This demographic profile was similar in most respects to the larger group of opposite gender stalkers with the exception of *gender*, same gender stalkers being significantly more likely to be female.

The duration of pursuit by this cohort of same gender stalkers ranged from two months to twenty years, with a median of twelve months. Again, this was not significantly different from the duration of stalking reported by their opposite gender counterparts. The most frequently employed means of contact with the object of their attentions was telephone calls (90%). One woman called her female victim more than twenty times a night, pleading for a relationship and variously claiming to be her daughter, her long-lost relative, and even that they were eligible to marry as she had had a sex change operation and was now a man! The victim changed to an unlisted phone number on several occasions but was repeatedly traced by the stalker who recommenced the barrage of calls.

Unwanted approaches were made by twenty-two subjects (76%), one woman driving for many hours to sit on the front porch of her victim's home in the country. Letters were sent or hand delivered by nineteen subjects (66%). A female who pursued her one-time physician took photographs of her as she conducted her hospital rounds. Subsequently she smothered the photos with lipstick kisses and then posted them to the hapless physician. Another wrote long letters demanding a relationship with her doctor, unconcerned that her victim was married with children because this meant she was 'more (sexually) experienced'.

Following and surveillance occurred in seventeen cases (59%). One infatuated woman purchased a year's gymnasium membership in order to attend aerobics classes and position herself behind her startled victim, compelling the latter to forfeit her gym membership. The stalker predictably followed suit. In another case the smitten stalker followed the *children* of her (married) love object as they walked home from school. An analysis of intrusion methods found, however, that same gender stalkers were significantly less likely to follow and approach their victim compared with their opposite gender counterparts.

Unsolicited material was sent by sixteen (55%) of this cohort. One female in pursuit of her office manager, a heterosexual single woman, sent the object of her attentions a selection of CDs by Canadian lesbian singer k.d. lang. Gifts from same gender stalkers were otherwise no more or less creative than those sent by opposite gender stalkers, flowers, chocolates and magazines predominating. Two cases, one female and the other male, sent pornographic magazines catering to the gay community.

Only three stalkers confined themselves to a single method of harassment (following, in the case of one male and repeated telephone calls by two females), with nineteen employing two to five methods and seven using practically every form of intrusion at their disposal. This pattern was not significantly different from that observed in opposite gender stalkers.

Threats were made by twenty-one same gender stalkers. In nineteen cases (nine female, ten male) the stalker threatened his or her victim, and twelve stalkers (six female, six male) threatened third parties. Four female and six male same gender stalkers made threats to both. An unemployed woman sent letters to her female counsellor of two years containing threats to shoot her and enclosed pictures of gravestones and a crucifix. Another who stalked her general practitioner made threats to 'eliminate' the victim's husband, and one female stalker threatened to kill her victim whom she (wrongly) believed was hindering her chances of marrying the man she admired from afar. One gay man felt powerless to control his ex-partner's harassment, since the stalker had threatened to inform both the victim's elderly mother and his employer of his homosexuality. The victim found the prospect of being 'outed' more distressing than actual physical violence.

Damage to property and pets was inflicted by 45% of same gender stalkers (six female, seven male). A spurned student kicked in her female teacher's classroom door, screaming obscenities, while an enraged and intoxicated woman drove her car over her ex-lover's dog. Occasionally, property damage serves other purposes: one woman tampered with her work colleague's computer so that she would be called upon to fix it, in the process brushing her breasts against the victim.

Attacks were made by eleven (38%) of the same gender stalkers on their victim, six by females and five by males. These were similar in nature to those reported by an earlier sample of stalking victims (Pathé & Mullen, 1997). One woman was punched, kicked and grasped around the neck by her young female student who was infuriated by being rejected by her. Sexual assaults occurred in two cases, one a gay man who touched his straight victim on the genitals, the other a woman who forcibly kissed her teacher-victim. In addition, the office worker described previously appeared to have frotteuristic as well as seductive motives when she brushed her breasts against her love interest while providing technical 'assistance'. Of nine (31%) who had a known offending history, five had committed previous violent offences against other individuals. Same gender stalkers in this series were no more likely than their opposite gender counterparts to have a prior history of offending, including violent offending. Furthermore, there were no significant differences in the incidence of property damage, violence (including sexual assaults), and threats between same and opposite gender stalkers.

The relationship between victim and his or her same gender stalker in this study was professional in eight instances (28%), the victim being their treating doctor in five of these (three female, two male), while three were students who stalked their teacher. A further eight stalkers and their victims had been casual acquaintances, while in seven instances (24%) contact between stalker and victim was initiated in the workplace. In four cases (14%; two female, two male) stalker and victim were ex-partners, while in two cases (7%) there was no prior relationship. Compared with opposite gender stalkers, significantly fewer instances of same gender stalking arose in the context of prior intimate relationships, while significantly more originated in the workplace.

Major psychiatric diagnoses were assigned to eleven same gender stalkers. Five manifested delusional disorders, one of erotomanic type, one persecutory and a further three with morbid jealousy (classified as delusional disorder, jealous type). Schizophrenia was diagnosed in three cases, one of whom had erotomanic delusions, and another subject had a bipolar disorder. In addition, there were two cases of morbid infatuation (categorized as delusional disorder, unspecified – see Chapter 8). There was a primary diagnosis of personality disorder in fifteen cases, most frequently borderline and dependent (four each), but also narcissistic (two) and antisocial (one), with four unspecified. A history of substance abuse was present in five (17%). This is not a significant departure from the diagnostic profile of the opposite gender sample, apart from an absence of paraphilias amongst the same gender group.

We have earlier proposed five categories of stalker on the basis of motivation and the context in which the stalking emerged (see Chapter 4.) There were group differences in stalking motive and typology between same and opposite gender stalkers, with more instances of resentful stalking among same gender stalkers and fewer involving rejection. It was not possible in one instance of same gender stalking to establish the motive with confidence. Eight same gender subjects (29%; six female, two male) were categorized as 'intimacy seekers':

Case example

Ms O, a 37-year-old clerk, was referred to our clinic by her (male) psychiatrist. This followed her eight-year pursuit of a married female doctor three years her senior. Ms O said she first met the object of her longstanding attentions as a psychiatric inpatient under her care. At that time, the victim was a psychiatry trainee who subsequently abandoned this career path as a consequence of her distressing harassment.

Ms O described an overwhelming sense of peace and tranquillity upon seeing the doctor for the first time, and there gradually emerged a conviction that they were destined to be a couple. She developed a strong desire for both a sexual and emotional relationship with this woman, but, given the doctor was also a woman, this was a source of some conflict. Ms O did acknowledge past homosexual relationships but had come to regard herself, at the time of meeting the doctor, as heterosexual. She resolved this by convincing herself that either her or her love object would undergo gender reassignment so that they could live as man and wife. Further, she became increasingly convinced that she and the doctor had been united as a couple in a previous life in which she was the male and her victim the female.

Ms O wrote the doctor a number of letters that were generally of a romantic nature. She made phone calls to the doctor's home and workplace, up to ten times a night, again addressing the doctor as her lover and relaying her plans for their perfect future together. She also attempted to approach the doctor on several occasions at her home.

At the time Ms O's infatuation began her life was in turmoil. She had had no sustained intimate relationships for many years and had become increasingly socially isolated, as well as experiencing serious financial difficulties. She had had a number of previous psychiatric admissions commencing five years prior to meeting the doctor, with a diagnosis of borderline personality disorder. There was no clear history of psychotic phenomena nor any sustained disorder of mood. She had no past history of stalking people of either gender. She was not prescribed any regular medication.

At interview, Ms O had a rather androgynous appearance. She was an intelligent and articulate woman who spoke candidly about her situation. She conceded that she had not actually elicited evidence that the doctor reciprocated her feelings, although felt that on several occasions she had sensed a warm and loving concern emanating from the doctor, albeit at a nonverbal level. It was noted that there were rather bizarre notions associated with Ms O's persisting infatuation, in particular those of the sex change and their union in a previous life, but these were not difficult to understand, since they enabled her to avoid the homosexual implications of her infatuation as well as to establish a claim to the legitimacy of her pursuit. It was noted also that Ms O did not advance any evidence from the doctor's behaviours or statements in support of her belief that a relationship would be possible. There were none of the paradoxical interpretations common to erotomania, no conviction that her feelings were reciprocated and no subsidiary ideas either about persecution or about organized schemes to keep her from her beloved. Ms O did not manifest any disturbance of mood and denied hallucinatory experiences.

Ms O's stalking and harassment of her former doctor was driven by her pathological infatuation with this woman. There was insufficient evidence that the infatuation arose out of a psychotic process but it appeared almost certainly on a substrate of borderline personality disorder and disturbed sexuality common to such characterological disturbance. Accordingly, antipsychotic medication was avoided in the first instance and she was offered supportive psychotherapy incorporating gentle confrontation with suggestions that the 'relationship' had now run its course and should be abandoned. Ms O gradually came to accept this, with the help of legal sanctions in the form of a protective injunction granted to the victim, who had thus far resisted such action on the advice of colleagues. Ongoing psychotherapy continues to focus on sexual identity and relationship issues.

In seven (25%; three female, four male) the stalking arose in response to *rejection* following, in three, the breakdown of an intimate relationship:

Case example

Ms X, a 30-year-old unemployed hairdresser, was referred to our clinic for assessment as a condition of a community-based correctional order. She had been convicted of stalking her former female lover. She said the two had met at a lesbian wedding and her friend, a 34-year-old journalist, soon moved into Ms X's flat. Theirs was a brief and tumultuous relationship; Ms X had a longstanding alcohol problem which had cost her several good jobs. She could not fund her drinking problem with social security payments alone and admitted to stealing money from her girlfriend. She became very jealous of her partner's relative affluence, interesting friends and supportive family, and began to accuse her of infidelity which her girlfriend repeatedly denied. Ms X none the less checked on her girlfriend's movements, frequently waiting up for her in a drunken state and berating her when she arrived home. On one such occasion, Ms X lunged at her partner (who had been working late to meet an urgent deadline), bruising her arm and tearing her jacket.

A week later, Ms X's girlfriend terminated the relationship and moved out. Ms X, both furious and panic-stricken, pursued her to her new residence and pleaded for her return. In addition to these approaches to her ex-girlfriend's home and workplace at any time of day or night, she repeatedly phoned her victim, wrote long, rambling letters and left soft toys with red satin hearts on her doorstep. Her communications generally vacillated between pleas for forgiveness and reconciliation, savage accusations of infidelity and threats of suicide or retaliation. During one drunken phone call she informed her horrified victim: 'I have a gun at my head and I'm going to blow my brains out, so you can hear what you've done'. Ms X began to appear at her ex-lover's home while she was away, scrawling obscene messages over her fence and upending rubbish bins. On one occasion she smashed a front window and bled over the lounge suite while awaiting her victim's return. Her terrified ex-lover immediately called the police but Ms X left before they arrived and no arrest was made. The victim was advised to apply for a restraining order, which Ms X breached on multiple occasions before being convicted of stalking. Her ex-girlfriend had long before left her job and moved to a secret address.

Ms X gave a history of troubled interpersonal relationships, having stalked two previous female partners, and restraining orders still operated in both cases. Morbid jealousy had plagued these relationships also, the second characterized by violence toward her partner and a serious motor vehicle accident caused by an argument and Ms X grabbing the steering wheel from her partner's hands. Ms X had seen various therapists since early adolescence. She described an abusive and chaotic upbringing, subsequent drug and alcohol abuse, promiscuity and a failed marriage in her teens, coming out at age 22. She had a prior criminal record that included prostitution, theft, drug possession, alcohol-related traffic offences and assault. Her erratic moods and periodic aggression had alienated most of her small social network and family.

Ms X was placed on a good behaviour bond and agreed to undergo drug and alcohol counselling. She also sees a psychotherapist but her attendance is erratic. She has, however, refrained from any further contact with her former lovers.

For a further four individuals in the rejected category, same gender stalking was precipitated by the breakdown of a friendship:

Case example

Ms K was a 28-year-old high school teacher who was referred by her local general practitioner (GP). She was, when first seen at the clinic, facing disciplinary proceedings arising from the persistent pursuit of the headmistress of a school at which she had been employed. The victim was in her fifties, married, with three teenage children. The stalker, despite having been transferred to a different school, despite the headmistress obtaining a court order prohibiting further contact and despite suspension from her job, was continuing to phone and to turn up at the victim's home.

Enquiries revealed that Ms K had been involved in similar stalking behaviour some five years earlier when she had persistently pursued a female lecturer at university who, like the current victim, was a married woman in her fifties with a number of children. This harassment had ended only when the lecturer took an extended overseas sabbatical and Ms K was persuaded to pursue her studies in another state.

Ms K, the only child of two professionals in senior positions in their respective callings, had a childhood as materially privileged as it was emotionally deprived. She was reared by a series of nannies and placed in a boarding school at the age of ten. Her relationship to her mother was always distant at best and that with her father markedly ambivalent. She had, as an adolescent, successfully striven to fulfil his immodest ambitions for her, attaining high academic distinction at school and the early years of university. Her first attempt, at the age of 20, to assert her independence over the choice of university course led to a rift that never entirely healed. She saw herself hence forward as a failure in her parents' eyes, a perception to which she responded by alternately either seeking to restore what she supposed to have been her parents' approval or fulfilling their worst prognostications about her inability and lack of direction.

Ms K had, in early adolescence, a close relationship with a school friend whose family she visited regularly and of whose mother she became inordinately fond. For several years she spent considerably more time in the company of this friend and her family than she did that of her own parents. When she was 16, this friend and her family moved overseas and other than letters in the first year they had no further contact. She found solace in a confiding relationship with an elderly teacher at the school. This woman continued to provide support to Ms K for the first year after she left the school but then the teacher retired and moved to a warmer climate, reducing their contact to the exchange of letters.

Ms K remained isolated in her late adolescence and early adult life, partly because of her commitment to the pursuit of high academic marks and partly because of her manner, which she acknowledged her peers experienced as aloof. When she moved into teaching, her isolation if anything increased. She shared few interests with her colleagues and, having considerable independent wealth to augment her teaching salary, she was conspicuously better off. As a teacher she was apparently talented but unresponsive to, or frankly dismissive of, the institutional and collegial demands that surrounded the classroom activities.

Ms K had had a series of heterosexual relationships but none had involved much, if any, emotional intimacy. Her chosen partners were her inferiors intellectually, socially and financially and were all either married or in another long-term relationship. She vehemently denied any homoerotic fantasies, let alone activities.

Ms K's first episode of stalking occurred in the context of what began as a mentoring relationship but which the lecturer, with presumably the best of intentions, had allowed to develop to the point that Ms K was visiting and even staying overnight with the lecturer and her family. This lady, like the headmistress at a later stage, seemed to have recognized Ms K's need for support and human contact. What they failed to see until too late was the insatiable nature of Ms K's appetite for care and concern. In both instances, when Ms K's demands began to become too intrusive the women attempted to extricate themselves from their involvement with her. Ms K responded by escalating her demands and by becoming intermittently angry at the perceived rejection. She wrote to, phoned and repeatedly approached the lecturer over a period of some six months and, when first seen, had been similarly stalking the headmistress for nearly a year.

Ms K claimed she was simply looking for a friend. She needed no interpretation to be offered for her to acknowledge that in part she sought both the mother she felt she had never had and a return of the idealized mother figure of her early adolescence. She sought from these women acceptance and admiration but her own insecurities fostered both escalating demands and a constant testing of their affection.

Eight same gender stalkers (29%; four female, four male) were categorized as 'resentful'. One of these was a local doctor who pursued a hospital administrator and made multiple death threats. He had lost his job through budget cuts for which he held the administrator responsible. Another 'resentful' stalker plagued the rooms of a cosmetic surgeon and threatened him with a knife because he was convinced his rhinoplasty rendered him effeminate and that the specialist's staff ridiculed him and spread rumours that he was homosexual.

In five individuals (18%, four female, one male) the stalking behaviours arose from social incompetence. Loneliness was the driving force for these individuals, two of whom had recently migrated to Australia (one from the Middle East and the other from the Philippines). One sought the companionship of her English teacher, with escalating demands on her victim's time. Although all five in this category strove for emotional intimacy none harboured any desire for a sexual relationship.

Victims of same gender stalking

Anecdotal reports suggest that victims of same gender stalking experience greater difficulties in their efforts to procure assistance compared with those stalked by the opposite gender. The victim's sexuality may be questioned, although only a minority of same sex pursuits in our series arose in the context of a former intimate relationship and most victims were heterosexual in orientation and practice. Homosexual overtones, regardless of the victim's sexuality, have been used to discredit the victim, one heterosexual journalist being asked by a cynical police officer whether he was a sex worker when he and his stalker met.

Many victims of same gender stalking allege that their complaints were not taken seriously. This is especially the case for female–female stalking, one woman commenting: 'As she [the stalker] was smaller and younger than me, they [the police] found my fear of her difficult to understand.' Given that *male* victims frequently report fears for their safety when confronted with the unwanted and relentless pursuit of a female (Pathé & Mullen, 1997) there is no reason to assume that female victims should feel any less intimidated.

In the study by M. Pathé et al. (in submission) information was available on twenty-two of the twenty-nine victims of same gender stalkers. All but three of these were heterosexual, most of whom being in stable relationships at the onset of the stalking. The overwhelming majority believed that their experience had had a deleterious impact on their psychological, interpersonal and/or occupational functioning. Seventeen (77%) had modified their usual activities as a direct consequence of being harassed. In thirteen (59%) social outings were curtailed to avoid the stalker, some victims driven by shame or humiliation to withdraw from family and friends. In ten (45%), work productivity diminished in response to the harassment, and in four cases the victim ceased work altogether. One victim – a well-built male who feared he might eventually be raped – drastically reduced his work hours to avoid travelling home in the dark. Six (27%) felt compelled to change their careers, and five (23%) moved residence in a bid to evade their stalker.

Additional security was sought by 64% of same gender victims, mostly in the form of unlisted telephone numbers, upgraded locks and the redirection of mail to private post office box addresses. One female teacher was provided with a security guard escort at work and another female victim, despite her stalker's diminutive stature, enrolled in self-defence classes.

Anxiety symptoms and feelings of powerlessness were acknowledged by 73% of the cohort, which was in accordance with larger, predominantly opposite gender stalking victim samples (Pathé & Mullen, 1997). The woman who had been subject to, amongst other things, her female co-worker's sexual advances at her computer workstation, was bitterly disappointed at the sluggish and ineffectual response of her employers and she ultimately moved to another department because 'it was easier to move me than [the stalker]'. The combination of her harassment, the unsympathetic response of her work superiors and the disruption and lost opportunities consequent upon the job change led to the development of a range of anxiety symptoms and psychosomatic disorders. She reported marked insomnia with recurrent nightmares of falling into an open grave and nobody coming to her rescue. She suffered panic attacks whenever she travelled alone and experienced constant tension, with headaches, muscle pain and bruxism requiring dental attention. She also developed a prominent startle reflex, knocking over a cup of water in our first interview in response to the abrupt onset of the air conditioner. This unfortunate woman had gained a substantial amount of weight through overeating and her inability to continue her gym classes, despite early morning vomiting most workdays. During this time she was also diagnosed with irritable bowel syndrome.

Same gender victims sought help from similar sources to stalking victims in general, most commonly turning to friends and family (73%), then police (60%), lawyers (45%) and the medical profession (41%). All but one of these, who openly acknowledged her prior intimate relationship with her stalker, reported dissatisfaction with the help that was received outside the family. There was a tendency for authorities to assume a sexual motive in such cases, despite increasing recognition of the heterogeneity of motives in opposite gender stalking cases. In some instances these assumptions appeared to justify desultory and sceptical responses to the complainant's plight. A female health professional who was subjected to a female client's repeated phone calls, letters, gifts and visitations felt ridiculed when her (also female) manager confidently assumed responsibility for the case ('because she thought her superior handling and heterosexuality made her immune to such attentions'), not that the victim or her stalker were homosexual nor was the motive a sexual one. Ironically, the client transferred her attentions to her new case manager.

Summary

Until recently our knowledge of same gender stalkers was limited to a series of case reports of so-called 'homoerotomania', most but not all of whom stalked the love object, as well as media reports of celebrities targeted by same sex fans. The phenomenon has generally been regarded as quite uncommon (Meloy, 1996), but the data emerging from victim studies (Pathé & Mullen, 1997; Hall, 1998; Tjaden & Thoennes, 1998) challenge this notion and raise questions about the nature and course of same gender stalking, as well as the relevance of present interventions. In the authors' series of 163 stalkers, same gender cases were by no means rare, comprising 18% of the sample. An analysis of the twenty-nine same gender stalkers suggests that they are notable more for their *similarities* to than their differences from opposite gender stalking cases, in a number of measures including their impact upon the lives of their victims. There were several significant departures, however, in that same gender stalkers in this study were more likely to be female and the prior relationship between stalker and victim arose less often from the breakdown of a former intimate relationship and more frequently within the workplace. Further, this group were less likely to harass their victims by following and unwanted approaches, these methods perhaps proving less essential in the repertoire of stalkers whose victims are, as it were, 'captive audiences' within the workplace. Same gender stalkers were more commonly motivated by resentment than their opposite gender counterparts and the absence of sexual predators amongst the same gender group was consistent with the finding that were no paraphilias diagnosed in these subjects. The psychopathological profile did not otherwise demonstrate any significant departure from the larger opposite gender stalker population. There was also no support in this study for a greater propensity for violence or threats among same gender stalkers.

Despite the similarities it appears that some stalking victims are confronted by sceptical and unsympathetic 'helping' agencies because they share their stalker's gender. Such responses may in part be fuelled by ignorance and homophobic attitudes, irrespective of the sexual orientation of victim *or* stalker. Same gender stalkers as a group may be no more dangerous than the opposite gender variety, but our data suggests that their victims suffer no less psychologically, nor could the disruption to their lives be regarded as trivial. Clearly it is important that stalking cases be judged not on the respective genders of stalker and victim but on the nature of the harassment itself and its impact on the lives concerned.

10

Stalking by proxy

In addition to the more direct forms of harassment described in earlier chapters, stalkers may involve other people or agencies in their attempts to communicate, contact or track their victim. We have termed those stalking activities that are perpetrated by others on the stalker's behalf 'stalking by proxy'. For the most part the involvement of others is unwitting. All manner of explanations may be offered by the stalker to encourage others to engage in these activities. Sometimes, friends and family members labour under the illusion that their loved one is in fact the *victim* of stalking at the hands of the true victim (e.g. see role reversal in Chapter 11). Some confederates are less concerned with the moral or legal implications, succumbing to bribes. In certain situations, such as delivery services, the transaction appears quite legitimate and may not arouse suspicion.

Victims may on occasion erroneously believe that others have been recruited by their stalker. They allege corrupt employees in telephone companies hired by the stalker to monitor calls or to interfere with traced calls, motor mechanics incited by the stalker to tamper with the victim's vehicle, or council workers recruited to watch the victim's home. These claims may have a delusional basis or reflect the overwrought reactions of a distressed victim driven beyond reason.

This chapter describes instances of individuals or agencies who have knowingly or unwittingly been suborned into assisting a stalker's pursuit and intrusions.

Private detectives

One of the more commonly recognized forms of stalking by proxy is the commissioning of private investigators to locate the victim and to monitor the victim's movements. The retainment of private security services allows the stalker indirect access to expensive and sophisticated means of surveillance. One private detective was paid a generous sum to follow his client's victim in a helicopter (Mullen et al., 1999). A woman who pursued a police officer hired a private investigator to photograph the man and obtain confidential details, including his police record number, passwords to his bank accounts and account numbers. This information was used to maliciously divulge information to criminals who had been arrested by the victim in the past (Silverman, 1998).

An infamous example in which the services of a private detective augmented a stalker's deadly repertoire was the tracking down and fatal shooting of American actress Rebecca Schaeffer by Robert Bardo. A private investigator was instrumental in locating Schaeffer's Los Angeles address through the California Department of Motor Vehicles, enabling Bardo to confront and murder the young star.

Private detectives are not commonly utilized as the cost is prohibitive for the 'average' stalker. In our experience they are more likely to be employed not by the stalker but by the stalking *victim* to provide personal protection or to gather evidence that may assist in the successful prosecution of the stalker.

There are anecdotal accounts of stalkers of celebrities who have obtained positions as security guards 'protecting' their famous target (Gross, 1994). In one case of noncelebrity stalking known to us, the perpetrator obtained a private investigator's licence in order to stalk his victim with relative impunity.

Case example

Mr Q had plagued his ex-wife since their marriage ended 18 months previously, breaking into the home she shared with her mother, vandalizing her property, besieging her with phone calls at work and home, staring through the bedroom window as she undressed and making repeated threats upon her life and that of her mother. Both women eventually obtained a restraining order but he breached this on countless occasions, once by attending his ex-wife's workplace (a legal firm), falsely accusing her of indecent acts against a niece and threatening a co-worker who demanded that he leave. He continued his campaign of harassment despite his impetuous second marriage to a Russian migrant. He then applied for a licence to establish his own private detective firm.

Despite his dubious history and his contempt for the restraining order, Mr Q was successful in the application and proceeded to outfit the company with a range of surveillance equipment, although his application for a gun licence was denied on the basis of the restraining order. His new wife joined him in this enterprise, assisting particularly with surveillance operations, always at the one address: that of Mr Q's ex-wife and mother-in-law, although his ex-wife was convinced that this woman knew nothing of the harassment nor even that her husband was previously married. She also suspected that his second marriage was one of convenience.

When the police felt unable to intervene in this man's persistent pursuit, since they considered his activities to be legal by virtue of his new-found occupation, the victim and her mother fled interstate, convinced he would one day kill them both. They now lead a sequestered lifestyle, which surprisingly, given their stalker's officially endorsed investigative skills, remains uninvaded.

Ordering or cancelling goods and services

Ordering goods that are then delivered to the victim is a relatively common means of recruiting innocent citizens to the stalker's campaign of harassment. Providers of various goods and services will naturally oblige, the usual examples being midnight pizza deliveries or flowers dispatched to the victim's address. One pizza delivery boy was instructed by the stalker to knock very loudly (at 1 a.m.) because the lady of the house was deaf! In some cases, stalkers have arranged for deliveries of firewood, manure and gravel and there are a few instances known to us where new cars, domestic appliances and entire lounge suites have arrived at the victim's address by order of the stalker. Stalkers have also subscribed to magazines on the victim's behalf; one of these was a weekly publication, such that the victim was forced to endure an onslaught of unwanted reading matter. Her efforts to cancel the subscription were initially ignored because the publishers were under the impression that she was seeking a refund without good cause. Monthly pornographic magazines arrived at another victim's address, creating embarrassment and exacerbating his feelings of fear and violation. Furthermore, his girlfriend of six months ended their relationship because she was unable to comprehend the magnitude of the problem, suspecting her boyfriend of leading some sort of 'secret double life'.

Stalkers may also *cancel* essential services in the victim's name. In one case the stalker persuaded the victim's local power company to terminate her electricity supply. Ironically, the victim reported greater difficulty in convincing the company of the deception than the stalker had apparently experienced in executing it: The victim was forced to stay the night with a friend before the power to her home was restored. She stated that she felt very vulnerable, fearing that she might at any time be plunged into darkness, rendering her easy prey for her tormentor.

Another tactic that has been adopted by some stalkers involves cancelling the victim's credit cards. A woman whose (ex-husband) stalker had reported her credit cards stolen experienced great embarrassment and inconvenience, and her temporary lack of funds heightened her sense of vulnerability. A similarly affected woman commented:

This [cancelled credit cards] was not only a terrible violation of my privacy. When the sales assistant discovered the card was stolen and I was suspected of fraudulent use it was the final straw . . . this guy is the criminal yet here I was having to defend myself to the police and the bank officials! I now avoid using any credit cards, because I feel great anxiety whenever I have to hand the card over . . . Of course, it means having to keep more cash in the house and that makes me pretty anxious also . . .

Finally, stalkers have on occasion advertised the *victim's* services. One placed job advertisements in local newspapers with the victim's contact details. In another case a man posted advertisements on the community bulletin board for his ex-girlfriend's (nonexistent) massage parlour, complete with her picture and contact numbers. These attracted a distressing barrage of enquiries at the victim's home and workplace (a primary school) from eager prospective clients and a less impressed school principal and police.

Friends and family

Stalkers will in some instances enlist friends, family or acquaintances to supplement harassing behaviours or even to 'stand in' for him or her so that the stalker creates the illusion of compliance with legal injunctions. Examples include persuading friends to repeatedly drive past the victim's residence (with or without the stalker on board) and friends and/or family members sharing surveillance of the victim. The wife of a man who stalked his female boss had been convinced that *he* was the one being stalked. At her husband's urging she made repeated abusive and threatening phone calls to the hapless victim, as well as accosting her at the local supermarket.

One young man promised his non-English-speaking migrant family that with their support he would win over the 'Australian lady of my dreams', a woman who had been friendly to him in a local store. This 'support' extended to family members joining him in renditions of romantic ballads in the street outside the woman's home, attired in T-shirts bearing the unfortunate victim's photograph! The victim ultimately moved interstate, believing that there was no other way to dampen the enthusiasm of her stalker or his family. She said that her fear and anger were tempered with embarrassment and guilt, as her pursuers had also intruded on her neighbours, adding wryly 'the singing was awful . . . .'

The criminal justice system

Courts can inadvertently facilitate the stalker's contact with his or her victim. The most frequent example of court-augmented stalking arises when the victim is required to testify in cases where the stalker is brought before the court on stalking or equivalent charges. Bringing stalker and victim face to face in the court room all too often serves to gratify the defendant's needs and to encourage continuing illicit communications. Paradoxically, the judicial process for some stalkers is perceived as an endorsement of their activities, especially by those defendants whose pursuit is driven by delusions. A famous example of court-mandated contact between stalker and victim was the stalking of actress and singer Madonna Ciccone, as reported by Saunders (1998, pp. 40–41):

In 1995 Robert Dewey Hoskins was arrested and charged with stalking and making a terrorist threat against Madonna, making terrorist threats against her personal assistant and her bodyguard and assaulting the latter. Hoskins was morbidly infatuated with the celebrity, alternately demanding they marry and, when rebuffed, threatening to 'slice her throat from ear to ear'. He scaled the wall of her home on several occasions, and was finally shot in the abdomen by Madonna's bodyguard during the ensuing struggle.

Madonna reportedly experienced nightmares about her deranged fan long after his arrest and remand in custody, but the ensuing trial proved to be a nightmare in its own right. Madonna, not surprisingly, was reticent to attend court and testify, so a detective in the case joined the media stake-out at her home to personally serve her with a subpoena when she emerged to go jogging. When Madonna ignored the subpoena, perhaps in the hope that compassion and commonsense would prevail, her attorney's pleas that the Material Girl [her hit record] was not a material witness were overruled in favour of the prosecution's argument that her testimony was critical in establishing that Hoskins' actions had subjectively put her in fear for her safety. A warrant was issued for Madonna's arrest, and the trial judge ordered that she guarantee her appearance by posting the equivalent of bail, in this case a sum of *US $5,000,000*.

In court, when asked how she felt about being face-to-face with the defendant, Madonna encapsulated the sentiment of so many stalking victims who have suffered at the hands of inflexible, even callous judicial processes when she responded:

Sick to my stomach . . . I feel incredibly disturbed that the man who has repeatedly threatened my life is sitting across from me and we have somehow made his fantasies come true [in that] I am sitting in front of him and that is what he wants.

Abrams & Robinson (1998) noted that 'some antistalking laws allow for gruelling cross-examination of the victim's past psychological history, which is similar to the revictimization that was seen with sexual assault cases, making the woman and her perceptions part of the offence . . . [I[mposing a standard of reasonableness opens the door to an examination of the victim's character, mental health, and stability'.

In a number of instances stalkers manipulate the legal system to establish courtroom contact by initiating spurious legal action against the object of their attention. Usually this takes the form of applying for a protective injunction against the victim, alleging that this person is stalking *them* (see Chapter 11). Gross (1994) reported the bizarre case of a woman who stalked her ex-lover and his wife, filing harassment, slander, assault and other charges against them. The stalker then acted as her own attorney and proceeded to 'verbally eviscerate' the defendants. Another stalker known to us failed in multiple appeals against her stalking conviction and a restraining order but then filed a civil suit against her victim, alleging slander, libel, defamation and perjury. Although she was unsuccessful legally, she was triumphant in achieving further contact with her distressed and weary victim, a victim who had been granted a protective injunction against the complainant in that same court five weeks earlier.

Other instances where the judicial system has effectively aided the stalker in his or her pursuit include a case in which the victim's (suppressed) address was inadvertently disclosed in court, and another where a victim's secret new address was provided to the subject of a restraining order by naïve court staff (apparently, to enable the stalker to keep clear of it!). One victim who had to give evidence at her stalker's trial complained that because she was required to continue her evidence after the lunch recess she was obliged to wait, alone and hungry in the court foyer, too scared to leave the building because there was only one small shopping centre nearby where she could purchase food and that was where the angry defendant had headed.

Lawyers are not immune to the manipulations of stalker clients. One victim's lawyer sent a registered letter to her ex-boyfriend who was stalking her to warn him that further harassment would result in legal action. The victim then received a letter from her ex-boyfriend's solicitor demanding a large sum of money which he (wrongly) claimed she owed him! The lawyer representing another woman whose ex-boyfriend refused to give her up began to make advances, stating: 'You can hardly blame [the stalker] . . . you're a very attractive lady' and when a protective injunction against the stalker was successful the lawyer conveyed her to an interview room at the back of the court, slipped his arm around her shoulders and told her: 'It's time you got yourself a *normal* man.' While his client was shaken and confused about this experience she was reticent to make an official complaint because 'it's just not worth it . . . with all that's happened [with her ex-boyfriend] who's going to believe *me?*'

When police fail to proceed with charges against the stalker or courts dismiss the case, they reinforce the power of the stalker, however unintended, and confirm the legitimacy of their quest (see Chapter 13). This may be the message conveyed to others also, diminishing the victim's credibility and supports. Examples abound where police have appeared more supportive of the stalker than the victim, especially in cases of ex-intimate stalking, in situations where the stalker is intelligent and plausible, which may be in contrast to an hysterical and erratic victim, and cases where the victim is physically attractive. Some victims complain that the reaction of law enforcement officers was experienced as further harassment and revictimization, one very attractive woman being told by police to 'remove the neon sign' from her forehead, implying that she invited the attentions of men and should therefore suffer the consequences.

By making spurious complaints against their victims, stalkers may also set in motion administrative harassment, as the victim is then subjected to investigation by various boards and tribunals. In one instance a man contacted the insurance broker of the ex-girlfriend he stalked, to advise that she had orchestrated a recent burglary at her home to claim the insurance, although *he* had been the real perpetrator. The woman was then subjected to an investigation. She told us:

I felt like the criminal . . . after all I'd been through nobody seemed able to comprehend my pain, and even though I was cleared – eventually – there was no attempt to apologise or to pursue the *real* criminal who wasted their time and resources; they still seemed to regard me as a party to it all, because Peter and I once dated. My reputation is tarnished . . . I feel like damaged goods.

There are also examples where the actions and persistence of stalkers have raised suspicions in the victim's workplace and prompted investigations into possible misconduct on the victim's part. One such case involved a male social worker in a community mental health service who was pursued relentlessly by a morbidly infatuated female client. The attitude of this man's colleagues and supervisor transformed from supportive and sympathetic (and relief that it was not them) to increasingly sceptical as the pursuit continued despite her 'failure to respond to reason'. Worse, the unfortunate social worker was refused his request to work in another part of the service, or at least to transfer the woman's care to another (preferably female) member of staff, 'because they thought I needed to *work it through* with her'! When eventually the woman comprehended his consistent rebuffs she phoned his supervisor to discuss their (fantasized) relationship, prompting a full departmental investigation. Ten months down the track the extremely disillusioned social worker left his job and is struggling to pay his legal costs. His name was cleared, but he no longer feels he has the confidence to return to his chosen profession. A similar case was reported in a popular health magazine (Silverman, 1998) involving a woman who stalked a police officer assigned to investigate her harassment of two psychiatrists. Despite the devastating effect the woman's activities had upon the detective's life, which had included hiring the services of a private detective to access confidential personal details as outlined earlier, he was subjected to an internal affairs investigation after some of his police colleagues became suspicious that the woman's activities may have been indicative of some sort of improper conduct on their colleague's part. Although the stalker was eventually imprisoned and the victim was cleared of any wrongdoing, it was at the cost of his marriage, his professional pride and his psychological well-being.

A woman whose approaches had been repeatedly rejected by her one-time psychiatrist (who had long before transferred her care to another therapist) complained to the medical licensing board, accusing him of sexual impropriety. Although he was later cleared of the allegations, the investigation caused the psychiatrist and his family much personal suffering. He declared that the entire process initiated by his stalker had damaged his reputation irreparably.

The medical profession

There are also disturbing accounts of the medical profession succumbing to the manipulation of stalkers. One victim's family doctor, who treated both her and the ex-husband who was stalking her, indiscreetly passed on her personal details to her stalker. He had in fact been apprised of the situation by the victim several months earlier when she consulted him about her disturbed sleep pattern but he uncritically accepted the ex-husband's allegations that the couple were reuniting. If he considered it strange that the victim had obviously not divulged her new address and phone number to this man he certainly did not dwell on it or concern himself that the woman might be placed at risk. We have also encountered instances in which medical receptionists have disclosed critical contact information to significant-other stalkers because the support staff were not acquainted with the risks. In one such case the treating physician was well aware of his patient's victimization at the hands of her estranged husband but had failed to alert his receptionist to the relevant security measures. In both examples the victim was forced to move to a new address and change her phone number, at considerable cost and inconvenience. Both have also changed their medical practice and practitioner.

From time to time we have also encountered psychiatrists and psychologists who, in the course of preparing reports for courts or legal counsel defending clients charged with stalking, have been seduced by very plausible defendants, with serious repercussions for the victim. One psychiatrist who interviewed the stalker-defendant for an hour concluded that the complainant – the defendant's psychotherapist – had in actual fact encouraged the defendant's advances. This was based entirely on the defendant's convincing but false account, without any reference to a wealth of objective, discorroborating information. Although in the course of the subsequent court proceedings the defendant's allegations were disproved, the victim's suffering was greatly exacerbated by the psychiatrist's preparedness to perpetuate the stalker's malicious portrayal of her.

The Church

The Church is another fiduciary body that has demonstrated its vulnerability to exploitation of this nature. One victim described her anger and disillusionment with the Church who, by providing support to her stalker, allowed his activities to continue and ultimately, she believes, helped him to evade prosecution. In this case, the stalker appeared to cultivate the sympathies of Church members by maligning her and endearing himself by presenting a picture of hypermorality. When the stalker was brought before the court on a charge of breaching a restraining order, the members provided glowing character references and naïvely recounted the defendant's many horror stories about the victim, all of which were the projections of the stalker's malevolent qualities.

Real-estate agents

Real-estate agents are a potential resource for stalkers. One was deceived by a stalker into attending the victim's residence with a view to selling the property. Several victims under our care have recounted instances where agents have been encouraged by stalkers to disclose crucial information, including the new address of the vendor-victim. When victims are forced to change residence as a consequence of stalking activities they may be too distressed and distracted to ensure that these details are withheld. Unfortunately, indiscretion of this magnitude can prove enormously costly.

Psychics

One morbidly infatuated woman sought the opinion of an astrologist regarding her future with her imagined paramour (her family physician). The astrologist unfortunately confirmed from the birth signs of both parties that they would indeed marry and she forecast a very happy future for them. Her beleaguered doctor did not share his ex-patient's excitement when she defied a restraining order to hand deliver the astrological charts to his surgery. In another case, a palmist predicted that her client (who had an erotomanic attachment to an artist) would die in the year 2000; this created an imperative for the fated stalker to step up her pursuit, so that she and her imagined suitor could wed and have a baby as soon as possible.

Motor vehicles

Stalkers can hire cars to conduct their surveillance activities, often with the intention of disguising their illicit presence. In effect, though, the behaviour instils considerable trepidation in their target, who becomes suspicious of every strange car in their street and especially fearful of any motor vehicle that travels behind them. One stalker hired a chauffeur-driven limousine and parked outside his victim's house. The chauffeur had never before been greeted by a screaming, knife-wielding young woman who clearly had *no* plans to accompany his client that night.

There are also examples where stalkers obtain personalized car registration plates to taunt their victim. One woman who absolutely refused to accept that her relationship with a businessman had ended obtained plates bearing the unusual surname of her ex-lover, then repeatedly drove her very recognizable vehicle past his workplace, screaming obscenities. Gross (1994) refers to the serial stalker in California who obtained two personalized license plates: ISTLKU and ISTLKU2 !

The media

The media contributes to the phenomenon of stalking in a number of ways. Many believe that the behaviour of the paparazzi who plague the lives of celebrities constitutes stalking in its own right, such that the term 'stalkerazzi' has been coined to describe them (Meloy, 1998b). Furthermore, their activities expose the readers of their tabloid newspapers to the personal lives of celebrities, promoting a false sense of extensive intimacy between celebrities and fans never before realized. In the Madonna Ciccone case, after her stalker was taken into custody the star's ordeal was far from over; the violation continued as she was then subjected to the scrutiny of the world press, with the media staking out her home. The ignorance and lack of empathy demonstrated by some reporters was astonishing, matched only by that of the Court and indeed of Robert Hoskins himself, portraying Madonna as unreasonable in her fears and heartless in seeking to prosecute this allegedly harmless eccentric.

Radio, television and cinemas variously foster the creation of such pseudo-intimacy. The accessibility of the famous individual through these media encourages in the suitably vulnerable the development of fantasized 'relationships'.

Media reporting of stalking cases is at times insensitive, and may encourage the stalker, with words such as 'husband' or 'boyfriend' rather than *ex*-husband and *ex*-boyfriend. Signer & Signer (1992) have observed that newspapers from time to time publish letters from stalkers in their 'personals' columns. They provide the following example, as it appeared in a Montreal newspaper in 1991. It was one of a series, probably written by the same man, who appeared to have erotomanic delusions:

Two years ago I was on Sherbrooke metro 1 cent dropped off me, one girl gave it to me. I said to her 1 cent is nothing, she answered me for good luck. One year ago she said to her girlfriend I am going to marry him. I saw her a couple of months ago. I am looking for her, but I cannot find her. I think she is German, many German girls know me. I am the most important for West. (Signer & Signer, 1992, p. 224)

Gross (1994) also provided an example of stalking via the print media, the stalker inserting menacing notes in the daily newspaper after the teenage girl with whom he sought a relationship began dating another man. They read: 'I'm out there. No telling what I might do.' and 'I'll be watching so I can catch you.' One stalking victim told us that the local newspaper regularly published her ex-fiancé's messages to her in the public notices section. This man, who had pursued and abused her since she ended their engagement nine months earlier, publicly demanded that she retract her statements to the police; these communications persisted, becoming increasingly intimidating over a six-week period, before the victim's lawyer threatened the paper's editor with legal action.

A talented singer/songwriter released a CD with lyrics directed at the ex-girlfriend he stalked, a mix of wooing, romantic songs and themes of being united in death. Attempts on behalf of the stalking victim to have a ban placed on the CD's release were unsuccessful. The victim heard her stalker's chilling descant over the airwaves while in a shop and was overcome; she can no longer bring herself to listen to any radio station, nor will she venture near shops where music is playing. She considers that the media and prominent people in the music industry have promoted her ex-boyfriend's intrusions at the expense of her well-being. She continues to lead an isolative existence largely bereft of once-pleasurable pursuits.

The Internet

It may be that the computer underworld, with its alternative universes, virtual realities, and cyberpunk counterculture, with the blurring of lines between fantasy and fact that it nourishes, will serve to quicken and potentiate the twisted fixations of the stalker . . . (Lloyd-Goldstein, 1998, p. 209).

With the advent of the Internet, the most ubiquitous of digital information networks, an additional vehicle for stalking has emerged. Electronic mail may constitute an exclusive mode of harassment or supplement existing forms of unwanted communication with the object of interest. The Internet can also facilitate the stalker's pursuit by furnishing him or her with intimate details about the victim from the wealth of personal data available in cyberspace. Currently, communication by email is restricted to a relatively small number of stalkers with the resources to access the network, although, increasingly, public venues such as libraries and Internet cafés offer these services. The advantages to a stalker of this newer form of communication are manifold. Digital information networks offer the user convenience and anonymity. Opportunities to be traced (and provide the victim with concrete evidence of harassment) are considerably reduced compared with telephone calls. Intruders may employ the services of 'anonymous mail redirectors', people who act for a fee as computer mail-boxes to protect individuals, including stalkers and networking paedophiles, by clouding the identities of the sender and source. As Cate (1996) pointed out: 'It is technologically impossible to monitor or control the content of Internet transmissions. The volume is simply too great. Moreover, monitoring [these] transmissions is undesirable in a society that values privacy because it would require service providers to read the 100 million private email messages that cross the Internet every day.'

Email messages are a potent addition to a stalker's armamentarium. Typically, multiple unwanted email messages are relayed to the object of harassment. Like its postal counterpart ('snail mail') such messages may or may not be overtly threatening but their capacity to induce fear and distress in the recipient is, in our clinical experience, substantial. For some stalkers, the pursuit is confined to the Internet (now commonly termed 'cyberstalking'), such that, increasingly, anti-stalking legislators in various parts of the globe have or are considering incorporating email harassment into the legal definitions of stalking (see Barton, 1995; Victoria Crimes Act). The Internet is in many respects an encouraging medium for stalkers, particularly as it 'allows communication with another person unconstrained by social reality' (Meloy, 1998b, p. 11). The Internet has spawned many a relationship that has foundered when face-to-face contact is made between the cyberspace correspondents and a less than perfect reality intervenes. These situations can precipitate a desperate or menacing flood of unwanted electronic communications from the rejected party, which may be combined with more old-fashioned methods of harassment.

Lloyd-Goldstein (1998, p. 209) described the Internet as a 'goldmine of online personal information' and the potential for misuse by stalkers cannot be overstated. Addresses, telephone and facsimile numbers, medical histories and photographs amongst other data can be accessed through these interconnected computer databanks. For instance, by typing in a name or phone number, one of the large telecommunications providers will supply free of charge additional information on the person of interest, including his or her address and even a road map to the victim's home. For a fee, however, stalkers can violate their victim's privacy on a much larger scale. The World-Wide Web offers a number of commercial online private investigator services, which can unearth information on an individual's legal history and assets, voting-registration records and even USA Social Security numbers. For a fee and 'a permissible purpose and screening process' one may access the most personal records. One of these will even allow access to a person's safe-deposit-box holdings. Incredibly, a specific home page for stalkers was set up in the USA for people wanting to stalk someone. The user specified the gender and region or city of their potential victim and the site then furnished a list of matches and telephone numbers/addresses for the stalking to begin. This absurd site has since shut down for obvious reasons (Pappas, 1997).

While victims of cyberstalking can exert some control over electronic intrusions by, say, disconnecting the telephone, he or she has much less influence over the flow of personal information to the stalker along the 'information superhighway'. In response to stalking incidents over the Internet as well as other privacy concerns, there are now sites that allow subscribers to sift through state, local and law enforce-ment Uniform Resource Locators (URLs) to see whether their names are listed. Services such as 'Cyber-Bodyguard' automate these searches, regularly scanning the Web and alerting subscribers by email if their name appears (Pappas, 1997).

On occasion, intimate details are volunteered by victims themselves. A naïve surgeon in the USA created his own website, which included photographs of his family and his luxury car (complete with registration number), details about each of his four children (including the schools they attended, their academic progress and sports achievements) and plans for the family's upcoming holiday. His enthu-siasm soon evaporated, however, when a disgruntled patient paid a visit to the family website. This led to a campaign of harassment spanning twelve months, when the stalker eventually succumbed to an illness for which he had held the doctor responsible. He followed the children as they walked home from school, scrawled graffiti over the surgeon's car and fence and repeatedly threatened the doctor and his wife. The terrified wife became increasingly bitter, blaming her husband for their ordeal and ultimately moving away with the children to a secret address. Devastated, the primary victim resigned from his hospital appointment on account of depression and deteriorating physical health, selling the family home and trading his beloved car for an unprepossessing second-hand vehicle.

Conclusions

Innocent disclosures, unwitting exploitations and inflexible systems that facilitate contact and communication between stalker and victim may all constitute stalk-ing by proxy. In most cases this form or extension of stalking creates dispropor-tionate distress to the recipient because it confirms to the victim that the rest of the world does not comprehend, trivializes or simply lacks sympathy for their pre-dicament. Worse, some may be viewed as willing accomplices. The sum effect is to heighten the victim's mistrust of others and isolate him or her from needed sup-ports. This situation lays fertile ground for imagined revictimization, which may also feature the co-opted services of others, as noted earlier and discussed further in Chapter 11.

As stressed in Chapter 13, victims must endeavour to enlist the support of others to maximize their protection against unwitting harassment. The information pro-vided need not be exhaustive but should convey the seriousness of the situation. It may be appropriate for victims to provide neighbours with a description of the stalker, or even a photograph. This applies also to work colleagues and security staff. Real-estate agents must be given clear instructions not to divulge any identifying information; this applies to any other agency where there is a potential for breaches of confidentiality. Many stalking victims harbour feelings of guilt or shame for their predicament, with consequent reticence to involve others, particularly strangers. They may avoid approaches to the aforementioned agents because their efforts to elicit help have thus far failed, and they feel increasingly helpless and pessimistic about the capacity of *anyone* to assist. Often, however, these approaches to would-be helpers engender community-spiritedness and protective responses, and mitigate the opportunities for stalking by proxy.

11

False victims of stalking

Introduction

Central to how stalking is constructed, both as a concept and in many jurisdictions as an offence, is the victim's perceptions of being harassed and rendered fearful. Given this subjective element it might be expected in some cases that there would be a genuine disjunction between the view taken of the behaviour at issue by the putative perpetrator and that of the complainant. Beyond such differences of perspective there is also a small proportion of individuals who claim to be stalking victims but who quite simply have not been subjected to the behaviour about which they complain.

Although false allegations of stalking have received scant attention in the literature to date, false victims of crime have been documented since biblical times in a number of cultures (Mohandie et al., 1998) and there is an expanding literature on intentional false reports of rape (Kanin, 1994), sexual misconduct (Gutheil, 1992), sexual harassment (Long, 1994; Feldman-Schorrig, 1995, 1996) and physical assault (Eisendrath, 1996).

Kanin (1994), who studied forty-five cases of falsely alleged rape presenting to a police agency over a nine-year period, observed that the false allegations served three main functions: to furnish an alibi, typically in the wake of regretted consensual sex or unwanted pregnancy; to inflict revenge, as in the case of a woman who retaliates against a rejecting male; and as a ploy to procure sympathy and attention. The author suggested that the attention seekers cause the least social harm because the alleged assailant is not identified, whereas, in about half the revenge seekers and most of the alibi group, the 'rapist' is named and in some cases wrongfully prosecuted. The study also found that false rape allegations are, in the main, the exclusive domain of women, since:

If rape were a commonplace victimization experience of men, if men could experience the anxiety of possible pregnancy from illicit affairs, if men had a cultural base that would support their confidence in using rape accusations punitively, and if men could feel secure that victimization could elicit attention and sympathy, then men also would be making false rape allegations. (Kanin, 1994, p. 89)

Some researchers postulate that, compared with sex crimes, 'Stalking as a behavior . . . is less threatening to the esteem of the claimant and thus represents an attractive option. Invasive and intrusive forensic procedures, such as rape kits, are also avoided' (Mohandie et al., 1998, p. 234). There are of course cases where the alleged stalking behaviours have encompassed sexual assault (see Case 4, p. 196). Furthermore, individuals who misrepresent themselves as stalking victims to elicit sympathy may well find that the response falls short of expectations, given the relative dearth of services available to stalking victims and the inappetency that has greeted many genuine cases.

The term 'false victimization syndrome' has been specifically applied to false stalking situations, for those stalkers who present themselves as *victims* of stalking. The Los Angeles Police Department data base suggests that false claims of this nature are rare (around 2% of all stalking cases.) They postulate that the phenomenon arises from 'a conscious or unconscious desire to be placed in the victim's role' (Zona et al., 1996). Mohandie and co-workers (1998) advanced a typology of related 'false victimization syndromes'. All of their cases consciously fabricated the alleged crimes, varying only by their characteristics, secondary gains and interventions. The authors referred to four cases of false reports of stalking documented in the literature since 1984, the perpetrator being unknown in all cases. They detailed a further three case histories encountered by law enforcement agencies, the identity of the alleged perpetrator being unknown in two. To these may be added the case of Australian entertainer Fairlie Arrow, who in 1991 alleged she was being stalked by an 'obsessive' fan, ultimately staging her own abduction with the aid of a male accomplice. She eventually confessed to her subterfuge, which was apparently motivated by her need to revive her flagging career. She was convicted of making a false complaint to police and was fined (Aus) $23 500, the money subsequently being raised by posing for *Penthouse* magazine (*Sydney Morning Herald*, 1992).

The aforementioned false claims of victimization were all conscious fabrications but other motivations or psychopathology may underlie false accusations. There are no published studies that have addressed the broader range of behaviours and diagnoses that can form a basis for fallacious allegations of stalking, or their management. Our clinic has assessed numerous stalking victims since 1994. Allegations of being stalked were found to be false in eighteen of these, all of whom were personally assessed, and in a further three instances the veracity of the victim's revelations was in doubt. While some of the eighteen pseudovictims conformed to the descriptions of false victims noted in the foregoing studies, it was clear that others were not deliberately confabulating and some in fact were frankly deluded.

This chapter examines this heterogeneous group of false stalking victims and presents a typology that assists our understanding of this phenomenon and informs treatment approaches. Given the paucity of studies in this area, we will draw upon the findings of our earlier series of twelve false victims of stalking (Pathé et al., 1999) to which a further six false victims have since been added (Cases 13–18, Table 11.1). In this study, victim accounts were judged to be false when they were clearly and repeatedly at odds with the available objective information. For those in whom the stalking was delusionally based, the claims were often inherently unlikely, if not frankly impossible. The benefit of the doubt was given to marginal cases where the victim's presentation was suspect, but where the presence of stalking could not be confidently excluded on the available evidence. These cases were not included in our false victim group.

Fourteen of the eighteen subjects were female, the cohort ranging in age from 25 to 55 years (see Table 11.1). Six of the subjects were referred by magistrates' courts, three by general practitioners, one by a general psychiatrist and eight were self-referred. Four had a documented history of mental disorder (delusional disorder, depression, schizoid personality disorder and dysthymic disorder in Cases 15, 5, 7 and 11, respectively.) Half the cohort had directly or indirectly experienced severe victimization in the past, five with corroborated backgrounds of spousal abuse, three a substantiated history of childhood sexual abuse, while another had witnessed a horrific industrial accident that had killed her son.

Three individuals who claimed to have been stalked were in fact stalking the person they accused, all of them appearing before the courts for such activities. Eight subjects had paranoid illnesses, which included delusional disorders with erotomanic and persecutory features (Cases 2, 6, 8, 9, 10, 13, 14 and 15), and in one instance schizophrenia with erotomanic delusions (Case 7). Three subjects had posttraumatic stress disorder (Cases 3, 17 and 11), the latter with superimposed major depression. One suffered a generalized anxiety disorder (Case 12) and another had a narcissistic personality disorder (Case 1). One subject was diagnosed with factitious disorder (Case 4) while the predominant diagnosis in Case 5 was malingering.

When compared with a group of 100 true stalking victims (Pathé & Mullen, 1997), there were no significant differences in age, gender or occupation between the false and genuine victims. However, whereas true victims were married or in de facto relationships in a third of cases, none of the fictitious victims was in a stable intimate relationship. Also, false victims tended to present earlier in the course of stalking, reporting a median duration of stalking that was only half that of true victims (twelve versus twenty-four months), although this difference failed to reach conventional levels of statistical significance owing to the broad range of stalking durations.

Pseudovictims were no more likely than their genuine victim counterparts to solicit the help of friends and family or police, but consulted lawyers and utilized

Table 11.1. Details on false victims

Case	Sex	Age	Occupation	Marital status	Relationship to 'stalker'	False victim category	Psychiatric diagnosis[a]
1	M	30	Actor	Separated	Estranged wife	Role reversal	Narcissistic PD
2	F	50	Computer programmer	Divorced	Neighbour	Delusional	Delusional disorder
3	F	30	Small businesswoman	Single	None	False revictimization	PTSD
4	F	30	Counsellor	Single	Ex-client	Factitious	Factitious disorder
5	F	35	Receptionist	Single	Acquaintance	Malingerer	Malingerer
6	F	50	Health professional	Divorced	Acquaintance	Delusional	Delusional disorder
7	M	35	Unemployed	Single	Acquaintance	Delusional	Schizophrenia
8	F	35	Health professional	Single	Colleague	Delusional	Delusional disorder
9	M	25	Unemployed	Single	None	Delusional	Delusional disorder
10	F	45	Welfare worker	Divorced	Neighbours	Delusional	Delusional disorder
11	F	55	Waitress	Widow	Work[b]	False revictimization	PTSD
12	F	40	Small businesswoman	Single	None	False revictimization	Generalized anxiety disorder
13	F	30	Secretary	Separated	Neighbour	Delusional	Delusional disorder
14	F	55	Cook	Divorced	Work	Delusional	Delusional disorder
15	F	45	Antique dealer	Single	Acquaintance	Delusional	Delusional disorder
16	F	40	Factory worker	Divorced	Work	Role reversal	Histrionic PD
17	F	35	Nurse	Single	Ex-intimate	False revictimization	PTSD
18	M	25	Tradesman	Single	Acquaintance	Role reversal	PD, unspecified

Notes:

[a] PD, personality disorder; PTSD, post-traumatic stress disorder.

[b] Stalked in the workplace and while on stress leave falsely believed she was under constant surveillance by worker's compensation fraud investigators.

Source: From Pathé et al., 1999: *British Journal of Psychiatry,* **174**, 170–2, 1999. Copyright 1999, the American Psychiatric Association. Reprinted by permission.

medical services such as general practitioners and psychiatrists significantly more often. Furthermore, while it was uncommon for true victims to seek the help of work colleagues or supervisors, eleven of the eighteen false victims solicited help from this source. There were proportionately more false victims embroiled in legal action: nine applied for restraining orders against their putative stalker, one was prosecuted for making false reports to police (Case 4), another went bankrupt through her inability to focus on her business (Case 3) and six were themselves convicted of stalking.

There were also noteworthy differences in the pattern of pursuit alleged by false victims. While there were no significant discrepancies between the two groups in their reporting of unwanted telephone calls, approaches, property damage and their receipt of unsolicited material, letters were less frequently acknowledged by false victims. The false victim group were also significantly more likely to allege following and surveillance. True and false victims were equally likely to report assaults and personal threats, but threats directed at a third party were substantially less likely to be reported by the latter group.

Eleven fictitious victims (61%) reported suicidal ruminations, as opposed to 24% of the genuine victim sample, and two-thirds described aggressive thoughts toward the purported stalker. None had acted on these, although a high proportion, all of them delusional, admitted to arming themselves (two with a gun, three with knives, two with baseball bats and another with illegally obtained capsicum spray), in preparation for their 'stalker's' anticipated attack.

Typology of false stalking victims

There are at least five broad contexts in which false claims of being stalked may emerge. The first is where a stalker pre-empts their victim's complaints by accusing the object of their unwanted attentions of being the initiator of the communications and approaches (Cases 1, 16 and 18). The second are those with severe mental disorders whose persecutory or erotomanic delusions encompass stalking (Cases 2, 6–10, 13–15). Third are those individuals who have been stalked in the past and who become hypersensitive to a possible recurrence such that they begin to see stalking in the perfectly innocent actions of others (Cases 3, 11, 12 and 17). Finally there are the two related groups, factitious victims (Case 4) and malingerers (Case 5).

Stalkers who claim to be victims

The perplexing and occasionally bizarre role reversal whereby the individual claiming to be the victim is in actual fact the *stalker* can arise in a variety of psychopathological contexts. The shame and humiliation experienced by certain narcissistic individuals in response to the termination of a relationship can provoke intense rage and retaliatory action in the form of false accusations and lawsuits in which the true victim is claimed to be behaving in the manner which has characterized their accuser.

Case example

Case 1: A 30-year-old struggling actor had been separated for two years from his attractive musician wife. He felt rejected and demeaned by her decision to end the marriage, repeatedly approaching her and demanding that she return. He kept her under surveillance, hiring private detectives to follow her and her female flatmate. He telephoned her home and workplace, alternately declaring his eternal love for her, and subjecting her to tirades of verbal abuse and threats. A telephone trace ultimately implicated him and he was convicted of stalking and sentenced to a noncustodial community supervision order, with a direction to undergo psychiatric assessment.

He was reluctant to be subjected to psychiatric scrutiny and strenuously denied that he had ever stalked his wife, appearing offended and resentful when his version of events was challenged. He was assigned a diagnosis of narcissistic personality disorder but was not found to be suffering any major mental disorder. He did not return for his second nor subsequent appointments and his co-operation with the conditions of his order was not enforced by his probation officer. Immediately the brief correctional order ended the stalking resumed, and his estranged wife, exhausted by his unrelenting pursuit and the apparent reluctance of police to assist, moved to a secret address interstate and as a precautionary measure obtained a restraining order. This further enraged the man and he promptly followed suit by applying for a similar order against her, in the process obtaining the details of her current address through an obliging court clerk. He alleged that his wife was harassing *him,* although there was no objective evidence for his claims. His wife was unfortunately required to return to her home state to appear in court alongside him. He rejected legal representation, delivering a dramatic courtroom performance, cross-examining his hapless victim mercilessly. Ultimately, astonishingly, the presiding magistrate granted the order against the true victim in the matter. She has since moved overseas while her now ex-husband, who has made no further contact, continues to revel in the resultant media attention which, although mostly negative, has provided the public exposure he craved.

Other processes may operate in these role reversals. It has been observed that some stalkers, by virtue of intrapsychic defence mechanisms such as projection and projective identification, attribute blame and a sense of threat and persecution to their victim (Meloy & Gothard, 1995; Kienlen et al.,1997). There are also documented instances of stalkers who come to regard themselves and their victims as one and the same. Perez noted: 'Most stalkers want some kind of union with the object [of their attentions]', and Wright and others described a process of 'fusion', whereby the stalker blends his or her personality into that of the victim. We have observed a number of instances in which the stalker has disarmingly remodelled his or her appearance to resemble that of the victim, some even appropriating other aspects of the victim's life.

Delusions of being stalked

An absolute conviction that one is being stalked may be encountered as part of a delusional system, usually of persecutory or erotomanic type. The sufferer harbours the belief that he or she is being stalked by one or more individuals, and may allege quite elaborate plots in which extensive networks of accomplices are recruited to monitor that person's every move.

It appears that, in recent years, society's growing awareness of the phenomenon of stalking is providing fresh material for delusional prepossessions. This is hardly surprising, given the centrality to many paranoid syndromes of experiences of being kept under surveillance, being followed and being harassed. The majority of deluded victims would not ordinarily be expected to present to psychiatrists but given that our clinic also provides a service for stalking victims we have had a unique opportunity to assess and offer treatment to a substantial number of individuals in this category.

Case example

Case 2: Ms AB, a 50-year-old divorcee, worked part-time as a computer programmer. She referred herself to our clinic, stating that she had been stalked for several years by a large network of people. She presented as an intelligent and articulate woman who had led a fiercely independent and celibate lifestyle since her marriage to her physically assaultive husband ended ten years previously. At the initial interview she was distressed and hyper-vigilant, fearing that other patients in the waiting-room were 'plants' hired to monitor her. She indicated that she first became aware that she was being stalked four years earlier, when she observed a male neighbour taking an inordinate interest in her activities. She maintained that this was prompted by his sexual interest in her, based on a series of innocuous events such as his whistling in the garden. She believed that her self-sufficiency and uninterest in his covert advances angered him, and his interest thereafter took a more malevolent course. She alleges that he circulated malicious rumours about her sexuality, painting her as a whore, deducing this from the furtive glances of work colleagues and, progressively, local shopkeepers and strangers passing in the street. She regarded her stalker as a very persuasive, influential man who could easily enlist the help of strangers to harass her wherever she went. She said that she was repeatedly followed when she was in her car, and unfamiliar cars tooted at her. Odd clicks convinced her that her telephone was bugged, and this, she contended, was the means by which her persecutors gathered knowledge of her movements.

Ms AB sought the help of police, lawyers, her local member of parliament and her telephone company. All were initially sympathetic, but later dismissive. Over the previous four years she had consulted three psychiatrists, each of whom advised her that she was mentally unstable and required medication. When she first attended our clinic, on the advice of a police constable who was himself feeling harassed by this unfortunate woman, she was notably sensitive to any indication of disbelief. At her third attendance, however, her level of distress and trust in her therapist were such that she agreed to a trial of the antipsychotic medication pimozide. She complied with the treatment, which was well tolerated at a relatively low dosage. The frequency of her diary recordings of suspicious incidents waned and she increasingly acknowledged the likelihood that some of the events over the years were benign and coincidental. Treatment, comprising pimozide and assistance in restoring her relations with family, friends and work peers, continues.

As noted in Chapter 8, erotomanic delusions may be primary, or secondary to a major psychiatric disorder such as schizophrenia. Individuals with erotomania are preoccupied with their imagined paramour, and, while it is common for individuals suffering erotomania to stalk their love object, in some instances they will come to perceive their love interest as the active pursuer (Segal, 1989; Prins, 1997). In the incubus syndrome, regarded as a variant of erotomania, the sufferer has delusions of imposed sexual approaches or intercourse at night by an unseen lover, the incubus (Raschka, 1979). Given the confidence of those with erotomanic delusions in the passionate persistence of their phantom lover it is perhaps not surprising to observe the delusion of being stalked arising in this context. Case 8 (see Table 11.1), for example, who developed erotomanic delusions in relation to a work colleague, was imprisoned for repeated breaches of the restraining order he had taken out against her. During her incarceration she alleged that he was bombarding her with seductive telepathic messages and upon her release she was convinced that he entered her home at night, made love to her as she slept and promised he would return to marry her.

The previously stalked

Genuine victims can subsequently become false victims, although there is no conscious intent on the part of these individuals to deceive. False reports instead arise out of the anxiety, fear and isolation that is so common to victims of stalking (see Chapter 13). Indeed, McCann et al. (1998) noted that, while fear reactions among crime victims in general diminish over time, precautionary behaviours may persist. Stalking victims exhibit a hypersensitivity and hypervigilance that can result in innocent situations being misperceived as threatening. Opportunities for reality testing are limited by their social isolation and mistrust of the supports that may well have failed them previously (Pathé & Mullen, 1997). Occasionally, these individual's groundless fears are actively reinforced by others; one woman who falsely believed she was still being monitored while her stalker served a prison term hired a private detective who had little difficulty in convincing her, despite the conspicuous absence of any evidence, that he had found two 'bugs' in her ceiling. This category features 'serial victims' who claim to have been targeted by two or more different stalkers over time.

Case example

Case 3: Ms TM was an attractive 30-year-old shop owner who was pursued by a stranger over an eight-month period. This man's predatory behaviours were sexually motivated, with obscene phone calls to her work and home, and on two occasions he stood outside her workplace and exposed his genitals to her. Ms TM's initial approaches to police were frustrated by their apparent reluctance to appreciate the seriousness of the behaviours, as well as their suggestion – based on her comeliness – that she might have encouraged these advances. She responded by avoiding police and other potential sources of help, instead abandoning her shop and returning to live with her parents. She maintained a vigil inside their home, noting any 'suspicious' happenings in the street outside. Eventually her parents, terrified for her safety as well as her sanity, insisted that police investigate, and the stalker was apprehended via a telephone trace.

The man was successfully prosecuted on a range of offences (stalking legislation had not been enacted at that time) and he did not continue his harassment of Ms TM. She remained quite disabled none the less, presenting to the clinic with symptoms of posttraumatic stress disorder (PTSD). She said she was unable to return to her job due to her severe anxiety, flashbacks and loss of confidence. She did not feel safe living alone in her flat, insisting that her mother accompany her everywhere. She isolated herself from friends, terminated her longstanding relationship with her boyfriend because of her mistrust of all men and attempted to thwart their advances by deliberately neglecting her appearance. Ms TM continued to spend long periods scanning the street of her formerly sleepy neighbourhood, noting the licence plate of any unfamiliar cars. Similarly, although she lacked the confidence to drive a motor vehicle, whenever she travelled with her mother she recorded details of any car that she suspected of tailing them, a camera at the ready to collect 'evidence'. She recorded phone calls on the answering machine, refusing to allow anyone to answer calls directly. Family and friends confirmed that her personality had changed drastically, from a staunchly independent, ebullient individual free from any prior contact with mental health services to an anxious, irritable, suspicious person.

These circumstances proved highly conducive to the genesis of subsequent allegations by Ms TM of victimization at the hands of unidentified stalkers. She angrily rejected family, police and therapists who pointed out the unsustainability of her charges, intensifying her efforts to collect evidence, so that she would eventually be vindicated by the police and courts as had happened in the past. Three further 'stalkers' were alleged, the first arising within weeks of the true stalker's prosecution. After two months of 'stalking' she became aware of the menacing presence of a different man whom she believed followed her in his car and threw rocks on the roof at home. There was no evidence to support these claims, nor to indicate that the behaviours were in any sense targeting her. Approximately six months later, while still reporting the strange noises at night (believed by her father to be possums), another 'stalker' emerged. He soon dominated her thinking, having innocently parked his car beside hers in a supermarket carpark. He supposedly followed her (although in a different vehicle), prompting her to insist that her mother speed through a red light, narrowly avoiding a traffic accident. She became convinced that this person was responsible also for two 'hang-up' phone calls that could not be traced.

Ms TM's treatment has focussed on the underlying PTSD, as well as assisting her family to deal with her difficult and disruptive behaviours. She sees a psychologist for cognitive-behavioural therapy, and there has been a significant improvement in anxiety symptoms to the point where she is able to leave the house unescorted, reports improved sleep patterns and is generally less vigilant. Working with a male psychologist has also enabled her to re-establish some trust in men.

The factitious disorder

In factitious disorders there is conscious simulation of physical or psychological symptoms in order to assume the sick role. As described for factitious sexual harassment, (Feldman-Schorrig, 1996), factitious victims seek gratification of dependency needs through adopting *victim* status rather than the sick role. These individuals, in addition to laying claim to victim status, invariably feign psychological symptoms, and occasionally physical symptoms, to support their allegations. This category should not be confused with malingering, although these individuals may acquire secondary motivations based on financial reward, or there may be a confluence of internal and external incentives for portraying oneself as a victim (Janofsky, 1994).

This category may also include cases who have genuinely experienced harassment in the past, with its associated rewards. These particularly include the gratification of dependency needs and receiving the sympathetic attentions of others. Subsequent (false) allegations of stalking serve to validate their identity as a victim, particularly if, through ineffectuality or scepticism, the authorities failed them in the first (genuine) instance. Victimhood becomes their career and potentially a permanent way of life.

Case example

Case 4: Ms V was a 30-year-old counsellor who worked for several years at a domestic violence clinic. She was referred to our clinic by a general practitioner after presenting to him complaining of anxiety and depressive symptoms consequent upon an eight-month history of being stalked. The referring doctor had not previously seen this woman and was not able to offer any additional background information. Ms V was a well-dressed, articulate woman.

She looked rather younger than her stated years and spoke in high-pitched girlish tones. She narrated an extraordinary series of events, which she conveyed in a dispassionate and vague manner, and the chronology of events was difficult to follow. She did, however, produce numerous items of 'evidence', including letters from the alleged stalker containing threatening and sexually explicit material, other unsolicited mail such as erotic magazines, itemized telephone bills in which she had highlighted countless unwanted calls, and photographs of obscene lipstick messages left on her bedroom mirror during a recent burglary at her home.

Ms V suspected that the culprit was a former client, but could not name any specific person. In spite of her rather homely appearance Ms V portrayed herself as very alluring to men, proudly alleging numerous affairs, mostly with work colleagues. She said a telephone trace failed to uncover the identity of her unwanted caller(s), which she alleged was due to a telephone company blunder. She said she had moved into another flat through fear, the rent being shared by a male acquaintance, although she said that he spent most of his time interstate. She took leave of absence at work because her productivity had diminished and her employers were perceived as unsympathetic. Ms V volunteered a range of subjective anxiety symptoms conforming to a diagnosis of PTSD, including insomnia, nightmares of being pursued by a faceless assailant, flashbacks to an alleged physical assault, intense fear of answering the phone, poor concentration and feeling edgy and irritable. She had earlier consulted a psychiatrist to arrange a disability allowance; he obliged, diagnosing PTSD.

By Ms V's account, her personal background was unremarkable. She had not experienced any significant illnesses and there was no history of drug use. She said she had dealt with several stalking cases in the course of counselling women in domestic violence situations, but denied any prior personal experience of stalking or other crimes. She claimed to be the only child of two adoring parents who were apparently unaware of their daughter's predicament. She was invited to bring them to one of our sessions but declined, stating 'it would be too upsetting for them.' Likewise, she refused permission to contact other relatives, friends, her mysterious flatmate or her employers, because 'they can't tell you any more than I've told you.' Indeed, she appeared to thwart all efforts to verify her story with outside sources.

Shortly after our first interview Ms V presented to our service unannounced, stating that she had been raped in her flat while investigating a noise outside in the middle of the night. She had called police and was examined by a forensic physician but there was no medical support for her allegations. She recounted, in detached legalistic terms, a vicious assault by a knife-wielding stranger.

Ms V was spending increasing amounts of time with lawyers and investigating police officers, as well as attending sexual assault counsellors. Police were perplexed by this woman, finding many anomalies in their investigation. This included the lack of evidence for the sexual assault and the likelihood that the small abrasions she sustained during the alleged assault were self-inflicted. They considered also that she was the probable author of the letters and the perpetrator of break-ins at her flat. Ms V was confronted with these concerns, and the lack of corroborative evidence for her allegations. She reacted angrily, threatening legal action against incompetent police, the examining forensic physician and the telephone company. She appeared so intent on 'beating' the sceptics that her fears for her safety and need to establish the identity of her 'stalker' were conspicuously subordinated. She never returned to our service, but her lawyers indicated she was continuing to receive 'counselling' with an unknown psychologist. We were later advised, some two years after her initial claims of being stalked and in the face of overwhelming evidence that she had fabricated her victimization, that Ms V was convicted of making false reports to police. She received a community-based disposition with an order to continue her existing counselling arrangements, albeit with a more enlightened therapist.

Symptoms and suffering associated with being a victim are relatively easily feigned, especially by an individual such as Ms V whose vocation brought her into regular contact with traumatized victims. Sparr & Pankratz (1983) have cautioned '[b]ecause the . . . condition's symptoms are mostly subjective, posttraumatic stress disorder (PTSD) can be easily simulated', an opinion recently endorsed by Freckelton (1997): 'diagnoses of PTSD are heavily dependent upon self-report and are not readily falsifiable nor easily disproved'. While monetary incentives existed for Ms V, in particular disability payments for PTSD, these were of less concern to her than the success of her 'condition' in eliciting support and satisfying her psychological need to be the recipient of legal, criminal justice and victim counselling services. Indeed, any secondary gains in her case were far outweighed by substantial personal losses; she emerged from court with a criminal conviction and humiliating media exposure, forfeiting her career and a comfortable lifestyle. Her disability payments were withdrawn and she now depends on social welfare.

The malingerer

Malingerers consciously fabricate or exaggerate claims of victimization for understandable external incentives, such as financial rewards or to evade criminal prosecution.

Case example

Case 5. Ms BR was a single 35-year-old receptionist who embezzled a large sum of money from her employer to fund escalating financial debts brought about by her gambling. Prior to her arrest Ms BR was a law abiding woman who devoted much of her time to church activities. She was the only child of hardworking Greek migrants who doted on her. Hers was a seemingly unremarkable childhood and she was held in high esteem by extended family and friends. A popular student, she received average grades at school and had remained in stable employment as a secretary since leaving school at 17. She dated men on a few occasions but had had no sexual relations because of her religious beliefs and upbringing. A male friend had introduced her to casino gaming machines two years prior to her arrest and for a time her gambling wins there and on horse races provided a welcome supplement to her income.

Ms BR had always prided herself on her efficiency and professionalism at work. When her father became ill with coronary heart disease and she was required to escort him to medical appointments to translate, her employer complained about her disruptive absences. She began to experience guilt and feelings of depression, finding solace in her gambling. Increasingly she dreaded her workplace, and was preoccupied with her 'escape' to the nearby casino after work. Despite her declining performance she spent increasing periods at the casino, in part to alleviate her dysphoria but also in a bid to win back the large quantity of money she had lost and repay accruing debts. She could rationalize her altered priorities because of her employer's apparent lack of compassion and because she had had to lie to her parents to obtain a loan, which she expected another win would repay. During this period, Ms BR found no time for her friends, some of whom were aware of her problem, and she shunned their efforts to assist. She accused a good female friend of 'jealousy', became argumentative with fellow parishioners and avoided church and family gatherings, ostensibly due to 'work commitments'. Her desperate bid to finance her gambling by stealing from her employer was exposed by the company's accountant and she made a full confession to police. She was released on bail and referred for psychiatric assessment.

Ms BR presented as an attractive woman who was distressed and tearful about the charges. In particular she was fearful that her parents would learn of her shameful behaviour and would disown her and return to Greece. She then contended that she was a victim, her gambling problem arising in the context of being stalked. She said that approximately four months previously she had met a Greek man on the train and that they had struck up a conversation. He had disclosed a few personal details but she knew little else about this man and did not speak with him again. However, on a few occasions she believed that she was being followed by the man, when she was in her car as well as on foot to and from the train station. She could not offer any explanation for his interest, although she thought that he seemed a little 'sleazy' when they had talked. She then claimed to receive some 'hang-up' calls at work and also at home, the latter whenever she was home alone 'like he was watching the house'. She recalls once receiving at work an anonymous bouquet of flowers which she 'knew' was from him; this was not witnessed by work peers because she dispensed with them immediately. She was vague regarding other unsolicited material, recalling that there had been a romantic card once, unsigned, which she was convinced came from her stalker, but there was no other correspondence and certainly nothing that arrived at her home address. Ms BR said she felt quite uneasy about this man's intrusions, which she perceived as threatening, although she could not recall receiving any specific threats.

He did, none the less, 'almost run me off the road' on two occasions after allegedly tailing her. Despite her concerns she did not approach police nor inform anyone else at that stage of her purported ordeal, nor had she documented any of these events nor retained any evidence. She claimed to feel 'ashamed' that she had originally spoken freely to this strange man and that people might suspect she had encouraged him.

Ms BR's allegations intensified as her court hearing approached. She gave dramatic accounts of strange noises in the night and shadows outside her window. She contacted her therapist (but not the police) several times, shrieking and sobbing and begging for protection. She gave clear descriptions of her pursuer's car, but never succeeded in obtaining its registration number. She appealed to her therapist and lawyer to suppress her name from the court proceedings out of concern, she said, that any publicity would increase her vulnerability to her stalker. She recounted her experiences to family, friends and work colleagues who responded with sympathy (even her employer) and was easily encouraged to seek monetary compensation for the psychological effects. When she learnt that monetary awards for victims of crime had been replaced, however, by a new scheme that offered free counselling sessions, she promptly withdrew her application.

Ms BR's account of her victimization was dramatic but inconsistent and could not be corroborated. When gently confronted with our suspicions that her allegations were fabricated Ms BR's initial defensiveness gave way to a tearful confession. Her allegations sympathetically reframed as a 'cry for help', she recounted some of the pressures of being an only child of non-English-speaking parents and her lifelong struggle to fulfil their hopes and dreams. She indicated that her secretarial job was unchallenging and that gambling provided a 'release' and introduced her to a wild and exciting facet of life. She was terrified of the prospect that her parents would discover her subterfuge, both her gambling and stealing and the subsequent false reports of stalking that she had hoped would protect her from the criminal justice proceedings and associated publicity. She did, however, consent to a family meeting with her therapist and a Greek translator during which her legal troubles were revealed. Further family sessions were productive, with Ms BR's parents showing some appreciation of the burden upon their daughter, and some easing of Ms BR's familial responsibilities was successfully negotiated. The elderly couple helped to support their daughter through her trial, which culminated in a community-based correctional order incorporating a requirement that she continue to receive counselling.

Ms BR's malingered claims of victimization were consciously intended initially to solicit the sympathies of family and friends shocked by her crime and to manipulate the outcome of her court case and avoid criminal prosecution, or at least public exposure of her crime. Subsequently she attempted to obtain crimes compensation on the basis of extravagant claims of psychological damage and financial loss. This illegitimate victim gave a dramatic but inconsistent and uncorroborated account of pursuit by an enigmatic, barely known stranger, who followed her, sent a card and some flowers and who telephoned her workplace and home. At no stage were his activities witnessed by others and the calls were always received when she was alone. Her tormented presentation was at odds with her behaviour. In particular, her movements were not obviously restricted by fear in the manner that characterizes the diffident stalking victim, Ms BR continuing to venture out alone at night to gamble.

Mohandie and co-workers (1998) deduced a number of descriptors that may be found in cases involving consciously fabricated claims of being stalked, many of which were in evidence in Ms BR's case. These include the relative lack of fear and feelings of vulnerability exhibited by false victims and their enlistment of significant others who rally around them. Discernible motives may well be present, but there is usually an absence of forensic evidence. The claims may arise in the context of situational stressors and family dynamics that include pressure within the family constellation. Other descriptors include the initial attributions of the complainant ('I am a victim' versus denial, disbelief, even self-blame in genuine victims); the presence of DSM-IV Cluster B personality disorders; a past history of manipulative and attention-seeking behaviour, and problems with the suspect, the false victim's notion of stalkers often being derived from portrayal of the latter in movies and magazine reports rather than real case dynamics. Instances of false stalking allegations purely for economic gain are rare in our experience, given the relatively small compensation and litigation-related monetary awards currently available to crime victims in this country.

The increased public attention accorded to the crime of stalking has generated a predictable rise in the number of victims coming forward in search of protection, counselling and/or monetary compensation. To date, services and resources have failed to keep pace, a situation familiar to rape victims before the appearance of rape crisis centres in the 1970s. Those confronted with stalking victims, whether they be health professionals, police, lawyers or the courts, generally have limited experience with these matters, hindering their capacity to recognize genuine suffering and offer appropriate intervention. Now, as in cases of rape and sexual harassment before it, we are finding that not all stalking victims are authentic and that a failure to identify these spurious and occasionally mischievous complaints early can prove detrimental on a number of counts.

Those who consciously or unconsciously make false complaints of being stalked prove costly and undermine the credibility of their genuine counterparts who in many contexts still struggle to have their experiences accorded the importance they deserve. Malingered victims, alert to this 'new' form of victimization as compensatable, deprive true sufferers, who have often incurred substantial financial losses in their efforts to evade their stalker, of limited public funds. The stalking victims we see typically consume a range of resources and our data indicate that *false* victims access a disproportionate share of legal, primary care and specialist psychiatric services. The cost to society of factitious disorders' subterfuge in particular can be substantial, as are the demands they place on law enforcement, and legal, psychiatric and victim resources. They may also place a considerable burden on other services to the point where such services themselves feel stalked. In one case, a locksmith was repeatedly approached by a deluded false victim demanding that he change her locks because she was convinced her 'stalker' continued to enter her home in the night. Another false victim, also deluded, made incessant approaches to her local member of parliament demanding that he '*do* something' to end her persecution.

Some categories of fictitious victims have remedial mental disorders and are truly tormented by their beliefs. Expedient treatment for individuals whose stalking has a delusional basis may in certain cases also diminish the risk to the falsely accused 'stalker'. The stalker who accuses his or her victim of harassment may succeed in obtaining a restraining order. Regrettably, this manipulation of the legal system all too often achieves its aim by bringing together both parties in the courtroom, further traumatizing the actual victim and gratifying the actual stalker's wish for revenge and/or contact with the object of his or her preoccupations.

Assessment and management of false stalking victims

In assessing stalking victims, it is essential to obtain as much objective data as possible. It has previously been noted in the diagnosis of factitious sexual harassment that the index of suspicion is heightened by 'a perplexing discrepancy between the plaintiff's apparent sincerity and the objective facts that seem to discredit her allegations' (Feldman-Schorrig, 1996), and this is equally pertinent to the false stalking victim. Feldman & Ford (1994, p. 30) have noted with respect to factitious disorders that 'doctors of such patients must be more than good diagnosticians; they must also be detectives.'

Although stalking has attracted more and more media exposure the actual details of the average stalking victim's experience tend to be limited to the more sensational. Assessing professionals, especially those familiar with stalking behaviours, will observe that the false victim's account lacks the consistency, plausibility and richness of detail evident in genuine cases. False victims are likely to present for help at an earlier stage than true victims, the latter frequently delayed by embarrassment, fear of being disbelieved or of being considered mad, or a failure to appreciate the seriousness of their predicament. Our analysis shows that false victims complain of the usual types of harassment, with the exception of receiving letters, where proof of these is not available. The two cases who claimed to receive letters, one with a factitious disorder and the other a malingerer, falsified these. Pseudovictims in our study were as likely as authentic victims to acknowledge personal threats from their stalker, but they rarely reported threats to significant others. This may in part reflect the egocentric nature of the false victim sample as a whole, the difficulty again of providing proof of threats to a third party and perhaps also the relative isolation of some of these individuals from other potential targets.

Other features that may alert the examiner to the illegitimate victim, irrespective of the underlying diagnosis, include: disorganized or convoluted histories that cannot be verified or are falsified by the available evidence; the engagement of multiple therapists, moving from one to another at the first hint of scepticism; and the possession of dossiers of 'evidence', the latter often proving to be of dubious significance. A repeated insistence that he or she is telling the truth and must be believed is found far more frequently. While psychotic false victims may present with bizarre accounts of stalking that can be discounted at the outset, genuine victims' stories can occasionally astound, attracting scepticism from practitioners less familiar with these cases.

There is a disproportionate representation of females in our series. This may in part be a reflection of the small population size. However, in larger studies of *bona fide* stalking victims males are likewise in the minority (see Chapter 3). It is conceivable that they are underrepresented in these studies because male victims may be less inclined to come forward for assistance compared with their female counterparts, particularly where harassment is relatively minor or involves same gender stalkers. Men in contemporary society are still largely discouraged from presenting as weak and needy, consciously or unconsciously. There are fewer incentives for them to falsely allege victimization.

Management of false victims rests with their early identification and treatment of the underlying disorder where indicated. Those with delusional disorders are notoriously difficult to treat owing to their lack of insight and refusal often to accept even small doses of antipsychotic medication. It is essential none the less to closely monitor this group because their fear and a perceived failure of others to take effective action can lead them to adopt their own desperate measures. One woman in our series armed herself with an unregistered shotgun and prepared to defend herself if *anyone* came to her door. Several others, tormented by their delusions of persecution, increasingly viewed suicide as the last remaining option. Another woman, whose disturbed mental state could be easily discerned by any observant lay person, paid tens of thousands of hard-earned dollars to unethical security consultants for the installation of surveillance equipment in her home. The same woman had a running account with a very obliging tradesman upon whom she regularly called to change her locks. While in this lady's case medication continues to be refused she has at least been rescued from financial ruin by accepting our advice (reinforced by a reputable private investigator and her lawyer) to refrain from spending any further money on useless security measures.

One must be alert to any opportunities that expand the false victim's information base and reinforce their self-perception as a victim. They should be excluded from support groups for crime victims, in particular those established for stalking victims.

Psychiatrists have an important role to play in assisting the courts to distinguish between valid and fallacious allegations of stalking, and the psychopathology that might underlie the latter. An improved understanding of the forces at play can assist in several key areas within the criminal justice system, including a more discerning approach to protective order applications and the minimization of trauma to falsely accused stalkers. The mental health professional can assist the court also in the disposition of convicted factitious 'victims' such as Case 4 by endeavouring to make the incomprehensible more comprehensible, and in those cases of false or grossly exaggerated victimization who seek monetary awards.

Summary

The vast majority of those who report stalking are genuine and despite acknowledgement of their plight through legislative changes, sympathetic media depictions, and the emergence in Australia and overseas of victim information/support groups, there remain many obstacles in the path of these individuals in their quest for personal safety and well-being. While it is not necessary to be suspicious of every self-designated stalking victim, this article delineates five broad categories of fictitious presentations, and some of the features that should alert clinicians and other professionals to their presence. We recognize that raising awareness of the phenomenon of false victims may appear at odds with the more pressing need to obtain recognition and help for the far greater number of legitimate victims but we are confident it will ultimately benefit our patients. With a more enlightened approach to the problem of dissembled victimization and relevant treatment measures, we are better positioned to ease the burden currently experienced both by true victims and by those driven by equally real distress and disturbance to make false claims.

12

Stalking and assault

Introduction

Stalking emerged as a significant social issue in no small part because it was presented as the harbinger of violent, and potentially homicidal, assault. Arguably the pre-eminent defining instance of stalking was the pursuit of actress Rebecca Schaeffer by a disordered fan who eventually attacked and killed her. This shocking example of the potentially lethal conclusion imminent in stalking was the stimulus to the first anti-stalking legislation (see Chapter 14). In other jurisdictions dramatic examples of stalking behaviours that culminated in serious or fatal physical violence provoked a public outcry that led to the initiating of anti-stalking legislation. In South Australia, for example, the initiative to introduce an anti-stalking Bill related to the killing of a personal assistant to a State Senator. The victim had been stalked by her estranged husband who followed her from one end of Australia to the other. Stalking was constructed initially as a form of threat. This all too easily converted stalking's importance into being not so much bolstered by the potential for violence but reduced to a message the meaning of which was a warning about imminent assault.

Associating stalking with dramatic instances that culminated in dreadful explosions of physical violence propelled stalking into prominence in the media, in the public mind and ultimately onto the legislative agendas of politicians. The advantages of this construction were manifest. One downside is that by focussing on the potential for physical violence raised by stalking it is possible to underrate, or even ignore, the pain and distress occasioned by persistent stalking in which no physical violence occurs (see Chapter 3). The other unfortunate, but inevitable, side effect of focussing in public presentations on the violent outcomes of stalking behaviour is that they will reinforce and amplify the victim of stalking's inevitable apprehensions about being attacked. The probability of assaults involving the infliction of physical and sexual violence occurring in association with stalking is the focus of this chapter. We would emphasize, however, that, although this is the most dramatic manifestation of the damage inflicted by stalkers, it is neither the commonest nor, excepting the extreme but fortunately rare examples of violence, is it necessarily the most distressing to the victim.

The lives of victims of stalkers may be laid waste without a hand being placed upon them. The constant intrusions, the fear and the sense of powerlessness can overwhelm the emotional resources of even the most robust of people without any assistance from the impact of direct physical attacks. However, quite reasonably, stalking victims almost always want a realistic appraisal of the risks of their being physically attacked. Equally police and courts seek guidance on the chances of individuals who have pursued a particular course of stalking presenting a future physical threat to the victim. Therapists similarly need some guidance about the probability of future violence in stalkers with whom they are working, or whose victims they are counselling.

Research in stalking has focussed primarily on documenting the level of violence, both against person and property. Few studies have been large enough to derive statistically significant associations between specific factors in the stalker, or their behaviour, and subsequent violence. Risk factors are simply this, statistically significant associations between the event and preceding occurrences. Risk factors do not presuppose, nor require, a causal connection between the risk factor and the predicted risk. For example, Monahan et al. (1999) found that a history of drug taking in the parents of a mentally disordered inpatient was a major risk factor for violence in that patient. A direct causal influence between parental indulgence and their child's aggressiveness many years later seems unlikely. Risk factors to be useful in constructing predictive actuarial algorithms require no quality other than a robust association to the predicted. In risk management, however, if you are to minimize the probability of an identified risk eventuating then a knowledge of the relevant causal connections are essential (Mullen, 1999).

Documenting the level of violence is the first stage. Establishing significant risk factors is the second. Deriving an effective predictive paradigm to identify high, low and medium risk groups is the third. The final stage is using such information to manage the risk and hopefully prevent, or at least minimize, the risk of violence. The stalking literature is still struggling in the first stage but as so often the unequal progress of knowledge in a new area has already resulted in hints about the other three stages.

Prior to stalking emerging as an organizing principle in this area of harassment there were studies that documented threatening and assaultive behaviours both in erotomanic pursuers and in stalking's immediate precursor, female harassment.

Erotomania and assault

Erotomania has, from its earliest recognition, been known to lead on occasion to violence (Esquirol, 1965/1845). Morrison wrote in 1848, 'erotomania sometimes prompts those labouring under it to destroy themselves, or others, for although in general tranquil and respectful the patient sometimes becomes unstable, passionate and jealous' (quoted in Enoch & Trethowan, 1979). Savage (1892) described a woman who became convinced, without grounds, that a romantic attachment existed between her and her doctor and that the doctor wished to marry her. Convinced that all that stood between her and her supposed lover was his wife, 'she found the wife was fond of chocolate creams and most ingeniously managed to introduce poisoned creams into the stock from which the doctor's wife bought her sweets. This resulted in several children being poisoned though the intended victim escaped' (Savage, 1892, p. 721).

Goldstein (1978, 1987) deserves the credit for being the first in modern times to draw clear attention to the potential for violence to occur as part of the stalking behaviour of erotomanics. Taylor et al. (1983) described four male erotomanics who were threatening and violent toward those that they believed stood between them and their supposed beloved. Leong (1994) reported on five cases of erotomania, referred for psychiatric assessment by the courts, all of whom had stalked the object of their affections, two of whom had made threats and one of whom had broken into the victim's house and another their car.

Erotomanics can resort to overt violence against the object of their affections motivated by rage at rejection or jealousy. Occasionally the assault may be an inadvertent by-product of the patient's clumsy attempts to approach the object of their attention (Mullen & Pathé, 1994b). Those believed to impede access to the beloved may also fall victim to the violence of an erotomanic. Taylor et al. (1983) and Menzies et al. (1995) found the violence to be directed most frequently at someone other than the object of the patient's affections, but in the series of Mullen & Pathé (1994b) and Harmon et al. (1995) the supposed beloved was the usual victim.

Mullen & Pathé (1994 a,b), in their studies of patients with pathologies of love, found that the object of the patient's disordered affection was at risk of violent assault. Of fourteen erotomanic patients assessed by the authors (Mullen & Pathé, 1994b), all of whom engaged in stalking behaviours, eight (57%) perpetrated physical or sexual assaults during the course of that harassment. In most instances the violence was directed against the target of their affection; however, three patients threatened and accosted third parties whom they perceived as impeding access to their beloved. In all, eleven attacks were committed against victims, six involving sexual assaults and five physical assaults. These assaults ranged from pushing and slapping to the fatal stabbing of one victim. Five patients (36%) also maliciously damaged their victim's property, most often vandalizing cars or causing extensive damage to homes. In all but one instance, assaults were committed by male patients. Violence was equally common among patients with pure erotomania and those whose erotomanic delusions emerged in the context of schizophrenia. This was a highly selected cohort seen in forensic practice and as might be expected was markedly skewed toward the inclusion of the more intrusive and violent examples of the erotomanic conditions. Nine patients had prior criminal convictions unrelated to their erotomanic preoccupations, most often involving physical and sexual assaults, one patient having a previous manslaughter conviction. The relationship between threats and subsequent violence in this study was variable. Only three of the eight assaultive patients had previously uttered threats. Indeed, the one patient who ultimately murdered his victim had used the least intrusive stalking methods, never directly communicating with his victim or approaching her, but rather engaging in surreptitious loitering and following.

Menzies and colleagues (1995) reported similar rates of aggressive behaviour in their study of male patients with erotomania. This study was the first specifically to examine potential predictors of dangerousness in this patient group. The authors compared the clinical and demographic characteristics of twenty-nine erotomanic patients who were distinguished on the basis of whether or not they had been assaultive. The cases in this study were derived from two distinct sources: (1) a clinical group consisting of thirteen inpatients assessed at two forensic mental health facilities in Canada, and (2) a sample of 16 patients derived from case reports of male erotomania published in the English language psychiatric literature. In the clinical group, the erotomanic delusions principally arose secondary to schizophrenia ($n=9$). Six of the patients were diagnosed with a coexisting Axis II disorder (in most cases antisocial personality disorder) and five presented with comorbid substance abuse or dependence. In contrast, the patients obtained from the published case reports were more likely to manifest erotomanic delusions in the context of depression or delusional disorder. Menzies et al. found that 46% of their clinical group ($n=6$) and 43% of the literature sample ($n=6$) exhibited 'antisocial' behaviour directly related to their erotomanic preoccupations. Antisocial behaviour was defined as physical harm to the victim or others, threats of physical harm or 'other potentially harmful behaviour'. The patients in the clinical group were reportedly equally likely to threaten or assault both the target of their affections and those perceived to be interfering in their quest for love. In the literature sample, antisocial behaviour was directed against perceived rivals or 'obstacles' in five of the six cases. The authors concluded that violence, when it occurred, was restrained (usually involving threats rather than physical attacks) and typically directed at a third party, rather than the object of affection.

The study by Menzies et al. confirmed the earlier findings of Mullen & Pathé (1994b) that erotomanic patients who assault are likely to have a history of other violent offending unrelated to their delusions. The results further emphasized the risk posed to third parties associated with the victim who were perceived as obstructing progress with the beloved.

Female harassment and assault

Jason and colleagues (1984) carried out two studies into female harassment by ex-partners. In their study of fifty women recruited by advertisement who were harassed after ending a relationship, fifteen (30%) were verbally or physically threatened or hit. No figures on assault as opposed to threat were provided. In their second study of forty-eight female undergraduates, three (7%) reported being threatened.

Stalking and assault

The first study to report on the incidence of assaults, on person or property, associated specifically with stalking was that of Zona et al. (1993). In this study, which proposed a typology of stalkers based on referrals to the Los Angeles Police Department Threat Management Unit (see Chapter 4), only two of the seventy-four stalkers were known to have physically assaulted their victims. Both cases involved stalkers classed in the 'simple obsessional' grouping, denoting for the authors that they had some form of prior relationship with their victims. The exact nature of the prior relationships in these two instances was not provided, nor were details regarding the nature or seriousness of the assaults against the victims. These 'simple obsessional stalkers' were also the most likely to damage their victim's property, although again the incidence of this behaviour was low (five out of thirty-five cases). None of the stalkers classed in the erotomanic ($n=7$) or love obsessional ($n=32$) groupings were reportedly violent toward their victims, and only one love obsessional stalker was known to have committed property damage.

An examination of the relationship between explicit threats to harm and subsequent violence in the study of Zona et al. (1993) revealed that few of the stalkers in this study acted on their threats. Although 65% of simple obsessionals threatened their victims, only 20% of this group of stalkers proceeded either to physically assault the victim or to damage their property. Similarly, while six love obsessional stalkers threatened their victims, only one subsequently damaged the victim's property. Most surprisingly, although 60% of erotomanic subjects made overt threats against their victims, none acted aggressively toward either the victim or their property. When the seventy-four stalkers in this study were considered together, over 70% of threats issued against the victims were not followed by assaults on property or persons. The incidence of threats and violence directed against third parties associated with the victim was not considered in this study.

The low incidence of violence in the study by Zona et al. (1993) precluded any attempts to examine for significant associations between characteristics of the stalker and assaultive behaviours. None the less, the findings provided an initial indication that stalkers with a prior relationship to their victim were the most likely to act violently, in terms both of assaults on the person and of property damage. The results also prompted early suggestions that the risk of violence associated with stalking may be minimal. However, the stalkers in this study were unlikely to be a representative sample, given that a significant proportion pursued film and television stars as opposed to ordinary citizens. These victims, by virtue of their fame are likely to remain inaccessible to their stalkers and well protected from unwanted intrusions.

Harmon and colleagues (1995, 1998) also examined factors contributing to violence in their excellent studies of stalkers referred to a New York Forensic Psychiatry Clinic. In their initial study of forty-eight individuals charged with harassment offences, 21% ($n=10$) were reportedly physically assaultative. In the majority of cases the violence was directed toward the target of attention, although two stalkers lashed out at third parties associated with the victim. Interestingly, assaultative behaviour was more common among stalkers said to have an amorous/affectionate attachment to their victim ($n=7$) than among those whose stalking was motivated predominantly by persecution and anger ($n=3$). While the authors were unable to analyse the contribution of psychiatric status and criminal histories to assaultative behaviour in this initial study, there were notably more patients in the amorous/affectionate group who were diagnosed with delusional illnesses (including erotomania).

The authors reported a significant correlation between threats of violence and subsequent assault among amorous stalkers, but not those in the persecutory group. Of the twelve subjects (40%) in the amorous group who made threats, five proceeded to assaults. In contrast, of the 10 (66%) persecutory/angry stalkers who threatened, only two subsequently assaulted their victims. Only 11% of amorous and 20% of persecutory stalkers assaulted the victim in the absence of threats.

In a subsequent study, Harmon and colleagues (1998) increased their sample size to 175 stalkers to enable further examination of the relationship between violence and offender characteristics. In the follow-up group, 61% ($n=104$) were classed as amorous/affectionate stalkers and 39% ($n=67$) persecutory/angry. The authors modified their earlier definition of violence to include not only physically assaultative behaviour, but also property damage and 'any physical contact' with the victim or a third party (including nonassaultative contact, for example, 'banging repeatedly on the victim's door', (Harmon et al., 1998, p. 240). Unfortunately, these behaviours were collapsed under the broad category of 'violent behaviour' and hence the actual incidence of assault, property damage and other forms of physical contact were not reported. On the basis of this definition, 46% ($n=81$) of stalkers exhibited violent conduct.

Contrary to their earlier findings, Harmon and colleagues (1998) reported that violence was not associated with the nature of the attachment, 48% of amorous and 45% of persecutory stalkers engaging in antisocial behaviour. However, the authors found a significant association between violence and the nature of the prior relationship between the stalker and victim. Over 65% of stalkers with an 'intimate' prior relationship (defined as spouses, romantic partners or family members of the victim) exhibited violent behaviour. This compared to 37% of those who were casual acquaintances, and 23% who were strangers to the victim. Psychiatric status was also significantly related to the incidence of violent behaviour. The most likely group to act aggressively were stalkers diagnosed with both an Axis II personality disorder and substance abuse, of whom 88% were violent. The next most assaultative groups were those diagnosed with a combination of Axis I and Axis II disorders (78% of whom were violent) and those diagnosed with substance abuse alone (73% violent). In contrast, patients who received only an Axis I diagnosis were the least likely to exhibit antisocial behaviour, with only 33% of these subjects reportedly violent. Thus the co-occurrence of personality disorder with either substance abuse or major mental disorder was associated with the highest incidence of violent behaviour.

An examination of the relationship between threats and subsequent violence again demonstrated that the majority of stalkers who threatened their victims subsequently acted upon their stated intentions (Harmon et al., 1998). A fifth of stalkers in the larger sample acted aggressively in the absence of any explicit threats; however, the majority who did not threaten also did not assault. The authors acknowledged that they were unable to reliably predict from the data which of the 20% of 'non-threateners' and the 60% of threateners would subsequently act violently toward their victims. None the less, the results further emphasize that the risk of escalation from stalking to assault is heightened in those with a prior intimate relationship with the victim and those with multiple psychiatric conditions, particularly the co-occurrence of personality disorder and substance abuse.

Psychiatric status was the principal dimension on which Kienlen and colleagues (1997) compared their group of stalkers. In their archival study of psychotic and nonpsychotic stalkers, a third (32%) were reported to have committed assaults. The incidence of violence was higher among the nonpsychotic (41%, $n = 7$), most of whom were diagnosed with an Axis II personality disorder or substance abuse, and lower in the psychotic (13%, $n = 1$). The victims assaulted by nonpsychotic stalkers were in each case a former sexual partner, the exception being one stalker who assaulted his mother. Over three-quarters of the stalkers in this study made verbal threats, 68% involving threats to harm or kill the victim, 20% to harm a third party and 12% to damage the victim's property. Nonpsychotic stalkers were significantly more likely to make threats (88%) compared to their psychotic counterparts (50%). The nonpsychotic were also more likely to follow through with their threats and intimidation, with over 50% acting on their threats.

The frequency and intensity of violence exhibited by the nonpsychotic stalkers in this sample was notable. Five of the seven stalkers who were assaultative committed more than one violent offence. The attacks included five physical assaults against the victim, four against third parties, a sexual assault against one victim and the murder of two victims. The nonpsychotic were more likely to brandish a weapon to intimidate their victim (47% versus 13%), although they were seldom used during attacks. Almost a quarter of the nonpsychotic stalkers assaulted a third party associated with the victim, a behaviour not observed in any of the psychotic stalkers. Consistent with other forensic samples of stalkers, seven nonpsychotic subjects had prior convictions for violent offending (five for assault, two for murder) as did two psychotic subjects (both involving physically violent offences). Clearly this was a highly selected group with a remarkable propensity for serious violence.

Sandberg et al. (1998) also reported that psychiatric inpatients who stalked or threatened hospital staff after discharge were more likely to be diagnosed with a personality disorder or erotomania than a matched comparison group of patients. In keeping with the other findings reviewed, some 94% of these patients had a previous history of fear-inducing or assaultative behaviour and were more likely to have a history of substance abuse than the comparison group.

Schwartz-Watts & Morgan (1998) directly compared the clinical and demographic characteristics of forty-two stalkers who were distinguished according to whether their harassment involved associated violence or not. There were no differences between the groups in terms of age, gender, marital status, education, history of substance abuse, or Axis I diagnoses. However, the violent stalkers were more likely to have been intimately involved previously with their victim.

Mullen et al. (1999) studied 145 stalkers to establish risk factors associated with threats and assault. Table 12.1 provides a revised and expanded analysis including a further twenty-three cases of stalking. Over a third of the victims in this study were attacked by their stalker. In addition some 6% of stalkers assaulted third parties who, they believed, were in some way impending their access to the target. In the majority of cases, the attacks constituted an impulsive lashing out in response to a rejection or perceived insult. The injuries inflicted were confined largely to bruises and abrasions. In fourteen cases, however, the victims were sexually assaulted, consisting of six indecent assaults and eight attempted or accomplished rapes. Assault was most prevalent among the rejected stalkers, eighty-four (59%) of whom attacked their ex-intimates. Half of the predatory stalkers (four) were also assaultative, usually committing sexual attacks against the victim.

Table 12.1. Frequency of threats and violence according to stalking typology

	$n=58$ Rejected (%)	$n=54$ Intimacy (%)	$n=24$ Incompetent (%)	$n=24$ Resentful (%)	$n=8$ Predatory (%)	Sig.
Threats to victim	74	51	25	87	37	0.000
Threats to third parties	47	41	8	42	0	0.001
Assaults on victim	59	24	21	29	50	0.001
Property damage	62	32	12	50	25	0.000

Note:
Sig., significance.
Source: Modified from Mullen et al., 1999.

Violence was less common among the intimacy seekers, the incompetent and the resentful, although a quarter of the stalkers in each of these groups did harm their victims.

Threats were made to the victim by 59% of stalkers and to third parties by 37%. Over a quarter threatened only the victim, 6% only third parties and 31% threatened both. The resentful (87%) and the rejected (74%) were the most likely to intimidate their victims with threats. Intimacy seekers made explicit threats against the object of their affection in over 50% of cases (see Table 12.1). The predatory and the rejected were the most likely to carry out their threats against the victim. The resentful were the least likely to act on their threats.

In keeping with the findings of Kienlen et al. (1997), nonpsychotic stalkers in our sample (Mullen et al., 1999) were more likely to assault than the psychotic (forty-three (44%) versus seventeen (26%)), although they were equally likely to threaten. Although specific psychiatric diagnoses were not associated with either threats or violence, subjects diagnosed with paraphilias and personality disorders were noted to be the most assaultative (six (55%) versus thirty-seven (45%), respectively).

Substance abuse was strongly associated with both threats and violence, as was a history of prior criminal offending. Of those who physically or sexually assaulted the victim, forty (69%) had prior criminal convictions. Such convictions were more prevalent among the predatory and rejected stalkers (six (86%) and twenty-eight (51%)) than in the other groupings. Although the prior relationship between the victim and stalker was not associated with overt threats, this factor was related to the risk of assault. Ex-partners were by far the most likely to assault (thirty-two, 64%), compared to stalkers encountered in work contexts (five, 25%), casual acquaintances (eleven, 32%) or strangers (six, 24%).

In order to detect the most salient predictors of violence Mullen et al. (1999)

entered the variables in regression analyses. Threats were predicted by prior convictions, substance abuse and typology (being highest among the resentful and rejected). Prior criminal convictions made the most substantial contribution. Property damage was predicted by both substance abuse and prior convictions. The risk of property damage was most strongly associated with substance abuse. Assault, as with threats, was predicted by prior criminal convictions, substance abuse and typology. Again for assault as for threats, it was prior convictions that accounted for the largest quantum of the variance.

The studies reviewed above are based on samples of stalkers. Victims are, however, in our view the most reliable source of information about intimidation, threats and violence. In practice many of the studies discussed above employed data from victim statements and victim impact reports to augment data direct from the stalker. It is unfortunate that the population-based studies of stalking victims performed to date give scant details of threats, property damage or assault. Hall (1998) provided data on the frequency with which her sample of 145 victims had been threatened or assaulted. She reported that 41% had been threatened, 43% had had their property damaged, 38% were hit or beaten and no less than 22% were the subject of a sexual assault. In addition eleven subjects in her series were kidnapped and two were victims of arson attacks. Pathé & Mullen (1997) in their sample of 100 victims reported similar rates of violence. In fifty-eight of the cases the stalkers had made overt threats, fourteen being directed solely at the victim, seven confined to family and or friends and a further thirty-seven threatened both victim and third parties. Assaults were reported by 36% of victims, seven of whom suffered predominantly sexual attacks. Property damage was reported by 36% of these victims. Threats preceded assault in 70% of cases. Assault was significantly more likely in victims who had had a former intimate relationship with the stalker.

Meloy (1998a, 1999) in important ground-breaking reviews of the relationship between threats and assault associated with stalking draws the following conclusions.

- Approximately half of all stalkers threaten the victim, the incidence being higher among those with a prior intimate relationship with the victim, or those with a real or imagined injury related to a business or professional relationship.
- The majority of those who threaten do not proceed to subsequent violence against the victim or their property. None the less, threats by stalkers should be taken seriously, as those who proceed to assault have usually issued prior 'warnings'.
- In approximately 15% of cases, the stalker is violent without prior threats.
- Violence usually occurs in approximately a third of cases, yet infrequently results in serious physical injury, most victims being grabbed, punched, slapped or fondled by the stalker.

Table 12.2. The frequency of threats and violence in stalking studies

Study	Sample $n=$	% Threats	% Assault	% Property damage
Zona et al. (1993)	74	45	3	8
Harmon et al. (1995)	48	46	21	NA
Harmon et al. (1998)	175	67	47[a]	NA
Meloy & Gothard (1995)	20	70	25	NA
Kienlen et al. (1997)	25	76	32	NA
Schwartz-Watts et al. (1997)	18	NA	39	NA
Pathé & Mullen (1997)	100	58	34	36
Hall (1998)	145	41	38	43
Tjaden & Thoennes (1998)	824	45	NA	30
Mullen et al. (1999)	145	64	36	40

Notes:

[a] includes physical assault, property damage and nonassaultative contact. NA, not available.

- The most likely victim of violence is the object of attention, followed by a third party perceived as impeding access to the victim.

Table 12.2 sets out the reported levels of assault in the currently available studies of stalkers and their victims. Reported rates for assault vary from 3% to 47%, most estimates lying in the 30%–40% range.

The studies of the violent behaviours associated with stalking have to date been based almost exclusively on highly selected populations in whom assault might be expected to be over represented. The studies of Pathé & Mullen (1997) and Hall (1998) on victims both gathered their samples in a manner that would be likely to recruit the more severely affected and, consequently, those at greatest risk of having been attacked. In the final analysis it will be properly conducted studies on random community samples gathering data from those who have been stalked that will provide the best picture of the prevalence of threats, property damage and assault in stalking situations. For the present we must work with the available information while retaining a healthy degree of scepticism about how far it can be generalized beyond the specific populations from which it derives.

Attacks on pets

An area of violence by stalkers that needs to be emphasized is that of attacks on the pets of victims. Hall (1998) reported in 13% of her victims that the stalker had killed or injured family pets. In Tjaden & Thoennes' (1998) study, nearly 10% of victims claimed that their pets had been killed or threatened. Victims seen in our clinic have recounted a number of horrific stories of pets being killed and maimed. They have reported dogs being poisoned, a cat being dismembered and sent back to the horrified victim in the post, goldfish boiled, poultry slaughtered, several dogs being deliberately run over by cars and one small dog being nailed to the distraught victim's front door.

Homicidal behaviour and stalking

A number of well-publicized cases of stalking have culminated in homicidal violence. Cases of the pursuit of the famous that have led to accomplished, or attempted, homicide include the killing of Rebecca Schaeffer and John Hinckley's attempted assassination of President Reagan. Malinquist (1996, p. 216) suggested that stalking can be connected to homicidal behaviour through what he refers to as 'self defeating patterns in love relationships that are not reciprocal, or in which one partner wishes to withdraw.' This attraction can be delusionally based but Malinquist suggested that the dynamics are more usually sadomasochistic, with continued attractions and approaches to those who flatly reject them. Like Meloy, he emphasizes the narcissistic aspects operative in the 'individuals self absorption with this one person' (ibid., p. 216). Such individuals can, according to Malinquist, resort to a final destructive act when they realize that their grandiose fantasies of establishing, or re-establishing, a relationship are unrealizable and that no alternative relationship could be of value.

There have been suggestions that the overall incidence of homicide in stalking is in the region of 2% (Meloy 1998a, 1999; White & Cawood, 1998). This statistic, it has been suggested, may even underestimate the true incidence of homicide, as the criminal offence of stalking is unlikely to be invoked in those cases where the offender ultimately murders the victim, being superseded by the more serious charge (Meloy, 1999). Such figures seem extraordinarily high. If we accept that the overall period prevalence of being stalked exceeds 1% per annum (see Chapter 2), and if we countenance a homicide rate of 2% in stalking, then stalking would, in and of itself, be expected to produce a homicide rate of 1 in 5000 per annum. This exceeds the known homicide rates in the USA of approximately 1:10000; in the UK of approximately 1:100000 and in Australia of approximately 1:50000 (Biles, 1982; Reiss & Roth, 1993; Malinquist, 1996). Clearly from these figures homicide rates in stalking cannot conceivably approach rates of 2% or even 0.2% for that matter. Homicide is fortunately a rare event (even if not rare enough). The risks of stalking having a fatal outcome will become clear only when there are adequate epidemiological studies and large enough forensic and clinical series. For the present the mortality associated with stalking must remain an open question.

Risk factors and risk management

At the time of writing, the studies on assault in association with stalking are too restricted by numbers and by selection criteria to generate the robust correlations from which risk factors can confidently be extracted. There are, however, a number of consistent findings that point toward a preliminary risk algorithm related to the probability of assault occurring as part of stalking.

The studies reviewed almost unanimously indicate that those being stalked by an ex-intimate are at a higher risk of being attacked than are those pursued by acquaintances or strangers (Zona et al., 1993; Kienlen et al., 1997; Schwartz-Watts & Morgan, 1998; Mullen et al., 1999). This can properly be used to support considerable caution in the management of those pursuing ex-partners or other ex-intimates. It does not, however, justify complacency with regard to probable violence in those stalked by, for example, strangers. First, the levels of assault by acquaintances and strangers remain high in reported series even if not as high as with prior intimates. Secondly, among the stranger stalkers are the predatory who are preparing for attacks of the most damaging type.

A number of studies indicate that those stalkers with major mental illness are less likely to become assaultative than nonpsychotic stalkers (Kienlen et al., 1997; Harmon et al., 1998; Mullen et al., 1999). This finding again needs to be interpreted with caution. Among the stalkers with major mental illness are included those with, for example, delusional jealousy. Morbid jealousy has a deservedly sinister reputation because of the frequency with which it is associated with violence directed against the partner believed to be unfaithful (Shepherd, 1961; Mowat, 1966; Mullen & Maack, 1985; White & Mullen, 1989; Silva et al., 1998). In the series of Mullen et al. (1999) there were six examples of morbid jealousy, all of whom were assaultative. The highest level of concern about future assault should be raised if, when evaluating a stalker with a paranoid illness, the content of their disordered preoccupations are found to be centred on the infidelity of the ex-partner, or in an intimacy seeker on the infidelity of the supposed lover. As research progresses, finer distinctions based on diagnosis will probably emerge with regard to assault. For the present it would be unwise for the clinician to ignore connections established in other contexts between violence and, for example, states involving particular delusional preoccupations (Hafner & Böker, 1982; Taylor, 1985; Link & Stueve, 1994).

Substance abuse is a marker for an increased probability of assaultive behaviour in the mentally disordered (Eronen et al., 1997; Steadman et al., 1998; Wallace et al., 1998; Soyka, 1999). Substance abuse has emerged as one of the most robust associations to subsequent violence in a wide range of individuals and situations. This association, not surprisingly, has been reported in studies of stalking (Harmon et al., 1998; Mullen et al., 1999). Those stalkers who are abusing alcohol and/or drugs are more likely to threaten, damage property, and attack than are their more abstemious confreres. As yet, no clinically useful distinctions have emerged between the abuse of particular substances.

In offender populations the nature and extent of prior convictions is one of the most robust predictors of future recidivism (Reiss & Roth, 1993). In the studies of stalkers, a similar association between a history of criminal convictions and subsequent assault has emerged (Menzies et al., 1995; Kienlen et al., 1997; Sandberg et al., 1998; Mullen et al., 1999). Violent or sexual offending in the past carries the highest risk, but any significant past criminal history, almost irrespective of the nature of the offending, increases the probability of assault in the stalking situation.

There have been repeated attempts to establish instruments that generate actuarial predictions about the risks of future violence (Monahan, 1981; Quinsey et al., 1998). Many such instruments attempt to elucidate personality factors believed to predispose to violent offending (Hare et al., 1990; Hart et al., 1994; Harris & Rice, 1997). At the time of writing, no studies of stalkers employing these fashionable aids to prediction (or is it stigmatization?) are available. Doubtless they will come. Violence in stalkers has been reported to be associated with prominent narcissistic personality traits and with borderline, histrionic, paranoid and psychopathic traits (Meloy, 1996; White & Cawood, 1998). Clearly this encompasses a wide range of characterological anomalies and will require refinement before such connections could contribute to the evaluation of the probability of future assault.

Threats should be regarded as promises. Like many promises, not all are fulfilled, but nevertheless they should be accepted as a commitment to future action until proved otherwise. Most stalkers who assault give warnings of their intentions by threatening (Pathé & Mullen, 1997; Harmon et al., 1998; Mullen et al., 1999). A significant proportion of stalkers who promise to hurt or injure keep their promises. Threats in the stalking context should always be taken seriously and should always be responded to as commitments to act. Further, threats are, in and of themselves, acts of violence. They are issued to frighten and intimidate, and for most stalking victims they amply succeed in those aims. The group of resentful stalkers, described by Mullen and colleagues (1999), who use threats as one of their central methods of creating distress in their target largely realize their intentions to hurt by the threat itself. This group seems less inclined to put the threats into practice. Even here, however, the threats are not always empty.

The motivation for the stalking would seem a likely candidate for at least contributing to predictions of the probability of assault. Unfortunately the motivations

of stalkers, and even their desires, can be contradictory and subjec
and change. The stalker pursuing a stranger they fondly believe is,
their one true love can become jealous, or can become enraged by
tions. Those pursuing an estranged partner may genuinely believe ....
intrusions are a function of their desire for reconciliation. All too easily, however,
the absence of the desired response from the ex-partner may ignite a vengeful rage.
The typology of Mullen and colleagues (1999) did demonstrate that stalkers of
different motivational types evidenced different frequencies of assault. These
results, although promising, do not as yet provide sufficient discrimination, in
themselves, to constitute guides to the risk of assault. They may, however, in concert
with other variables, help to identify high-, low- and medium-risk categories.

The ability to sort stalkers into high-, medium- and low-risk categories is a first
stage in establishing a useful algorithm for predicting the probability of assault. No
single study so far has the numbers to allow such calculation. A meta-analysis of a
number of existing studies is tempting, but in our view the populations studied,
and the methods of data-gathering, are still too disparate to justify combining
results in this manner. The existing studies are also hampered by selection processes
that almost certainly produce an overrepresentation of the violent and assaultative
stalker. For prediction, we need to know about who *does not* act violently as well as
who does.

A low-risk category should define a population with a probability of assaulting
their victim, or an associate of the victim, of less than 5%, over say the next year.
We know from stalking research, and more importantly from risk assessment
studies in general, that lower rates of assault are associated with:

 1 Not being a substance abuser.
 2 Being female.
 3 Having no criminal record.
 4 Not making threats.
 5 Not being severely personality disordered.
 6 Being employed.
 7 Having an adequate social network.
 8 Being a stranger to your target.
 9 Not being a rejected or predatory stalker.
10 Being compliant with treatment.

These almost exclusively negative attributes may yet be able to identify a low-risk
group when appropriately weighted and combined. For now, however, they can be
promoted merely as possible reassurance, but as reassurance that should be viewed
with a sceptical if not frankly jaundiced eye.

A high-risk group should include those with a greater than 70% or 80% chance
of proceeding to assault. The characteristics of the high-risk group can be advanced

with somewhat more confidence, in no small part because the existing studies contain so many such individuals. Increasing the risk of assault are:

1 Substance abuse.
2 A history of criminal offending, particularly sexual and violent offending.
3 Being male.
4 Making threats.
5 Having a personality disorder.
6 Pursing an ex-intimate.
7 Being unemployed.
8 Being socially isolated.
9 Having high levels of anger directed at the victim.
10 Having an intense sense of entitlement.
11 Fantasizing about assault (usually sexual).
12 Planning for an attack.
13 Having a facility with violence (this includes an interest in, and access to, guns).

White & Cawood (1998) in their extremely useful guide to threat management of stalking also suggested that the presence of depressive symptoms and suicidal threats should be regarded as risk factors. This fits with clinical experience, although it has yet to be confirmed in systematic studies. Again the existing data do not allow appropriate weight to be assigned to the separate risk factors let alone identify the three or four that best define a high-risk group.

Conclusions

Stalking is in and of itself a form of violence perpetrated by one individual against another. It is also a form of violence that may be the harbinger of assault. Studies have suggested remarkably high rates of assault associated with stalking and some commentators have advanced terrifying estimates of the risks of injury and death for victims of stalking. The substantive studies so far published are on highly selected groups and almost certainly overestimate the strength of the association with assault. This being said, victims of stalking are at risk of being assaulted by their stalker. The true risks of assault, although probably much lower than many current estimates, are almost certainly substantial. Given the frequency of stalking behaviours there is an urgent need to develop risk assessment profiles and, even more importantly, effective risk management strategies. The priority is to identify those with a significant probability of proceeding to assault and intervening to prevent that progression. This we believe will usually be attained by therapeutic interventions rather than forms of preventive detention, although only time and properly conducted studies will reveal whether that belief has real substance.

13

Reducing the impact of stalking

Introduction

The clinical studies reviewed in Chapter 3 demonstrate the destructive impact of stalking on its victims. Being stalked can induce depression, anxiety and chronic stress. The syndrome of posttraumatic stress disorder (PTSD) has been used here, as in so many areas of trauma and victimization, to describe and delineate the psychological sequelae of stalking. PTSD offers a label that encompasses the increased fear and arousal experienced by many victims, the deliberate avoidance of reminders of the harassment, and intrusive re-experiencing phenomena such as nightmares. Given the frequency with which stalking victims report such symptoms, the focus in this chapter is on the clinical management of these forms of psychological disturbance.

The efficacy of supportive, cognitive behavioural and pharmacological therapies in the treatment of traumatic stress has been reported, particularly for those individuals exposed to combat, sexual assault or natural disasters (for comprehensive reviews see Shalev et al., 1996; Foa & Meadows, 1997). To our knowledge, however, the utility of these treatments in the management of stalking victims has yet to receive empirical support. Unlike other forms of traumatic stress that involve life-threatening but relatively circumscribed events, stalking can present a more complex dynamic for the clinician as victims experience repeated and often prolonged trauma. The situation is akin to that of victims of domestic violence and, like them, stalking victims may present to health professionals during the course of their victimization. The management strategies reviewed in the latter part of this chapter are proffered as a guide, based on the authors' experience of treating stalking victims.

We should emphasize at this point that it is not our intention to 'pathologize' the suffering of these individuals. Like many victims exposed to traumatic events and disasters, those who are stalked do not invariably manifest psychological disturbance or other ill-effects as a consequence. None the less, we continue to see stalking victims who are so disturbed by their experiences that they require, and indeed request, clinical intervention.

Alleviating psychological distress and rebuilding confidence and trust are primary goals in the clinical management of victims of stalking. However, for most victims (especially those who continue to endure harassment) it is also crucial to address personal safety needs. A first priority in situations where the stalking is ongoing is to ensure that strategies are in place to protect the victim and his or her loved ones, as well as to discourage the stalker's intrusions. Victims of stalking desperately seek an end to the unwanted pursuit and this is often, not surprisingly, the most effective means of overcoming their psychological suffering. In those instances where it is not possible to effect immediate change in the victim's situation, supportive therapy and practical advice may prove beneficial to the victim's adjustment and assist in reducing the chances of progressing to physical assault. Ending the stalking does not per se always produce a full or immediate recovery from the stress-related symptoms. Victims often require continued intervention in order to regain self-confidence, trust and interpersonal competence.

As we have previously noted, stalking is a behaviour and a crime to which we are all potential victims. Although there are no strategies or precautions we can adopt that will guarantee immunity from the attentions of a stalker, this chapter commences with a discussion of common sense preventative measures that may contribute to minimizing the probabilities of being stalked. For those who find themselves the target of a stalker, we present a range of safety strategies and responses to circumvent the stalking and halt its progression to long-term harassment.

Preventative approaches

Stalking victims frequently ask how they might have avoided their ordeal. Could they have handled their situation differently in its earliest stages to stop the stalker in their tracks, as it were? Should they have 'seen it coming'? Individuals who have never had the misfortune to be victimized in this way are also curious to know whether there are any 'warning signs' of a would-be stalker, and counteractive strategies to ward them off.

Recognising the would-be stalker

Obviously, the stalker's history is significant but this may not be known to the future victim. The stalker may have convinced the victim that a former lover lied or set them up, or the seriousness of any past convictions is minimized. Some victims who have subsequently contacted their stalker's ex-partners have learnt that they, too, had been subject to similar harassment, in some instances ceasing only because the stalker formed a new relationship. Some stalkers had even continued to harass their previous partners while courting their next targets, without the knowledge of either victim.

There may exist early warning signs in the relationship which any prospective partner would be well advised to heed. Possessiveness, hypersensitivity, dependence, jealousy and moods that oscillate between extremes of undying devotion and angry rejection may all be observed in the potential stalker and may be instrumental in the healthy partner's decision to terminate the relationship. Stalking can in some instances commence while the couple are still together, particularly in instances of morbid jealousy, where the incensed partner checks upon his or her lover's movements by following, monitoring and phoning their workplace and other proposed destinations. While extricating oneself from such pathological situations is the only logical choice available to victims, this may well be the point at which the stalking commences or escalates. Some victims, in a manner similar to that of battered spouses, may then return to their tormentor in a desperate effort to appease them and to alleviate temporarily threats to their own and others' safety. This apparent ambivalence serves only to convince the stalker that persistence wins out and enhances the difficulties and risks of any future attempts to end the relationship.

Declining and terminating relationships

Few of us receive any tuition during the course of our lives in managing difficult social situations such as unexpected persistence from would-be suitors or ex-lovers, former friends or work associates. Gross (1994) emphasizes the wisdom of conveying clear messages to unwanted suitors or those who refuse to 'let go' of relationships. As discussed later in this chapter, if you do not wish to pursue a relationship with a person (be it romantic, a friendship or a business alliance), state this plainly and unequivocally. That a large proportion of stalkers are socially incompetent individuals who fail to grasp obvious, let alone subtle social cues necessitates that you be straightforward and unambiguous. The declaration 'I do not want a relationship with you' succinctly conveys your wishes and requires no further explanation. This statement should be delivered personally and directly to the pursuer, preferably in a public place or other venue where you feel safe. Do not use the telephone or a letter to convey this statement, as this gives the pursuers the opportunity to protest that they did not receive or understand your message. Your wishes should be delivered in a firm and reasonable manner that allows the pursuer to maintain his or her dignity and avoid giving them further reasons, particularly resentment or anger, to harass you. Upon receiving this message, a reasonable person, however disappointed, will ultimately respect your decision and withdraw. If they persist in making unwanted contact, your wishes are being deliberately disregarded, rather than misinterpreted (except in a minority of cases who may be deluded and prone to reinterpret the words and actions of the object of attention – see Chapter 8). Persistence on this scale at least confirms that your decision to terminate or decline the relationship was sound and justified.

Having delivered this message, do not engage in any further discussions with the pursuer or indulge them in counter-argument, debate or negotiation. You are not obliged to provide explanations for your decisions to anybody, particularly one who has persisted in unwelcome behaviour. Indeed, providing explanations often gives the pursuer the opportunity to challenge your decision. The statements 'I'm sorry, but I'm just not interested in a relationship at the moment' or 'I'm too busy for this right now' may imply that you could be interested in a relationship some time in the future. Worse, 'I already have a boyfriend' may be interpreted as 'I'd go out with you but for my boyfriend' with occasional tragic results as desperate stalkers have attempted to eliminate what they believed to be the only obstacle to the desired relationship.

As a final word of warning, do not attempt to 'let them down easily' by gently delivering your message in instalments – this serves only to prolong the relationship from which you are trying to extricate yourself. These situations are often uncomfortable, many of us preferring to be conciliatory and sensitive to the other person's feelings, even when they have shown a callous disregard for ours. However, this approach does not necessitate that you be rude or offensive; rather, the imperative is to be firm, both in your approach and your convictions. Attempts to let the other down gently may convey that you are undecided or ambivalent about what you want, and instil hope in the pursuer that persistence will eventually be rewarded.

Protecting personal information

Be selective about disclosing your personal details. Limit the distribution of your home address and telephone number to trusted service providers, ensuring that your records will be kept confidential. Where possible, provide a business address in those situations where you are asked to disclose contact details. One should consider establishing a post office box address for correspondence; this will also circumvent the theft of confidential letters from a private letterbox. Those who do not have a post office box should at least install a secure or lockable letterbox, so that the stalker cannot intercept correspondence. Victims occasionally receive disconnection or cancellation notices from service providers (e.g. telephone or electricity companies) because accounts stolen from their letterbox remain unpaid.

Ensure that all personal mail that is old or irrelevant is destroyed, rather than simply discarded. Some stalkers will rifle through the victim's rubbish in search of valuable personal information, such as credit card details from banking statements, or telephone numbers from phone bills.

The advent of the Internet has presented a further avenue for the access and abuse of a veritable wealth of personal information about us. Guidelines for minimizing cyberspace security breaches are discussed in Chapter 10.

Celebrity victims

Despite public figures being, of necessity, more attuned to the problem of stalkers and security needs, some continue needlessly to place themselves at risk. A staggering amount of intimate information is broadcast daily in the print media (particularly popular magazines) and on radio and television. It is still not uncommon to hear a media personality extolling the virtues of their favourite restaurant, holiday venue, new car, or even their children's local playground. Those with a public profile should avoid or at least minimize the disclosure of personal information. This strategy may conflict with the agenda of media publicists and employers for whom popular celebrities who are 'accessible' and 'down-to-earth' guarantee better ratings and advertising revenue. However, given the growing number of celebrities reporting unwanted intrusions by overzealous fans there is no longer room for complacency.

For some fans, the disclosure of intimate details about their idol is cause for disillusionment rather than encouraging the pursuit of a closer relationship with the celebrity, inciting attacks on the celebrity or third parties:

Mark Chapman's decision to kill his hero John Lennon may have been triggered by an article published in October 1980. The piece examined Lennon's life as an eccentric semi-recluse, dominated by his Japanese wife Yoko Ono. He did not emerge as an idealist, but rather as an extremely rich 40-year-old who watched daytime television and who amused himself speculating on property. Chapman felt so deeply upset by his icon that he decided to kill him. (Ritchie, 1995, p. 66).

De Becker (1997) advises his portfolio of famous clients to refrain from conducting interviews in, or allow any photographs of, their homes. Disclosing information about one's home in particular gives stalkers the impression of intimacy with the victim and conveys the message that their home is not 'off limits'. Such interviews can also provide valuable clues regarding the precise location of the celebrity's residence. Of course, many celebrities now jealously guard their privacy, and it is the paparazzi – whose behaviours may constitute stalking in their own right (see Chapter 10) – who expose celebrities' most intimate secrets, however exaggerated or fabricated, to the outside world.

Strategies to combat stalking

Since stalking is not a uniform behaviour with a singular motivation there is no single, effective strategy for eradicating it. The best strategies for dealing with stalking are those that take into account the individual circumstances, including the nature of any prior relationship between the victim and the stalker, the methods used to harass and the chronology of events. Nevertheless, various authorities have proposed a number of overarching strategies to combat the problem. It should be emphasized that there is no consensus regarding the general utility and effectiveness of these techniques; indeed, certain approaches draw vehement debate from some groups according to whether, or how, they should be applied. A review of these techniques follows, with particular emphasis on those we have found to be beneficial in our clinical practice.

Informing others

Victims should inform various trusted people that they are being stalked. Neighbours, workmates or friends who are unaware of the victim's predicament can inadvertently disclose important information to the stalker. It is useful, where appropriate, to provide others with a photograph or description of the stalker, so that they can be alerted to any intrusions. One victim attending our clinic actually posted photographs of her stalker all around the neighbourhood, asking people to report any sightings of the man to her or the police, as she had a restraining order prohibiting his presence in that area.

Where children are also potential secondary targets it is important that they be instructed in basic safety drills (including having the phone numbers of emergency services beside the phone) and that their school is notified of the situation and security arrangements; again, a snapshot of the stalker should be made available to relevant staff.

Helping agencies

Victims should also contact appropriate helping agencies, such as victim support organisations, mental health clinics, domestic and sexual violence programmes where applicable, or the police (Orion, 1997; National Victim Center, 1998). Ideally, victims should approach those groups or organizations who can claim some familiarity with stalking and who can assist them to devise an individualized response plan, although there is a lamentable dearth of such services in most communities. In our experience, although more generalist helping agencies such as family doctors or local police make earnest attempts to assist stalking victims, they may, through unfamiliarity with these behaviours, suggest approaches that are likely to inflame or escalate the situation and thus exacerbate the victim's distress and confusion. These services are likely to be more useful in providing referrals to agencies with the requisite expertise to provide stalking victims with sound and effective advice aimed at controlling the stalker's intrusions and minimizing further damage and disruption to the complainant.

In dealing with police, victims should provide as much objective documentation as possible (see below). A stalking victim who has been sufficiently organized to keep times and dates of various incidents will ease the often onerous task of typically underresourced law enforcement agencies who may be confronted with a complex trail of behaviours spanning months or even years, some of which do not of themselves constitute criminal behaviour. Victims who feel their complaints are not given proper weight can request to speak with a more senior police officer. Many who receive cursory treatment at the hands of the junior constable manning the front desk are unaware of this option, or indeed the existence of more specialized police units who may be more sensitive to the needs of victims. It is helpful if one or two specific officers can be assigned to the case, as the police will be spared much time and the victim unnecessary distress by avoiding the retelling of his or her story on multiple occasions to unfamiliar staff. It is also easier to appreciate a course of criminal conduct if the officer concerned is well-acquainted with the wider context of each new complaint. When police do investigate a victim's complaint it is essential that the victim receive some written record of this, such as an incident report, which may be important in any future legal proceedings. It is not advisable to rely solely on police record keeping, as a number of victims known to us who did not keep duplicate reports were later told that the police documentation had since been 'lost'.

While in some instances police involvement may incense stalkers because it effectively underscores the victim's determination to end the behaviour, it can contribute in other cases to bringing the harassment to an end. Stalkers who persist in their activities, despite being cautioned by police, are clearly signalling, in all but a minority of psychotic cases, their *intention* to stalk and their awareness that their behaviour is unwanted. Hence, seeking police assistance at the earliest opportunity may bring stalking to a halt in some cases. In other cases it may at least succeed in gaining the co-operation and sympathies of the police and the courts. Conversely, a verbal warning by police with a failure to follow up any subsequent transgressions with definitive legal action gives a very clear message to the stalker that he or she is immune to legal sanctions. Such dereliction sends an equally clear and painful message to the victim that the 'system' is not taking the situation seriously.

Support organizations can play a critical role in these early stages of harassment. They can provide emotional support for the victim and information about stalking, as well as advise about strategies to deal with the stalking. These bodies can also refer victims to specialist treatment services when additional support appears necessary. Most of these organizations are easily accessible on the Internet (usually applying the search term 'stalking'), or can be accessed via toll-free telephone listings. Some of these support organizations are listed in Appendix A and are further discussed later in this chapter. The National Victim Center (1998) suggests that when contacting helping services, persons identify themselves as stalking victims (as opposed to a generic 'crime victim'), in order to reinforce to staff that their personal information is to be securely filed and that no information can be provided to others without the victim's prior knowledge and approval. (It is of course important that victims emphasize this in their dealings with *any* agency.)

Avoiding contact and confrontations

In most instances when approached or contacted by their stalker, the victim reacts or responds in some way to these advances. Often this is in an attempt to reason with the perpetrator and negotiate an end to the pursuit. Typically, the victim cannot help but convey that he or she is fed up and angry. Others who avoid any verbal response to their stalker may none the less unwittingly gratify the stalker's need to connect with the object of attention by, say, returning unsolicited gifts or letters to their sender. It is strongly recommended that any contact between the stalker and their victim be actively avoided and that this rule be strictly and consistently adhered to, regardless of the victim's frustration levels or however compelling the need to renegotiate with the stalker (de Becker, 1997; Orion, 1997; Westrup, 1998).

When a person first becomes aware of a stalker's attentions they should, wherever possible, inform their pursuer in firm and unambiguous terms that they do not want any further contact from him or her. This message should be conveyed once only, in a clear and dispassionate manner that avoids threatening or humiliating language. (Some victims find it helpful to rehearse the announcement first, alone or role-played with a therapist or a trusted friend.) Victims must resist the stalker's attempts to engage them in any further dialogue. Ongoing communications will only reward the stalker's efforts to maintain contact, instil hope or reward optimism that perseverance will eventually be crowned with the desired relationship, and invariably prolong the stalking.

This 'no contact' approach, derived from applied behaviour analysis and reinforcement theory, contends that any contact with the stalker, however intermittent, reinforces the unwanted behaviour. A common example is the victim who is telephoned incessantly. If the victim resists answering the telephone (many authorities suggest that victims use an answering machine to screen calls and capture any intrusions), even the most determined stalker will, eventually, desist. However, if the victim, typically out of sheer frustration, responds on the twentieth occasion, the message to the stalker is that persistence (in this case twenty phone calls) will eventually be rewarded with contact from the object of attention. It could be expected that the harassment will intensify in the short term using this nonreinforcing approach, but extinction of the unwanted behaviours is the usual result, although the time course for this is variable and frequently difficult to predict. One stalker referred to our clinic telephoned her hapless victim 666 times in a twenty-four hour period, eventually abandoning this method when her (traced) calls remained unanswered. (The actual number of calls was apparently coincidental, the stalker denying any Satanic significance!)

In a number of instances known to us stalkers have provoked their victim into making contact with them in order to undermine the victim's credibility or to lure them into potentially damaging situations. One of the commonest examples is the stalker who takes out a restraining order against the victim, with conditions that effectively entrap the victim, leading to their arrest for breaching the order. A ludicrous example was that of Kim, a stalking victim whose mother lived alone in an apartment block adjacent to the residence of Craig, Kim's ex-boyfriend and stalker. When Kim threatened to take legal action against her pursuer, Craig responded by convincing a magistrate that she was harassing *him*, and – to Kim's dismay and disbelief – he was granted a restraining order that prohibited her from venturing within 200 metres of Craig's home. One evening, Kim was called by her mother's 'neighbour' (in truth, Craig feigning the neighbour's foreign accent) alerting her that her mother had 'collapsed' at home. Without reflecting on the legalities of the situation, Kim hastened to her mother's address, where she was greeted by two police officers. They had been contacted by the 'victim' Craig 'in a very distressed state', alleging that Kim had threatened to kill him and was on her way. Although the actual state of affairs was eventually elucidated, the true victim and her mother suffered considerably as a consequence of Craig's malicious actions. Despite the revocation of the restraining order and the stalker's arrest for making false reports to the police, Kim's mother felt so unnerved by the events that she moved out of her apartment to another daughter's address. She did in fact collapse some weeks later from a stroke. Kim blames the stress of the stalking and expresses profound guilt for bringing Craig into her family's lives. (For further discussion of role reversal, see Chapter 11).

In another case of stalker provocation, a suicidal woman informed by police that the ex-husband she had stalked for over two years had reached 'breaking point' and might assault or even kill her, responded: 'Good. That way *I* die and *he* gets punished.' Her harassment at that point escalated. As a further example of victim-initiated contact that backfired badly, famous horror story author Stephen King once hired a private detective to investigate a man who had stalked him over a six-month period and who had publicly alleged it was King, and not Mark Chapman, who shot John Lennon. King was advised not to show his stalker any fear:

So I walked past him in the town, and said: 'Take care'. That's all. Later that day he plastered the town with his 'newsletter' saying I threatened him. He said I grabbed him around the neck and said: 'Take very good care, because on some dark night I may come and get you.' That's a total psychotic distortion of what really happened. (Ritchie, 1995, p. 69)

While the 'no contact' approach is likely to be of benefit to many victims, it may be a rather more difficult undertaking in situations such as workplace or neighbour stalking, where the two parties must interact on a frequent basis. Some victims simply cannot resist an opportunity to appeal to logic, unable to accept that their pursuer, who appears to be of normal intelligence and not obviously demented, will not eventually see reason if the victim can invest sufficient time and energy into persuading them. Moreover, it is not uncommon for many stalking victims to reject or react harshly to the 'no contact' strategy, perceiving it to be an unfair approach that allows the stalker to 'walk all over them' or 'get away with it'. There is no doubt that stalking is unjust, but the overriding objective with this approach is to ensure the victim's safety and effect an end to the harassment. Victims can do little if anything to directly change their stalker's behaviour but they can certainly modify their *own* actions; this is in many cases the most effective strategy available to them.

Documentation

Stalkers often leave tangible evidence of their harassment, common examples being answering machine messages, letters, cards and unwanted gifts. Most recipients of these communications are frightened and repulsed, and their natural inclination is to destroy, discard or return the items or messages. Others are driven by guilt, embarrassment or a need to protect loved ones to conceal this evidence. It is strongly recommended, however, that victims retain all materials received from, and document incidents perpetrated by, their stalker, for the purposes of investigation and prosecution.

Victims should keep and date all taped answering machine messages, as well as any notes, cards, letters, gifts or other items received. We advise victims to avoid handling these (ideally, place them in a plastic document sleeve) and to store the items in a secure location such as a lockable cupboard. In addition, it is wise to maintain a log of any unwanted approaches, or instances of following and surveillance. Where possible, victims should make copies of any materials or correspondence associated with the stalking, including copies of any police reports filed, as noted above. We have encountered several instances in which the stalker has broken into the victim's home and stolen the only documentation of the harassment. In one such case, the victim was dismayed to find that the police had 'misplaced' their copies of her statements and multiple incident reports, and the telephone company records of the stalker's calls to her home were incomplete. Another victim with meticulous records spanning a twelve-year campaign of harassment lost all of these – her only copies – when her flat burnt down under suspicious circumstances. As a consequence of these experiences we now advise victims to keep a duplicate copy of all their documents at a separate, secure location. This advice is offered with some reservations, given its potential for encouraging a situation where an obsessive follower is confronted by an obsessive victim. The stalker's driven and preoccupied pursuit erodes and potentially destroys the fabric of his or her existence. Equally though, an increasingly pervasive identity as victim and obsessive gathering of evidence of that victimization can add another dimension of distress and disruption to that already imposed by the stalking itself.

The evidence cited can be invaluable to any future legal proceedings against the offender, particularly in helping to establish a course of conduct (see Chapter 14). To this end, the National Victim Center (1998) recommends that, in addition to documenting all stalking incidents, victims file police reports of any illegal acts that occur during the course of the stalking, such as breaking and entering, theft or assault. If possible, victims should collect photographic evidence, with dates, of any physical injuries or property damage sustained. Where it is safe to do so, photographing the stalker's surveillance activities (e.g. tailing the victim in his or her car) may also constitute useful collateral. At the very least the victim should endeavour to note down the licence plate of any suspicious car. It is essential to keep pens and writing material in the car at all times. (One unprepared but resourceful victim searched frantically for a pen to document her stalker's car registration number, ultimately improvising with a lipstick!)

Telephone harassment

One of the commonest methods employed by stalkers to communicate with their victim is repeated telephone calls. Most victims respond by changing their phone number, a frequently recommended and seemingly logical strategy. This approach, however, is often ineffective in bringing about an end to the harassment, such that some authorities discourage recipients of persistent telephone calls from obtaining new phone numbers (Schaum & Parrish, 1995; de Becker, 1997). Aside from being an expensive exercise, stalkers can be quite resourceful when faced with the challenge of obtaining the new listing (several stalkers boasting to us about the speed with which they succeeded in this task). The experience of having a stalker violate the victim's privacy in this way can be very damaging, further undermining the victim's sense of control and confidence in their so-called protectors. Instead, victims are advised to connect an answering machine to their phone to intercept and record the stalker's calls. De Becker (1997) suggested that victims recruit a friend to record the message on the answering machine, in order to thwart those stalkers who continue to call simply to listen to their victim's voice (de Becker further recommends that the friend be the same gender as the victim, so as not to provoke a stalker who mistakenly perceives competition). It is recommended that the victim then obtain a second, unlisted phone number for all their personal or business calls, being exceedingly circumspect about who is made privy to the new listing. Employing this approach, it is hoped that the stalker will continue to call on the answering machine line, oblivious to the fact that a second line exists. This serves multiple purposes, capturing the stalker's unwanted calls for any future legal intervention, eliminating the problem of inadvertent reinforcement and ensuring that the victim retains the confidence to use the telephone. The latter is an important issue, as a fear of answering the phone can greatly exacerbate a stalking victim's social isolation and vulnerability. Further, for many stalking victims the ringing of a telephone is a potent trigger to marked anxiety symptoms, even years after the telephone harassment has abated. Some have found that recent developments in telephone technology that allow for different tones according to the identity of the caller have been helpful in removing the unpredictability and apprehension associated with a ringing phone.

Restraining orders

The use of restraining or nonmolestation orders against stalkers is a contentious issue. The National Victim Center (1998) advises victims to at least consider obtaining a restraining order against their assailants, as any violation of the order may be punishable by a fine or (less often) imprisonment. However, they sensibly caution victims against developing a false sense of security from any such protective injunction, since these orders can only be enforced once breached, and in some jurisdictions they are limited to instances where the stalker is a former spouse (see Chapter 14).

Drawing from her own experience of being stalked for many years by a former erotomanic patient, psychiatrist Dr Doreen Orion (1997) is sceptical about the use and effectiveness of restraining orders. She argues that in her situation the multiple violations of restraining orders by her assailant were not treated seriously by the police. The police actually *warned* Orion's stalker against further breaches but – as is so often the case – failed to prosecute her when she disregarded their directions. Orion considers that such warnings serve only to embolden stalkers because, as has been noted earlier, the message to the stalker is that police have no intention of taking action. In some cases, stalkers have interpreted such inaction as a vindication, even denunciation, of the victim. Orion argues that restraining orders are unlikely to be effective against two classes of stalker in particular: (1) ex-intimates, many of whom have invested too much in their relationship and may become humiliated and enraged if the victim makes any effort to legally prohibit further contact; and (2) erotomanic or other delusional stalkers, whose attachment to the victim is based on a fantasized and idealized relationship such that legal orders are either entirely irrelevant to their quest, or simply a test of their love and devotion.

De Becker (1997) also queried the effectiveness of restraining orders against certain categories of stalker. In his opinion, restraining orders are most likely to be effective against a reasonable person who has limited emotional investment in his

or her relationship with the victim, and no history of violence. Protecti
may be useful against a casual acquaintance or business client who stalk
Becker concurs that they are more likely to inflame estranged spouses or partners
who have a deep emotional investment in the victim. In our experience, the majority of these stalkers possess an overwhelming sense of entitlement to their partner
and family. Rejection is experienced by these individuals as personally humiliating
and a powerful justification for their continued pursuit of the perpetrator of their
narcissistic wound. It is not surprising that the compounding public humiliation
these stalkers perceive with the imposition of a restraining order can precipitate an
escalation in stalking behaviours. This may include violence, occasionally of murderous proportions.

Victims who do obtain restraining orders should be mindful that the period
immediately following the issuance of the order may be one of heightened risk of
physical danger. This is a time that is highly emotionally charged for both stalker
and victim. In perhaps the most tragic and extreme example of this, in a six-week
period during 1989, four Californian women were killed by their ex-partner stalkers after each had obtained a restraining order to prohibit further harassment; ironically, one of these was clutching a purse that contained the newly issued order
(Montesino, 1993; Gross, 1994).

When restraining orders are contemplated, it is preferable to initiate an application *early* in the course of harassment. In our experience, stalkers who fail to appreciate that their behaviour constitutes a nuisance and source of distress to the object
of attention may be capable of receiving this message when a restraining order is
issued. A court order received in the early stages of a stalker's pursuit conveys the
victim's attitude at the outset, and is likely to be more effective than one that is
obtained after months or even years of stalking, when the stalker's emotional investment in the relationship has intensified and the stalker may well be left to wonder
'Why now?'. One stalker at our clinic was in fact convinced that because his victim
applied for a restraining order two years into their imagined 'relationship' she had
begun seeing someone else! De Becker (1997) also cautioned against the use of
restraining orders in response to threats or an escalation in stalking behaviours, as
this usually signals that the perpetrator is intensely involved in the stalking dynamic
and may become enraged by the added dimension of a legal rein on their behaviour.

Finally, it should be borne in mind that restraining and nonmolestation orders
are a *civil* remedy, the contravention of which rarely attracts prison sentences and
regrettably pits the victim against the accused (the exception being anti-stalking
legislation in the UK, which enables court-initiated restraining orders – see
Chapter 14). Victims may be better advised to pursue criminal charges against their
perpetrator, invoking anti-stalking laws or other charges such as theft, assault or
threats to kill, if applicable. This approach diffuses some of the fervour encountered

in victim-initiated civil interventions as the criminal charges are brought by police. This may also reduce the demands on the victim in the court process including the face-to-face contact between victim and defendant. Stalking charges are gradually finding greater use as a first-line approach to stalking offences (as opposed to restraining orders), as police and the judiciary become increasingly familiar with their application. An important advantage of criminal rather than civil remedies is that prosecution under anti-stalking laws offers greater flexibility in sentencing and more serious penalties than civil approaches. Legal sanctions raise the stakes sufficiently high for a substantial number of stalkers to abandon their quest.

Expert opinion and anecdotal evidence suggest that restraining orders may be counterproductive for many stalking victims. Meloy and others (1997), in contrast, contended that the extant domestic violence research supports the use of these orders in reducing the risk of violence in this specific context and in affording protection to battered women. In our opinion, obtaining restraining orders should not be regarded as a routine procedure in the management of stalking. We recommend that victims consult with professionals, preferably specialists in the area of stalking or threat management, to determine whether a prohibitive order is likely to be beneficial given the individual circumstances of their case. In general terms, the use of restraining orders should best be perceived as a useful adjunct to other legal proceedings initiated early in the course of stalking. Obtaining a restraining order should not bring with it expectations, at least in the immediate term, of protection and resolution of harassment.

Self-defence training

Some authorities recommend that stalking victims consider incorporating self-defence training into their safety plans (Shrapnel, 1997). As well as imparting skills that protect one's physical integrity, self-defence training can have an empowering effect. In conjunction with other forms of support, instruction in self-defence techniques can help to diminish feelings of helplessness and vulnerability, and assist the victim to regain a sense of competence and self-respect. We do not endorse the use of weaponry in this approach, and although some victims feel reassured when carrying repellent aerosol weapons their use in many jurisdictions is outlawed. We are particularly concerned about the acquisition of potentially lethal weapons by distressed stalking victims whose judgement may be impaired by fear, thus producing a high potential for injury to innocent parties. For those stalking victims who do not perceive their lives as already ruined, there can be little doubt about the effects of such a tragedy on their future. Our other major concern is that a substantial proportion of stalking victims experience suicidal thoughts and the access of suicidal people to lethal weaponry is not ordinarily encouraged. By the same token, a number of stalking victims will admit to homicidal feelings toward their stalker, and the presence of weapons again enhances the risks that action of this nature will be undertaken, however compelling the mitigating circumstances. One victim of stalking with whom we dealt did kill his stalker when enraged and intoxicated. He was convicted of murder, the court discounting as provocation the eighteen-month history of severe harassment and repeated intrusions that had been inflicted not only on him but on his wife and children.

Some victims do feel more secure with a personal (duress) alarm. Those that are centrally monitored will ensure a prompt police response. One of our victims strapped her alarm to her chest like an essential item of underwear; she eventually discarded it, but not for some fourteen months after her stalking had ended.

Workplace practices

While workplace stalking is in many cases the product of individual psychopathology in the employee, the role of organizational and management practices in fostering the instability and tension that can culminate in some cases of workplace violence and stalking has earlier been emphasized. Of course, stalking at work can also be an extension of stalking in other settings, especially by ex-intimates.

It is important that those harassed in the workplace report the matter to their superiors, who should in turn consult more senior staff where appropriate. It is desirable in most situations that work colleagues also be informed, for the safety of the primary victim as well as the security of co-workers. Employers have responded in some instances by the development of specific security procedures, including security guard escorts for the victim, co-workers screening the victim's calls and special carparks that offer the victim greater protection or proximity to their work location. In situations where a stalker's actions threaten other workers, safety drills have been developed and increasingly consideration is being given to the use of corporate restraining orders.

Above all, it is incumbent upon senior management to acknowledge the potential gravity of the situation and promptly address it. The following vignette demonstrates some of the difficulties encountered in cases of workplace stalking, the lack of appropriate action by management in this case serving to perpetuate the stalker's behaviour.

Case example

A single 26-year-old registered nurse was stalked by a 38-year-old divorced neurologist at the hospital at which they both worked. At a social function one evening, Dr M sensed that the nurse was attracted to him by the way she sat across the room from him. He subsequently began calling the woman at work and at home, requesting that she meet with him. She politely declined on each occasion, stating explicitly that she had no desire to pursue a relationship with Dr M nor to receive any further approaches from him. He was impervious to her wishes and the telephone calls, mostly to the victim's home late at night, continued. During these calls Dr M implored his victim to 'give in to her undeniable lust' for him but when the nurse tired of appealing to the logic she expected of a professional in his position and refused to respond to the calls at all, her pursuer crammed the tape on her answering machine with messages. Notes were also left on the windscreen of the woman's car at work, even during her night shifts; these alternately questioned the woman's unresponsiveness and declared his 'undying love' for her.

At work, Dr M followed the nurse around. He frequently followed her home and waited in his car outside her residence. Gifts often appeared at work and on one occasion a taxi load of flowers arrived at her home late at night, which repulsed and embarrassed the woman. She began to experience anxiety symptoms and hypervigilance as a consequence of her stalker's ubiquitous presence and feared that she was becoming 'paranoid'.

The victim's suspicions that Dr M was mentally unstable were confirmed when he confided to her on a number of occasions that he was hearing voices and felt suicidal. Although anxious to alert authorities to Dr M's behaviour and impaired state, his victim was concerned that suspension or revocation of the doctor's licence to practise might precipitate retaliatory violence toward her, if not suicidal behaviour. Her concerns were not without basis, since Dr M's letters had in recent months become increasingly menacing and derisive. Such intimidation finally convinced her to alert the hospital administration and senior medical staff to the problem that she had endured for almost eighteen months. Their reactions ranged from patronizing ('You should be flattered by all the attention he's giving you') to irresponsible ('Don't worry, you're not the first one he's done this to'). When the victim indicated that she had no choice but to report the situation to the police and the medical registration board, her employers conceded that some 'limits' should be imposed on Dr M's behaviour. Several private meetings were convened between senior staff, the administration and Dr M, during which he was instructed to refrain from approaching or otherwise contacting his fellow employee. His behaviour, however, persisted, with worsening malevolence. Further meetings followed and finally a disciplinary hearing recommended Dr M take sick leave and seek psychiatric assistance. Dr M was allowed to return to work, albeit in a nonclinical capacity, less than a week later.

For professional reasons, which were by no means unrelated to the toll Dr M's unending harassment had had upon her emotional well-being and the ineffectual if not negligent workplace management practices, the victim left the hospital to take up a position in another state. This brought an abrupt end to the stalking, although at considerable personal cost. A friend has since informed her that Dr M had transferred to another hospital and was apparently continuing to stalk female colleagues with appallingly little professional censure.

It is crucial that management staff in any work environment establish guidelines to deal with employees who present problematic and threatening behaviours. If in the first instance counselling or mediation cannot address the problems underlying the harassment (be they personal or contextual to the organization), termination of employment of the workplace stalker may ultimately be indicated. If dismissal is in fact the optimal course it is preferable that this be undertaken at the earliest possible juncture, as recommended in the termination of other unwanted relationships. De Becker (1997, p. 162) pointed out: 'a problem employee is easier to terminate before he makes a substantial emotional investment in the job, before the minor issues become causes, before disappointments become disgruntlements'. De Becker further cautioned that in dealing with difficult terminations, organizations must strive to protect the dignity of the dismissed individual, keep the discussion focussed on the future rather than the problems and failures leading to his or her termination, cite general rather than a multitude of specific reasons for this course of action, and not be drawn into further negotiation.

Other security measures

Stalking victims should strongly consider a home security check. Often, there are units within local police branches that offer this service, but victim support agencies and reputable security companies can also assist in this regard. Relatively simple measures to improve home security include changing locks, and installing deadlocks, lockable windows, exterior motion sensor lights and peepholes in doors. Trimming shrubbery, especially near windows, is also recommended.

We advise stalking victims to invest in a mobile phone so that they can call for help in an emergency. Unfortunately, since these devices can be another medium for stalker intrusions, we remind clients that cellular phone calls can be scanned and they should be wary of broadcasting identifying information during their conversations.

It is desirable that stalking victims avoid routines that provide the stalker with a predictable schedule for the object of their attentions. Various authorities advise victims to take different routes when travelling to the same location. In some cases, victims have departed unexpectedly for weekends away with friends. These trips have had the added advantage of alleviating some of their fear and isolation.

Stalking victims should strive to have their address and other contact details removed from all public records, including the electoral roll, libraries, business cards, driver's licence, car registration and medical registries.

Clinical management of stalking victims

Education and supportive counselling

Victims of stalking commonly consult general practitioners, mental health professionals or other helping agencies. They may seek an appraisal of the stalker's potential for violence, or an opinion regarding the likely course and duration of the stalking. Some are simply trying to make sense of the bizarre behaviours and communications of their stalker. For those who are still active targets, the clinician must primarily focus on assisting the victim to attend to issues of personal safety and security. Health professionals would be well advised to familiarize themselves with community agencies, including victim support services, that can provide further assistance to stalking victims and to refer the victim as appropriate. As we have noted, in many jurisdictions – including our own – there is a regrettable lack of co-ordinated services for these individuals. However, there is at least a growing awareness of the need for specialist services in law enforcement, criminal justice and mental health fields. Although it is desirable to encourage the stalking victim to initiate contact with the relevant agencies the clinician occasionally must adopt a more active advocacy role, particularly where the victim's functioning is compromised by fear or they are too overwhelmed by hopelessness and helplessness to effectively access the help they require.

It is not unusual for victims of stalking to endure months, if not years, of harassment before enlisting the services of a professional. For some, earlier attempts to enlist the help of other agencies, particularly police and the legal profession, have met with little success or have actually proved counterproductive. These victims commonly allege that their complaints were trivialized. Not a few of the victims who have come to our service have previously encountered implied or direct accusations that they encouraged the stalker's attentions or that they should be flattered by them. One police sergeant, in response to a middle-aged professional male making a complaint about being stalked over many months by a young woman, asked the victim whether the young woman was attractive. When the victim rather confusedly responded that he supposed she could be seen as such, the policeman replied: 'Well aren't *we* the lucky one!' These ineffectual and insensitive reactions serve to exacerbate the complainant's feelings of guilt, powerlessness and alienation, and many are then at a loss to know how to proceed. When presented with a victim of stalking it is therefore essential to adopt an accepting, encouraging and nonjudgemental attitude if the risk of adding to the victim's distress is to be minimized.

It is also crucial early in the victim's presentation to forge a trusting alliance with them. By the time these individuals consult a clinician, their disillusionment and mistrust can be pervasive and they may have become as a consequence quite isolated from their customary supports. It is important to acknowledge the victim's fears for their privacy and to reassure them that any information, including personal contact details, will remain confidential and secure. Other staff, including nonclinical administrative staff, must be attuned to the issues and should be reminded never to disclose information to any third party regarding this client, unless prior approval has been given by the client or their treating clinician. This message will need to be repeated whenever there are staff changes.

Allaying fears, especially those that may be unrealistic, is a fundamental, although occasionally neglected step in establishing a therapeutic relationship with the stalking victim. While it may be more constructive to acknowledge realistic safety concerns than to dismiss or trivialize the victim's fears, particularly for those for whom the stalking continues and for whom the fear is well founded, it is none the less important to diminish or eliminate those concerns that, rather than representing a tangible or realistic fear, are the product of the victim's anxious state.

In addition to providing a supportive, educational and advocacy role, the clinician must address the psychological morbidity produced by the stalking experience. Treating health professionals should be mindful of the fact that, in some instances, victims of stalking seek to relieve intolerable symptoms by 'self-medicating' with alcohol or other substances. A comprehensive treatment plan for victims of stalking must address not only the primary and largely observable symptoms of psychological and physical distress, but also the frequent concomitants. These can include alcohol and other psychoactive substance abuse, relationship discord and general hostility to others that impede the victim's social and occupational functioning as well as thwarting rehabilitative efforts. In the early stages of treatment it is also important for clinicians to consider that victims with high levels of psychic arousal and who demonstrate marked avoidance patterns are likely to be poor candidates for more intensive therapies that focus on the exploration and elaboration of the distressing experiences. These include cognitive-behavioural techniques such as systematic desensitization, which require the client to be exposed to feared situations (Shalev et al., 1996). For these victims, the priority is to reduce anxiety and arousal and to provide a supportive foundation before attempting to proceed with other forms of symptom reduction.

Cognitive-behavioural approaches

For many victims of violent crime, the traumatic and threatening event breaches previously held assumptions about their safety. Often a belief in the individual's strength and resilience is replaced by feelings of extreme vulnerability. The confidence most of us share to a greater or lesser degree in the reasonable and predictable nature of our world is shattered, to be replaced by an expectation of danger and unpredictable harm. Psychological therapies such as cognitive restructuring attempt to correct these erroneous posttraumatic assumptions and evaluations about the world. The approach also targets the relationships between triggering stimuli and responses in the victim. For example, cognitive-based approaches for victims of natural disasters typically seek to challenge the victim's subsequent appraisals of the world as being imminently dangerous and threatening. Unfortunately, in the case of stalking, the victim's assumptions and evaluations about their safety may be valid, as some remain vulnerable to persisting indiscriminate harm. While cognitive restructuring techniques can be valuable in the treatment of stalking victims they should focus on rebuilding a realistic and viable sense of safety for the victim.

Cognitive-oriented therapies are useful when endeavouring to correct the assumptions that underlie pathological forms of anxiety and depression. The aim is gradually to assist the victim to acknowledge that (1) being in safe situations even if it reminds the person of their stalking is *not* dangerous; (2) experiencing anxiety or other distressing symptoms does *not* lead to a loss of control, and (3) remembering a traumatic and fear-provoking incident is *not* the equivalent of re-experiencing it.

Strategies that seek to restructure the victim's morbid perceptions of the world are likely to benefit those victims whose stalking and harassment has ceased. They may also be appropriate for those individuals whose victimization is ongoing, yet whose arousal is sufficiently manageable to attempt more direct methods to minimize their fear in relatively safe situations. The latter should, however, always be undertaken in conjunction with measures to optimize the victim's security and overcome the continuing intrusions of the stalker.

Clinicians must focus not only on the stalking victim's fear and overt symptomatology, but equally on their *avoidance*. Victims frequently avoid both internal (e.g. thoughts or memories) and external cues associated with the stalking, such as the ringing of the telephone, or places and persons associated with the stalker. In most instances their avoidance is rewarded by a reduction in distress. Avoidance responses, although understandable, may in the long term exacerbate the victim's perceived or actual feelings of isolation. Although avoidance of threatening situations or cues is a reasonable and adaptive response, when avoidance extends to other areas of the victim's life (e.g. avoidance of leaving home or going to work), alienation from supports and social and vocational opportunities may ultimately impede the victim's recovery.

Avoidance may respond to behavioural techniques such as prolonged exposure and stress inoculation, which aim to assist victims gradually to resume abandoned activities and manage the associated anxiety. Prolonged exposure usually requires victims to confront their fears through a gradual process that increases the nature (imagined versus real) and the duration (brief versus extended) of the exposure as well as the subject's level of arousal (low versus high; Foa & Meadows, 1997). During the initial stages of this approach the victim may be asked to imagine a feared event for a brief duration that involves relatively low arousal. As the victim learns to tolerate the imagined exposure to the avoided stimuli, the duration and level of arousal can be gradually increased. It is preferable at this stage to introduce other strategies that assist the victim to manage their anxiety *as it occurs*, such as relaxation training. Some authorities advocate the use of techniques such as eye movement desensitization reprocessing (EMDR), which may allow the individual to deal with their traumatic memories without requiring that they experience the extremes of hyperarousal (van der Kolk et al., 1994). The use of these cognitive and behavioural techniques in conjunction with supportive therapy may be effective in assisting the victim to re-enter avoided situations without experiencing intolerable fear or distress.

Pharmacotherapies

Creamer & McFarlane (1999) have recently noted the dearth of randomized clinical trials of pharmacological agents in the treatment of stress-related syndromes. Medication is none the less an important adjunct to nonpharmacological approaches in sufferers with severe symptoms and in the treatment of comorbid psychiatric disorders. The selection of medication must be guided by the side effect profile of these agents, minimizing as far as possible any iatrogenic contribution to the victim's distress and disability. The prescribing clinician must also be mindful of the occasionally protracted course of stress-related syndromes, and hence the potential requirement for long-term chemical treatment.

Selective serotonin reuptake inhibitor (SSRI) antidepressants have demonstrated efficacy in the treatment of stress-related symptoms. In some studies SSRIs such as fluoxetine produced a marked reduction in overall symptoms that could not be attributed solely to their antidepressant actions (van der Kolk et al., 1994). These agents have been reported to ameliorate numbing and arousal symptoms, at least in victims of civilian trauma (Friedman, 1998). SSRIs are an attractive choice in the pharmacological treatment of stress-related syndromes as they have also proved effective in alleviating comorbid conditions such as alcohol abuse and dependence, depression and panic (Brady et al., 1995).

While monoamine oxidase inhibitor (MAOI) antidepressants are claimed to diminish PTSD symptoms, particularly re-experiencing phenomena, there is little information on the efficacy of the reversible MAO-A inhibitor moclobemide. Tricyclic antidepressants have long been employed in the treatment of stress syndromes. They have shown some benefit with re-experiencing symptoms and in cases with severe insomnia (Creamer & McFarlane, 1999). The 5-hydroxytryptamine (5-HT) antagonist cyproheptadine has also proved beneficial in sleep-disturbed patients with PTSD, by reducing nightmares (Gupta et al., 1998). Although we have used cyproheptadine with some success in Vietnam veterans with chronic war-related nightmares, we have had only modest success to date with victims of stalking.

Benzodiazepines are prescribed widely as anxiolytics and hypnotics for stress-related symptoms. While they may produce a reduction in anxiety symptoms and insomnia, some authors are not convinced of their usefulness in PTSD and related conditions (Gelpin et al., 1996). Tolerance and dependence are a significant problem with the benzodiazepines, especially in individuals who may already exhibit comorbid substance abuse/dependence.

Antiadrenergic agents have also been recommended in the treatment of acute stress reactions, particularly propranolol and clonidine (see Friedman et al., 1993; Friedman, 1998). Other agents that have also been trialled, with variable results, include anticonvulsants, narcotic antagonists and antipsychotic medication (Friedman, 1998).

In our clinic, which tends to see predominantly the more severely affected stalking victims, medication is not infrequently employed, either as a short-term measure to diminish overwhelming anxiety symptoms or to treat comorbid major depression. SSRIs are generally better tolerated in this (usually) antidepressant-naïve group. Unfortunately, in our experience SSRIs may produce or exacerbate cognitive dysfunction such as short-term memory impairment, a side effect of significant concern to high-functioning individuals who may already be struggling to hold down demanding jobs. We have tended to limit our usage of benzodiazepines, given the predictably protracted course of harassment in many cases, problems of abuse or dependence associated with these medications, their exacerbating effects on cognitive impairment and their disinhibiting properties in individuals who may be experiencing suicidal or even homicidal ideation. When prescribed, benzodiazepines are viewed as an effective means of bringing extreme distress under rapid control, but emphasis is placed on the role of psychological measures in achieving control over negative emotional states and self-efficacy in the long term. Despite these intentions, benzodiazepines may occasionally be continued as an adjunct to nonpharmacological therapies in selected cases.

We have also used moclobemide in one stalking victim with a range of stress-related symptoms. The patient had previously been trialled on SSRI medication, which was discontinued due to intolerable headaches. The reversible MAO-A inhibitor produced a marked reduction in depressive and anxiety symptoms, and, to a lesser extent, symptoms of avoidance and numbing. The patient also reported a significant diminution in the frequency of nightmares, such that she was no longer fearful of falling asleep. This resulted in improved energy levels and, ultimately, her return to work.

We have employed tricyclic antidepressants with mixed success. They have generally been prescribed for those individuals who have succumbed to intolerable side effects on the newer antidepressants. Their effectiveness has been most evident in cases exhibiting a comorbid major depressive illness and prominent arousal symptoms. These agents are far more toxic in overdose compared with the newer generation of antidepressants. Appropriate precautions must therefore be taken if they are to be prescribed in this population, in which a high prevalence of suicidal ideation has been reported (Pathé & Mullen, 1997). Antipsychotic agents are rarely a consideration in treating stalking-related PTSD, although they are first-line drugs in the treatment of a small number of individuals who present as stalking victims, but who are subsequently found to be deluded (see Chapter 11).

Family/partner therapies

It is often useful to involve family members or partners of the stalking victim in therapeutic interventions. Significant others frequently share in the primary victim's distress, as a consequence of either the indirect effects of the stalking (e.g. lifestyle disruptions, altered relationship dynamics) or directly, when they too become targets for the stalker's threats and assaults. Family members and partners can be a valuable resource, especially in determining the motivations of the stalker, and constitute an essential supportive foundation for the victim. It is imperative that they receive education about stalking and its impact as well as being alerted to the safety issues. They too will require support and, in some cases, referral for individual counselling. Often significant others seek advice about managing the uncharacteristically erratic or hostile behaviours of the victim. They are also understandably concerned about the likely long-term impact of the stresses on the victim. Some families who are contemplating radical life changes, such as moving house (to a foreign country in some instances), seek the therapist's guidance in these decisions. Here an awareness of the nature of the stalking and its underlying motives can avert enormous sacrifices which may fail to resolve the problem.

Occasionally family members or partners are critical of the victim, blaming him or her for encouraging or becoming involved with the stalker (such disapproval frequently surfacing with the benefit of hindsight). Some express frustration at the victim's apparent lack of strength and inability to 'move on'. Of course, none of these responses are constructive and deprive the victim of the trusting and nonjudgemental alliances that will facilitate his or her recovery. The therapist must tackle counter-therapeutic ignorance by educating significant others about the phenomenon of stalking and shifting blame from the victim to where it properly belongs, with the stalker.

Group therapies

It has been noted earlier that victims of stalking frequently perceive their experiences as unique and incomprehensible to the rest of society. They report the failure of others to appreciate the burden and implicit threat posed by the stalker's behaviour, and many come to feel abandoned and alienated from their usual supports. Group therapies, in the form of self-help or support groups, can play a useful role in the rehabilitation of the stalking victim. These groups can diminish the victim's sense of isolation and alienation. They provide a supportive environment in which participants experience mutual understanding, validation and trust, and a safe venue for sharing their anger, frustration and loss. These groups can also be a valuable resource, as victims exchange helpful strategies, reading material, details of agencies or individuals who may have proved helpful and share security tips and equipment.

Ideally, therapeutic support groups should be facilitated by a clinician who is well grounded in the issues faced by victims of stalking, including the complex psychological sequelae. The role of the therapist includes enhancing and maintaining mutual support among members, and retaining a focus on proactive measures that take account of members' safety and rehabilitation needs.

In addition to providing a supportive forum for victims to share their experiences, another important objective of therapeutic groups is the reduction of psychological distress. This is achieved by instructing group members in techniques to manage symptoms of anxiety, panic, anger and/or depression, and assisting them in their effective application. To this end, the trained facilitator and group member set realistic goals, such as the gradual resumption of activities avoided or abandoned due to the stalking, which are reviewed during the course of the group. This should ideally be supplemented with objective measures to assess the progress of individuals and the efficacy of the therapeutic approach. This approach, combining a structured component aimed at restoring those aspects of the victim's functioning compromised by stalking with the fluidity of group discussions, can be very beneficial to a victim's social competence and self-efficacy, although this effect is greatest in those cases who are no longer being stalked.

Support organizations for stalking victims

Since the mid 1990s several prominent support organizations have been founded which specifically address the needs of stalking victims and their families. These organizations play an invaluable role in providing educational and safety information for victims, in addition to much needed emotional support. The majority of organizations, such as Survivors of Stalking (SOS) and the National Anti-Stalking and Harassment Campaign and Support Association (NASH), were founded by stalking victims disillusioned with existing services. SOS was established in Florida in 1995 by Renee Goodall, a former stalking victim who was harassed for almost a year by a man who refused to accept the termination of their brief romantic liaison (Marino, 1995). In her efforts to find assistance, Ms Goodall encountered fragmented services who were unable to offer constructive advice regarding optimal safety and legal options, as well as unsympathetic professionals, especially law enforcement and criminal justice personnel. The inadequacy of services catering to the needs of stalking victims prompted her to establish a nationwide organization in the USA, which, like most support groups of its kind, operates as a community-funded nonprofit organization providing a telephone helpline service accessible

throughout the USA. The organization states that its primary role is to provide information regarding:
- immediate safety concerns and safety strategies,
- state anti-stalking laws and available legal options,
- victim's rights and the operation of the criminal justice system,
- referrals to local mental health professionals, and
- information for dealing with the police, filing incident reports and documenting evidence for future prosecutions (see Marino, 1995).

SOS is one of several groups established in the USA specifically to assist victims of stalking and can be accessed by a toll-free number in each US state (see Appendix A).

NASH was founded in 1995 in the UK by a woman who also had first-hand experience of stalking, and the lack of appropriate services for victims. Dr Evonne von Heussen-Countryman was stalked for over seventeen years by a professor who made repeated telephone calls to her home, kept her young children under surveillance, poured acid on her car and on one occasion held her captive in her home and attempted to sexually assault her in the presence of her children (Orion, 1997). Her many attempts to seek police intervention and initiate criminal charges against her assailant met with the advice that it was 'her word against his', a 'domestic matter' (despite her never having been even casually acquainted with the man), or that the perpetrator's actions were not illegal. His harassment gradually abated after many years, only for Dr von Heussen-Countryman's daughter later to become the target of two separate stalkers, one of whom sexually assaulted her. The inadequacy of the police response to both her own and her daughter's ordeals led Dr von Heussen-Countryman to become a vocal activist in the campaign for the introduction of anti-stalking legislation and appropriate services for stalking victims in the United Kingdom. The group she founded and continues to direct has been instrumental in establishing community support groups for stalking victims, disseminating educational material on stalking and providing a telephone helpline that provides victims with practical advice as well as emotional support.

The increasing recognition in recent years of stalking as a prevalent behaviour that can cause substantial damage to its various victims has resulted in the appearance of specialist services and support organizations for victims of this crime. Despite the expansion of our knowledge of stalking and to a lesser extent that of service provision, in most communities there remains a regrettable lack of appropriate services to address the needs of stalking victims. Several of the victims treated at our clinic travel large distances to use our specialized service. Recently, one such individual established her own support group in her local area and has invited one of our therapists to act in a consultative role to the group. At a time when many governments are retreating from public health service funding and provision, it is an unfortunate reality that those who seek local support organizations for stalking often must establish such services on their own initiative. Despite the frustration this apparent apathy produces for many victims, the experience of forming a support group can be an empowering one, which is often experienced by the victim as instrumental in regaining the self-confidence, autonomy and personal effectiveness that have frequently been eroded by the stalker's actions.

The task of forming support organizations or groups is, however, beyond the capacity of many stalking victims, some of whom are virtually paralysed by fear and helplessness. Those who continue to be stalked may be too absorbed by their current problems, or have such a sense of foreshortened future that they cannot contemplate active participation, or they are understandably reticent about involving themselves in activities with the potential for public exposure and its attendant risks. The stalking victim should none the less be encouraged to become an active participant in the quest to eradicate stalking from his or her life. Involvement in activities such as compiling resources for stalking victims, reviewing the anti-stalking legislation or even writing to local politicians reinforces the message that victims are ultimately responsible for their own safety and protection (a function no one else can provide on a daily basis) and fosters independence and greater self-efficacy.

Associated issues in treatment

As noted in Chapter 3, the experience of a traumatic or threatening event alone is not sufficient to produce prolonged stress symptoms. It is likely other *individual* vulnerabilities contribute to the development and nature of the ensuing psychological disturbance. It is important that clinicians consider the role of such factors in the treatment of stalking victims, as a failure to do so may frustrate rehabilitative efforts. These include the patient's habitual coping style, past psychiatric history and exposure to prior traumatic experiences (see van der Kolk et al., 1996).

In addition to the psychological sequelae of stalking, the *physical* health of stalking victims may be compromised by chronic stress and the effects of deteriorating diet, poor sleep, the memory impairment that comes with being constantly preoccupied and highly aroused (such that one of our diabetic patients 'forgot' to take her insulin), and self-destructive urges. A failure to attend to the victim's physical ill-health by appropriate referral and encouragement to comply with medical advice may also hamper progress on the psychosocial frontier.

The victims of ex-intimate stalkers are typically fearful of further relationships and lack faith in their competence to judge the suitability of any future partner. While the more extreme and maladaptive aspects of this reaction can be addressed in the course of cognitive and supportive therapies, the restoration of trust in other people may never be complete and victims generally accept that, up to a point, such caution may prove adaptive to future self-preservation. While victims cannot be blamed for being stalked, we have encountered a number of instances of individuals with a history of embarking upon relationships somewhat precipitously and recklessly, disregarding aspects of their partner that might normally be cause for concern. These are the individuals, often women, who may have married after only a brief courtship; one stalking victim with such a history had been married twice previously after brief courtships and was barely 25 years old when she sought our help for stalking by her estranged fiancé. She had known this man for less than six months. Unlike the majority who are stalked by ex-intimates, these victims may actually enter a new relationship while the harassment is continuing or soon after its resolution. For these victims, treatment must also focus on developing less potentially destructive relationship patterns.

Finally, in addition to being attuned to the safety needs of the victim and endangered third parties, therapists who treat stalking victims must also be cognisant of their own personal safety issues. Although thankfully rare, it is conceivable, especially in cases of resentful or rejected stalking, that those involved in the victim's treatment – and whom the stalker perceives as obstructive to their cause – may become the target of angry revenge. If there is any doubt about the therapist's vulnerability they should at the very least ensure optimal security practices at their rooms and in their private life. Ideally, treatment of these victims should be conducted in a setting in which other staff are present and there is an appropriate level of physical security, such as the clinic in which we operate. A further advantage for therapists in group as opposed to solo practices, the importance of which cannot be overstated, is the opportunity this provides for readily accessible, informal debriefing with colleagues in an atmosphere of understanding and confidentiality.

Conclusions

> to some extent, the imprint [of trauma] is indelible and hence immutable by current methods . . . attempts to cure chronic PTSD by reversing its 'etiological' mechanisms should be reconsidered and replaced by more realistic goals, for example vocational rehabilitation, family counseling, and control of adverse health practices. (Shalev et al., 1996, p. 178)

The therapeutic techniques and interventions reviewed in this chapter have demonstrated efficacy in the treatment of patients with stress-related symptoms, suggesting that they may also have a potential role in the treatment and management of stalking victims. However, the clinical management of these victims is a complex undertaking for treating professionals, given the variable and often chronic course of the stressor and the range of deleterious effects it can produce in the victim. The treatment of stalking victims requires an individually tailored approach that takes into account the specific context and circumstances of the harassment. The management of stalking victims has as its primary objective the alleviation of the victim's distress and the restoration of interpersonal, social and occupational functioning, while recognizing that for those victims who continue to be pursued, such methods must always be accompanied by strategies that promote the safety of the victim and any other parties at risk.

Defining and prosecuting the offence of stalking

Introduction

The constellation of acts that constitute stalking, when considered individually, often may seem innocuous to the uninvolved observer and their threatening nature may be far from immediately apparent. When repeated over time, however, the actions of the stalker all too often take on an altogether more sinister import for the object of these unwanted attentions. Although 'stalking' is a new word, the behaviour itself is not new to the criminal justice system, having been dealt with in various ways by the courts since at least the eighteenth century. The recent media fascination with the stalking of high-profile victims, and cases where the pursuit of former intimate partners has culminated in violence, highlighted problems with existing legal responses. Largely as a result of agitation in the media, stalking has come to be regarded as both new and increasingly prevalent, requiring immediate political and legislative responses. Although in fact not new and possibly not even increasing in frequency, it is true that existing criminal, civil and common laws, despite being available to prosecute stalking-related conduct, have proved largely insufficient either to deter the perpetrator of stalking or to protect the victim. The laws that existed in most jurisdictions prior to 1990 applied to single illegal acts, rather than taking into consideration the repetition of an act, which may change not just its gravity but its very nature. In short, existing legal approaches were ill equipped to deal with offending that is constructed of the oft-repeated act, each instance of which may be legal or at worse a nuisance, but the totality of which is a damaging and distressing infliction. Rather than modify and strengthen existing laws to deal with stalking, legislators throughout many Western nations have instead acted swiftly to criminalize this behaviour specifically.

Since 1990, there has been a rapid proliferation of anti-stalking legislation, beginning in the USA and extending to Canada, Australia, the UK and New Zealand. Similar laws are now being considered or enacted in continental Europe. Such laws have been fervently promoted by legislators keen to be seen as 'doing something' and equally enthusiastically received by a public and media increasingly concerned with vulnerability to crime. In the popular arena, the introduction of anti-stalking laws has been wholeheartedly welcomed, but for many jurists, civil libertarians and liberals the new legislation is highly contentious. The framing of anti-stalking laws has been troubled by the issue of defining a criminal activity that comprises a series of actions that, when taken individually, often constitute legitimate behaviour (e.g. sending letters or flowers or waiting outside a person's home or workplace). In creating a legal definition of stalking, legislators have broadly prohibited contacts and communications that occur on 'two or more occasions' and which render the recipient fearful. The thinking behind such binary regulations may be that requiring a greater number of prohibited acts leaves victims vulnerable to an escalation to violence before the necessary elements of the offence have been fulfilled. It is because these laws require so few – and potentially such inoffensive – acts to establish the offence of stalking that they all too easily may cross the line between prohibiting and punishing illegal behaviours and intruding on legitimate activities.

The blurred boundaries between what constitutes legitimate and illegal behaviours have vexed the development and application of anti-stalking laws. These laws raise compelling legal issues, especially in the USA, where constitutionally protected rights and behaviours have been considered by some to be infringed by anti-stalking laws. Anti-stalking legislation equally raises important questions about the nature of social interactions in Western industrialized societies, particularly when a person can at least in theory be convicted of a criminal offence on the basis of several, from their point of view perhaps well-intentioned, contacts with someone who chooses to perceive this behaviour as threatening. None the less, anti-stalking laws in our opinion filled a gap in the criminal and civil law that previously permitted effective intervention only after a harasser had caused physical harm to the victim and that largely ignored the enormous potential harm inflicted by inducing persistent fear and apprehension in the victim.

This chapter reviews the development of anti-stalking laws, particularly in the USA where the first legislation was enacted and issues related to the constitutionality of anti-stalking laws have been most widely canvassed. Legislation introduced in Australia and the UK to address stalking is also examined in the light of the criminal justice issues raised by this new category of offending. This chapter focusses on the definitions applied to stalking and the attempts made to limit the offence to prevent inadvertently making legitimate activities illegal. We also examine the relative importance that different jurisdictions have placed on the intentions of the stalker versus the subjective reactions of the victim. The advantages and disadvantages of legislation in the USA, Australia and the UK are analysed, placing emphasis on the proper application and the potential misuse of these laws. At the outset we need to acknowledge both our biases and our limitations. We are mental health professionals not lawyers. We are moved more by the distress of victims and the destruction wrought in the lives of stalkers themselves than by issues of proper legal process. That being said, we are not unaware, at an intellectual level, that issues of legal process underpin basic aspects of civil society of even more significance and moment than the fate of stalkers and their victims. Our reading of the legal literature is an exegesis performed for clinicians and other nonlawyers by clinicians. *Caveat lector.*

Early attempts to prosecute stalking-related behaviours

Although the categorization of stalking as a criminal offence is a late twentieth century phenomenon, examples of attempted prosecutions of similar conduct can be found in eighteenth and nineteenth century criminal law. However, because stalking was not recognized socially or legally as a distinct form of offending, attempted prosecutions of such conduct had to correspond to existing offences, such as assault or battery.

A prosecution for stalking-like behaviour was brought before the English courts in the case of *Dennis v. Lane*, in 1704. Dr Lane, a physician, persistently pursued Miss Dennis, a young heiress, against the wishes of her mother. Having once made romantic advances to Miss Dennis, Dr Lane was forbidden by her mother to approach her daughter's residence, but he disregarded those instructions and entered her house, attempting to gain access to Miss Dennis' chambers. When the fearful mother and daughter departed on a trip to London, he followed the pair, occupying an adjacent room at an inn where they had stayed the night. The following morning as Miss Dennis was approaching her coach, Dr Lane assaulted one of the men accompanying her, stating that he would force Miss Dennis from them. He was brought before the courts for the assault some months later. Still incensed by his being denied access to Miss Dennis, Dr Lane assaulted a barrister who had previously escorted her to London, beating him severely with a cane outside the courthouse. Dr Lane was detained and again brought before court for the assaults. The court ruled that his behaviour was good cause to require a 'security of the peace'. He was ordered to provide £400 as security to ensure that he would 'keep the peace' for a year and one day, although records fail to indicate the success of this remedy.

Almost a century and a half later, another English case, *Regina v. Dunn* (1840), provides one of the most detailed accounts of stalking recorded, in this case undoubtedly involving erotomania. The defendant, Richard Dunn, Esquire, a barrister by profession, pursued Miss Angela Coutts for nearly a year. In August 1838, Miss Coutts received two letters from Dunn, a person then unknown to her. On the basis of the language contained in the letters, Miss Coutts assumed an 'insane person' was responsible and discarded them. In the same month, Dunn followed Miss Coutts to a hotel where she was lodging. Annoyed that this stranger had somehow managed to place his card in her room, Miss Coutts moved to another hotel. Dunn bombarded her with letters at the new hotel, tried to enter the building and made frequent unwanted approaches to her in public. Miss Coutts began to be accompanied by a male servant, whose protection she felt she needed. The contents of one particular letter that Miss Coutts received caused her to fear for her personal safety and she made a complaint to the courts. Richard Dunn was apprehended and ordered to provide £500 as 'security of the peace' and to procure a surety of the same amount from a third party in the event that he broke the peace. He could not provide the required sureties and was placed in custody at York Castle until the hearing. However, by that time, Miss Coutts had left the district and, 'induced to hope that such annoyance would not be renewed' did not direct any further legal proceedings against Dunn. He was subsequently discharged from custody.

Upon release, Dunn went to London (near the Coutt's family home in Piccadilly) and resumed his pursuit, sending Miss Coutts letters and packages, following her and her friends, watching her at places she frequented and accosting her on the street, at church and on vacation. Being greatly alarmed for her safety, Miss Coutts applied for and received a warrant to apprehend Dunn in December 1838. Richard Dunn was again unable to provide the required sureties of the peace and was taken into custody for a short period. Once released, he continued his harassment of Miss Coutts throughout 1839. In May of that year, he sent her a letter proposing that they meet. The letter contained the ominous sentence 'If you refuse this request, you will, when it is too late, repent a course, the consequences of which will sooner or later fall on yourself and your family' (*Regina v. Dunn*, 1840, p. 943). Miss Coutts restricted her daily activities and ensured that she was always accompanied by a friend and a male servant, living in daily fear that Dunn would commit some act of violence against her. She again sought recourse from the courts, this time requesting that Dunn be ordered to find sufficient sureties for keeping the peace and thereby restrained from further 'molesting, annoying and terrifying' her.

In her application to the court, Miss Coutts was required to submit 'articles of the peace' (a written oath) that showed a reasonable basis for her fear of bodily harm and that a threat had been alleged against her. The court determined that 'Articles of the peace are not sufficient unless they shew a threat. The threat need not be in words, but may be inferred from a course of conduct' (ibid., p. 939). The articles of the peace submitted by Miss Coutts were deemed insufficient to establish the requisite fear and the charges against Dunn were dismissed.

Recognizing the miscarriage of justice that resulted from the limitations inherent in the legal system at the time, the judges concluded the case by stating:

Perhaps the law of England may be justly reproached with its inadequacy to repress the mischief, and obviate the danger, which the prisoner's proceedings render too probable; and we may naturally feel surprised if none of the numerous Police Acts have made specific provisions for that purpose (*Regina v. Dunn*, 1840, p. 949).

Unfortunately the judges' prescience was largely ignored. Although 'sureties of the peace' attempted to *prevent* offensive acts before they occurred, they offered little discouragement to the infatuated or determined stalker. Thus, while the 'mischief' and 'danger' presented by stalkers was evident to the courts in 1840, no legal mechanisms were available to prosecute this form of conduct. Any prosecution of stalking behaviour had to be mounted on the basis of existing criminal or civil offences that sought to punish crimes against the individual (e.g. assault or trespass), the community (e.g. Public Nuisance Acts) or more recently, within the context of the family (e.g. Domestic Violence and Matrimonial Proceedings Acts).

The criminal laws and torts employed primarily to prosecute stalking conduct were assault, harassment, menacing, intimidation, terroristic threatening, malicious communications, or trespass (see Guy, 1993; McAnaney et al., 1993; Home Office, 1996). Pursuing offenders under these laws provided some recourse for victims, but as a systematic means to address the activities associated with stalking, they proved inadequate for several reasons. First, criminal laws related to assault, menacing or intimidation address discrete incidents that are illegal in and of themselves, in contrast to the myriad activities used persistently to harass the victim of stalking, which taken individually may often constitute no offence. The use of such laws to prosecute stalking would require multiple prosecutions of the offender. An effective prosecution under such circumstances would be so drawn out as to deter victims who are reluctant to repeatedly provide essential testimony. Secondly, most anti-harassment offences are classed as summary offences or misdemeanours. As a consequence the penalties associated with them are limited (typically fines) and certainly unlikely to dissuade most stalkers or afford the victim any protection. Finally, laws such as menacing require an immediate threat of violence against the victim, which is not applicable to many stalking situations where threats, if they exist at all, are rarely explicit but largely implicit in the course of following or surveillance.

Civil law remedies, such as restraining or nonmolestation orders, were another means by which stalking victims could attempt to protect themselves against repeated intrusions and unwanted communications. To obtain a restraining order or its equivalent, however, the onus is on the victim to make an application to the court and to provide sufficient evidence of an imminent threat against his or her physical safety (Guy, 1993). This petitioning process is frequently associated with lengthy delays between application and hearing and involves the expense of hiring counsel. Many jurisdictions restrict issuing restraining orders to intimate or ex-intimate relationships, thereby excluding those circumstances where a victim is pursued by an acquaintance or stranger (Sohn, 1994; Home Office, 1996). The greatest limitation of restraining orders, however, is the notorious difficulty of enforcing them. Often referred to as 'paper shields' (Smith, 1995), in practice these orders do little to abate stalking and frequently serve to intensify the anger and determination of the perpetrator (Walker, 1993; Mullen & Pathé, 1994b).

Criminal and civil laws could in theory be stretched to extend their scope to stalking, but these laws failed to reflect the unique nature of stalking behaviour, which involves a *series* of related and seemingly legitimate actions, as opposed to single or unrelated and clearly illegitimate offences. In practice, any effective legal action against stalking usually required a physical assault against the victim or damage to property. Criminal justice intervention was all too often stalled until the stalker 'did something'. Jane McAllister, herself a victim of stalking, testified to the US Senate Judiciary Committee Hearings on Antistalking Legislation in 1992:

the police were not insensitive, but they were stymied. The man violated almost every area of my life, but had broken no law. The police worked with me to prevent an assault but, in the final analysis, said there was nothing they could do till an assault occurred. (National Institute of Justice, 1996, p. 2).

At the same hearings, Mrs Sandra Polard, the mother of a young stalking victim testified that:

despite the threats he has made against our lives, despite his repeated violations of restraining orders, despite the professional assessment of him as dangerous, both the District Attorney and our own attorney have said that nothing can be done until he has 'done something'. What is the 'something' they must wait for him to do? Kidnap [my daughter]? Rape her? Kill her? . . . (Cited in Walker, 1993, p. 273)

It was this gap in the law, which in practice if not in theory permitted effective intervention only after escalation to violence that prompted consideration of a more effective and specific legislative response to the problem of stalking. Feminist critics argued that, rather than introduce laws specific to stalking, there should be a strengthening and proper enforcement of existing anti-harassment laws, which would demonstrate a greater commitment by governments to address systemic violence against women (e.g. making restraining order violations punishable by significant terms of imprisonment; Way, 1994). In the end, however, the pressure was for something to be done about stalking, and for obvious political and some practical legislative reasons, the response of governments has been to create with specific anti-stalking statutes, a new category of offending.

The development of anti-stalking legislation

The 1989 murder of popular American sitcom actress Rebecca Schaeffer was the impetus for the introduction of anti-stalking legislation in California. Schaeffer was by no means the first celebrity to suffer the unwanted attention of a disturbed fan, nor the first victim of an escalation from stalking to violence. However, she was the first *high-profile* victim in the USA (and possibly worldwide) to be fatally attacked by a stalker and her death has virtually become synonymous with the public outcry and media pressure that culminated in the instigation and passage of the world's first anti-stalking statute (see Gilligan, 1992; Resnick, 1992; Anderson, 1993; Sohn, 1994).

Schaeffer's death received intense media attention, both in relation to the circumstances of the murder and the seemingly bizarre motives of the perpetrator. Characterizations of a 'deranged' stranger easily able to correspond with, and locate, his victim helped to reinforce a social anxiety that emphasizes vulnerability to crime and suspicion regarding the intentions of others. While the public outrage over Schaeffer's death was sufficient to galvanize a political response to this behaviour (Bureau of Justice Assistance, 1996) the murders of four women from Orange County, California, in 1989, also highlighted the gaps in existing laws to deal with stalking. In each case, the victim had been pursued by an ex-intimate partner prior to her murder, despite legal intervention to obtain restraining orders in response to the ongoing harassment (Guy, 1993; Montesino, 1993). The highly publicized deaths of these five women stimulated public demand for a response to stalking. The political response was by any standards rapid. California State Senator Edward Royce, the representative for Orange County, sponsored a Bill in 1990 making stalking a criminal offence. The Bill was passed in September 1990 and came into effect on 1 January 1991. The California Penal Code defined the offence of 'stalking' as:

any person who wilfully, maliciously, and repeatedly follows or harasses another person and who makes a credible threat with the intent to place that person in reasonable fear of death or great bodily harm . . . (CAL PENAL CODE 646.9(A))

'Harasses' was defined as:

a knowing and wilful course of conduct directed at a specific person which seriously alarms, annoys or harasses the person, and which serves no legitimate purpose. The course of conduct must be such as would cause a reasonable person to suffer substantial emotional distress, and must actually cause substantial emotional distress to the person. 'Course of conduct' means a pattern of conduct composed of a series of acts over a period of time, however short, evidencing a continuity of purpose. Constitutionally protected activity is not included within the meaning of course of conduct. (CAL PENAL CODE 646.9 (e–g)

A credible threat was defined as 'a threat made with the intent and the apparent ability to carry out the threat so as to cause the target of the threat to reasonably fear for his or her safety'. The statute's sentencing provision initially carried a maximum term of one year's imprisonment and/or a US $1000 fine for an initial conviction, with enhanced penalties if the perpetrator violated a court order or subsequently committed another stalking offence against the same victim within seven years (two to four years' imprisonment).

In less than nine months, the Californian legislature had conceived and passed the first law to prohibit stalking. The primary legal elements of this offence were: (1) a course of conduct over a period of time that evidenced a continuity of purpose to harass, alarm or annoy a person; and (2) a credible threat with the specific intent to place a person in reasonable fear of death or great bodily harm. Although each of these elements (an 'act', a 'threat' and an 'intent') appear relatively straightforward, a closer examination reveals considerable legal complexity.

The act

The first necessary element for the offence of stalking is the performance of the requisite 'act'. In California, the act requires a course of conduct against a victim involving harassment or following. The statute stipulates that the perpetrator must perform a 'series of acts over a period of time, however short, evidencing a continuity of purpose'. While 'series of acts' is not defined, US courts have interpreted this to mean acts performed on two or more occasions (*People v. Heilman*, 1994). Furthermore, it is unclear from the wording 'however short' whether these acts can be perpetrated within the space of several hours in order to constitute stalking.

The Californian statute also requires that the victim suffer substantial emotional distress due to the actions of the stalker. This distress is measured both subjectively (i.e. the victim must actually suffer significant emotional distress) and objectively (employing the standard of what a 'reasonable person' would be expected to experience). The inclusion of an objective assessment of suffering ensures that the offence is not wholly contingent on the sensitivities or vulnerabilities of each victim.

Other US states have subsequently grappled with the issue of how to define the 'act' requirement in anti-stalking laws. Jurisdictions have either adopted the Californian approach, requiring the perpetrator to engage in a 'course of conduct', or have specified activities that constitute stalking within the statute (see Michigan, p. 262). It is argued that those states that list prohibited activities are unlikely to fall to constitutional challenges as potential stalkers are put on notice as to what behaviour is illegal (Walker, 1993). Conversely, many states have chosen not to specify stalking activities for fear that courts will limit prosecutions only to those behaviours so proscribed (National Institute of Justice, 1996), although this is yet to occur in any US appellate court.

The threat

Under the Californian statute, having established that the perpetrator performed the necessary act, the prosecution must also prove that a credible threat was directed at the victim and that the stalker possessed the means to execute that threat[1]. The threat must be made against the victim or a member of the victim's family and must involve death, great bodily harm or fear for one's safety. This provision was included to ensure that the perpetrator intended to cause harm to the victim, thus protecting inoffensive or legitimate behaviours from being captured by the offence (Guy, 1993; Boychuk, 1994).

The requirement of a credible threat, however, fails to acknowledge that many stalkers never make explicit threats against their victim (Orion, 1997; Mullen et al., 1999), or, if they do threaten, do not possess the necessary means to effect them. To further complicate matters, many stalkers, as has been emphasized, have the intention not to harm the victim but to express their love or wish for reconciliation. The requirement to make a specific and credible threat effectively nullifies stalking activities that occur in the absence of any verbal or written threat, without recognizing that a significant threat is usually implied in the course of conduct (e.g. disclosing an intimate knowledge of the victim's daily routine). Although initially regarded by the Californian legislature as necessary to establish intent, the requirement of a credible threat poses significant difficulties for the enforcement of stalking laws (see Saunders, 1998). As a consequence, few US states have included this element in their anti-stalking laws, instead providing both for explicit threats and for the recognition that certain behaviours, whatever the perpetrator's claimed intentions, would be expected to cause a reasonable person to feel threatened (Bureau of Justice Assistance, 1996).

The intent

The final provision of the Californian law is the 'intent' requirement. In those statutory offences that do not expressly include intention in the definition, and in common law offences, there is a rebuttable presumption that an essential ingredient in every criminal act is *mens rea* [guilty mind]: that is, that the accused

---

[1] California amended its statute in 1994 to include either explicit or implicit threats, but the law retains the requirement that the perpetrator possessed the intent and the apparent ability to carry out the threat.

possessed a criminal intention or knowledge of the wrongfulness of the act (Burke, 1976). Criminal offences may vary according to whether general intent is sufficient (i.e. that the perpetrator's illegal actions were voluntary or wilful) or whether specific intent is required (i.e. that the offender possessed an additional culpable mental state during the commission of the offence, e.g. to place the victim in reasonable fear of harm or death).

The role of the perpetrator's intentions in the crime of stalking is a vexed issue. Poorly handled it has the potential to compromise fundamental elements of criminal law as well as the ability to successfully prosecute stalkers. It is generally considered a prerequisite of the criminal law that, in order to obtain a conviction, the offender must have intended to commit the crime or have been reckless as to the consequences of their actions. In practice intent is usually assumed, but it is open to the defence to raise the issue of criminal intent in all except the rare offences not requiring any intent (e.g. parking offences). The requirement that an offender possess the intent to harass or harm a victim can raise profound problems with the offence of stalking. As mentioned, many stalkers do not intend to harm or alarm; instead they may possess the, albeit misguided, intention to establish or attempt to re-establish a relationship with the object of their attention. Despite their pursuit of the object and the fear this elicits, if the requirement for a guilty intent is retained in the absence of any specific aim to harass or harm, such stalkers could not be convicted of an offence. A West Australian man was charged under the state's stalking law for repeatedly approaching and intruding on a woman he had met briefly while repairing the photocopier at her workplace. Following this brief business contact, the man made repeated visits to the woman's workplace and later to her home. These unwanted approaches persisted for seven years and did not abate when the woman obtained a restraining order. When the man was finally brought to court under the new anti-stalking laws, the magistrate acquitted the defendant on the basis that he did not believe he had intended to intimidate or frighten the woman. The magistrate in his judgement opined 'I don't think he was intimidating her, he was just being persistent. He was being like a little puppy dog wagging its tail' (*The West Australian*, 2 February, 1996). Similar enforcement difficulties with anti-stalking laws may be encountered with the lesser element of general intent, if courts are not satisfied that a defendant's intentions were 'malicious'. That some stalkers suffer psychiatric conditions that effectively preclude the formation of criminal intent further renders this provision problematic in practice.

In response to the difficulties that intention poses for the prosecution of certain stalkers, several jurisdictions have adopted a minimum level of intent. Anti-stalking legislation in sixteen US states[2] does not require any proof that the defendant

---

[2] Alaska, District of Columbia, Florida, Indiana, Iowa, Maine, Michigan, Minnesota, Nevada, New Hampshire, North Dakota, Utah, Vermont, Virginia, Washington and Wisconsin.

intended to cause fear, alarm or any untoward effect. Instead, if the victim was subjected to behaviour likely to frighten or alarm a reasonable person, then the crime of stalking has been committed. In these jurisdictions, it is necessary only to demonstrate that the defendant intended to commit *the act* that caused the victim to fear. In effect, the victim's perceptions, reactions, vulnerabilities and sensitivities become the critical elements that define a stalking event, rather than the intentions of the defendant. We thus have a victim-defined crime, which is virtually unique. The nonlawyer usually finds such a proposition neither surprising nor troubling, but lawyers, with very good reason, are often less sanguine about overturning one of the most venerable and central tenets of the criminal law.

The absence of traditional criminal intent requirements in several anti-stalking laws has been praised by victim advocates for ensuring that most, if not all stalkers, can be effectively prosecuted. However, in recognizing that psychiatric illness may be of central relevance to the emergence of stalking behaviour, it is from a mental health perspective both poor practice and policy that few of these anti-stalking laws contain provisions requiring the psychiatric assessment of such offenders (Fritz, 1995). If it is prevention, not mere punishment, that is to guide the progress of anti-stalking laws, then it is essential that such laws contain provisions for mandatory assessment and mandated treatment when indicated.

Other elements

The Californian law states that 'constitutionally protected activity' is not included within the meaning of the statute and specifically exempts acts of stalking that occur during labour picketing. Other US states have similarly exempted lawful demonstrations, journalists, process servers and private detectives to ensure that selected members of the community who possess a 'legitimate purpose' can lawfully conduct their business without fear of, or nuisance from, anti-stalking laws. However, what constitutes a 'legitimate purpose' or 'constitutionally protected activity' has been the subject of debate in US appellate courts (see below). For example, an anti-abortion protester in the USA was charged with stalking an abortion clinic director, after she repeatedly followed the director, suggested that the latter should get a bullet-proof vest and disclosed an intimate knowledge of the layout of the director's home (cited in Faulkner & Hsiao, 1994). Political protest groups argue that such behaviour is consistent with lawful demonstration and contend that stalking laws potentially infringe these rights to free speech. It remains to be seen how US courts will deal with the issue of what constitutes legitimate or constitutionally protected behaviour. The impact of the sociopolitical persuasions of the judges hearing these cases may be an intriguing variable.

In summary, the first anti-stalking law to be enacted has been praised for being narrowly defined legislation that is unlikely to infringe constitutional rights (Guy,

1993; Boychuk, 1994) and simultaneously criticized for failing adequately to address the realities of stalking (McAnaney et al., 1993). The Californian statute was framed to err on the side of constitutionality, as evidenced by its requirements of specific intent, objective reasonableness of the victim's response, and a credible threat. The statute served as a model for most of the legislation that followed in the USA, although few states adopted the elements of the 1990 code in its entirety. Most states framed their legislation in response to local and highly emotive cases of stalking, each state giving greater or lesser emphasis to the rights of the victim and the accused. Therefore, despite anti-stalking statutes sharing a common purpose to prohibit ongoing harassment and intimidation, no single legal definition of stalking exists and there is considerable variation in the application and sanctions of laws in each US state.

Stalking statutes in other US states and Canada

Since 1992, each US state has introduced anti-stalking legislation, or has amended existing criminal statutes to address stalking behaviours. In what has been described as a 'torrent of legislation' (McAnaney et al., 1993), thirty states enacted anti-stalking legislation in 1992 and an additional nineteen jurisdictions passed anti-stalking laws in 1993. The US Federal Government has also legislated to prohibit interstate stalking and malicious communications. (See the Interstate Stalking Punishment and Prevention Act, 1996, and the Communications Decency Act, 1995.) Following this stampede to legislate, Canada introduced a criminal harassment provision to deal with stalking-related conduct in 1993. Provided below are examples of anti-stalking legislation from several US states and Canada, which emphasize the variation in the law and highlight special provisions used in conjunction with this offence.

Florida

Misdemeanour stalking occurs when a person 'willfully, maliciously, and repeatedly follows or harasses another person'. This offence attracts a maximum penalty of one year's imprisonment. If, during the course of stalking, the perpetrator makes a credible threat with the intent to cause the victim to reasonably fear death or bodily injury or continues to stalk despite a court-imposed prohibitive order, this constitutes *aggravated* stalking, a felony offence punishable by up to five years' imprisonment.

The provisions of the Florida anti-stalking statute have been criticized for being overly broad in their definition and potentially unconstitutional (Guy, 1993; Thomas, 1993; Faulkner & Hsiao, 1994). (Up to 1997, Florida's anti-stalking law has been challenged 26 times in appellate courts (Office of Justice Programs,

1997).) As a misdemeanour offence, the law requires only that a perpetrator repeatedly harass or follow the victim, in the absence of any threat. It is argued that such conditions allow the mere presence of a person to be punished, thus making it difficult to distinguish legal from illegal behaviour (Thomas, 1993). However, the statute requires that the conduct be 'malicious' and it is to be hoped that this element ensures that only offensive activities are prosecuted. The other contentious aspect of the Florida law is the provision that a victim's emotional response to stalking need not be reasonable. The law does not include an objective measure of harm, requiring the victim only to suffer substantial emotional distress. By neglecting to include an objective standard of harm, each case may be judged on the idiosyncratic responses of the victim, leaving the law open to becoming arbitrary and oppressive.

Illinois

Stalking occurs when a person threatens another with the intent to place that person in reasonable apprehension of death, bodily harm, sexual assault, confinement or restraint, and 'in furtherance of the threat' follows the person or places the person under surveillance on at least two occasions. The statute provides a special provision that restricts bail for aggravated stalking where the court determines that the release of the accused would pose a significant threat to the physical safety of the victim.

The provisions of this law have also been subject to criticism. The statute initially required a threat to *precede* at least two instances of following or surveillance. This element created difficulties similar to those encountered in California, whereby stalking activities that occurred in the absence of an explicit threat could not be prosecuted. (The Illinois statute was modified to require either an explicit or implicit threat conveyed at any time, but on at least 2 occasions (see Bureau of Justice Assistance, 1996).) The restrictive bail provision was included to assure the safety of the victim in cases where no condition of release (e.g. a restraining order) was felt to offer reasonable protection. However, detaining an accused prior to trial may increase the presumption of guilt (Strikis, 1993) and deprive a defendant of liberty without sufficient evidence. A well-publicized case in Chicago highlighted the difficulties with this 'no bail' provision. A woman alleged that her ex-husband made a threatening phone call and intimidated her at her place of work, a pizza shop. The accused was charged with stalking but acquitted by a jury, who felt that the woman made the allegation out of anger over their recent divorce proceedings. Unfortunately, the man had already spent 132 days in gaol under the state's no-bail provision (Faulkner & Hsiao, 1994). Following difficulties with the application of this provision, the statute was amended to ensure that procedural guidelines are employed for 'no-bail' hearings, although this element remains contentious.

Michigan

The Michigan code has been described as the strongest anti-stalking law in the USA. The code defines stalking as a willful course of conduct involving repeated harassment that causes a reasonable person to feel terrorized, frightened, intimidated, threatened, harassed or molested. A course of conduct is defined as two or more noncontinuous acts. Harassment consists of conduct that includes, but is not limited to:

- following or appearing within the sight of that individual,
- approaching or confronting that individual in public or private property,
- appearing at the workplace or residence of that individual,
- entering or remaining on property occupied or owned by that individual,
- contacting the individual by phone,
- sending mail or electronic communications to the individual, or
- sending or placing an object on that individual's property.

As mentioned previously, the Michigan law does not require any intention on the part of the defendant to cause the victim fear or harm. Rather, the defendant must intend only to commit the *act* that causes the victim to fear. Thus, a person could, without wrongful intent, appear *within the sight* of another on two occasions, and so long as the other person is frightened by this conduct, then the crime of stalking has been committed. The statute requires that the victim's response be objectively reasonable, however, which should ameliorate to some extent concerns regarding the law's vulnerability to misuse.

West Virginia

The West Virginia statute was framed to address stalking in the context of domestic violence. The statute initially defined stalking as to intentionally follow, lie in wait or repeatedly threaten a person with whom the defendant had resided or had a sexual relationship. The law was amended in 1994 to extend its application to circumstances in which the perpetrator 'seeks to establish a personal or social relationship'. Therefore, while the law retains an emphasis on intimate or former intimate stalking, it has broadened its scope to include those wishing to establish other interpersonal relationships. The penalties for stalking in West Virginia are less draconian than in other states, a first offence attracting a maximum six month sentence, while aggravated stalking and second offences are punishable by up to one year's imprisonment.

Canada

The Criminal Harassment provision (1993) in Canada requires the defendant to engage in conduct that consists of repeated following or communicating, besetting or watching a place where the person happens to be, or engaging in threatening conduct. This conduct can be directed either to the intended object or another person known to him or her and must cause the object reasonable fear for his or her safety, or the safety of the other known person. The law requires either a specific intent to harass, or a recklessness standard, whereby the defendant should have known that such conduct would result in harassment. This offence is punishable by up to five years' imprisonment on indictment or six months on summary conviction. In a departure from most US laws, the Canadian offence does not refer to a 'course' of conduct. Although the defendant must 'repeatedly' follow or communicate with the victim, the acts of watching, besetting or threatening are not qualified by the need for repetition. Consequently, a person may be found guilty if he or she performs one of these acts on only *one* occasion. This increases the risk that inoffensive activities may be prosecuted as stalking, although the use of an objective measure of harm should help to curtail misuse of the law.

Summary

This brief review demonstrates the variation in the definitions applied to stalking and the essential elements required to establish the offence. The majority of American states drafted their laws in accordance with the original Californian model. However, enforcement difficulties associated with the credible threat and specific intent provisions resulted in a broadening of the original provisions in many states. In sixteen jurisdictions, traditional criminal responsibility elements have been minimized in anti-stalking laws, with the perceptions and reactions of the victim becoming the defining elements of the offence, usually qualified by those being consonant with the reactions of a reasonable person. As prohibited conduct must occur on only two occasions in order to constitute criminal stalking, the potential of these laws to inhibit a person's legitimate behaviour is not insignificant. Given the boundary difficulties associated with this offence, a discourse emerged among legal academics in the early 1990s regarding the ability of the laws to withstand constitutional challenges. Coinciding with this debate was the commission of a model code on anti-stalking legislation by the Federal Government. This code was developed in order to promote uniformity in state laws and to strengthen them to withstand any constitutional challenges, although its success in achieving these aims has yet to be established.

The constitutionality of anti-stalking laws in the USA

The swift introduction of anti-stalking laws throughout the USA in less than three years, prompted concern as to whether the laws were drafted with sufficient clarity and regard for constitutional rights (see Guy, 1993; McAnaney et al., 1993; Thomas, 1993; Boychuk, 1994; Faulkner & Hsiao, 1994). The primary bases on which these laws have been argued as potentially unconstitutional are *vagueness* and *overbreadth*. The doctrine of vagueness operates under the due process clause of the Fourteenth Amendment of the US Constitution, which requires that legislation be written with sufficient clarity to enable a person of common intelligence to ascertain the boundaries of lawful conduct and behaviour (Thomas, 1993; Faulkner & Hsioa, 1994). The US Supreme Court held in *Connally v. General Constr. Co.* (1926), that 'a statute which either forbids or requires the doing of an act in terms so vague that men of common intelligence must necessarily differ as to its application, violates the first essential of due process of law'. Thus, the creation of a new criminal offence must be sufficiently explicit to inform members of the community what conduct will render them liable to its sanctions. It must also be framed with sufficient specificity to ensure that police and other law enforcement personnel will not enforce the law in an arbitrary or discriminatory manner. A statute in which lawful and illegal conduct cannot be determined from its language may be deemed vague and in such a case be struck down. The expression 'void for vagueness' has become embedded in the language of American Constitutional law.

The doctrine of overbreadth prohibits a criminal law from sweeping so broadly as to encompass constitutionally protected activity. This doctrine applies only to statutes that inhibit First Amendment rights of freedom of speech and expression (Hueter, 1997). (While freedom of movement is not a right enshrined in the US Constitution, it is generally accepted as falling within the scope of First Amendment rights and hence is applicable under the doctrine of overbreadth (Hueter, 1997).) A statute may be found overbroad if, in addition to prohibiting activities that are not constitutionally protected, it includes within its scope activities that are protected by the Constitution. Hence, while a law may be designed to capture illegal conduct, if it substantially infringes a constitutional right, it will be found overbroad and struck down. To argue successfully that a law is overbroad, however, it must be shown that the protected right is a significant aspect of the law's target and that there is no satisfactory method to sever the law's unconstitutional applications from its constitutional ones (Walker, 1993).

The legal discourse that emerged in North America centred on whether anti-stalking laws were likely to be vulnerable to challenges on the bases of vagueness and overbreadth. It was concluded almost universally that, while the narrowly drawn provisions of California's law were unobjectionable, the broader scope of laws such as Florida's were likely to be both unconstitutionally vague and overbroad. Unfortunately, the bulk of this discourse occurred prior to constitutional challenges being addressed by appellate courts and this speculation proved premature. (The earliest constitutional challenges to anti-stalking laws were heard in appellate courts in late 1994 and 1995 (National Institute of Justice, 1996).) While trial courts in North America have struck down anti-stalking laws on the basis of vagueness or overbreadth, upon appeal superior courts have generally upheld the legislation. At the time of writing, only a handful of American states have suffered the striking down of their stalking statutes on the basis of being unconstitutional.

The first anti-stalking law to be struck down by an appellate court was in Massachusetts, in 1994: *Commonwealth v. Kwiatkowski*. In this case, the defendant was barred by a restraining order from telephoning his ex-wife and approaching her residence. On the night of his arrest, the defendant called his ex-wife at 2.45 a.m. on the pretext that one of their children had had a nightmare. Having gained his ex-wife's attention he then told her that he wanted to re-establish their relationship. However, when he bluntly questioned whether she had any men in her apartment, his ex-wife hung up. Her phone immediately rang again, prompting her to take it off the hook. Two hours later the defendant arrived at his ex-wife's house with their children, at which point she called the police. The defendant left, but shortly afterward telephoned his ex-wife and said, 'This is war. I'm going to get you'. The defendant was arrested and subsequently convicted of stalking.

On appeal of conviction, the appellate court agreed with the defendant's claim that the stalking statute was vague. According to the judgement, the statute was faulty in the definition of 'repeatedly harasses'. The statute defined harassment as 'a knowing and willful pattern of conduct or series of acts'. The court held that under this definition, in order to repeatedly harass the defendant must perform at least *two series of acts* (i.e. at least four separate acts). As the defendant had not engaged in a repeated series of harassment, his conviction was overturned.

Several other American states have suffered the striking down of their anti-stalking statutes on the basis of vagueness. In *Oregon v. Norris-Romine/Finley* (1995) it was successfully argued in consolidated cases that the state's anti-stalking statute was unconstitutionally vague. Both defendants were charged with violating stalking protective orders, which can be issued by a law enforcement officer who has probable cause to believe that a person, 'without legitimate purpose, intentionally, knowingly or recklessly engages in repeated and unwanted contact'. The court ruled that the meaning of 'legitimate purpose' was not apparent from a reading of the statute, rendering the law vague. The charges against the defendants were dismissed and the statute struck down. The Oregon appellate court subsequently found the state's law unconstitutional in *Starr v. Eccles* (1995). In this case, Starr sought to dismiss a stalking protective order brought against him by his former psychologist. Starr consulted Eccles with his wife when they were having marital difficulties. The couple subsequently divorced, though Eccles briefly continued to treat Starr's ex-wife. Starr claimed that his ex-wife and former psychologist were having a sexual affair and were conspiring to ruin him. On the basis of this belief, he allegedly made up to thirty unwanted contacts with Eccles, including blocking his passage on a crossway, harassing his family when he was out of town, making lewd gestures and taking photographs of Eccles in a parking lot, and threatening that he would 'get' his former psychologist. Eccles obtained a stalking protective order against Starr. In filing for a dismissal of the order, Starr argued on his own behalf that the statute violated his right of access to public places, abridged his right to travel, was overbroad and unconstitutionally vague (especially the phrases 'legitimate purpose' and 'repeated and unwanted contact'). Relying on the judgement in *Oregon v. Norris-Romine/Finley*, the court held that 'legitimate purpose' was vague and reversed the stalking order on that basis alone. Unfortunately, it chose not to address the arguments related to overbreadth and right of access to public places and travel.

In *State v. Bryan* (1996) the Kansas anti-stalking law was found unconstitutionally vague on the basis that it did not include any objective guidelines to determine whether a stalker's actions were alarming, annoying or harassing to the victim. The defendant successfully argued that the crime of stalking 'depends on the sensitivity of the complainant', a concept rejected by the court, which subsequently interpreted the statute to include a 'reasonable person' standard. More recently, in *Long v. The State of Texas* (1996) the court relied on a prior vagueness precedent to strike down the state's anti-stalking provision. The court was particularly concerned that the stalking law could inhibit the lawful exercise of free speech (making several references to political protesting) and criticized the absence of a clear 'reasonable person' standard. It was suggested that a staggering 800–900 stalking cases were dismissed in Texas as a result of the ruling (Anon., 1997), although a new law addressing these limitations was promptly passed following this decision.

The model anti-stalking code for American states

In October 1992, the US Congress commissioned the National Institute of Justice to develop a model anti-stalking code for the states that would be both enforceable and constitutional. The model code was seen as important in resolving problematic aspects of the state laws, which probably arose as a result of legislators drafting the laws more with the imperatives of public relations in mind than constitutional concerns. Although the intention was for the states to adopt the code uniformly, none of its recommendations regarding the definition and punishment of stalking was binding. As a result, American states have adopted only those elements that are consistent with their agenda for prosecuting stalking. The objective of the code to bring uniformity to state anti-stalking laws has largely failed.

The model code (Bureau of Justice Assistance, 1996, Appendix A) defines stalking as a 'purposeful' course of conduct directed at a person that would cause reasonable fear of bodily injury or death, either to oneself or a family member and that actually induces such fear. The code requires that the defendant 'has knowledge or should have knowledge' that such fear is a likely consequence of the behaviour. A course of conduct is defined as 'repeatedly maintaining a visual or physical proximity to a person or repeatedly conveying verbal or written threats or threats implied by conduct . . .'. 'Repeatedly' means on two or more occasions. The code suggests that states 'consider requiring mental evaluations and counselling as part of sentences imposed on convicted stalkers and as part of conditions for pre-trial release, probation or parole', a salient and in our view critical issue that has been overlooked, or disregarded, in the majority of stalking statutes.

While the model code was intended to provide constitutionally rigorous recommendations, the 'intent' requirement of the code has been criticized as potentially vague. The code effectively ascribes what amounts to a negligence standard for the offence (i.e. that the defendant has knowledge or 'should have knowledge' that the victim will be placed in fear). The 'should have knowledge' clause has been argued as being vague, particularly when coupled with 'maintaining a visual or physical proximity to a person' (Faulkner & Hsiao, 1994). While the 'reasonable person' standard should minimize any misuse of the code, the minimum standard of *mens rea* employed renders it vulnerable to challenges on the basis of vagueness, in contradiction to its stated purpose to be constitutionally enforceable.

North American anti-stalking laws: a summary

The categorisation of stalking as a criminal offence in the USA has been a swift and contentious exercise. By no means a new behaviour, stalking rapidly came to be regarded as an urgent issue requiring political and legislative action. Although the option of modifying and strengthening existing anti-harassment laws was available, legislators instead chose the politically popular response to criminalize this form of behaviour in specific anti-stalking legislation.

Between 1990 and 1993, each American state enacted laws or amended existing statutes to prohibit stalking. The speed with which these laws were enacted is noteworthy, given that the problem of stalking was well entrenched in North America. The cumulative effect of lobbying by the women's movement and domestic violence groups was undoubtedly instrumental in demonstrating the need for laws to address violence against women. However, feminist critics argued that the 'speedy criminalization' of one aspect of this problem was a knee-jerk reaction that served public relations imperatives for governments, as opposed to a desire to address systemic violence in society (Way, 1994). The observation that politicians, as public and often reviled figures, frequently draw the attention of disgruntled and deluded stalkers also has not escaped critics trying to explain the rapid response to stalking. Finally, the media fascination with stalking and its role in harnessing public awareness and outrage to the problem were also instrumental in galvanizing a political response. Undoubtedly each of these factors was influential to varying degrees in the decisions by states to enact anti-stalking laws. None the less, it is the *haste* with which these laws were enacted that has increased the probability that inadvertent behaviours will be prosecuted as stalking, as well as the likelihood that the laws may be rendered unconstitutional.

The other notable aspect of anti-stalking laws is their lack of uniformity. Stalking as a criminal offence varies considerably between the US states. Whereas California requires a stalker to intend to cause distress to his victim, in Michigan it is the perceptions and the reactions of the victim to a course of conduct that define whether stalking has occurred. Emphasizing the responses of the victim of stalking ensures greater enforcement of anti-stalking laws, yet this is largely at the expense of traditional elements of culpability, any compromise of which may increase the likelihood that inadvertent behaviours are seen as stalking. Although the model anti-stalking code was commissioned with the express purpose of providing a constitutionally enforceable model that states could adopt uniformly, these objectives do not appear to have been achieved.

There was broad public agreement, albeit orchestrated by the media (a far from disinterested party), that legislative measures to address the problem of stalking were required. Stalking is a harmful course of conduct, with deleterious effects on the victim's social, emotional and occupational functioning. However, it is the extent to which these laws capture legitimate or inadvertent behaviours in addition to 'genuine' stalking that is a critical issue. Fearing that victims may be vulnerable to escalation to violence as the number of contacts increase, legislators have prohibited unwanted forms of contact that occur on as few as two occasions. Frequently, these actions need not be accompanied by malicious intent or threatening behaviour. While defining the boundaries of what constitutes harmful and inoffensive contacts is undoubtedly complex, limiting the legal definition of stalking to two nonconsensual contacts is a far cry from the actual experience of this behaviour. Although anti-stalking laws will capture genuine stalking, the potential for these laws to capture inoffensive (although unwanted) behaviours or social interactions cannot be discounted.

Anti-stalking laws in the USA continue to come under constitutional scrutiny in appellate courts, and it remains to be seen in what form they will survive. Research to assess the effectiveness of the legislation continues and an annual report on stalking presented to the US Congress will provide an ongoing source of valuable information to those curious of the future directions of anti-stalking laws. (See the US Department of Justice Web site (www.usdoj.gov) for the Annual Report to Congress on Stalking and Domestic Violence.)

Australian anti-stalking legislation

Australian law is based on the common law of England and Wales, as well as on State and Federal legislation. While Australian courts continue to interpret and apply the common law in given cases, they not infrequently refer to North American (particularly Canadian) judgements and North American decisions are increasingly influencing legislative initiatives in Australian states (e.g. the use of victim impact statements and defences such as the battered woman syndrome). In general terms, it was not unexpected that once anti-stalking laws were established in North America a campaign to introduce similar legislation in Australia would be forthcoming. Like the experience in North America, the publicized murders of women in the context of ongoing harassment by ex-intimate partners and the public outrage accompanying these cases were catalysts for anti-stalking laws in Australia (McMahon & Davids, 1993; Goode, 1995). While many Australian state laws prohibited harassment, intimidation or malicious communications, the option to strengthen such laws was, as in the USA, passed over in favour of the creation of a new criminal offence.

Between 1993 and 1995, anti-stalking laws were passed in each Australian state and territory.[3] The first Australian state to introduce anti-stalking legislation was Queensland, followed in quick succession by New South Wales (NSW), South Australia (SA), Victoria, Western Australia (WA), the Northern Territory (NT), Tasmania and the Australian Capital Territory (ACT). An examination of Australian anti-stalking laws demonstrates that they were modelled on the North American laws that preceded them and similarly, they vary according to their definition, application and sanctions. The following section provides a comparison of the primary elements of anti-stalking laws in each Australian jurisdiction in order to illustrate variations in, and novel applications of, the laws.

Conduct requirements

Most Australian states specify conduct that constitutes the offence of stalking. In Queensland, SA, Tasmania, Victoria, ACT and NT, prohibited acts include:
- following,
- loitering outside the place of residence of the victim or some other place frequented by the victim,
- entering or interfering with the victim's property,
- giving offensive material or leaving such material for the victim to find,
- keeping the person under surveillance, or
- acting in any other way that could reasonably be expected to arouse the victim's apprehension or fear.

---

[3] Stalking offences for each state and territory can be found at the following: Australian Capital Territory, *Crimes Act* (section 34A, 1–4); New South Wales, *Crimes Act* (section 562AB, 1–4); Northern Territory, *Criminal Code* (section 189 1–2); Queensland, *Criminal Code, 1993* (section 359A, 1–7); South Australia, *Criminal Law Consolidation Act* (section19AA 1–5); Tasmania, *Criminal Code* (section 192 a-f); Victoria, *Crimes Act* (section 21A, 1–5); Western Australia, *Criminal Code* (section 338D 1–2; 338E 1–4).

Victoria additionally includes 'telephoning, sending electronic messages to, or otherwise contacting, the victim or any other person'. Queensland prohibits a person from harassing, intimidating or threatening a victim, or performing acts of violence against the victim or a relative, friend, employer or associate. In NSW, stalking is prosecuted under the offence of 'stalking, intimidation with intent to cause fear for personal safety'. Initially, this offence applied only to people who were, or had been, in a domestic or sexual relationship with the victim, although a subsequent amendment broadened the law to include nonintimate relationships.

The majority of states require the prohibited conduct to occur on two or more occasions. In Tasmania and WA, however, there is no reference either to a course of conduct or the number of acts required to constitute stalking. Consequently, a person may be found guilty if he or she performs a prohibited act on only *one* occasion. Like the Canadian harassment provision, this signals a significant departure from all other anti-stalking laws, which distinguish the offence on the basis that it relates to a course of conduct, as opposed to one act. The risk that inadvertent behaviour will be prosecuted as 'stalking' is greatly increased in these states (e.g. Tasmania prohibits 'leaving offensive material where it is likely to be found by a person' in its stalking law), although it is to be hoped that the provision that specific intent must accompany the crime may lessen misuse of the law.

Intention

Most Australian states require the perpetrator of stalking to possess intent to cause physical or mental harm to the victim or another person, or intent to cause apprehension or fear. However, Queensland does not require any intention to cause harm or distress; rather, the perpetrator must intend that the victim be aware that the behaviour is directed at him or her. In Victoria, the law demands either specific intent or the lesser requirement that an offender intends to cause harm or fear 'if that offender knows, or in all the particular circumstances that offender *ought to have understood*, that engaging in a course of conduct of that kind would be likely to cause such harm'. This latter clause ascribes a state of mind that is related more to recklessness than intention (Wiener, 1995).

The response of the victim

The majority of state anti-stalking laws are surprisingly vague in relation to the required response of the victim. Queensland requires the course of conduct to cause a reasonable person to believe that an act of violence is likely to happen. However, the victim is not required to actually experience any emotional effect. Similarly, in both NSW and the ACT, the prosecution need not prove that the victim actually feared personal injury as a result of the defendant's actions, thereby abandoning the need for either a subjective or objective standard of harm. Victoria requires the subjective experience of physical or mental harm yet does not include an objective assessment of this response. In the remaining states, although the laws specify that the offender must intend to cause harm or apprehension, there is no elaboration regarding whether the victim must subjectively experience such an effect.

Thus, only one Australian state requires that a victim's response to stalking be reasonable. With the exception of Victoria, no states require the subjective experience of distress or fear. The majority of states have resolved that fear or harm should not be prerequisites to establish the offence of stalking, to ensure that resilient or otherwise unaffected victims of stalking are not denied legal recourse.

Penalties

In most Australian states, stalking is punishable by up to two to three years' imprisonment. Offences that involve aggravation typically attract a maximum penalty of five years' imprisonment. Victoria's maximum penalty for stalking is ten years' imprisonment, one of the most severe penalties imposed for stalking in the world. This is peculiarly harsh, given that Victoria does not provide a scale of offending (i.e. aggravation) or an objective measure of suffering and ascribes the criminal responsibility of recklessness to the offence.

Exemptions or defences against a charge

Queensland and Victoria provide defences against the charge of stalking if it can be shown that the conduct was for the purposes of a genuine industrial, political or other public dispute, or was carried out as part of official duties related to the enforcement of the criminal law or the protection of public revenue. In WA, it is a defence that the accused acted either with lawful authority or with a 'reasonable excuse'. The majority of states, however, do not provide within the legislation itself any exemptions or defences against the charge of stalking.

Special provisions

South Australia's anti-stalking law contains a novel provision that amounts to a double jeopardy protection clause. This provision states that:

(a) a person who has been acquitted or convicted on a charge of stalking may not be convicted of another offence arising out of the same set of circumstances and involving a physical element that is common to that charge, and
(b) a person who has been acquitted or convicted on a charge of an offence other than stalking may not be convicted of stalking if the charge of stalking arises out of the same set of circumstances and involves a physical element that is common to the charge of that other offence.

Thus an offender cannot be convicted of stalking if the series of acts were related to, and part of, another offence (e.g. a paedophile convicted of sexual assault cannot also be prosecuted for stalking, if following and surveillance were related to the preparation for the assault). Similarly, an offender convicted of stalking cannot also be prosecuted for trespass, for example if this occurred during the commission of the offence. The SA government included these provisions to ensure that the offence of stalking is not used to 'load up' an indictment in cases where a series of crimes have been committed (Goode, 1995). Early sentencing statistics suggest that the inclusion of these provisions is warranted in all other states. For example, in Victoria, the charge of stalking was most often included in a series of offences against defendants. Only in fewer than a third of cases was stalking the principal (i.e. most serious) charge for which a defendant was sentenced (Department of Justice, 1997, 1998). The feared 'loading up' is occurring, with suspected paedophiles in particular being charged with stalking. This is probably at least in part because in the state of Victoria the maximum sentence for stalking may be far higher than that for substantial sexual offences of, for example, indecent exposure or indecent assault.

Victoria's anti-stalking law also contains a contentious provision. If satisfied on the balance of probabilities that a defendant has stalked another person and is likely to continue to do so, the courts may grant an intervention order. The magistrate or judge must necessarily find that the defendant has stalked in order to grant such an order. Thus, a person may be labelled a 'stalker' in the absence of any criminal conviction related to such behaviour and on the basis of a civil standard of proof (Wiener, 1995).

Summary of Australian anti-stalking legislation

Following the enactment of anti-stalking legislation throughout North America, each Australian state passed complementary laws between 1993 and 1995. The Australian laws were modelled on the North American codes that preceded them and they similarly vary according to their definition, application and penalties. In the absence of a written constitution of the American type with its Bill of Rights, or a separate Bill or Charter of Rights, Australian law is not restricted to the same extent by those constitutional imperatives that operate in the USA or in Canada. Despite this, most Australian states have made some attempts to limit anti-stalking laws from capturing legitimate activities. The majority of anti-stalking laws require specific or general intent to cause harm or fear to the victim in order to establish the offence. However, unlike the US laws, Australian jurisdictions typically do not require the victim to experience any ill effects due to the actions of the defendant. If the intention to cause physical or mental harm is proved, the reactions of the victim (or lack thereof) are deemed irrelevant. Where Australian laws become increasingly problematic is in those states that require minimum standards of culpability or the performance of only *one* act in order to constitute 'stalking'. Coupled with the lack of any subjective or objectively reasonable harm, such conditions increase the likelihood that anti-stalking laws will be applied against essentially inoffensive or inadvertent behaviours.

Recognizing the potential for misuse and abuse of these laws, the SA government introduced a protection clause that disallows the offence of stalking to be used as a 'loading up' mechanism against an accused. Such provisions help to ensure that stalking is recognized and, more importantly, treated as a serious offence, rather than a useful adjunct to augment a case against a disliked offender. As initial sentencing statistics indicate that stalking is infrequently the principal charge brought against an accused, the use of such protection clauses appears justified in all anti-stalking laws.

In the last decade, Australian law has become increasingly inclined to follow some US legislative initiatives and the swift introduction of anti-stalking legislation in each state is another indication of this tendency. However, in adopting anti-stalking laws, Australian legislators and legal academics had the opportunity to evaluate the laws in practice in the USA and Canada and the legal and constitutional issues that had arisen in attempting to define the boundaries and necessary elements of this offence. In light of this, it is discouraging that several states failed to include safeguards that reduce misuse or abuse of anti-stalking laws. It is also unfortunate that, given this opportunity, little debate occurred among Australian legal academics regarding the need for new laws to deal with stalking, the potential advantages and disadvantages of anti-stalking legislation and methods to minimize these laws encompassing legitimate conduct. While critical public debate concerning proposed laws is frequently of little consequence to legislative decision-makers, the lack of scrutiny of legislation that has the potential to impact on both individual rights and the nature of social interactions is surprising.

The United Kingdom: the Protection from Harassment Act

The introduction of anti-stalking laws in the USA and Australia led to public calls in the UK for similar laws to be enacted. This campaign was advanced by the National Anti-Stalking and Harassment Campaign and Support Association. The UK tabloid press ably placed stalking on the national political agenda, providing a plethora of cases involving the pursuit of celebrities (particularly members of the Royal family), strangers or ex-intimate partners. Wells (1997) succinctly expressed the beliefs underscoring the push for stalking laws, both in the UK and elsewhere: that violence/stalking is increasing, that something must be done to address this and that legislation, as a vehicle for social change, is the appropriate means to achieve this. While stalking was touted as a 'growing menace' (Turl, 1994), British legislators were cautious in adopting a position on how to address this problem. Academics questioned whether existing criminal and civil laws[4] were sufficient to deal with this behaviour and the impact any extension of the law would have on legitimate activities (Allen, 1996; Wells, 1997).

A Private Member's Bill to criminalize stalking was introduced in the House of Commons in May 1996, but failed to receive a second reading. In the following months, the Government sought community responses to the problem in its consultation paper, 'Stalking: The Solutions' (Home Office, 1996). After reviewing the existing civil and criminal laws, the Home Office concluded that current laws did 'not afford sufficient protection to the victims of stalking' and proposed two new criminal offences, and a new tort of molestation, to deal with stalking. Although these recommendations were not accepted in their proposed form by the Government, two offences to deal with stalking behaviours were subsequently introduced in the Protection from Harassment Act (1997).

The Protection from Harassment Act came into force in June 1997 and applies to England, Wales, Scotland and Northern Ireland. (The Protection from Harassment (Northern Ireland) Order (1997) is a separate provision.) The Acts prohibit two forms of antisocial behaviour: 'harassment' and 'putting people in fear of violence'. As applied to England, Wales and Northern Ireland, the harassment clause states that:

A person must not pursue a course of conduct:
a) which amounts to harassment of another, and
b) which he knows or ought to know amounts to harassment of the other.

The Act does not provide a definition of 'harassment', although a course of conduct must involve at least two acts that cause the victim alarm or distress. This provision does not apply if the person demonstrates that the conduct was pursued for the purpose of preventing or detecting crime or that in the particular circumstances the pursuit of the course of conduct was reasonable. Harassment is classed as a summary offence and attracts a maximum six-month term of imprisonment. Any breach of the Act may become the subject of a claim in civil proceedings by the victim, whereby damages may be awarded for any anxiety and financial loss caused by the harassment.

---

[4] British courts have attempted the prosecution of stalking-related behaviours under criminal offences such as grievous bodily harm; assault; the Telecommunications Act (1984); the Malicious Communications Act (1988); the Public Order Act (1986). Civil remedies involving 'non-molestation' orders have also been employed under the Family Law Act (1996) and the Domestic Violence and Matrimonial Proceedings Act (1976).

The second offence, 'putting people in fear of violence', more closely resembles the anti-stalking laws introduced in North America and Australia. According to the Act:

A person whose course of conduct causes another to fear, on at least two occasions, that violence will be used against him is guilty of an offence if he knows or ought to know that his course of conduct will cause the other so to fear on that occasion.

The use of male terms being generic for male and female here. Conviction on this offence on indictment is punishable by a maximum five years' imprisonment, while summary conviction attracts a maximum six months' imprisonment. A person convicted either of harassment or of putting people in fear of violence may be subject to a court-imposed restraining order that prohibits the defendant from further engaging in these activities. If the defendant continues a prohibited course of conduct with this order in effect, this attracts a sentence in accordance with the 'fear of violence' category. Both offences rely on a minimum standard of *mens rea* whereby the defendant 'knows or ought to know' that the consequences of his or her conduct will be frightening to the victim, although the victim's perceptions and response to the actions are emphasized for the 'fear of violence' offence. Neither offence requires an objective measure of harm, although a subjective response is required for the indictable charge.

A separate provision for Scotland is contained in the Act. If a person is found to have pursued a course of conduct that amounts to harassment (i.e. causing alarm or distress on at least two occasions), the victim may make a claim in a civil proceeding referred to as an 'action of harassment'. The court may award damages to the victim or grant a nonharassment order, if satisfied on the balance of probabilities that this is necessary to protect the victim from further harassment. Any breach of a nonharassment order is an offence punishable by a maximum five years' imprisonment on indictment, or six months on summary conviction. Therefore, in Scotland, it is necessary to establish both a pattern of harassment and a breach of an imposed order before the courts can evoke criminal sanctions against the defendant's behaviour. This contrasts with the other UK jurisdictions, whereby restraining orders may be imposed *in addition to* other penalties following a course of harassment.

In essence, the Protection from Harassment Act, as applied to England, Wales and Northern Ireland, provides a scale of offending for crimes of stalking. The offence of 'putting people in fear of violence' amounts to a form of aggravated stalking punishable by a significant term of imprisonment, whereas harassment acts as a 'catch all' offence that should ensure the conviction of those offenders who cannot be prosecuted under the more restrictive aggravated crime. Scotland does not provide a scale of offending, although it establishes a significant maximum penalty for those stalkers who clearly persist in a course of harassment.

The Protection from Harassment Act has been, at the time of writing, in use for eighteen months and its effectiveness in proscribing and punishing the behaviour of stalkers remains to be assessed. While the offences of harassment and putting people in fear of violence require a low standard of criminal intent, and fail to include an objective measure of harm, that is balanced to some extent by the inclusion of provisions that allow courts to impose restraining orders as a condition of sentencing. Any subsequent prohibited contact with the victim constitutes violation of such an order, potentially punishable by a prison sentence with a significant maximum penalty. If enforced, this system may provide an incentive for some stalkers to discontinue harassment of the victim, as well as enable early intervention in those cases where stalkers fail to desist. That the courts at sentencing may impose these restraining orders further eliminates difficulties traditionally encountered with the victim-initiated system, such as lengthy and potentially dangerous delays between application and hearing, the expense of petitioning the court and hiring counsel and the victim incurring the wrath and resentment of the perpetrator.

In comparison with the USA and Australia, legislators in the UK have been relatively circumspect in their response to the problem of stalking. Seemingly less encumbered by the need to offer a fast and politically popular solution, the result has been a more tightly framed law that attempts to limit its scope to offensive behaviours, while providing both civil and criminal remedies. Although the ill-defined offence of harassment is particularly vulnerable to misuse, the aggravated offence of putting people in fear of violence may be less likely to be employed against inadvertent behaviours. Unlike other anti-stalking laws that require the victim to experience fear, alarm or distress, this offence requires the fear that violence will be used against the victim. While this provision would be strengthened by the inclusion of an objective assessment of fear, the wording of the law attempts to limit the application of the offence to potentially harmful conduct. Furthermore, the linking of provisions for restraining orders and civil damages to the criminal offences should offer a reasonable deterrent for those who continue to flout the law, while affording the victim earlier intervention if harassment persists. The laws are still unlikely to encompass the behaviour of all stalkers, although the recognition that a range of remedies is required is welcomed.

The prosecution of stalking: summary and conclusions

In less than a decade, a new category of offending has been established in many Western nations. Since 1990, anti-stalking legislation has been enacted in the USA,

Australia, the UK, Canada and New Zealand (New Zealand prosecutes stalking under its Harassment Act (1997)) and other countries, particularly in continental Europe, are actively considering introducing similar legislation. Stalking has rapidly come to be perceived as a new and increasingly prevalent anti-social behaviour. Such beliefs gain considerable currency in those societies with 'law and order' agendas that value governments that are seen to be tough on crime and open to the needs of victims. The criminalization of stalking is a natural extension of such cultural beliefs and legislative agendas. However, whether these laws prove sufficient effectively to prevent and punish stalking is questionable. Stalkers vary considerably according to their motives, their psychiatric status and their response to management and treatment. Laws that fail to include a *range* of remedies to address this variation are unlikely to offer an effective solution. With the exception of a handful of US statutes, most laws have failed to consider the value of including mental health evaluations and intervention as part of the sentences imposed on convicted stalkers. Similarly, the concept of treatment has been eclipsed by the desire for punishment. Whether anti-stalking laws prove effective may ultimately depend heavily on the motivations and psychiatric status of the offender, as well as the willingness of the criminal justice system to view the offence seriously (Abrams & Robinson, 1998).

Defining the offence of stalking is undoubtedly a complex and problematic endeavour. The constellation of behaviours associated with stalking frequently involves legitimate and otherwise innocuous activities, such as telephone calls, letters, sending 'gifts', or approaches in public. Requiring as few as *two* prohibited actions to constitute the offence will assist the proscription of behaviour prior to an escalation to violence. However, in the absence of sufficient safeguards, these laws increase the likelihood that inadvertent and legitimate behaviours will be regarded, and prosecuted, as 'stalking'. While the first anti-stalking law attempted to minimize such an effect by requiring specific intent, a threatening course of conduct and an objective standard of harm, enforcement difficulties have led to a subsequent watering down of such protections and an extension of the scope of anti-stalking laws. Thus, according to the model anti-stalking code of the US Federal Government, a person could be convicted if, on two occasions, he or she purposefully maintains a 'visual proximity' to a victim who is rendered reasonably fearful by this conduct. Broad requirements such as these certainly ensure that prosecution difficulties encountered by jurisdictions with more restrictive provisions are avoided. However, that such behaviour would constitute criminal stalking is far removed from the experiences of the victims whose circumstances prompted these laws.

The public often looks to the criminal justice and legal systems to prohibit and punish antisocial behaviour, yet there are natural limits to what the law can do to help to protect victims and prevent unwanted forms of conduct. It remains to be seen whether anti-stalking laws in their current form will prove an effective remedy to the problem of stalking, and, in many jurisdictions, in what form these contentious laws will eventually survive.

Assessing and managing the stalker

Introduction

Approaches to managing stalking behaviours have been discussed at various points in the book, most particularly in the chapters on the stalker typology and on erotomania. The focus has been, to this point, almost exclusively on how best to end the stalking behaviours. The extent of the disruption that stalking brings to the life of the perpetrator as well as the victim has been acknowledged but rarely given attention. Sympathy for the stalker is not a proposition with immediate appeal. And yet these are often a lonely, inadequate, disturbed, if not frankly mentally ill, group of human beings. Their stalking reflects a range of influences among which can be remediable mental disorders as well as modifiable characterological and social skills deficits. Furthermore, it is the distress and disruption experienced by the stalkers that can potentially be used as a lever to alter their behaviour and release the victims from continuing distress and disruption.

A false dichotomy is often created in the management of mentally disordered offenders between the social imperatives of prevention and punishment and the health responsibilities of treatment and care. The issue of how to respond to a mentally abnormal offender is sometimes presented as a choice between either responding to the claims of the victim and the wider society or responding to the needs of the offender. For many, even raising the issue of mental disorder in the context of criminal offending is at best an irrelevant obfuscation, and at worst a ploy to help the perpetrator escape his or her just deserts. Stalking is a particularly good example of a behaviour which is criminal (in most jurisdictions) but in which mental disorder can, and not infrequently does, play a causal role. To ignore the role of remedial mental disorders is to do a disservice not just to stalkers but to their victims.

Fining, confining and otherwise coercing a stalker driven by erotomanic delusions is, quite apart from the injustice, futile. As prevention it will not work. As punishment it will not work. As correction it certainly will not work. The victim's best hope for long-term delivery from being stalked by this type of person is effective treatment of the stalker's delusional state. At the other extreme there are angry narcissistic individuals bent on asserting control and exacting revenge on those with the temerity to reject their advances. Such individuals may respond to judicial sanctions. They may even deserve to be at the wrong end of such sanctions. Equally, if their behaviour is not to recur, therapy may well have a role. The choice between criminal sanctions and therapy is not one of either/or. The choice should be pragmatic: what balance of judicial sanction and therapy will best end the present stalking and best reduce the chances of future stalking?

Stalking may well reflect, as Emerson et al. (1998) argued 'intricate social processes', but if the stalker's psychopathology is a necessary, even if a far from sufficient, cause, then treating that psychopathology will stop the stalking. Stalking can quite legitimately be used to illustrate arguments about such matters as social pathologies, gender inequalities and distortions in human relatedness. If, however, the primary aim is to relieve victims of the burden of being stalked then it would be foolish to ignore the role of the stalker's psychopathology and to pass up the chance of stopping the stalking by attending to those disorders. There is also an imperative, from a health professional's perspective, to provide treatment to those with an illness and a disorder that are either causing distress or contributing to disability. Many stalkers need treatment irrespective of their offending. That that treatment may well reduce their future offending is a bonus.

The assessment and management of stalkers with significant psychopathology does not differ, in most respects, from the management of those with similar mental disorders who do not stalk. The stalking behaviour does, however, provide a particular context in which assessment and treatment occurs. Those who work in forensic mental health services are no strangers to managing those in whom offending and mental disorder coexist and interrelate. One of the problems is to prevent further offending during the course of treatment. Neither victims nor the criminal justice system are particularly tolerant of allowing the stalking to continue while the treatment has 'time to work'. In some stalkers a moratorium can be negotiated on their stalking activities. The willingness to accept this temporary cessation in some is encouraged by judicial sanctions or parole conditions. In some, however, the stalkers recognize that they have a problem that requires help and they will accept curbing their activities as the price of that help. In the deluded it may also be possible to negotiate a respite from stalking by entering into a dialogue with the patient's sane part, which exists even in the maddest of minds. In others they will not, or cannot, curb their persistent intrusions and harassment. Here containment may be necessary in hospital, if their mental state justifies civil commitment, or in prison, if the courts so decide. (We have found treating stalkers in prison a practically difficult and unrewarding exercise.) In practice, when managing stalkers in the community there are not infrequently recrudescences of their stalking activities, particularly in the early stages of therapy. While health practitioners never collude with, or condone, such activities, minor relapses stalking cannot be an indication, in and of themselves, for abandoning treatment. This is so if for no other reason than that they are almost universal. Fortunately many such episodes are surreptitious and go unnoticed. The only reason the clinician knows they have occurred is because the patient has told them. It is our custom to make clear to stalkers that if they continue to offend the fact they are being seen in the clinic will not provide them with indemnity against the legal consequences of their actions. In practice the treatment of stalkers is on occasion interrupted or totally disrupted by their arrest and imprisonment on further charges.

Stalkers evoke considerable fear. Even among our experienced staff who have worked for years with seriously violent offenders and some of the worst sex offenders in the state, there is considerable wariness about being involved in managing stalkers. Of all the groups of offenders encountered in our services it is almost always about the stalkers that students and newly recruited staff express most apprehension. The stalker has become a culturally sanctioned bogyman. Fantasies abound of these men and women sitting in the clinic, or on the ward, ever vigilant for another potential victim on whom they can fix their unwanted attentions. Staff need education and reassurance about the realities of stalkers. Whatever the risks attendant on managing stalkers the probability is very low of the stalker transferring their unwanted attentions onto the therapist. Therapists, of all types, are at risk of being stalked by their lonely, fantasizing, affection- and attention-hungry patients and clients. By the time the stalkers reach our clinic, however, they have chosen their target and are rarely in the market for a replacement.

Assessment

The information base required to assess a stalker differs little from that required for any full clinical evaluation. One needs details of past assessments, management strategies and their effects, or lack thereof. Ideally one needs some independent source of information in the form of a relative or friend, but this is frequently absent in the assessment of stalkers. One needs as much detail about the stalking behaviours as possible. The latter often comes in the form of witness statements and victim impact reports. Courts are sometimes reluctant to disgorge this type of information but they should be pressed as it is often invaluable. When referrals come from the criminal justice system the stalker's full criminal record needs to be provided. Although we would not make direct contact with the victim of a stalker, we are treating it as essential, especially where the harassment may be continuing, that the authorities involved with the victim are made aware of appropriate services to which the victim can be referred. This is essential to the safety and well-being of the victim, but will also assist the management of the stalker, by eliminating any counterproductive or reinforcing responses on the part of the victim.

Assessing stalkers is often complicated by their having been compelled to attend by a court order, a Mental Health Act provision or simply by threats as to the consequences of not attending. The compelled, not to say coerced, client or patient is rarely easy to engage. Further complicating the initial assessment may be the context of a court-mandated examination, the results of which may have serious implications for the patient. It is an ethical obligation to ensure that the patient knows the purposes of the examination, knows to what extent, if any, the interview can and will be held confidential and to what extent it will be communicated to the court or other agency. Often coerced, equally often denied the protections of medical confidentiality, they are usually righteously indignant. These are bad foundations for a free-flowing and frank assessment process.

Insight in stalkers is often conspicuous by its absence. Their capacity to deny, minimize and rationalize are matched in our experience only by sex offenders. An approach was made directly to our clinic by a woman facing extensive charges arising out of stalking a celebrity over a period of years. She requested an examination by a 'stalking expert' to provide her with a certificate stating she was not a stalker. The receptionist offered an appointment some two weeks hence. Initially this was accepted, but less than an hour later the woman phoned back for an earlier appointment. Then followed a series of phone calls, demands to speak to doctors and directors, some of which were put through to clinical staff. Over the next week there were multiple phone calls, letters and persistent intrusions, particularly directed at one receptionist, demanding the immediate issuing of this certificate declaring her free from the tendency, or even capacity, to stalk.

The initial phase of the assessment is usually best given over to allowing the stalker both to express resentment and to provide an account of events. As has been noted, often such accounts are characterized by self-justification and the minimizing, or denial, of their harassing behaviours. On occasion, however, a frank disclosure of their stalking may be provided. Such candidness can be motivated either by contrition or by self-righteousness. It is unwise at this stage for the clinician to be drawn into an argument about the nature and extent of the harassment, particularly given that in most such assessments there is adequate documentation of the stalking from victim and witness statements. Having the stalker confirm such details can be forgone. At a later stage in the assessment it can be of value to confront the stalker with the accounts of his or her activity, but this is unhelpful when still attempting to establish rapport.

It is usually more productive to frame questions about the stalking in a manner that is nonjudgemental, if not frankly collusive. Thus, asking: 'What drove you to these actions?' is likely to elicit a more ready response than enquiries as to why the stalker intruded and harassed by phoning, following, etc. Equally, asking about 'attempts to communicate' and 'efforts to meet' the other person allows the stalker to describe behaviours without being immediately forced to justify those actions. We find intimacy seekers in particular respond well to reframing stalking in terms of a quest. As full an account as possible should be obtained of the stalkers' aims and objectives in stalking. Why they have committed themselves to this course of action and what they believe they will gain from the pursuit need to be spelled out.

Exploring the what and the why of the harassment needs to be amplified by enquiries directed at the impact of the stalking on the *stalker*. How much time is occupied by the stalking behaviours? How long do they spend thinking about the target? What have been the costs to the stalker of their campaign? How long do they think they can continue to pay the price of this quest in terms of time, money, energy and emotional turmoil? Having defined the costs it is then possible to explore the benefits. What has the stalker gained so far from his or her behaviour? What, if anything, has been the satisfaction?

Framing questions in this way is not just a collusive trick to obtain more information. It is the beginning of an attempt to lay the groundwork for changing those behaviours. Focussing attention on the costs of the behaviour for the stalkers is in part beginning the process of persuading them to change, or to be more professional, cognitively restructuring their attributions and commitments. An important step on the path to change can be to have them admit how unproductive has been the stalking in terms of advancing their aims and how costly for them has been this failed enterprise. The frankly deluded, or totally self-deceived, may well remain impervious to such approaches, protected as they are by an absolute conviction in their eventual vindication, or the ultimate success of their quest.

The assessment of any stalker must involve a thorough mental health evaluation. This is familiar territory for the mental health professional and differs not at all from good standard practice in clinical and forensic evaluations. Their history and mental state needs to be elucidated. In these cases a particularly thorough evaluation of their personality characteristics and habitual way of responding to life's challenges is often helpful. Structured and standardized personality assessments can be of considerable potential use as an addendum to the clinical evaluation. Equally, detailing their social networks, if any, and their interpersonal competencies and difficulties is even more important than in standard evaluations. A full relationship history should be obtained from all stalkers, not just the rejected.

Substance abuse can often contribute both to the nexus from which stalking emerges and toward the emergence of more intrusive and violent behaviours. A thorough history of the stalker's substance use is therefore essential. In those whom one suspects of more than the usual modesty in revealing these habits it is useful to include a physical examination, looking for stigmata of alcohol abuse or intravenous drug usage. In addition, where available, one should perform urine and blood screens for drugs, and liver function tests, which are potentially revealing of alcohol-related damage.

Assault is always of concern in stalking situations. Evaluating the probability of such behaviour requires a systematic (or even standardized) risk assessment, taking into consideration the relevant factors both stalker-specific and general (see Chapter 12). There is now a multitude of guides on assessing the risks of assault. These include: Harris & Rice (1997), Quinsey et al. (1998), Scott (1977), Snowden (1997) and Mullen(1999).

The assessment, when completed, should allow at least a preliminary answer to the following questions about the stalker:

1 What, if any, is the nature of their current mental disorder?
2 Is there a history of mental disorder and how has this been managed in the past?
3 What are the salient personality vulnerabilities?
4 What evidence is there of substance use and misuse?
5 What are the motivations for the stalking behaviours?
6 What is the context from which this individual's stalking arose and the factors that tend to sustain the behaviour?
7 What is the likely future course of the harassment?
8 What is the probability of assault? (This is expressed cautiously in terms of *probable risk*. There is a real danger, particularly when reporting to courts, of covertly encouraging, or justifying, sentencing not for what the individual has been convicted but for offences they might in the future commit.)
9 What is their current social situation and their social support networks?
10 What can the role of therapy be in ameliorating and preventing the stalking?
11 What therapy does the individual require for any mental disorder? (This is irrespective of the likely impact of such treatment on the stalking behaviours – although fortunately it is difficult to imagine effective treatments that aggravate stalking rather than potentially ameliorate that behaviour).

Management

The management of the stalker has the following elements:

Management of any continuing mental disorder

Those stalkers with mental disorders are managed no differently, as far as the disorders themselves are concerned, from any other patient with that condition. Delusional disorders are found relatively frequently among stalkers, particularly intimacy seekers. The management of these disorders has been discussed in

Chapter 8. Suffice to say that the management of these conditions is often outside of the experience of those working in the general mental health services but will soon become familiar to those with a special interest in stalkers. Similarly, social deficits and personality problems are common in this group and require focussed and often long-term remedial therapy.

Depressive disorders should not be ignored or dismissed as self-pity. In the occasional case, dramatic results are obtained by the simple expedient of providing adequate antidepressant therapy. We favour the use of the selective serotonin reuptake inhibiters (SSRIs), with clomipramine as a second-line treatment. Those choices are based on the claimed efficacy of these medications in depression complicated by obsessional phenomena and impulse control problems. Even in those stalkers where depression is thought to be reactive to the problems created subsequent to commencing stalking it is still important to adequately treat the altered mood if other treatment approaches are to have a chance.

Those whose stalking is driven by sexual impulse disorders may also benefit from serotonergic medication such as SSRIs, and these may be preferable to antiandrogens for predatory stalkers with severe or chronic depression. Anxiety disorders, especially social phobia, can be instrumental in the evolution of stalking behaviours. When these are addressed through the appropriate combination of medication (we use SSRIs or the reversible inhibitor of monoamine oxidase-A (RIMA) moclobemide) and behavioural therapies the results can be quite gratifying.

Management strategies targeted at the stalking behaviours

Stalking is a time-consuming, resource-consuming, emotionally draining and usually ultimately futile activity. Stalkers, even those caught up in a delusional system, generally have some realization, however partial, of the costs and self-defeating nature of their behaviours. Changing those behaviours is in part about helping them to focus on the negative impacts on them of continuing to stalk.

Stalking is damaging to victims yet most stalkers deceive themselves into believing such behaviours will further their aims of either attracting or reconciling with the object of their unwanted attentions. Even those stalkers pursuing agendas of revenge or vindication rarely admit to themselves the extent to which they are damaging their victims. Providing information about the impact of stalking in general and of their stalking in particular is part of therapy (in our view even with the deluded). Strategies for encouraging victim empathy borrowed from sex offender treatment programmes can usefully be applied with many stalkers. While we do not have the benefit of group therapy for stalkers and the opportunities for emotional expression and recognition that such groups may facilitate, efforts are made in individual work with stalkers to improve the accuracy of their processing of social information, especially their awareness of other people's desires and perspectives.

This is most usefully achieved through role playing of various day-to-day social situations encountered by the stalker, challenging their beliefs about the impact of stalking on victims generally, and on their victim(s) specifically. As for sex offenders, videos of stalking victims recounting their distressing experiences can be a useful adjunct, as are media reports of other cases and film portrayals.

Stalking is sustained, in no small part, because the behaviour is gratifying in and of itself. Despite this, few stalkers admit to themselves that they find the stalking rewarding. They explain their actions to themselves as being necessary to attain their goal (be that goal a relationship or retribution or whatever). It can be useful to expose the intimacy seekers' use of their stalking behaviours as a substitute for an intimate relationship, rather than a path to any such goal. Similarly the rejected can sometimes be helped to understand that they have substituted the stalking for the lost relationship. As a result they can neither re-establish a connection to, or free themselves from, their ex-partner. The incompetent suitors can occasionally be made to realize that their behaviour is a crude caricature of establishing a relationship which is doomed to failure and with which they are fooling themselves. The resentful stalkers have poured all their pain and spleen into the pursuit of people who in practice are largely irrelevant to the real issues. They can sometimes be encouraged to an understanding that their 'pursuit of justice' is being lost sight of in the short-term gratifications of punishing a minor and possibly innocent party.

The stalker, by the time he or she reaches a mental health professional, has invested in the pursuit considerable resources both personal and often financial. To abandon their pursuit would be to lose face. It is important to attempt to move them to a position where they can abandon the stalking without feeling humiliated or robbed. One female stalker who refrained from contacting her victim (a former boss) during the bail period was so incensed when the magistrate commented that she had been 'a very good girl' that she immediately resumed her pursuit. Unfortunately stalkers have often been exposed to attempts to make them stop stalking which involve what they perceive as threats, punishments and insults. They may have responded to such coercive tactics by becoming self-defensive and assertive about their rights. By reframing their actions as 'understandable' but ultimately counterproductive and damaging, they can sometimes be manoeuvred into abandoning the stalking as an act of generosity or of enlightened self-interest.

Stalkers are almost universally socially impoverished and isolated individuals. The stalking would have been unlikely to have emerged let alone have been sustained if they had had adequate peer relationships, let alone intimate relationships. Loneliness, isolation and a lack of feedback about their behaviour from those whose opinion they value, are among the prerequisites of such stalking. Improving social networks, equipping them with the skills to acquire and maintain friendships, helping them to establish and utilize confiding relationships are often critical elements in ending and, more importantly, preventing a relapse into, stalking.

These approaches can perhaps be illustrated in the approach to an intimacy seeker in which therapy broadly follows the following path:

1 The focus of the stalker's concerns are gradually shifted from the target's actual or potential love for the stalker to the stalker's love for the target. The stalker's motivations are reframed in terms of the stalker's hopes, investment and desires. His or her view of the target is reframed from the attributes of the victim to the positive qualities with which he or she has endowed the loved one. This moves the centre from the unknowable feelings, qualities and intentions of the target to the feelings and judgements of the stalker.

2 Establish how important is this love. In particular elucidate the stalker's prior loneliness and lack of other relationships. Assist the stalker to see how much has been invested in the hoped-for relationship. This moves the stalker toward understanding his or her love as a product of the situation and being sustained by feelings and judgements, not the imagined feelings of the target.

3 Focus on concrete examples of the loved one's supposed expressions of love and gently indicate that they could be interpreted very differently. This begins the process of confronting the stalker with the reality of the situation which he or she has (with naturally the best of intentions) brought about. The stalker is now trapped in a distressing situation largely of his or her own making.

4 Help the stalker to identify the costs to him or her of stalking: time, energy, emotions, the humiliations, etc.

5 Using the stalker's distress and losses as a starting point, begin the process of confronting him or her with the distress and disturbance inflicted on the target.

6 Move to a position where the stalker can abandon the quest with dignity, to extricate himself or herself from an 'embarrassing' relationship. The target has proved unworthy. The stalker tried, did his or her best. The stalker didn't mean to do it but the loved one was frightened and caused distress. Time to move on.

7 Begin the process of building real relationships and investing affections in more realistic objects (even if that is only a dog).

Connecting, or reconnecting, stalkers to a social world is one of the most important elements, not only in terminating stalking but in preventing relapse. The intimacy seekers had often never established adequate social networks. The rejected, if they ever had such connections, often lost them with the breakdown of the relationship and as a result of their subsequent stalking. The stalkers we see have usually sacrificed jobs and what friends and acquaintances they ever had to the process of stalking. Encouraging their involvement with other people is all the more necessary if their impoverished social world is not to form a basis from which stalking re-emerges. Those stalkers with whom we can claim a sustained success of stalking behaviours have often been those who acquired new social activities and new relationships (however superficial). But this is not just a 'relationship cure', as it is essential to avoiding further victimization in future relationships.

One stalker was encouraged to join a sports club rather than pursue her usual lonely long-distance running. This rapidly provided a social network and social life she had never previously possessed. The stalking was abandoned and never recurred. Another was persuaded to stop unsuccessfully seeking work in his profession (in which he was known and feared) and accept an unskilled labouring job. Having exchanged the prospect of a highly paid position for the reality of a low paid job he transferred the immense energy previously focussed on stalking his ex-wife into work. Within two years he had formed a partnership with a man he met at work, running a demolition business, earning far more than ever before and with a totally new, and closer, group of friends. He not only stopped harassing his ex-wife but even managed to apologize and establish very occasional appropriate contact.

Conclusions

This chapter, and to some extent this book, has emphasized the contribution of psychopathology to stalking and the contribution of therapy to stopping those behaviours. Stalking is as much, or more, a social pathology. The focus on the mental health aspects in part reflects our professional orientation but in part it also reflects pragmatism. It is not easy to treat delusional disorders or modify narcissistic character traits, but it is far easier, and quicker, than altering societies. Therapy is aimed, in no small part, at overcoming the social disabilities of the stalker. Certainly, adequate social function and acquiring 'good enough' social networks are central to managing stalking. Although the psychopathological and social pathological interact and sometimes overlap, they do not occupy different worlds.

There is perhaps a degree of naïve enthusiasm for the results of therapy apparent in this book. Delusional disorders are difficult to treat but when one starts from the assumption that they are untreatable then they become untreatable. Personality disorders are difficult to modify but again defining them as unchangeable makes them unchangeable. In managing stalkers one will have spectacular failures, but there will be successes. We believe there are more successes when the task is approached with optimism and even enthusiasm. Time and systematic studies will eventually clarify what works and what only flatters the therapeutic egos of professionals. Till then it is important for the sake of stalkers and their victims to treat what can be treated, and modify that which is open to modification, in an attempt to bring this miserable and destructive behaviour to an end.

Appendix A: Victim services

USA

National Victim Center

2111 Wilson Blvd, Suite 300,
Arlington, VA, 22201, USA
  See website at www.nvc.org/
  Provides information on stalking and safety
  procedures for victims: referral service for
  victims of crime.

Survivors of Stalking (SOS)

PO Box 20762
Tampa, FL, 33622, USA
  See website at www.soshelp.org/
  Provides a list of support groups for
  stalking victims, in addition to phone
  counselling, safety information, support
  and referral information.

CANADA

Canadian Resource Center for Victims of Crime

141 Catherine Street, Suite 100
Ottawa, Ontario K2P 1C3, Canada
  Provides legal and other information for
  victims of crime.

UNITED KINGDOM

National Anti-Stalking and Harassment Campaign and Support Association (NASH)

Bath Place Community Venture,
Bath Place, Leamington Spa,
CV31 3AQ, UK.
  Provides support, information and
  telephone counselling for victims of stalking.

Suzy Lamplugh Trust

14 East Sheen Avenue
London SW14 8AS
  Telephone: 0181 392 1839
  See website at: www.suzylamplugh.org/
  This is the national charity for personal
  safety. It aims to create a safer society and
  enable people to live safer lives, providing
  practical personal safety advice for anyone,
  anywhere.

AUSTRALIA

Victims Referral and Assistance Service

GPO Box 4356QQ,
Melbourne, Victoria 3001, Australia
  Telephone: (03) 9603 9797 (Melbourne
  metropolitan area).
  Telephone: 1800 819 817 (outside
  Melbourne area).
  Support and referral service for crime
  victims.

Victim Support Service

11 Halifax Street,

Adelaide, South Australia 5000, Australia
Offers support, information, and
counselling for victims of crime, their
families and friends.

Victims of Crime Bureau

Level 6, 299 Elizabeth Street,

Sydney, New South Wales 2000, Australia
Telephone: (02) 9374 3000 (Sydney
Metropolitan Area).
Telephone: 1800 633 063 (Outside Sydney
area).
Twenty-four hour telephone counselling
and referral service.

Victims of Crime Assistance League NSW

Telephone: (02) 9743 1636 (Sydney).
Telephone: (02) 9426 5826 (Newcastle).
Provides support group to assist
rehabilitation of crime victims.

Assisting Victims of Crime – Western Australia

Sixth Floor, 81 St George's Terrace,

Perth, Western Australia 6000, Australia
Telephone: (09) 322 3711 (Perth
metropolitan area).
Telephone: 1800 818 988 (Outside
metropolitan area).

Appendix B: Important anti-stalking Acts/statutes

AUSTRALIA

Australian Capital Territory: Crimes Act (section 34A, 1–4),

New South Wales: Crimes Act (section 562AB, 1–4),

Northern Territory: Criminal Code (section 189, 1–2),

Queensland: Criminal Code (section 359A, 1–7),

South Australia: Criminal Law Consolidation Act (section19AA, 1–5)

Tasmania: Criminal Code (section 192, a–f),

Victoria: Crimes Act (section 21A, 1–5),

Western Australia: Criminal Code (section 338D, 1–2; 338E, 1–4).

CANADA

Criminal Harassment Law, 1993

NEW ZEALAND

Harassment Act, 1997.

UNITED KINGDOM

Protection from Harassment Act, 1997

USA

California: CA PENA § 646.9 (West 1990)

Florida: FLA. STAT. Ch. 784.048 (Supp 1993)

Illinois: 720 ILCS 5/12–7.3–7.4, 5/13–14–5 (1993)

Michigan: MICH. COMP. LAWS ANN § 750.411h-I (1993)

West Virginia: W.VA.CODE § 61–2–9a (Supp 1993)

Legal cases and references

Legal cases

Commonwealth v. Kwiatkowski (1964) 637 Supreme Judicial Court of Massachusetts.

Connally v. General Constr. Co. (1926) 269 U.S.385, 3.

Dennis v. Lane (1704) 87 English Reports (Queens Bench), 887–8.

Long v. The State of Texas (1996) 931 S.W.2nd, 285.

Oregon v. Norris-Romine/Finley (1995) 134 Court of Appeals of Oregon.

People v. Heilman (1994) 25 Cal.App.4th 391.

Regina v. Dunn (1840) 113 English Reports (Queens Bench), 934–49.

Starr v. Eccles (1995) 136 Court of Appeals of Oregon.

State v. Bryan (1996) 73, 9. Kansas Superior Court.

References

Abel, G. G., Becker, J. V., Cunningham-Rathner, J., Mittelman, M. & Rouleau, J.-L. (1988) Multiple paraphilic diagnoses among sex offenders. *Bulletin of the American Academy of Psychiatry and Law*, **16**, 153–68.

Abrams, K. M. & Robinson, G. E. (1998) Stalking. Part II. Victims' problems with the legal system and therapeutic considerations. *Canadian Journal of Psychiatry*, **43**, 477–81.

Alcott, L. M. (1997) *A Long Fatal Love Chase*. New York: Dell Publishing.

Allen, M. J. (1996) Look who's stalking: seeking a solution to the problem of stalking. *Web Journal of Current Legal Issues*, **4**, 1–18. (See: www.webjcli.ncl.ac.uk)

American Psychiatric Association (1980) *Diagnostic and Statistical Manual of Mental Disorders*, 3rd edition. Washington, DC: APA.

American Psychiatric Association (1987) *Diagnostic and Statistical Manual of Mental Disorders*, 3rd edition – Revised. Washington, DC: APA.

American Psychiatric Association. (1994) *Diagnostic and Statistical Manual of Mental Disorders*, 4th edition. Washington, DC: APA.

Anderson, S. C. (1993) Anti-stalking laws: will they curb the erotomanic's obsessive pursuit? *Law and Psychology Review*, **17**, 171–85.

Anon. (1997). Stalking law. *Legal Matters*. (www.oag.state.tx.us)

Australian Bureau of Statistics (1996) *Women's Safety, Australia, 1996*. Canberra: Commonwealth of Australia.

Barton, G. (1995) Taking a byte out of crime: E-mail harassment and the inefficiency of existing law. *Washington Law Review*, **70**, 465–90.

Baruk, H. (1974) Delusions of passion. In M. Shepherd & S.R. Hirsch (Eds.) *Themes and Variations in European Psychiatry* (pp. 375–84). Bristol: John Wright & Sons.

Bastie, Y. (1973) Paranoia passionelle. *Annales Medico-Psychologiques*, **131**, 639–49.

Baum, A., Gatchel, R. J. & Schaeffer, M. A. (1983) Emotional, behavioural, and physiological effects of chronic stress at Three Mile Island. *Journal of Consulting and Clinical Psychology*, **51**, 565–72.

Baum, A., Cohen, L. & Hall, M. (1993) Control and intrusive memories as possible determinants of chronic stress. *Psychosomatic Medicine*, **55**, 274–86.

Baumeister, R. F. & Wotman, S. R. (1992) *Breaking Hearts: The Two Sides of Unrequited Loves*. New York: Guilford Press.

Benjamin, W. (1968) *Charles Baudelaine* (A. Zohn, Tranls.). London: Verso.

Biles, D. (1982) *The Size of the Crime Problem in Australia* (2nd edition). Canberra: Australian Institute of Criminology.

Bisson, J. & Shepherd, J. P. (1995) Psychological reactions of victims of violent crime. *British Journal of Psychiatry*, **167**, 718–20.

Bleuler, E. (1950) *Dementia Praecox or the Group of Schizophrenias* (J. Zinkin, Transl.). New York: International Universities Press. (Original work published in German in 1911).

Boast, N. & Coid, J. (1994) Homosexual erotomania and HIV infection. *British Journal of Psychiatry*, **164**, 842–6.

Boss, M. B. (1949) *Meaning and Content of Sexual Perversions*. New York: Grune & Stratton.

Bowlby, J. (1969) *Attachment*. New York: Basic Books.

Boychuk, M. K. (1994) Are stalking laws unconstitutionally vague or overbroad? *Northwestern University Law Review*, **88**, 769–802.

Brady, K. T., Sonne, S. C. & Roberts, J. M. (1995) Sertraline treatment of comorbid posttraumatic stress disorder and alcohol dependence. *Journal of Clinical Psychiatry*, **56**, 502–5.

Brenner, M. (1991) Erotomania. *Vanity Fair*, September, 86–149.

Breslau, N., Davis, G. C., Andreski, P., & Peterson, E. (1991) Traumatic events and posttraumatic stress disorder in an urban population of young adults. *Archives of General Psychiatry*, **48**, 216–22.

Breslau, N., Kessler, R. C., Chilcoat, H. D., Schultz, L. R., Davis, G. C. & Andreski, P. (1998) Trauma and posttraumatic stress disorder in the community: the 1996 Detroit area survey of trauma. *Archives of General Psychiatry*, **55**, 626–32.

Bureau of Justice Assistance (1996) *Regional Seminar Series on Developing and Implementing Antistalking Codes*. Washington, DC: US Department of Justice.

Burgess, A. W., Baker, T., Greening, D., Hartman, C., Burgess, A., Douglas, J. E. & Halloran, R. (1997) Stalking behaviors within domestic violence. *Journal of Family Violence*, **12**, 389–403.

Burke, J. (1976) *Osborn's Concise Law Dictionary*, 6th edition. London: Sweet & Maxwell.

Burton, R. (1621) *The Anatomy of Melancholy*. Numerous reprints and editions.

Buss, D. M. (1994) *The Evolution of Desire: Strategies of Human Mating*. New York: Basic Books.

Caplan, L. (1987) *The Insanity Defence and the Trial of John W. Hinckley, Jr*. New York: Dell.

Cate, F. H. (1996) Cybersex: regulating sexually explicit expression on the Internet. *Behavioral Sciences and the Law*, **14**, 145–66.

Cockram, J., Jackson, R. & Underwood, R. (1992) Perceptions of the judiciary and intellectual disability. *Australian and New Zealand Journal of Developmental Disabilities*, **18**, 189–200.

Coleman, F. L. (1997) Stalking behavior and the cycle of domestic violence. *Journal of Interpersonal Violence*, **12**, 420–32.

Cooper, S. (1998) Helen Razor: On the razor's edge . . . *Forte Magazine*, 1 October, 21.

Creamer, M. & McFarlane, A. (1999) Post-traumatic stress disorder. *Australian Prescriber*, **22**, 32–6.

Davidson, L. M. & Baum, A. (1986) Chronic stress and posttraumatic stress disorders. *Journal of Consulting and Clinical Psychology*, **54**, 303–8.

de Becker, G. (1997) *The Gift of Fear: Survival Signals that Protect us from Violence*. London: Bloomsbury.

de Clérambault, G. (1942) Les psychoses passionelles. In *Oeuvres Psychiatriques* (pp. 315–22). Paris: Presses Universitaires de France. (Original work published in French in 1921).

de Rougemont, D. (1950) *Passion and Society* (M. Belgian, Transl.). London: Faber & Faber. (Original work published in French)

Department of Justice. (1997) *Stats Flash: Stalking*. Victoria: Criminal Justice Statistics and Research Unit.

Department of Justice. (1998) *Stats Flash: Stalking Statistics*. Victoria: Criminal Justice Statistics and Research Unit.

Dietz, P. E., Matthews, D. B., Martell, D. A., Stewart, T. M., Hrouda, D. R. & Warren, J. (1991a) Threatening and otherwise inappropriate letters to members of the United States Congress. *Journal of Forensic Sciences*, **36**, 1445–68.

Dietz, P. E., Matthews, D. B., Van Duyne, C., Martell, D. A., Parry, C. D. H., Stewart, T., Warren, J. & Crowder, J. D. (1991b) Threatening and otherwise inappropriate letters to Hollywood celebrities. *Journal of Forensic Sciences*, **36**, 185–209.

Dill, D. L., Chu, J. A., Grob, M. C. & Eisen S. V. (1991) The reliability of abuse history reports: a comparison of two inquiry formats. *Comprehensive Psychiatry*, **32**, 166–9.

Drevets, W. C. & Rubin, E. H. (1987) Erotomania and senile dementia of Alzheimer type. *British Journal of Psychiatry*, **151**, 400–2.

Dunlop, J. L. (1988) Does erotomania exist between women? *British Journal of Psychiatry*, **153**, 830–3.

Eisendrath, S. J. (1996) When Munchausen becomes malingering: factitious disorders that penetrate the legal system. *Bulletin of the American Academy of Psychiatry and Law*, **24**, 471–81.

Eliot, T. S. (1930) *Dante in Selected Essays*. New York: Harcourt.

Ellis, P. & Mellsop, G. (1985) De Clérambault's syndrome – A nosological entity? *British Journal of Psychiatry*, **146**, 90–5.

Emerson, R. M., Ferris, K. O. & Gardner, C. B. (1998) On being stalked. *Social Problems*, **45**, 289–314.

Eminson, S., Gillett, T. & Hassanyeh, F. (1988) Homosexual erotomania. *British Journal of Psychiatry*, **154**, 128–9.

Enoch, M. D. & Trethowan, W. H. (1979) *Uncommon Psychiatric Syndromes*. Bristol: John Wright & Sons.

Eronen, M., Tiihonen, J. & Hakola, P. (1997) Psychiatric disorders and violent behavior. *International Journal of Psychiatric Clinical Practice*, **1**, 179–88.

Esquirol, J. E. D. (1965) *Mental Maladies: A Treatise on Insanity*. (R. de Saussure, Transl.). New York: Hafner. (Original work published in in French 1845.)

Evans, D. L., Jeckel, L. L. & Slott, N. E. (1982) Erotomania: a variant of pathological mourning. *Bulletin of the Menninger Clinic*, **46**, 507–20.

Faulkner, R. P. & Hsiao, D. H. (1994) And where you go I'll follow: the constitutionality of anti-stalking laws and proposed model legislation. *Harvard Journal on Legislation*, **31**, 1–62.

Feldman, M. D. & Ford, C. V. (1994) *Patient or Pretender: Inside the Strange World of Factitious Disorders*. New York: John Wiley & Sons.

Feldman-Schorrig, S. (1995) Need for expansion of forensic psychiatrists' role in sexual harassment cases. *Bulletin of the American Academy of Psychiatry and Law*, **23**, 513–22.

Feldman-Schorrig, S. (1996) Factitious sexual harassment. *Bulletin of the American Academy of Psychiatry and Law*, **24**, 387–92.

Fergusson, D. M. & Mullen, P.E. (1999) A historical perspective. In D. M. Fergusson, P. E. Mullen (Eds.). *Childhood Sexual Abuse: An Evidence Based Perspective* (pp. 13–33). Thousand Oaks, CA: Sage Publications.

Finkelhor, D. (1984) *Child Sexual Abuse: New Theory and Research*. New York: Free Press.

Fisher, M. (1990) *Personal Love*. London: Duckworth.

Foa, E. & Meadows, E. (1997) Psychosocial treatments for posttraumatic stress disorder: a critical review. *Annual Review of Psychology*, **48**, 449–80.

Follingstad, D. R., Rutledge, L .L., Bery, B. J., Hause, S. E. & Polek, D. S. (1990) The role of emotional abuse in physically abusive relationships. *Journal of Family Violence*, **5**, 107–20.

Freckelton, I. (1997) Psychological damages and their aftermath. *Psychiatry, Psychology and Law*, **4**, 107–8.

Fremouw, W. J., Westrup, D. & Pennypacker, J. (1997) Stalking on campus: the prevalence and strategies for coping with stalking. *Journal of Forensic Sciences*, **42**, 666–9.

Freund, K. (1990) Courtship disorder. In W. L. Marshall., D. R. Laws & H. E. Barbaree (Eds.) *Handbook of Sexual Assault* (pp. 195–207). New York: Plenum Press.

Freund, K. & Blanchard, R. (1986) The concept of courtship disorder. *Journal of Sex and Marital Therapy*, **12**, 79–92.

Friedman, M. J. (1998) Current and future drug treatment for posttraumatic stress disorder patients. *Psychiatric Annals*, **28**, 461–8.

Friedman, M. J., Charney, D. S. & Southwick, S. M. (1993) Pharmacotherapy for recently evacuated military casualties. *Military Medicine*, **158**, 493–7.

Frijda, N. H. (1986) *The Emotions*. Cambridge: Cambridge University Press.

Fritz, J. P. (1995) A proposal for mental health provisions in state anti-stalking laws. *Journal of Psychiatry and Law*, **23**, 295–318.

Gaddall, Y. Y. (1989) De Clérambault's syndrome (erotomania) in organic delusional syndrome. *British Journal of Psychiatry*, **154**, 714–6.

Gelpin, E., Bonne, O., Peri, T., Brandes, D. & Shalev, A. Y. (1996) Treatment of recent trauma survivors with benzodiazepines: a prospective study. *Journal of Clinical Psychiatry*, 57, 390–4.

Giannini, A. J., Slaby, A. E. & Robb, T. O. (1991) De Clérambault's syndrome in sexually experienced women. *Journal of Clinical Psychiatry*, 52, 84–6.

Gillett, T., Eminson, S. R. & Hassanyeh, F. (1990) Primary and secondary erotomania: clinical characteristics and follow up. *Acta Psychiatrica Scandinavica*, 82, 65–9.

Gilligan, M. J. (1992) Stalking the stalker: developing new laws to thwart those who terrorize others. *Georgia Law Review*, 27, 285–342.

Goldstein, R. L. (1978) De Clérambault in court: a forensic romance? *Bulletin of the American Academy of Psychiatry and Law*, 6, 36–40.

Goldstein, R. L. (1987) More forensic romances: De Clérambault's syndrome in men. *Bulletin of the American Academy of Psychiatry and Law*, 15, 267–74.

Goode, M. (1995) Stalking: crime of the nineties? *Criminal Law Journal*, 19, 21–31.

Gross, L. (1994) *To Have or to Harm: True Stories of Stalkers and their Victims*. New York: Warner Books.

Gupta, S., Popli, A., Bathurst, E., Hennig, L., Droney, T. & Keller, P. (1998) Efficacy of cyproheptadine for nightmares associated with posttraumatic stress disorder. *Comprehensive Psychiatry*, 39, 160–4.

Gutheil, T. G. (1992) Approaches to forensic assessment of false claims of sexual misconduct by therapists. *Bulletin of the American Academy of Psychiatry and Law*, 20, 289–96.

Guy, R. A. (1993) The nature and constitutionality of stalking laws. *Vanderbilt Law Review*, 46, 991–1027.

Hacking, I. (1995) *Rewriting the Soul: Multiple Personality and the Sciences of Memory*. Princeton, NJ: Princeton University Press.

Hafner, H. & Böker, W. (1982) *Crimes of Violence by Mentally Abnormal Offenders* (H. Marshall Transl.). Cambridge: Cambridge University Press.

Hall, D. M. (1998) The victims of stalking. In J. Reid Meloy (Ed.) *The Psychology of Stalking: Clinical and Forensic Perspectives* (pp. 113–37). San Diego: Academic Press.

Hall, R. L. (1989) Self-efficacy ratings. In D.R. Laws (Ed.) *Relapse Prevention with Sex Offenders* (pp. 137–46). New York: Guilford Press.

Hare, R. D., Harpar, T. J., Hakstian, A. R., Forth, A. E, Hart, S. D. & Newman, J. (1990) The revised psychopathy checklist: reliability and factor structure. Psychological assessment. *A Journal of Consulting and Clinical Psychology*, 2, 338–41.

Harlow, H. F. (1974) *Learning to Love*. New York: Aronson.

Harmon, R. B., Rosner, R. & Owens, H. (1995). Obsessional harassment and erotomania in a criminal court population. *Journal of Forensic Sciences*, 40, 188–96.

Harmon, R. B., Rosner, R. & Owens, H. (1998) Sex and violence in a forensic population of obsessional harassers. *Psychology, Public Policy, and Law*, 4, 236–49.

Harris, G. & Rice, M. (1997) Risk appraisal and management of violent behavior. *Psychiatric Services*, 48, 1168 – 76.

Hart, B. (1921) *The Psychology of Insanity*. Cambridge: Cambridge University Press.

Hart, S. D., Hare, R. D. & Forth, A. E. (1994) Psychopathy as a risk marker for violence: development and variation of a screening version of the revised psychopathy check list. In J. Monahan

& H. J. Steadman (Eds.) *Violence and Mental Disorder* (pp. 81–98). Chicago: University of Chicago Press.

Hayes, M. & O'Shea, B. (1985) Erotomania in Schneider-positive schizophrenia. *British Journal of Psychiatry,* **146**, 661–3.

Hazelwood, R. R., Dietz, P. E. & Burgess, A. W. (1989) *Autoerotic Fatalities.* Boston, MA: Lexington Books.

Holahan, C. J. & Moos, R. H. (1991) Life stressors, personal and social resources, and depression: a 4-year structural model. *Journal of Abnormal Psychology,* **100**, 31–8.

Hollender, M. H. & Callahan, A. S. (1975) Erotomania or De Clérambault syndrome. *Archives of General Psychiatry,* **32**, 1574–6.

Home Office. (1996) *Stalking – The Solutions: A Consultation Paper.* London: Lord Chancellor's Department.

Hueter, J. A. (1997) Lifesaving legislation: but will the Washington stalking law survive constitutional scrutiny? *Washington Law Review,* **72**, 213–40.

Hunter, R. & McAlpine, I. (1963) *Three Hundred Years of Psychiatry, 1535–1860* (pp. 196–7). Oxford: Oxford University Press.

Janofsky, J.S. (1994) The Munchausen syndrome in civil forensic psychiatry. *Bulletin of the American Academy of Psychiatry and Law,* **22**, 489–97.

Jason, L.A., Reichler, A., Easton, J., Neal, A. & Wilson, M. (1984) Female harassment after ending a relationship: A preliminary study. *Alternative Lifestyles,* **6**, 259–69.

Jaspers, K. (1963) *General Psychopathology* (7th Edition) (J. Hoenig & M.W. Hamilton, Transl.). Manchester: Manchester University Press.

Jones, C. (1996) Criminal harassment (or stalking). (See: www.chass.utoronto.ca: 8080/~cjones/pub/stalking)

Kanin, E.J. (1994) False rape allegations. *Archives of Sexual Behaviors,* **23**, 81–92.

Kessler, R.C., Sonnega, A., Bromet, E., Hughes, M. & Nelson, C.B. (1995) Posttraumatic stress disorder in the national comorbidity survey. *Archives of General Psychiatry,* **52**, 1048–60.

Kienlen, K.K., Birmingham, D.L., Solberg, K.B., O'Regan, J.T. & Meloy, J.R. (1997) A comparative study of psychotic and nonpsychotic stalking. *Journal of the American Academy of Psychiatry and Law,* **25**, 317–34.

Kierkegaard, S. (1987) *Either/Or* (H.V. Hong & E.H. Hong, Transl.). Princeton, NJ: Princeton University Press. (Original work published in Danish in 1843.)

Kierkegaard, S. (1996) *Papers and Journals: A Selection* (A. Hannay, Transl.). Harmondsworth, Middx: Penguin Books.

Kraepelin, E. (1921) *Manic Depression Insanity and Paranoia* (M. Barclay, Transl.). Edinburgh: ES Livingston. (Original work published in German in 1913).

Krafft-Ebing, R. (1886) *The Psychopathia Sexualis.* London: Panther.

Krafft-Ebing, R. & Chaddock, C. (1904) *Text Book of Insanity.* Philadelphia: F.A. Davies. (Original work published 1879.)

Kretschmer. E. (1918) *Der Sensitive Beziehungswahn.* Berlin: Springer-Verlag. [Selection translated as 'The sensitive delusion of reference'. In M. Shepherd & S.R. Hirsch (Eds.) (1974) *Themes and Variations in European Psychiatry* (pp. 153–195)]. Bristol: John Wright & Sons.

Kurt, J.L. (1995) Stalking as a variant of domestic violence. *Bulletin of the American Academy of Psychiatry and Law,* 23, 219–30.

Lagache, D. (1947) *La Jalousie Amoureuse.* Paris: Université de France.

Lardner, G. (1995) *The Stalking of Kristin: A Father Investigates the Murder of his Daughter.* New York: Onyx.

Leong, G.B. (1994) De Clérambault syndrome (erotomania) in the criminal justice system: Another look at this recurring problem. *Journal of Forensic Sciences,* 39, 378–85.

Lewis, C. T. & Short, C. (1879) *A Latin Dictionary.* London: Oxford University Press.

Lindsay, W.R., Olley, S., Jack, C., Morrison, F. & Smith, A.H.W. (1998) The treatment of two stalkers with intellectual disabilities using a cognitive approach. *Journal of Applied Research in Intellectual Disabilities,* 11, 333–44.

Link, B. & Stueve, A. (1994) Psychotic symptoms and the violent/illegal behavior of mental patients compared to community controls. In J. Monahan & H. Steadman (Eds.) *Violence and Mental Disorder* (pp. 137–59). Chicago: University of Chicago Press.

Lion, J.R. & Herschler, J.A. (1998) The stalking of clinicians by their patients. In J. Reid Meloy (Ed.), *The Psychology of Stalking: Clinical and Forensic Perspectives* (pp. 163–73). San Diego: Academic Press.

Lloyd-Goldstein, R. (1998) De Clérambault on-line: a survey of erotomania and stalking from the Old World to the World Wide Web. In J. Reid Meloy (Ed.) *The Psychology of Stalking: Clinical and Forensic Perspectives* (pp. 193–212). San Diego: Academic Press.

Long, B. L. (1994) Psychiatric diagnoses in sexual harassment cases. *Bulletin of the American Academy of Psychiatry and Law,* 22, 195–203.

Lopez, G., Piffaut, G. & Seguin, A. (1992) Psychological treatment of victims of rape. *Psychological Medicine,* 24, 286–8.

Lovett Doust, J. W. & Christie, H. (1978). The pathology of love: some clinical variants of De Clérambault's syndrome. *Social Science and Medicine,* 12, 99–106.

Low, P. W., Jeffries, J. C. & Bonnie, R. J. (1986) *The Trial of John W. Hinckley, Jr.: A Case Study in the Insanity Defence.* New York: Foundation Press.

Lowney, K. S. & Best, J. (1995) Stalking strangers and lovers: changing media typifications of a new crime problem. In J. Best (Ed.) *Images of Issues: Typifying Contemporary Social Problems* (pp. 33–57). New York: Aldine De Gruyter.

MacCulloch, M. J., Snowden, P. R., Wood, P. J. W. & Mills, H. E. (1983) Sadistic fantasy, sadistic behaviour and offending. *British Journal of Psychiatry,* 143, 20–9.

Macpherson, J. (1889) *An Introduction to the Study of Insanity.* London: Macmillan.

McAnaney, K. G., Curliss, L. A. & Abeyla-Price, C. E. (1993) From imprudence to crime: anti-stalking laws. *Notre Dame Law Review,* 68, 819–909.

McCann, I. L., Sakheim, D. K. & Abrahamson, D. J. (1998) Trauma and victimization: a model of psychological adaptation. *Counseling Psychologist,* 16, 531–94.

McCann, J. T. (1995) Obsessive attachment and the victimization of children: can anti-stalking legislation provide protection? *Law and Psychology Review,* 19, 93–112.

McConaghy, N. (1993) *Sexual Behavior: Problems and Management.* New York: Plenum Press.

McEwan, I. (1997) *Enduring Love.* London: Jonathan Cape.

McMahon, M. & Davids, C. (1993) Anti-stalking legislation: a new strategy in the fight against domestic violence? *Socio-legal Bulletin*, **10**, 4–7.

Malinquist, C. P. (1996) *Homicide: A Psychiatric Perspective.* Washington, DC: American Academic Press.

Marino, T. W. (1995) Looking over your shoulder: public has misconceptions on whom stalkers are. *Counseling Today, October*, 1–21.

Martin, J., Anderson, J., Romans, S., Mullen P. & O'Shea, M. (1993) Asking about child sexual abuse: methodological implications of a two stage survey. *Child Abuse and Neglect*, **17**, 383–92.

Meloy, J. R. (1989) Unrequited love and the wish to kill: diagnosis and treatment of borderline erotomania. *Bulletin of the Menninger Clinic*, **53**, 477–92.

Meloy, J. R. (1992) *Violent Attachments.* North Vale, NJ: Aronson.

Meloy, J. R. (1996) Stalking (obsessional following): a review of some preliminary studies. *Aggression and Violent Behavior*, **1**, 147–62.

Meloy, J. R. (1997) The clinical risk management of stalking: 'Someone is watching over me. . .'. *American Journal of Psychotherapy*, **51**, 174–84.

Meloy, J. R. (1998a) A clinical investigation of the obsessional follower: 'she loves me, she loves me not. . .'. In L. Schlesinger (Ed.), *Explorations in Criminal Psychopathology*, (pp. 9–32). Springfield, IL: Charles C. Thomas Press.

Meloy, J. R. (1998b) The psychology of stalking. In J. Reid Meloy (Ed.) *The Psychology of Stalking: Clinical and Forensic Perspectives* (pp. 2–23). San Diego: Academic Press.

Meloy, J. R. (1999) Stalking: an old behavior, a new crime. *Psychiatric Clinics of North America*, **22**, 85–99.

Meloy, J. R. & Gothard, S. (1995) A demographic and clinical comparison of obsessional followers and offenders with mental disorders. *American Journal of Psychiatry*, **152**, 258–63.

Meloy, J. R., Cowett, P., Parker, S., Hofland, B. & Friedland, A. (1997) Do restraining orders restrain? *Proceedings of the American Academy of Forensic Sciences*, **3**, 173.

Menzies, R. P. D., Fedoroff, J. P., Green, C. M. & Isaacson, K. (1995) Prediction of dangerous behaviour in male erotomania. *British Journal of Psychiatry*, **166**, 529–36.

Michael, A., Zolese, G. & Dinan, T. G. (1996) Bisexual erotomania with polycystic ovary disease. *Psychopathology*, **29**, 181–3.

Mohandie, K., Hatcher, C. & Raymond, D. (1998) False victimization syndromes in stalking. In J. Reid Meloy (Ed.) *The Psychology of Stalking: Clinical and Forensic Perspectives* (pp. 226–56). San Diego: Academic Press.

Monahan, J. (1981) *The Clinical Prediction of Violent Behaviour.* Washington, DC: US Government Printing Office.

Monahan, J., Steadman, H. J., Appelbaum, P. S., Robbins, P. C., Mulvey, E. P., Silver, E., Roth, L. H. & Grisso, T. (1999) Developing a clinically useful actuarial tool for assessing violence risk. *British Journal of Psychiatry* (Suppl.), in press.

Money, J. (1988) *Gay, Straight, and In-Between: The Sexology of Erotic Orientation.* Oxford: Oxford University Press.

Montesino, B. (1993) 'I'll be watching you': strengthening the effectiveness and enforceability of state anti-stalking statutes. *Loyola Entertainment Law Journal*, **13**, 545–86.

Mowat, R. R. (1966) *Morbid Jealousy and Murder*. London: Tavistock.

Mullen, P. E. (1990) A phenomenology of jealousy. *Australian and New Zealand Journal of Psychiatry*, **24**, 17–28.

Mullen, P. E. (1991). Jealousy: the pathology of passion. *British Journal of Psychiatry*, **158**, 593–601.

Mullen, P. E. (1997) Disorders of passion. In D. Bhugra & A. Munro (Eds.) *Troublesome Disguises: Underdiagnosed Psychiatric Syndromes* (pp. 127–167). Oxford: Blackwell Science.

Mullen, P. E. (1999) Dangerousness, risk and the prediction of probability. In M. G. Gelder, J. J. López-ibor & N. C Andreasen (Eds.) *Oxford Textbook of Psychiatry*. Oxford: Oxford University Press, in press.

Mullen, P. E. & Maack, L. H. (1985) Jealousy, pathological jealousy and aggression. In D. P. Farrington & J. Gunn (Eds.) *Aggression and Dangerousness* (pp. 103–26). New York: Wiley.

Mullen, P. E. & Pathé, M. (1994a) The pathological extensions of love. *British Journal of Psychiatry*, **165**, 614–23.

Mullen, P. E. & Pathé, M. (1994b). Stalking and the pathologies of love. *Australian and New Zealand Journal of Psychiatry*, **28**, 469–77.

Mullen, P. E., Pathé, M., Purcell, R. & Stuart, G. W. (1999) A study of stalkers. *American Journal of Psychiatry*, **156**, 1244–9.

Munro, A., O'Brien, J.V. & Ross, D. (1985) Two cases of 'pure' or 'primary' erotomania successfully treated with pimozide. *Canadian Journal of Psychiatry*, **30**, 619–21.

National Institute of Justice (1996) *Domestic Violence, Stalking, and Antistalking Legislation. Annual Report to Congress*. Washington, DC: US Department of Justice.

National Institute of Justice (1997) *The Crime of Stalking: How Big is the Problem?* Washington, DC: U S Department of Justice.

National Victim Center. (1998) Safety Strategies for Stalking Victims. (See: http//: www.nvc.org).

Office of Justice Programs (1997) *Domestic Violence and Stalking: The Second Annual Report to Congress under the Violence Against Women Act*. Washington, DC: US Department of Justice.

Orion, D. (1997) *I Know You Really Love Me: A Psychiatrist's Journal of Erotomania, Stalking, and Obsessive Love*. New York: Macmillan.

Panton, J. H. (1978). Personality differences appearing between rapists of adults, rapists of children, and non-violent sexual molesters of children. *Research Communications in Psychology, Psychiatry and Behavior*, **3**, 385–93.

Pappas, C. (1997) To surf and protect. (email: cbpappas@hiwaay.net).

Parton, N. (1979) The natural history of child abuse: a study in social problem definition. *British Journal of Social Work*, **9**, 431–51.

Pathé, M. & Mullen, P. E. (1997) The impact of stalkers on their victims. *British Journal of Psychiatry*, **170**, 12–17.

Pathé, M., Mullen, P. E. & Purcell, R. (1999) Stalking: false claims of victimization. *British Journal of Psychiatry*, **174**, 170–2.

Perez, C. (1993) Stalking: when does obsession become a crime? *American Journal of Criminal Law*, **20**, 263–80.

Peters D. S., Wyatt, G. E., & Finkelhor, D. (1986) Prevalence. In D. Finkelhor (Ed.) *A Source Book on Child Sexual Abuse* (pp. 15–59). Beverley Hills, CA: Sage.

Peterson, G.A. & Davis, D.L. (1985) A case of homosexual erotomania. *Journal of Clinical Psychiatry,* **46,** 448–9.

Phillips, S. P. & Schneider, M. S. (1993) Sexual harassment of female doctors by patients. *New England Journal of Medicine,* **329,** 1936–9.

Poe, E. A. (1967) The man of the crowd. In D. Galloway (Ed.) *Selected Writing.* Harmondsworth, Middx: Penguin Books. (Originally published 1840.)

Prins, H. (1997) Dangerous obsessions – some aspects of jealousy and erotomania. *Psychiatric Care,* **4,** 108–13.

Proust, M. (1980) *Remembrance of Things Past* (F. Scott-Moncrieff & T. Kilmartin, transl.). New York: Random House. (Originally published in French 1913–22).

Quayle, S. (1994) Harassed by a rash of male patients. *Australian Doctor, May,* 28.

Quinsey, V. L., Harris, G. T., Rice, M. E. & Cormier, C. A. (1998) *Violent Offenders: Appraising and Managing Risk.* Washington, D.C.: American Psychological Association.

Raschka, L. B. (1979) The incubus syndrome: a variant of erotomania. *Canadian Journal of Psychiatry,* **24,** 549–53.

Raskin, D. E. & Sullivan, K. E. (1974) Erotomania. *American Journal of Psychiatry,* **131,** 1033–5.

Ray, I. (1839) *Medical Jurisprudence of Insanity.* Boston: Little & Brown.

Reis, A. & Roth, J.A. (1993) *Understanding and Preventing Violence.* Washington, DC: National Academy Press.

Resnick, R. (1992) California takes lead: States enact 'stalking' laws. *National Law Journal,* **4**(36), 3.

Retterstøl, N. & Opjordsmoen, S. (1991) Erotomania – erotic self-reference psychosis in old maids: a long-term follow-up. *Psychopathology,* **24,** 388–97.

Ritchie, J. (1995) *Woman's Day,* February, pp. 66–72.

Romans, J., Hays, J. & White, T. (1996) Stalking and related behaviors experienced by counseling center staff members from current or former clients. *Professional Psychology: Research and Practice,* **27,** 595–9.

Rudden, M., Sweeney, J. & Frances, A. (1983) A comparison of delusional disorders in women and men. *American Journal of Psychiatry,* **140,** 1575–8.

Rudden, M., Sweeney, J. & Frances, A. (1990) Diagnosis and clinical course of erotomanic and other delusional patients. *American Journal of Psychiatry,* **147,** 625–8.

Sandberg, D. A., McNiel, D. E. & Binder, R. L. (1998) Characteristics of psychiatric inpatients who stalk, threaten, or harass hospital staff after discharge. *American Journal of Psychiatry,* **155,** 1102–5.

Saunders, R. (1998) The legal perspective on stalking. In J. Reid Meloy (Ed.) *The Psychology of Stalking: Clinical and Forensic Perspectives* (pp. 28–49). San Diego: Academic Press.

Savage, G. H. (1892) Jealousy. In H. D. Tuke (Ed.) *Dictionary of Psychological Medicine* (pp. 720–23). London: Churchill.

Schaum, M. & Parrish, K. (1995) *Stalked: Breaking the Silence on the Crime of Stalking in America.* New York: Pocket Books.

Scheler, M. (1954) *The Nature of Sympathy* (P. Heath, Transl.). London: Routledge & Kegan Paul. (Original work published in German in 1912).

Scheler, M. (1961) *Ressentiment* (W. W. Holdheim, Transl.). Free Press: New York. (Original work published in 1910.)

Schwartz-Watts, D. & Morgan, D. W. (1998). Violent versus nonviolent stalkers. *Journal of the American Academy of Psychiatry and Law*, **26**, 241–5.

Schwartz-Watts, D., Morgan, D. W. & Barnes, C. J. (1997) Stalkers: the South Carolina experience. *Journal of the American Academy of Psychiatry and Law*, **25**, 541–5.

Scott, D. (1995) The social construction of child sexual abuse: debates about definitions and the politics of prevalence. *Psychiatry, Psychology and Law*, **2**, 117–26.

Scott, P. D. (1977) Assessing dangerousness in criminals. *British Journal of Psychiatry*, **131**, 127–42.

Scruton, R. (1986) *Sexual Desire: A Philosophical Investigation*. London: Weidenfeld & Dicolson.

Seeman, M. V. (1978) Delusional loving. *Archives of General Psychiatry*, **35**, 1265–7.

Segal, J. H. (1989) Erotomania revisited: from Kraepelin to DSM-III-R. *American Journal of Psychiatry*, **146**, 1261–6.

Segal, J. H. (1990) Erotomania, obsessive love not uncommon but difficult to treat. *The Psychiatric Times: Medicine and Behavior*, **7**, 22–4.

Shalev, A., Bonne, O. & Eth, S. (1996) Treatment of posttraumatic stress disorder: a review. *Psychosomatic Medicine*, **58**, 165–82.

Shepherd, M. (1961) Morbid jealousy: some clinical and social aspects of a psychiatric symptom. *Journal of Mental Science*, **107**, 687–704.

Shrapnel, R. H. (1997) *Personal Protection at Home and Abroad*. Singapore: Times Books International.

Signer, S. F. (1989) Homo-erotomania. *British Journal of Psychiatry*, **154**, 729.

Signer, S. F. & Cummings, J. L. (1987) De Clérambault's syndrome in organic affective disorder. *British Journal of Psychiatry*, **151**, 404–7.

Signer, S. F. & Isbister, S. R. (1987) Capgras syndrome, de Clérambault's syndrome, and *folie à deux*. *British Journal of Psychiatry*, **151**, 402–4.

Signer, M. & Signer, S. F. (1992) Erotomania in the personals column. *Canadian Journal of Psychiatry*, **37**, 224.

Silva, J. A., Ferrari, M. M., Leong, G. B. & Penny, G. (1998) The dangerousness of persons with delusional jealousy. *Journal of the American Academy of Psychiatry and the Law*, **26**, 607–23.

Silverman, N. (1998) Terror of the stalker. *Good Medicine*, August, 36–39.

Simon, R. I. (1996) Workplace violence. In Simon, R. I. (Ed.) *Good Men do What Bad Men Dream* (pp. 237–77). Washington, DC: American Psychiatric Press.

Singer, I. (1966) *The Nature of Love*. Volume 1, *Plato to Luther*. New York: Random House.

Singer, I. (1987) *The Nature of Love*. Volume 2, *Courtly and Romantic*. Chicago: University of Chicago Press.

Smith, S.L. (1995) Developments in United States criminal law. *Criminal Law Journal*, **19**, 90–1.

Snowden, P. (1997) Practical aspects of clinical risk assessment and management. *British Journal of Psychiatry* (Suppl.) **32**, 32–4.

Sohn, E. F. (1994) Antistalking statutes: Do they actually protect victims? *Criminal Law Bulletin*, **30**, 203–41.

Solomon, R. C. (1976) *The Passions*. New York: Doubleday.

Solomon, R. C. (1980) Emotions and choice. In A.O. Rorty (Ed.) *Explaining Emotions* (pp. 251–81). Berkeley, CA: University of California Press.

Soyka, M. (1999) Substance abuse, psychiatric disorder and disturbed behaviour. *British Journal of Psychiatry,* in press.

Sparr, L. & Pankratz, L. D. (1983) Factitious posttraumatic stress disorder. *American Journal of Psychiatry,* **140**, 1016–9.

Steadman, H. J., McGreevy, M. A., Morrissey, J. P., Callahan, L. A., Robbins, P. C. & Cirincione, C. (1993) *Before and After Hinckley: Evaluating Insanity Defence Reform.* New York: Guilford Press.

Steadman, H. J., Mulvey, E. P., Monahan J., Clark Robbins, P., Appelbaum, P. S., Grisso, T., Roth, L. H. & Silver, E. (1998) Violence by people discharged from acute psychiatric inpatient facilities and by others in the same neighbourhoods. *Archives of General Psychiatry,* **55**, 393–401.

Stein, M. B. (1986) Two cases of 'pure' or 'primary' erotomania successfully treated with pimozide. *Canadian Journal of Psychiatry,* **31**, 289–90.

Stone, A. A. (1984) *Law, Psychiatry and Morality.* Washington, DC: American Psychiatric Press.

Strikis, S. A. (1993) Stopping stalking. *Georgetown Law Journal,* **81**, 2771–813.

Tallenbach, H. (1974) On the nature of jealousy. *Journal of Phenomenological Psychology,* **4**, 461–8.

Taylor, P .J. (1985) Motives for offending among violent and psychotic men. *British Journal of Psychiatry,* **147**, 491–8.

Taylor, P. J., Mahendra, B. & Gunn, J. (1983) Erotomania in males. *Psychological Medicine,* **13**, 645–50.

Thomas, K. R. (1993) How to stop the stalker: state antistalking laws. *Criminal Law Bulletin,* **29**, 124–36.

Tjaden, P. & Thoennes, N. (1998) *Stalking in America: Findings from the National Violence against Women Survey.* Washington, DC: National Institute of Justice and Centers for Disease Control and Prevention.

Turl, P. (1994) 'Stalking' is a public problem. *New Law Journal,* **144**, 632–3.

Ungvari, G. S. & Mullen, P. E. (1997) Reactive psychoses. In D. Bhugra & A. Munro (Eds.) *Troublesome Disguises: Underdiagnosed Psychiatric Syndromes* (pp. 52–90). Oxford: Blackwell Science.

Updike, J. (1997) *Forward to The Seducer's Diary.* Princeton, NJ: Princeton University Press.

Urbach, J. R., Khalily, C. & Mitchell, P. P. (1992) Erotomania in an adolescent: clinical and theoretical considerations. *Journal of Adolescence,* **15**, 231–40.

US Congress (1992) Senate Committee on the Judiciary: Antistalking Legislation, Hearing 29 September 1992 on S.2922, A Bill to Assist the States in the Enactment of Legislation to Address the Criminal Act of Stalking Other Persons. 102nd Congress, 2nd Session.

van der Kolk, B. A., Dreyfuss, D., Michaels, M., Shera, D., Berkowitz, R., Fisler, R., et al. (1994) Fluoxetine in posttraumatic stress disorder. *Journal of Clinical Psychiatry,* **55**, 517–22.

van der Kolk, B. A., McFarlane, A. C. & van der Hart, O. (1996) A general approach to treatment of posttraumatic stress disorder. In B. A. van der Kolk, A. C McFarlane & L. Weisaeth (Eds.) *Traumatic Stress: The Effects of Overwhelming Experience on Mind, Body and Society* (pp. 417–40). New York: Guilford Press.

Walker, J. M. (1993) Anti-stalking legislation: does it protect the victim without violating the rights of the accused? *Denver University Law Review,* **71**, 273–302.

Walker, L. E. & Meloy, J. R. (1998) Stalking and domestic violence. In J. Reid Meloy (Ed.) *The Psychology of Stalking: Clinical and Forensic Perspectives* (pp. 139–61). San Diego: Academic Press.

Wallace, C., Mullen, P. E., Burgess, P., Palmer, S., Ruschena, D. & Browne, C. (1998) Serious criminal offending and mental disorder: a case linkage study. *British Journal of Psychiatry,* **172**, 477–84.

Walker, L. E. A. (1989) *Terrifying Love: Why Battered Women Kill and How Society Responds.* New York: Harper and Row.

Warchol, G. (1998) *Bureau of Justice Stats Special Report* (Workplace Violence, 1992–6).

Way, R. C. (1994) The criminalization of stalking: an exercise in media manipulation and political opportunism. *McGill Law Journal,* **39**, 379–400.

Wells, C. (1997) Stalking: the criminal law response. *Criminal Law Review,* 463–70.

Westrup, D. (1998) Applying functional analysis to stalking behavior. In J. Reid Meloy (Ed.) *The Psychology of Stalking: Clinical and Forensic Perspectives* (pp. 275–94). San Diego: Academic Press.

Westrup, D. & Fremouw, W.J. (1998) Stalking behavior: a literature review and suggested functional analytic assessment technology. *Aggression and Violent Behavior,* 3, 255–74.

White, S.G. & Cawood, J.S. (1998) Threat management of stalking cases. In J. Reid Meloy (Ed.) *The Psychology of Stalking: Clinical and Forensic Perspectives* (pp. 296–315). San Diego: Academic Press.

White, G.E. & Mullen, P.E. (1989) *Jealousy: Theory Research and Clinical Strategies.* New York: Guilford Press.

Wiener, D. (1995) Stalking: criminal responsibility and the infliction of harm. *Law Institute Journal,* January, 30–3.

Wilcox, B. (1982) Psychological rape. *Glamour,* pp. 232–3 and 291–6.

Wilson, G.D. & Cox, D.N. (1983) Personality of paedophile club members. *Personality and Individual Differences,* **4**, 323–9.

Wright, J.A., Burgess, A.G., Burgess, A.W., Laszlo, A.T., McCrary, G.O. & Douglas, J.E. (1996) A typology of interpersonal stalking. *Journal of Interpersonal Violence,* 11, 487–502.

Writer, L. & Blackman, J. (1993) Fanatic obsession. *Who Weekly,* May, 42–3.

Zona, M.A., Sharma, K.K. & Lane, J. (1993) A comparative study of erotomanic and obsessional subjects in a forensic sample. *Journal of Forensic Sciences,* **38**, 894–903.

Zona, M.A., Lane, J. & Moore, M. (1996*)* The psychology and behaviour of stalkers. Unpublished paper presented at the American Academy of Forensic Sciences Annual Meeting, Nashville, TN.

Zona, M.A., Palarea, R.E. & Lane, J. (1998) Psychiatric diagnosis and the offender–victim typology of stalking. In J. Reid Meloy (Ed.) *The Psychology of Stalking: Clinical and Forensic Perspectives* (pp. 70–84). San Diego: Academic Press.

Index